LANGUAGE UNGOVERNED

LANGUAGE UNGOVERNED

Indonesia's Chinese Print Entrepreneurs, 1911–1949

Tom G. Hoogervorst

SOUTHEAST ASIA PROGRAM PUBLICATIONS
AN IMPRINT OF CORNELL UNIVERSITY PRESS ITHACA AND LONDON

Southeast Asia Program Publications Editorial Board
Mahinder Kingra (ex officio)
Thak Chaloemtiarana
Chiara Formichi
Tamara Loos
Andrew Willford

Copyright © 2021 by Cornell University

All rights reserved. Except for brief quotations in a review, this book, or parts thereof, must not be reproduced in any form without permission in writing from the publisher. For information, address Cornell University Press, Sage House, 512 East State Street, Ithaca, New York 14850. Visit our website at cornellpress.cornell.edu.

First published 2021 by Cornell University Press

Library of Congress Cataloging-in-Publication Data

Names: Hoogervorst, Tom, 1984– author.
Title: Language ungoverned : Indonesia's Chinese print entrepreneurs, 1911–1949 / Tom G. Hoogervorst.
Description: Ithaca [New York] : Cornell University Press, 2021. | Includes bibliographical references and index.
Identifiers: LCCN 2020046682 (print) | LCCN 2020046683 (ebook) | ISBN 9781501758225 (hardcover) | ISBN 9781501758232 (paperback) | ISBN 9781501758249 (epub) | ISBN 9781501758256 (pdf)
Subjects: LCSH: Popular literature—Publishing—Indonesia—History—20th century. | Popular literature—Indonesia—Chinese influences. | Malay literature—Indonesia—Chinese influences. | Chinese—Indonesia—History—20th century. | Printing—Indonesia—History—20th century. | Language and culture—Indonesia—History—20th century. | Literature and society—Indonesia—History—20th century. | Languages in contact—Indonesia—History—20th century.
Classification: LCC PL5080.5 .H66 2021 (print) | LCC PL5080.5 (ebook) | DDC 495.17/9598—dc23
LC record available at https://lccn.loc.gov/2020046682
LC ebook record available at https://lccn.loc.gov/2020046683

To Amy

To preserve the testimony of creative thinkers and to render
their manuscripts accessible to international research is an act
of profound civic importance whereby we affirm our identity and
maintain the life and continuity of our cultural heritage. The cultural
heritage is not a dusty monument, a souvenir of the past restricted
to a scholarly élite, but the focus of a form of "ancestor-worship"
which vitalizes and enriches later generations.

Léopold Sédar Senghor

**Maka barang siapa mengira bahasa Melajoe ada gampang
dipeladjarin, ialah terang sekalian soedah omong kosong dan
bion betjoes bahasa Melajoe.**

Kwee Tek Hoay

Taal is soms klank, soms teeken, maar altijd gedachte.

Gerrit Jacob Nieuwenhuis

Contents

Acknowledgments	xi
List of Abbreviations	xv
Note on Transliteration	xvii
Introduction: A Prism into the Past	1
1. Connected Language Histories	28
2. On Good, Bad, and Ugly Malay	51
3. Printing, Pulp, and Popularity	77
4. Competing Expressions of Modernity	101
5. The Humoristic and the Invective	125
Epilogue: An Important Historical Monument	150
Appendix	161
Notes	177
References	207
Index	235

Acknowledgments

When the Royal Netherlands Institute of Southeast Asian and Caribbean Studies (Koninklijk Instituut voor Taal-, Land- en Volkenkunde; KITLV) granted me the opportunity to investigate a large corpus of primary texts, written in colonial times by Chinese-Indonesian authors, one of my first questions to colleagues around the world was "Which particular topic would you like me to look into?" The replies were, of course, intriguingly diverse. Many researchers and community members expressed interest in Chinese contributions to Indonesia's anticolonial movement, women's emancipation, education, or healthcare. Some urged me to look specifically at Medan, Makassar, Semarang, or Pontianak, while others proposed to prioritize the ways minorities are "othered" in colonial and postcolonial contexts. Occasionally people advised me to quit my research at once, asserting that a career in the humanities is a surefire path to poverty-stricken irrelevance, especially compared to biomedical science, law, or economics. And yet, a still bigger group—including colleagues who had retired from precisely those lines of work—insisted that people's connection to their cultural heritage forms the essence of their self-worth. To have an equal playing field, they repeatedly pointed out, people first need to know where they come from.

The present book is unlikely to satisfy even minimally so divergent a range of objectives, but it has been immensely valuable to participate in these ongoing processes of meaning-making. At times, it felt as if I was learning to prepare a complicated dish, for which all attendant gourmands recommended their own favorite ingredients. I was unable to include everything, but my cooking certainly benefited from these pieces of advice. As my grandmother reminded me, *Staatsblad kalah sama sobat* (The Official Gazette never surpasses a friend), and I have been lucky to consult with so many along the way.

This book has benefited immensely from the correspondence and conversations I was fortunate to have with Tom van der Berge, Elizabeth Chandra, Charles Coppel, Dwi Noverini Djenar, Christina Firpo, Roel Frakking, FX Harsono, Hoko Horii, Marian Klamer, Esther Kuntjara, Didi Kwartanada, Elizabeth LaCouture, Ravando Lie, Maya Liem, Sutrisno Murtiyoso, Shin Mun Ng, Gert Oostindie, Katja Paijens, Jan van der Putten, Siew-Min Sai, Claudine Salmon, Roshni Sengupta, Rizal Shidiq, Tim Shortis, Josh Stenberg, Evi Sutrisno, Eric Tagliacozzo,

Patricia Tjiook-Liem, and Wu Xiao An. I am also deeply grateful to my colleagues who have carefully read and critically commented on chapters of my book: Adriaan Bedner, Ward Berenshot, Crystal Ennis, Ajay Gandhi, Radhika Gupta, Ariel Heryanto, Rosemarijn Hoefte, Jay Huang, Peter Keppy, David Kloos, Koos Kuiper, Grace Leksana, Fan Lin, Waruno Mahdi, Arnout van der Meer, Willem van der Molen, Henk Schulte Nordholt (whose idea it was to embark on this project), and Maja Vodopivec. Since my knowledge of the Hokkien language would be most charitably described as passive, I also thankfully acknowledge the help of Sim Tze Wei and the late David Kwa for answering my queries on that language. Another frank acknowledgement of debt goes to the excellent team of Cornell University Press, in particular to Sarah Grossman, Karen Hwa, and to the anonymous reviewers for their valuable feedback.

I am equally appreciative to those who have spared neither time nor trouble to help me access primary sources while showing kind interest in my work: Hueimin Chen, Anita Dewi, Pak Is (Isnain), Jeffrey W. Petersen, Marije Plomp, Rheny Pulungan, the late Harianto Sanusi, and Tim Yap Fuan. When the entire KITLV collection was moved to the Leiden University Library in 2014, it was Alfred Schipper who personally ensured that the fragile Sino-Malay newspapers remained in place intact, so that they could eventually be digitized. Saskia van Bergen, Isabel Brouwer, Ben Companjen, and Laurents Sesink have been tremendously helpful in creating an online portal administered by the Leiden University Library, where much copyright-cleared material can now be accessed digitally. Three people have done many of the above things combined: Azmi Abubakar, Oei Hiem Hwie, and Myra Sidharta were always willing to indulge in intellectual conversations, yet must be praised even more for their heroic, self-funded efforts to make publicly available an important part of Indonesia's heritage. I also convey my utmost gratitude to Caroline Chia, Doreen Lee, Natalie Ong, and Seng Guo Quan, dear fellow-travelers who have tolerated my presence in various parts of the world and made my days of library research substantially more interesting. Last but not least, I am indebted to the Netherlands Organisation for Scientific Research (NWO) for their financial support of this research through an Innovational Research Incentives Scheme (Veni) and to KITLV for funding the digitalization of the periodicals *Sin Po* and *Hoakiao*, and for providing me with a vibrant, multidisciplinary research home.

The beginning of my academic career comprised grand plans to work on the Javanese language, to which I am ancestrally connected. In a curious quirk of fate, I found myself applying for a postdoctoral project to investigate the textual heritage of Indonesia's Chinese-descended communities. One year prior to this academic point of no return, I married into a family of Chinese-Indonesian origins. My parents-in-law, Joyce Go and Peter Heru Utomo (Kho San Hauw), never ceased to support this pleasantly unexpected twist in my scholarly path. My wife, Renate, redressed the balance by immersing herself in Javanese poetry, dance, batik, and cuisine, whereas our daughter, Amy, seems fascinated by all sides of her heritage. Both put a smile on my face every day and encourage me to reach for the impossible.

List of Abbreviations

C	consonant
Cn	Cantonese
coll.	colloquial
D	Dutch
dial.	dialect
excl.	exclusive
Ha	Hakka
Hk	Hokkien
hon.	honorific
incl.	inclusive
KITLV	Koninklijk Instituut voor Taal-, Land- en Volkenkunde (Royal Netherlands Instititute of Southeast Asian and Caribbean Studies)
lit.	literally
Md	Mandarin
Ml	Malay
S	Straits
Tc	Teochew
THHK	Tiong Hoa Hwee Koan (Chinese Association)
V	vowel
VOC	Vereenigde Oostindische Compagnie (Dutch East India Company)

Note on Transliteration

This book contains several transliterated words and sentences from Malay and Chinese varieties. As the different romanizations often contain sociolinguistically relevant information, I respect the original spelling of my sources, with the exception of evident typos or punctuation errors. Vernacular Malay was romanized in different ways, depending on the time, location, editorial policy, and degree of standardization. A Dutch-style romanization was in use in the Netherlands Indies, whereas an English-style romanization prevailed in British Malaya. At present, a modern Malay/Indonesian orthography is used throughout the Malay-speaking world, whereas the Pėh-ōe-jī system is the best known romanization of Hokkien.

Keeping in mind that the different spelling systems were far from consistent, table 1 provides a rough overview. Note that /õ/ represents a nasalized vowel, whereas /ʰ/ marks an aspirated consonant (in Chinese loanwords). In romanized Malay from the Straits, /i/ and /u/ in closed syllables were written respectively as <e> and <o>, corresponding to their regional pronunciation in that position.

TABLE 1 Overview of spelling systems used

PHONEME	MALAY			HOKKIEN
	INDIES	STRAITS	MODERN	PĖH-ŌE-JĪ
/ai/	ai~ae~aij~ay	ye~ai	ai	ai
/au/	au~auw	ow~au	au	au
/c/	tj	ch	c	ch
/cʰ/	tjh~dj	chh	c	chh
/e/	e~é~è	e~ay	e	e
/ə/	e~ĕ~ê	e~ŭ~Ø	e	Ø
/i/, /ɪ/	i~ie	i~ee	i	i
		CeC		eC
/j/	j~i~ij~y	y	y	j
/ɟ/	dj	j	j	j
/kʰ/	kh~g	kh	k	kh
/ɲ/	nj	ny	ny	
/ɔ/	ouw	oh	o	o·
/pʰ/	ph~b	ph	p	ph
/ʃ/	sj	sh	sy	
/tʰ/	th~d	th	t	th
/u/, /ʊ/	oe	u	u	u
		CoC		
/w/	w	w	w	
x	ch	kh	kh	
/õ/	Ø	Vⁿ	Ø	Vⁿ

MAP 1. Locations mentioned in this book

LANGUAGE UNGOVERNED

INTRODUCTION
A Prism into the Past

After a few chats, Stalin fell in love with Nadya, and not long afterwards Nadya the ironmonger's daughter was embraced as a "comrade" by the Dictator of Russia!

School kids these days have become famously useless! The moment they've learned how to wear short skirts, get bobbed haircuts, and speak English or speak Dutch, all they're good for is going to the cinema, spinning the gramophone, and dancing around; they're totally incapable of anything else!

Even worse are people who dress to impress
Except for big shots, they notice nobody
Poor guys should not behave incorrectly
Lest they are looked down on by the girls.

Kongkou poenja kongkou Stalin djadi perliep sama Nadya, dan tida lama poela Nadya anaknja si toekang besi dipoengoet "toengtji" oleh Dictator Rusland!

Memang anak-sekolahan sekarang soeda kesohor tida goenanja! Mentang-mentang soeda bisa pake rok-pendek, ramboet di Bobit-her (bobbed hair) Inglis-spik atawa Olan-sprek, bisanja tjoema nonton bioscoop, poeter gramafoon, dansa-dansa sadja, laen-laennja sama sekali tida bisa!

Lebiän jang soeda berpake rebo

Salaennja Baron marika khoabo
Kaloe sie miskin djangan tjerobo
Dipandang rendah oleh sie tjabo.[1]

On the previous page are three excerpts taken respectively from a journalistic article, a theater play, and a poem. They are all written in colloquial Malay, of the variety used in colonial times by Indonesia's urban Chinese. They all reveal fragments of social issues that ran through the 1920s and 1930s. They all contain more than a grain of satire. But they also share something deeper. None of the texts can be fully appreciated, or in fact understood, through their English translations alone. Ignoring the Malay source texts means missing out on crucial information to contextualize these accounts. It would obscure, for example, that Chinese words were used for "chat," "comrade," "notice nobody," and "girl," English words for "bobbed hair" and "speak English," and Dutch words for "in love," "speak Dutch," and "big shot." Indeed, slang pertaining to social life was often Chinese-derived, whereas words from European languages signaled cosmopolitanism. No less importantly, it would obscure that many English and Dutch words were deliberately misspelled, as if burlesquing the language hierarchies colonialism exerted. Oscillating between China, Indonesia, and the West, the wordsmiths behind these texts indefatigably produced such linguistic subtleties in their articulations of the everyday. In translation, the above passages are quotidian. In their original language, they are entertaining, playful, and irreverent. Their narrative content (what is being told) is deeply inscribed in the language itself (how it is told), in particular through the choice of words. This is to some extent the case with all texts, but it is particularly so with writings produced under unequal power relations by authors with plurilingual competencies.

This book approaches language as a prism into the past. Through a focus on late colonial Malay, as used by the urban Chinese, it aims to better understand its speakers and their lived experiences. Many writers from this community relied on the press to navigate the world they inhabited. As pioneers of commercialized printing and brokers of popular culture, their language practices left a deep imprint on the wider society. They consciously adopted a language characterized by versatility and resistance to formalization. The main argument of this book, then, is that a linguistic reading of vernacular texts—placing language in conversation with history and culture—is key to make sense of the society that slowly transformed into Indonesia, and the position therein of its Chinese minority. I treat linguistic development and social change as co-constitutive: language describes and defines new lifeways but is also expanded and enriched by them. At the same time, experiences of in-betweenness, oppression, and shifting cultural orientations translate into literary production and linguistic creativity. To put it succinctly: vernacular language, mass culture, and colonial modernity produce each other.

This connected exploration of language and history leads us almost organically to the Chinese-Indonesian printing tradition. Unlike the vast majority of colonial-era documents from the Netherlands Indies, which were written in Dutch, these texts appeared in romanized Malay. By investigating the linguistic character of these sources, I attempt to add empirical depth and cultural texture to the historical conditions in which they were forged. These insights stretch beyond the confines of established academic fields (history, linguistics, literary studies, anthropology, etc.) and engage with the transdisciplinary themes of plurilingualism, counterhegemonic discourses, and the pleasure of reading. In doing so, this book pivots on three main questions: Why did Indonesia's Chinese minority adopt Malay, study it, influence it, and eventually produce knowledge in it? What outcomes did this linguistic choice foster for the broader society? How can one study the experiences of the colonized by investigating, simultaneously, their texts and the language in which they were written?

The lynchpin of this book is a rich array of novels, periodicals, educational materials, poetry, and plays, commonly classified as "Sino-Malay." These publications offer otherwise unavailable vistas into life in Indonesia's late colonial cities. Their authors were Chinese men and women who had made the former Netherlands Indies, present-day Indonesia, their home. For many, their liminal status led them to embrace Malay printing. Being racialized as foreign, occupying an interstitial position in society, and writing in the local lingua franca, they depended on the press for market information, education, legal and medical advice, conflict resolution, and much-coveted career prospects in journalism.[2] Initially, the Malay printing industry was dominated by Eurasians, who regularly employed Chinese writers and typesetters on their editorial boards. The archipelago's first Chinese-run newspapers appeared in the late nineteenth century, although collaborations with Eurasian editors remained the norm into the early twentieth century.[3] My analysis starts with an event that took place not in Indonesia, but in China: the Revolution of 1911, when supporters of Sun Yat-sen finally succeeded in overthrowing the Qing dynasty. As a result of this victory, the Indies Chinese became more assertive and politicized, as did their books and newspapers. It was also a time of large-scale urbanization, growing interethnic tensions, and Indonesia's first mass organizations.[4] The Sino-Malay print culture of this period embodied the experiences of a group wedged between European elites, indigenous masses, and a self-confident China. Simultaneously, it continued to satisfy society's need for popular entertainment.

All the new media, technologies, sounds, images, influences, interactions, and clashes of the early twentieth century found each other in the urban sphere. Batavia (currently Jakarta), Surabaya, Semarang, and other cities became breeding grounds of industrialization, institutional transformations, notions of progress, individualism, physical health, and the influx of capital—a series of interrelated phenomena we have come to see as "modernity." Yet modernity is a tricky concept, and its understandings differ across time, place, and culture. Without paying attention to language, this elusive phenomenon is easily discussed in ways that subject people's experiences to the translations of others.[5] To many Chinese and "indigenous" Indonesian authors, the word *kemodernan* (modernity) centered around novelty and opposition to tradition, as it did globally. Yet compared to its European usage, the word carried strong negative connotations from the outset. Many new things, after all, were introduced by Western imperialist forces, who simultaneously held the power to undermine time-honored traditions. Modernity was a product of revision as well as destruction.[6] It was both embraced and feared. Yet what scholars might refer to as "alternative modernity" or "competing narratives of modernity" was rarely phrased as such in the Sino-Malay discourse. If anything, social change inspired by the Republic of China was articulated as revivalism of lost traditions, rather than their substitution. When discussing positively charged notions of modernity, writers unequivocally invoked the term *kemadjoean* (progress).[7] Technological innovation, for example, was systematically categorized as *kemadjoean*. Conversely, the latest European fashion, Western dances, and previously unthinkable types of male/female relationships were categorically dismissed as *kemodernan*, though they could only exist by virtue of *kemadjoean*.

Such translational asymmetries are indispensable to contextualize people's lived experiences under colonialism. They exemplify the centrality of language—in particular vernacular language—in socially and racially stratified societies. The Netherlands Indies featured a complex linguistic landscape. Most ethnic Chinese came from Hokkien-speaking backgrounds, but they were not necessarily literate in that language, and many used Malay, the regional lingua franca, in everyday interactions. The necessity to learn Malay arose predominantly in the cities. It granted people from various backgrounds access to the colonial administration, commercial information, the press, and communities with which contact would have otherwise remained minimal. The vast majority of people sought fluency in "vernacular" rather than classical or literary Malay. Vernacular language, as defined by Mikhail Bakhtin, is "the language of life, of material work and mores, of the 'lowly,' mostly humorous genres (*fabliaux, cris de Paris*, farces), the free speech of the marketplace."[8] It is a continuous dialog rather than a top-down mandate. While the vernacular is not explicitly antielitist, its subtle and not-so-subtle defiance of regimes of authenticity is indissoluble. The Malay vernacular was perceived—by both European scholars and indigenous literati—as ungrammatical, excessively influenced by foreign languages, and of a low literary quality. Yet over time, it was able to generate a discourse powerful enough to undermine hegemonic notions of literacy and, in doing so, rankle the colonial establishment.

This type of Malay did what no prestigious language could achieve: it carved out liminal spaces to express the "cacophony of the streets" in all its complexities, confusions, and contradictions.[9] It was ungoverned, and powerfully so.

The Malay print culture displays significant historical differences from its European antecedents. As the colonial system precluded all opportunities for rational and critical engagement with the government, a "public sphere" in the Habermasian sense was unable to take root in the Netherlands Indies. Nevertheless, the Malay press was crucial to the development of participatory politics and a civil society, creating an Indonesian public sphere on its own terms.[10] Within the constraints and power hierarchies in place, it enabled groups and individuals not necessarily connected to state power to observe, describe, discuss, and shape the social change around them. Over time, the printing industry grew sufficiently multivocal to accommodate conflicting cultural values, ideological claims, and particularistic interests. It developed in tandem with a commercialized mass culture. In that sense, mass printing contributed not to the decline of Indonesia's public sphere, as has conventionally been argued for western Europe, but to its survival. Only through a convergence of interests of mercantile elites, entrepreneurial authors, and knowledge-hungry audiences was the Malay press—and in particular the Sino-Malay press—able to largely emancipate itself from European control. When it did so, Malay print culture began to differ substantially from its western European counterparts, including in its ability to connect different geographical, ethnic, religious, and ideological "publics" on a scale thus far unheard of.

Interethnic print languages such as Malay stood at the cradle of three interrelated processes: protonational resistance, the formation of an "imagined community," and nation-building avant la lettre. As was first argued by Benedict Anderson, the emergence of nationalism in ethnolinguistically variegated societies resulted from print capitalism, "the commercialized, secularized, nongovernmental, and nonphilanthropic production of texts for a popular audience."[11] This trajectory was anything but smooth. In the Netherlands Indies, as in most colonial settings, true liberalism, free enterprise, and other social characteristics one might innocently associate with a term like "print capitalism" were seldom in evidence.[12] Besides staying in the good books of the authorities, it was crucial for publishers to create audiences, make esthetic choices, and develop a language that was both comprehensible and entertaining. If print capitalism stood at the cradle of Indonesian nationalism, it was preceded and overshadowed by a distinct process that could be named "print entrepreneurship." Print entrepreneurship, as I define it, is the mass production by private entities of enjoyable, widely accessible, visually attractive, and culturally adaptive texts. As such, it can be seen as a fundamental aspect of cultural entrepreneurship more broadly.[13] Fiction, poetry, and sensationalized journalism stood at its core. The term "entrepreneurship" also connotes a sense of pioneering and innovation. It was due to the efforts of print entrepreneurs that romanized Malay developed from merely a tool for teachers, accountants, priests, and pharmacists into a means for the literate masses to make sense of the modernizing world around them. While industrialized printing had been a Dutch introduction into the Indies, the Chinese (and a number of Eurasian) print entrepreneurs were the first to consciously target the rising middle classes as the patrons of popular entertainment. As had been the case elsewhere, "the colonized became consumers."[14]

The chief entrepreneurial aspect of Chinese printing in the Indies was its multitude of genres, including newspapers, short stories, novels, poetry, and educational material. Print entrepreneurship meant being involved in highly politicized journalism and highly lucrative fiction at the same time. The language of these divergent publications was likewise heterogeneous. Even the Malay of individual authors could fluctuate between formal and colloquial, and between Chinese-affected and broadly understandable. Certain thematic strings cut across all genres: traditional "Eastern" values, public probity, Chinese chauvinism, social change, and a troubled relation with Dutch colonialism, its power hierarchies, and prescriptions of modernity. All materials were furthermore part of the same circulatory networks. They were written by the same authors, printed by the same publishing houses (on the same cheap paper), and punctuated by the same advertisements. The prolificacy of Chinese print entrepreneurs skewed the colony's flow of knowledge. They enabled people from various backgrounds to perceive themselves as active participants of urban life. They stimulated literacy in romanized Malay, which became a vehicle of popular culture throughout the Indies. Indeed, many Sino-Malay writers targeted the entire plebeian Malay-speaking world, including Javanese, Sundanese, Eurasians, Arabs, Indians, and others. Their publications were not infrequently marketed as "for all races" (*oentoek segala bangsa*). Several other communities also wrote in Malay, yet the Chinese played an outsized role and had the largest output.

Information on individual print entrepreneurs is rather spotty. The works and exploits of prominent figures—such as Lie Kim Hok (1853–1912), Kwee Tek Hoay (1886–1951), Tan Boen Kim (1887–1959), Tio Ie Soei (1890–1974), Liem Thian Joe (1895–1962), Kwee Thiam Tjing (1900–74), Kwee Kek Beng (1900–75), Njoo Cheong Seng (1902–61), Nio Joe Lan (1904–73), Liem Khing Hoo (1905–45), Tan Boen Soan (1905–52), Tan Hong Boen (1905–83), and Pouw Kioe An (1906–81)—have been described in quite some detail.[15] Next to their journalistic and editorial activities, most of them wrote monographs and poetry. Successful Sino-Malay fiction could also migrate to the stage of popular theater. Kwee Tek Hoay, for example, became a successful dramatist midcareer. Several entrepreneurs established their own printing shops, started one or more journals, and owned other businesses. In addition, many were involved in educational reform and Chinese cultural revivalism. There is not a great deal this book can add to the existing literature about the above individuals. Much less can be known about the more obscure protagonists. Many wrote anonymously or under pseudonyms, making it difficult to reconstruct the contexts in which they operated. Anonymity was especially commonplace in publications that insulted powerful people and institutions. We do know that the agents involved in the production and consumption of Sino-Malay print culture came from all walks of life. They included members of the affluent elites (*tjabang atas* or *kaoem Packard*), urban middle classes, and sojourners moving in transregional circuits. Most authors were men, but women writers played important and scantily researched roles as well.[16] A small number was born in China, yet the vast majority of print entrepreneurs came from the Netherlands Indies, in particular the cities of Java.

Indonesia is home to one of the world's largest overseas populations of ethnic (Han) Chinese, following Thailand, Malaysia, and the United States. The presence of innumerable mixed-race families, combined with a widespread reluctance to self-identify as Chinese, makes it difficult to calculate their precise number.[17] I use the umbrella term "Chinese-Indonesians," teleologically, to include the full range of Chinese-descended individuals behind the production and consumption of Sino-Malay texts, notwithstanding their diverse regional origins, linguistic proficiencies, cultural orientations, political allegiances, and degrees of admixture with Indonesia's other peoples. In colonial times, the Chinese used a variety of competing terms to refer to themselves. My usage of "Chinese-Indonesian" does not imply the existence of a static, homogeneous group. Nomenclature is in fact a recurring challenge, with no English term being universally accepted. Most Indonesian scholars prefer the term *Tionghoa* (Chinese), a Hokkien loanword into Malay/Indonesian. In English, "Chinese-Indonesians," "Sino-Indonesians," "Indonesian Chinese," or "Indies Chinese" are all in regular use.[18] To my mind, the term "Indonesian" has validity even in a late colonial context.[19] By the mid-1920s, journalists writing in Malay widely referred to their country under its current name, two decades before it became a politically viable entity. While "Indonesian" was not their prevailing identity at the time, the majority saw their future in the archipelago, not in China. A terminological acknowledgement of their Indonesianness furthermore reflects a sense of belonging shared by most Chinese-Indonesians at present.

Nevertheless, this is no book about all Chinese-Indonesians, who in 1930 amounted to 724,499 men and 465,515 women. A focus on Sino-Malay print culture partly (but not entirely) excludes the perspectives of women, rural populations, and people who could not read Malay. Historically, the majority of

Indonesia's Malay-literate Chinese were townspeople. In 1930, 11.7 percent of the urban population of Java—Indonesia's most populous island—was registered as part of the Chinese population. This book foregrounds these communities, and particularly the educated—and, occasionally, self-taught—social classes with access to romanized Malay, but not necessarily to the colony's governing elite.[20] The majority was legally required to settle in Chinatowns, located near the center of most Indonesian cities. Other sizable Chinese groups had established themselves on the countryside of eastern Sumatra, western Kalimantan, and the Malay Peninsula. Many of them were speakers of Hakka, Teochew, or Cantonese. They initially had difficulties communicating with outsiders and only belatedly entered the Malay-speaking world, so that these groups likewise do not form the focus of this book.[21]

In terms of geographical coverage, this book prioritizes cities with Chinese-run Malay printing presses, such as Batavia, Bogor, Sukabumi, Semarang, Solo, Surabaya, Pontianak, Makassar, Padang, and Medan, where Sino-Malay texts were produced and consumed, and where most authors grew up and worked. These cities were in many ways better connected to the British Straits Settlements (Singapore and Penang)—where Malay likewise functioned as a print language used by people of Chinese origins—than to the remote interior of the Netherlands Indies. British Malaya, Sumatra, and Java exhibit deep connections on a cultural and linguistic level. Their markets for popular entertainment were likewise intertwined, with novels, poetry, music, and theater performances routinely traveling across the boundaries of empire. This book therefore adopts a transborder scope. It examines the ways Sino-Malay texts resonated across the wider Malay-speaking world, but also how they were influenced by events outside Indonesia, such as the Chinese Revolution. It also takes into account themes that resonated elsewhere in Southeast Asia and the colonized world more broadly, including the dilemmas of modernity, culture formation in diasporas, and agency-through-language. Print entrepreneurship universally relied on transregional brokers, urban middle classes, and vernacular languages. At the same time that Chinese entrepreneurs successfully mechanized their commercial networks, plurilingual competencies, and printing companies in the Netherlands Indies and British Malaya, agents from the Indian Subcontinent did the same in several Indian Ocean port cities, albeit for a more homogeneous readership.[22]

Sino-Malay texts portray—often in subtle ways—a community that vacillated between the ancestral homeland, recipient society, and colonial system to which they were inextricably linked. Chinese-Indonesian history abounds in these journeys of belonging, some of which were specific to the archipelago and others exemplary to migration in general. As with Chinese-descended communities worldwide, they were feared and exploited by imperial regimes and modern nation-states alike. Due to their oft-assumed economic prowess and mercantile connections, many such groups "have largely flourished in postcolonial states and yet are considered politically alien, or alienable, when conditions take a turn for the worse."[23] The history of Indonesia's Chinese communities, then, reads like a record of partial acceptance at best and racialized violence at worst. It features successive centuries of assimilation—voluntary or otherwise—interwoven with not-so-subtle discrimination and, up to recent times, a reluctance to recognize their contributions to the nation's cultural palimpsest. Shifting political loyalties, or accusations thereof, constitute an equally familiar theme. These predate the timeframe of this book. From the 1890s, Chinese businessmen from Southeast Asia proved instrumental to China's modernization and were welcomed into the fold of its nationalistic movement.[24] Increased contacts between communities of different provincial and linguistic origins helped to solidify a pan-Chinese consciousness and strengthened the position of Mandarin as a link-language. The Sino-Malay print culture rose to prominence amidst these waves of nationalism, anticolonialism, Chinese reformism, resinicization, but also opportunism to arise within the colonial system.

In Indonesia, as elsewhere in Southeast Asia, Chineseness was a legally imposed category as much as an ethno-linguistic identity. The established paradigm of "overseas Chinese" insufficiently reflects these realities, as many people so designated saw themselves as permanent settlers rather than eternal subjects to the ancestral land. This is especially the case for Southeast Asia's acculturated Chinese communities, known self-referentially as *Peranakan* or *Baba* in the Malay-speaking world. An important intervention in this regard is Shu-Mei Shih's concept of a Sinophone, which takes as its starting point the ethnic, linguistic, and cultural heterogeneity of Chinese Others living outside mainland China. By emphasizing (Sinitic) languages rather than race, nation, and/or ethnicity, Sinophone studies have been fruitfully applied in Southeast Asian contexts where Chineseness—in its full sociolinguistic diversity—gave rise to literature, cinema, music, and performances that differed markedly from those of China.[25] Yet in the case of Indonesia, such an approach would exclude the majority of subject matter. Java, Sumatra, Borneo, and other islands have attracted (male) settlers from China's southern provinces from precolonial times, generating processes of acculturation that spanned over many more centuries than they did elsewhere. Eventually, not-speaking-Chinese became a prevailing reality for many Chinese-descended families.[26] This situates Chinese-Indonesians at the margins of the Sinophone, if not outside its palisade. And yet, Chineseness—actively achieved as well as externally ascribed—was crucial to their cultural productions from late colonial times.[27] In the context of Indonesia, but also Cambodia, Myanmar, and the Philippines, it is hardly fruitful to deemphasize race in favor of language, given that "Chinese people are discriminated against by not being allowed to forget that they are Chinese, even when their families have lived in those countries for generations and they do not speak Chinese languages at all." As Ien Ang put it, many families are Chinese by descent, not by consent.[28]

Sino-Malay Texts

At this point we must introduce the characteristics of Sino-Malay publications, their linguistic features, reception (up to present times), accessibility, and criteria for selection. In the following section I will discuss methods to examine Chinese-Indonesian experiences through the crucible of language, before finally presenting the chapter outline. This book focuses on a geographically scattered, ideologically incoherent corpus of newspapers, novels, advertisements, short stories, educational books, biographies, instruction manuals, poetry books, songs, theater plays, and linguistic publications. I cherish no aspirations to canonize so noisy and internally discordant a corpus, whose writers quarreled with each other as much as with outsiders. Instead, I offer glimpses, as Virginia Woolf put it so evocatively, into "its rubbish-heap, its record of vanished moments and forgotten lives told in faltering and feeble accents that have perished."[29]

I use "Sino-Malay" (*Melajoe-Tionghoa*) as a categorical shortcut for writings in Malay by people of (partly) Chinese origins. "Malay" here strictly refers to the language of these texts, which differs from those of ethnic Malays. At the same time, Sino-Malay is best approached as a fluid category defying easy categorization. From the 1920s, the Dutch authorities classified Sino-Malay publications as distinct from their indigenous counterparts,[30] yet reality is always more complicated. Editorial boards were heterogeneous, as were audiences, and even ethnicity is an insufficient yardstick to extricate the Sino-Malay print culture from that of other groups. It was not uncommon for writers of non-Chinese backgrounds to situate their stories in Chinese settings and vice versa. Many authors were furthermore anonymous, with their ethnic (and gendered) identity forever sealed in mystery. Taking into account this fluid nature, a watertight definition of the term "Sino-Malay" would be impossible to formulate. A rigid treatment of Sino-Malay literature as an autonomous corpus has furthermore obstructed its appreciation as part of Indonesia's early literary canon.[31] It is equally difficult to demarcate this print culture chronologically. Chinese-descended authors have always remained active in Indonesia's literary scene, yet Indonesia's independence in 1945 encouraged a gradual assimilation into the nation's postcolonial mainstream. The scope of this book ends in 1949, when the last Chinese editors adopted the national Indonesian orthography. The period of Indonesia's

Japanese occupation (1942–45) forms a hiatus, as almost all Sino-Malay publications were banned under this regime, to be partly revived afterward.

The authors, editors, journalists, playwrights, and comedians behind Sino-Malay texts typically had access to multiple languages and cultures. In this regard, their position in society was akin to that of other in-between groups spearheading theater, music, cinema, and other forms of popular entertainment, such as Parsis in India, Armenians in West Asia, or Jews in Europe and the United States.[32] Unlike Yiddish, the Malay used in Chinese productions was written in a script readily available to other ethnicities, making them even more accessible and popular. A number of writers had received Western education in addition to their homegrown knowledge of Malay. Yet their linguistic horizons stretched far beyond the European/non-European bilingualism seen among indigenous intelligentsia of other colonial contexts.[33] Many authors had also received some Chinese education, granting them access to ideas from China and Singapore. Chinese print entrepreneurs were by no means alone in embracing the vernacular—this was also done by indigenous, Eurasian, and Arab writers—but they were arguably the most plurilingual. Here, class and proximity to power must also be taken into account. While many of Indonesia's Peranakan elites and indigenous "bourgeois nationalists" could best express themselves in Dutch and belatedly adopted standard Indonesian, Chinese print entrepreneurs exhausted the full range of vernaculars at their disposal. Their prominence in Malay printing and popular culture was a thorn in the side of the colony's intellectual gatekeepers, who had formed an archetypal "alliance of nativist elitism and institutional Orientalism."[34] Even today, the Chinese are rarely credited for their historical importance in this domain, which ranks among the first phenomena to overstep the boundaries of locality and ethnicity.

In view of their multiple linguistic competencies, it is somewhat misleading to categorize the Chinese of the former Netherlands Indies as "native speakers" of either Chinese or Malay. As Vicente Rafael has pointed out in the context of Philippine plurilingualism, "whenever I am asked what my native language is, I always hesitate to respond. I cannot point to a single one without feeling that I might be betraying the others. . . . Whatever I happen to be speaking at the moment is always commingled and contaminated with a whole train of other languages I grew up speaking and hearing in the past and to this very day."[35] Chinese communities in the Netherlands Indies, too, had many "motherless tongues," to borrow his term. Numerous men and women attained fluency in languages they acquired later in life. Especially in the informal sphere, their speech formed a complex amalgam. Profuse borrowing from Hokkien rendered their in-group Malay hard to understand for outsiders. Yet, as true print entrepreneurs, most

Chinese writers could strategically switch to a generic Malay also in use among Eurasians, Arabs, Indians, and indigenous peoples.

This de-ethnicized, urban Malay constituted a spectrum of dialects and registers, known interchangeably as Low Malay (*Melajoe Rendah*), Bazaar Malay (*Melajoe Pasar*), or Batavian Malay (*Melajoe Betawi*). Somewhat confusingly, the term Low Malay also denoted a certain administrative register—sometimes called Service Malay (*dienst-Maleisch*)—used between Europeans and indigenous people in diplomacy, the press, and legal proceedings.[36] Few Chinese with Malay proficiency took the latter variety seriously. They categorically denounced the Malay of Dutchmen as too European in its grammar, too classical in its lexicon, or both at the same time. It made for stiff if not incomprehensible reading, at least in the eyes of Java's vernacular audiences. For this reason, cartoons, comic strips, and advertisements only achieved maximum outreach when they appeared in the correct type of Low Malay. In turn, Low Malay could have only become as popular as it did by virtue of a highly visual media culture, facilitated by technological developments and financed by commercial advertising. Many Chinese authors had come to embrace the term "Low Malay," undermining its pejorative power and the fact that it was foisted upon them by others. Its success was closely linked with other strands of cultural entrepreneurship, such as popular theater and Indonesia's budding film industry.[37] The convergence between language and image, textuality and visuality, and moralism and sensationalism stood at the core of this exciting mass culture.

Of considerably higher prestige, yet still below Dutch, was the literary idiom of Malay elites. It was called High Malay (*Melajoe Tinggi, Melajoe Atas*) or Riau Malay (*Melajoe Riouw*), after the area where the purest Malay was allegedly spoken. The colonial administration had long sought to mechanize this hegemonic variety, although Service Malay prevailed among Europeans.[38] Dutch universities, the Netherlands Bible Society, the Royal Batavian Society of Arts and Sciences, the KITLV, and other research institutions proved decisive in making "languages objects of knowledge, so that their speakers could be made subjects of power."[39] High Malay was standardized in 1901 by the Sumatra-born linguist Charles Adriaan van Ophuijsen (1854–1917). Throughout the early twentieth century, many Dutch editors attempted to emulate this standard, with varying degrees of success. Pioneering in this regard was the Balai Poestaka (Commission for Popular Literature; D: Commissie voor de Volkslectuur), founded in 1908, which promoted a more respectable type of Malay and issued publications deemed appropriate for indigenous readers.[40] Yet such "civilizing" efforts did little to curb the power of Chinese print entrepreneurs, who had unapologetically and irrevocably integrated the Malay language—their Hokkienized version of it, but also Low Malay in general—into the vibrant realm of popular culture. Different factions continued to exploit Malay for different purposes, and for a moment it seemed as if the Chinese had the upper hand.

The Malay of Chinese print entrepreneurs was colored—if not enhanced—by their plurilingual competencies. In written form, its grammar was not too distinct from that of other urban communities from the same region. Lexically, however, the preponderance of European and Chinese words made Sino-Malay texts difficult to fully comprehend for the uninitiated, including for most of today's readers. Rather than treating their translingual practices as artificial or exaggerated, I argue that it was an existential part of their liminal identity. The ancestral language of most authors, a Chinese variety known in Southeast Asia as "Hokkien," asserted a strong lexical impact on the writings intended for Peranakan audiences.[41] Other Sinitic languages, such as Cantonese, Hakka, and Teochew, barely influenced Java's Malay. Words from Dutch and other European languages were equally ubiquitous in Sino-Malay texts and in vernacular Malay print culture more generally. As the Sumatra-born intellectual Armijn Pané (1908–70) wondered out loud, "At times we ask ourselves, what is the use of quotations in French, German, Latin. The majority of these citations is not translated, nor is it even clarified what they mean."[42] Indeed, indigenous writers with access to High Malay, many of whom were of Sumatran origins, were seldom positive about the cultural productions from Java's cities. It was no different the other way around.

Such sentiments were more than classist pronouncements buttressed by delusions of linguistic purity. From the 1910s, indigenous authors started to compete against their Chinese and Eurasian colleagues in the marketplace of Malay printing.[43] To distinguish themselves from their Chinese competitors, some indigenous journalists wrote in a type of Malay that was closer to the colonial standard. This was the case, for example, with the Islam-oriented literary scene in Medan, North Sumatra, which emerged in the 1920s and lasted until the 1960s.[44] In the cities of Java, too, Indonesian nationalists of Javanese, Sundanese, and Madurese origins substituted their locally flavored Malay—in 1909 they still referred to it as Java-Malay (*bahasa Melajoe-Djawa*)[45]—for what had become known as Indonesian (*Bahasa Indonesia*) in the mid-1920s. Both were offshoots of the same Malay tongue, but only the latter enjoyed the endorsement of language planners. During the *Soempah Pemoeda* (Youth Pledge) of October 28, 1928, Bahasa Indonesia was declared Indonesia's unitary language.[46] Yet, while writers who knew better passionately disparaged the Low Malay of Chinese authors, the latter responded in kind by ridiculing the artificial language of their snobbish detractors.

An academic foray into Sino-Malay print culture must take into account the language and contents of the material, but also its scattered accessibility and political legacy. There is no better time to do so than the present. Academic freedom has improved drastically since the fall in 1998 of Indonesia's second president, Suharto (1921–2008), whose exclusionary brand of social engineering sought to minimize the visibility of ethnic Chinese and erase their culture from the public domain. Suharto's rise to power in 1966 meant the end of "all Chinese schools, mass organizations, mass media, use of Chinese characters, personal names, and names for firms/shops."[47] His Orde Baru (New Order) regime also imperiled private collectors of Sino-Malay publications. As the dictum went, "the Chinese language was treated like a drug and its use banned."[48] It is no surprise, then, that Indonesia's academic efforts to reassess the position of its Chinese minority are of recent pedigree. These days it has become difficult to keep track of newly established museums, conferences, seminars, Zoominars, workshops, public lectures, exhibitions, book launches, and other events dealing with Chinese-Indonesian culture and history. Yet even though the Sino-Malay print culture arguably constitutes one of the bedrocks from which modern Indonesian literature has sprung, the amount of book-length monographs dedicated to this topic remains limited.[49] A reacquaintance with the Sino-Malay textual heritage, therefore, stands high on the agenda of many young Indonesian scholars.

This proliferation of interest in Chinese-Indonesian texts constitutes somewhat of a historical anomaly. During colonial times, no international library took the acquisition of these publications seriously. The KITLV, tasked from 1851 with the collection of Indies/Indonesia-related materials, only started to systematically collect Sino-Malay novels in the late 1960s. The Universiti Kebangsaan Malaysia did so from 1973.[50] On their absence in university curricula, Charles Coppel pointed out in the 1970s:

> It is striking that most studies of the development of the Indonesian language and Indonesian literature ignore (or relegate to a footnote) this Sino-Malay literature. In part, this has no doubt been due to the difficulties of obtaining access to it, but I suspect that there are other factors at work. In our departments of Indonesian Studies and in Indonesia today, the Sino-Malay dialect is regarded with some disdain as being sub-standard Indonesian, rather comical and hence of dubious value. No-one would suggest that this now dead dialect should be a model for Indonesian style today, but is it therefore worthless? One might as well throw out Shakespeare's writing from the purview of our English departments, if suitability for contemporary style is to be the criterion.[51]

Sino-Malay fiction became internationally known through the scholarship of Claudine Salmon, whose extensive bibliography remains the standard work of reference. Before this vital intervention, the material was at best mentioned in passing and at worst ignored altogether by the world's experts on Indonesian literature.[52] Academic attention to Sino-Malay literature grew in the 1990s, both in Indonesia and abroad. A still relevant portrait is given in this period by Henk Maier:

> Many of the books mentioned in Salmon's book never went through a second printing. None of them made it to the Indonesian school textbooks. Many of them are now available in only one or two libraries in the world. This residuality does not necessarily imply irrelevance and indifference, however. It rather suggests the existence of a distinct circuit, with a vitality and a desire to experiment on its own, and with its own forces and rules, which cannot fail sooner or later to penetrate the canon. The residual circuit formed by Chinese-Malay printed materials shaped its own themes and initiated its own discussions, propelled along by a group that may have been gradually pushed into the ideological and cultural margins of society, but which even so retained a voice that was heard and that demanded a reaction. It is a telling fact that the Chinese-Malay community in the Indies continued to generate so many publications, so many novels, in a climate that became increasingly repressive in the literary and, more widely, in the political sphere.[53]

The bulk of Sino-Malay material is found in Indonesian libraries and private collections. These publications are indulged as curiosities from a forgotten time, including by Indonesians of non-Chinese origins and non-Indonesians of Chinese origins. They are collected by passionate aficionados and sold on social-media platforms. Their academic use, however, faces a number of challenges. As Malay has changed rapidly over the past century, many linguistic nuances are incomprehensible to contemporary readers. More importantly, most Indonesian libraries lack fully functional and up-to-date cataloguing systems to infer the actual location of specific titles, so that one is usually redirected to Singapore, Kuala Lumpur, Melbourne, Sydney, Auckland, Leiden, or Ithaca (NY). Yet the situation is quickly improving. A recent initiative, the Museum Pustaka Peranakan Tionghoa (Chinese-Indonesian Literature Museum) in Tangerang, houses numerous unique Sino-Malay publications and accommodates public events.[54] Indonesia's National Library has digitized 122 Sino-Malay novels at the time I am writing this, accessible through the Indonesia Heritage Digital Library website. Plans to revitalize Jakarta's Pusat Dokumentasi Sastra H. B. Jassin (H. B. Jassin Literature Documentation Center) and Surabaya's Medayu Agung are ongoing, but the future of these important libraries is unclear at this point.

It would be fair to say that Sino-Malay texts are currently in the process of being rediscovered by Indonesian and international students. This generally takes place in Indonesian Studies rather than Chinese Studies departments. Courses on Sino-Malay literature have recently been taught at the University of Indonesia (Depok), Petra University (Surabaya), and other institutions, during which the works of Kwee Tek Hoay and Njoo Cheong Seng have proven especially popular. Further testimony to this renewed interest are a number of online repositories: the aforementioned Indonesia Heritage Digital Library (National Library of Indonesia), the Chinese-Indonesian Community Documents Collection from Java (University of Washington), the Monash University Library's Asian Collections, and the Sino-Malay Texts (Leiden University Library and KITLV).[55]

At this point the corpus and data selection for this book merit some further comment. As with vernacular writings more broadly, much Sino-Malay material was not seen as worthy of preservation at the time it was issued. The total amount of Chinese-owned journals has been estimated at around seventy in 1935,[56] yet comparatively few of these ended up in university libraries. Many sources have not been preserved anywhere, and their short-lived existence can only be deduced from other publications in which they are mentioned. In some cases, owners or heirs of private collections lost, sold, or discarded their Sino-Malay material but held onto Chinese-language publications, indicating a difference in prestige.[57] While Chinese-Indonesians and their allies increasingly perceive Sino-Malay publications as important cultural heritage, the extant material is thinly scattered across different libraries, secondhand bookstores, and private collections. Most primary texts investigated in this book belong to the KITLV collection and are currently stored at the Leiden University Library.[58]

In terms of periodicals, I have chiefly drawn from *Sin Po* (New Newspaper; Batavia, 1910) and *Hoakiao* (Overseas Chinese; Surabaya, 1923).[59] With around ten thousand daily circulations in the 1920s, *Sin Po* was one of the biggest newspapers in the Netherlands Indies.[60] Established amidst the euphoria of the Chinese Revolution, it was a forward-looking and proudly nationalistic mouthpiece of predominantly left-wing pro–Sun Yat-sen factions. In addition to its Malay daily, *Sin Po* published a homonymous Chinese daily (from 1921) and a Malay weekly (from 1923), which contained a variety of cultural and political items and a short supplement in Dutch. Like many other Sino-Malay newspapers, *Sin Po* was sympathetic to Indonesian nationalism, albeit in a non-participatory way. Initially, the board was able to promulgate its pro-China stance without much interference from the colonial government. This relative lack of supervision generally afforded Chinese journalists more room for expression than their indigenous counterparts. In the 1930s, however, the political inconsequence of *Sin Po* and other pro-China newspapers quickly dissipated after they published a series of vehement anti-Japanese pieces, attracting Dutch censorship as a consequence.

The semiweekly periodical *Hoakiao*, edited by Kwee Hing Tjiat (1891–1939), was smaller in its scope and likewise attracted a pro-China readership. The authorities never took it seriously enough to warrant much comment.[61] Both *Sin Po* and *Hoakiao* targeted readers across the Netherlands Indies, especially those interested in nationalism, politics, and culture. I imagine they could be purchased in every town where sufficient numbers of Chinese entrepreneurs had set up shop, but the precise circulation of Sino-Malay periodicals has never been accurately charted.

In addition to these digitized sources, I have browsed through various miscellaneous materials—often in fragile condition—in the dispersed archives of the British Library, the Chinese-Indonesian Literature Museum, the Cornell University Library, the Fadli Zon Library, the Fisher Library (Sydney University), the H. B. Jassin Literature Documentation Center, the Matheson Library (Monash University), the Medayu Agung Library, the National Library of Indonesia (both the Perpustakaan Nasional Indonesia and the Perpustakaan Nasional Salemba Raya), the National Library of Singapore, and the National Library of the Netherlands.

Words that Unlock Worlds

Language history is largely absent from the otherwise extensive oeuvre of Chinese-Indonesian studies.[62] Much scholarship has recently prioritized local-level histories, influential community members, and contributions to the Indonesian nation. This is clearly in response to persistent and inaccurate stereotypes portraying the Chinese as socially aloof, economically exploitative, and unwilling to engage with nation-building.[63] As a result, more is known about the lives of prominent individuals, including individual print entrepreneurs, than about the Malay they adopted or the print culture they helped create. The available publications on language are few in number and chiefly examine localized Sinitic languages, Chinese loanwords into Malay, and contemporary language practices.

While this book investigates Sino-Malay printing through the lens of language, it does so without writing exclusively or even chiefly for a linguistic readership. Language offers fruitful transdisciplinary avenues to scrutinize texts dealing with popular entertainment, cultural loyalties, and colonial hierarchies. The ability of polyglots to creatively and strategically mobilize their linguistic resources has been described as "translanguaging," a framework that treats plurilingual discourses not as collectives of opposing language identities, but as cohesive systems of interactional communication. Lydia Liu, investigating the hybrid, fast-evolving language of the colonized vis-à-vis the hegemonic language of colonizers, proposes the term "translingual practice."[64] Unlike code-mixing, lexical borrowing, or bilingualism, a focus on the translingual enables a deeper engagement with linguistic (self-)styling and its power—especially in unequal settings—to inscribe meaning, forge shared identities, and perpetuate exclusionary practices. In the context of this book, it allows for an integrated study of Sino-Malay print culture and its linguistic plurality, which encompassed Malay, Hokkien, Dutch, Javanese, Mandarin, and other languages.

The Indies Chinese, as well as other in-between groups, excelled in these translingual practices. A combination of plurilingualism and access to different registers of Malay underpinned their mastery of puns, jokes, and swear words. As such, they were perfectly configured to produce popular culture, which by definition contains elements of humor, playfulness, and vulgarity. Their enlarged vocabularies helped them to articulate, challenge, and satirize experiences of the everyday. Much indeed revolved around words, including loanwords, neologisms, archaisms, ethnonyms, insults, puns, stretched meanings, and specialized contexts. Words constitute the landmarks of cultural progress, social complexity, and knowledge exchange between communities in contact or conflict. Words, famously, have the power to differentiate people along the lines of class, gender, and ethnicity. Malay speakers with belletrist pretensions, for example, avoided European vocabulary, while those keen to showcase their Western education saturated their prose with Dutch, English, German, French, and even Latin. Avid followers of Chinese politics interspersed their Malay with Mandarin, while traditionalists preferred Hokkien. The deliberate misspelling (cacography) of words became a translingual device to mark boorish provincialism as opposed to suave urban slickness. The study of these linguistic clues, then, has the potential to lay bare strategies of selfing and othering that prevailed among Chinese speakers of Malay, but were by no means limited to them.

This book is not the first to examine colonial experiences through a linguistically informed analysis of vernacular texts. In this arena, I have found ample inspiration in scholarship on Africa. Mohamed Adhikari's *Straatpraatjes* (Street Talk)—named after a satirical newspaper column in the early twentieth century—casts a unique light on Cape Town's language history, social life, and popular culture through the "Coloured" variety of Afrikaans. Jan Blommaert's *Grassroots Literacy* presents an ethnographically inspired study of nonelite Swahili texts and the way their writers lose voice upon encountering globalized literary regimes. Ziad Fahmy's *Ordinary Egyptians* traces Egypt's modern national identity and its solid footing in a popular mass culture in the Cairene dialect.[65] Each in their own way, these works foreground colonial-era texts in the vernacular, demonstrating a vast array of methods to examine the language practices they exhibit. My own analysis is based on words and translingual practices, yet approaches prioritizing grammar, visual markers, or the material dimensions of texts-as-objects can be equally fruitful. I follow these scholars in displaying the source texts alongside their English translations, as the latter can never accurately replace the former in terms of content, style, quality, and esthetic evocativeness. Doing so furthermore introduces a layer of verifiability to my interpretations.

Sino-Malay publications, not unlike the African examples mentioned above, were written in the vernacular of the urban masses deprived from access to European languages. This Low Malay idiom thrived amidst and despite the exclusionary practices of colonialism. It became an "enforcer of complex language behavior,"[66] able to assume formal, humoristic, poetic, practical, Chinese-like, European-like, educated, or abusive properties as the context demanded. It connected readers and writers from different regional, social, and ethno-religious backgrounds. In doing so, it did what neither Dutch nor the legitimated standard Malay could achieve: to capture the everyday life of people whose aspirations, anxieties, and antics would have otherwise vanished into the mists of time. In this regard, the element of humor is insightful above all else. It was by no means limited to slapstick, although that certainly had an important place as well. In Sino-Malay texts, playful humor often dovetailed with serious frustration. It provided an instrument to gently poke holes in the colonial system, the power hierarchies it encapsulated, the loss of tradition it caused, and the limitations it imposed. Not unlike today's online activists defying authoritarianism, Chinese print entrepreneurs adeptly wielded translingual puns, as double interpretability provided some protection against their censors and detractors.

The hierarchical nature of the Netherlands Indies informs this book's linguistic analysis. On the one hand, the choice to write in the vernacular—rather than Dutch, High Malay, or Service Malay—pits the Sino-Malay print culture against the master narrative. As the logic of colonialism has it, nonknowledge of the vernacular is something enviable and indicative of an elevated social status.[67] Vernacular texts, then, intrinsically have some subelite if not counterhegemonic tendencies. On the other, they are not to be romanticized as "freed from the dominance, if not taint, of the Eurocentric-Enlightenment epistemic framing of histories, worldviews and prescriptives."[68] If one takes into account the racialized and gendered contexts in which they were written, it would be perverse to expect no tincture of bigotry in their pages. Neither should they be seen as unquestionable gold mines of historiographic value. As in most textual corpora, the relation between the written word and the lived experience was characterized by tension rather than equivalence, leaving many things unknown.[69] Yet, it is precisely in disagreement and contention—in the translated, the syncretic, and the cacophonous—that the potential of language is stretched to its fullest and, hence, becomes the most meaningful. Many examples in this book indeed originate from heated arguments on the cultural and/or political issues of the day.

In the same way that scholars interested in the social life of commodities can "follow the things themselves,"[70] those keen to explore language development can follow trails of words, expressions, and grammatical structures. Many of the insights so generated carry historical value, akin to the ones derived from objects, buildings, and archives. In the colonial context, it is hard to miss the various terms and phrases coined as part of the discourse on race. The Indies Chinese found themselves in a particularly delicate position, caught between the fires of Chinese nationalism, colonial conservatism, and the Indonesian struggle for emancipation and independence. The rather specific insults exchanged between these opposing factions present an exercise in linguistic scrutiny. Western-educated Peranakans risked being castigated as *holan-holanan* (fake Dutch), *gila barat* (obsessed with the West), *baoe kedjoe* (smelling like cheese), *belepotan mentega* (smeared with butter), and *baba tjat* (painted Babas).[71] At the same time, their knowledge of European languages proved extremely useful to articulate experiences of discrimination. Translingual proficiency thus provided grease for the wheels of emancipation. This is perhaps best illustrated by a brief extract from *Hoakiao*. In a 1926 plea to recognize the value of Sino-Malay journalists, its editors lamented their subordinate position in the Netherlands Indies press landscape. To discuss concepts that "pure" Malay was at the time unable to communicate, they deliberately infused their prose with the Dutch words *suprematie* (supremacy) and *rassenwaan* (racial mania):

| We feel that the time has come to let go of the delusion of Western supremacy and throw aside the racial mania that still lurks within. | Kita merasa soedah tjoekoep temponja, impian suprematie Barat dilepasken dan rassenwaan jang masi sadja mengerem diboewang kasamping.[72] |

In addition to challenging the "intellectual" underpinnings of colonialism, journalists also sought to improve their own communal position. Those dynamics can likewise be investigated by following the words. A case in point is the legal position of the Chinese, which remained a controversial topic throughout the late colonial period. Many Indies-born Chinese loathed their government-imposed racialization as "foreign orientals" (D: *Vreemde Oosterlingen*, Ml: *bangsa Timoer Asing*), especially since the colony's Japanese subjects had from 1899 luxuriated in the same legal privileges of Europeans.[73] This was even extended to ethnic Chinese from Japanese-occupied Taiwan. As one commentator put it with no shortage of indignation: "he could be the rudest coolie or biggest crook, and yet his congener, though a subject of the Netherlands, has to be content with a lower legal position, even if he holds an academic title from a Dutch university."[74] Eventually, a growing number of Chinese did obtain the legal status of European, especially from the 1920s. They became "equated" (D: *gelijkgesteld*, Ml: *disamaken, dipersamaken, diglekstel*), or—to use the parlance of British colonialism—part of the European and Allied races. In a mixed Malay-Hokkien idiom, such individuals were commonly derided as *blanda toenphoa* (1.5-guilders-Europeans), a snide reference to the postage of an application letter for legal equation (Ml: *masoek blanda*, D: *gelijkstelling*). In Dutch, they were dismissed as *Staatsblad-Europeanen* (Gazette Europeans), as their newly acquired European status was publicly announced in the *Indies Gazette*. The mannerisms associated with them provided fertile grounds for additional linguistic sarcasm. One poem, published in 1926 in *Sin Po*, accuses them—simultaneously, as if part of a package—of fetishizing European languages, modern clothes, and capitalist aspirations:

Hey, readers, don't you know me yet?	Zeg, pembatja, U belon kenal ikke ini?
My name is Ch.S.H. Lie	Naamnja van my jaitoe: Ch.S.H. Lie.
Of course I've been equated with the Europeans around here	Tentoe al glykstel met Europeaan disini,
My servants call me: Sinjo Charly	Myn bedienden panggil ikke: sinjo Charly.
When I get married, I want to look for a rich girl	Ikke kaloe kawin, wil zoeken meisje jang kaja,
Who always wears a skirt, never a blouse	Jang altyd pake rok dan tida kenal kabaja,
With a modern haircut, able to speak Dutch	Kapselnja moet jang modern, Hollandsch sprekennja bisa,
That's my ideal, that's what I long for.	Dat is myn ideaal, jang di-inginken oleh saja.[75]

Once again, texts of the above sort can only be fully understood though their linguistic peculiarities. The Dutch pronouns, interjections, and other parts of speech symbolize the pathos of uprootedness, but in other contexts they might convey genuine practices of self-styling. The use of *Sinjo*, an appellation mostly reserved for Eurasians, adds to the mockery. True Europeanness—the hidden message seems to be—will always remain out of reach. The Dutch words associated with invasive culture, such as *rok* (skirt), *kapsel* (haircut), *Hollandsch spreken* (speaking Dutch), and of course *modern*, sharply contrast with the Malay *kabaja* (blouse) representing tradition. In the same vein, and in the same artificially Europeanized Malay idiom, the poem proceeds to travesty a Westernized Peranakan girl. Wearing revealing clothes, she shamefully admits that her complexion is darker than that of Europeans, compelling her to use skin-whitening powder. As Sino-Malay satirists regularly pointed out, and as Rey Chow demonstrates for the postcolonial experience more broadly, "unattained *tones* of whiteness" tend to manifest themselves simultaneously in the realms of language and body politics.[76] Europeanization and its (un)desirability is linguistically inscribed. It is most vividly expressed through narrative content fused with linguistic style, yielding—in the case of the poem in question—a bumbling Malay-Dutch aberration:

Even though it's not allowed, I could not care less	Maskipoen zoo verboden, ikke toch wil niet perdoeli,
I always wear the most modern clothes money can buy	Altyd myn pakean de modernste, jang bisa dibeli
Sleeveless, revealing cleavage; too bad my skin is a bit dark	Zonder mouw, dada onbedekt, jammer myn huid beetje zwart katjiwa sekali,
But that's no problem, you know, Virgin powder is very cheaply priced.	Maar perkara ketjil, hoor, bedak Virgin toch prysnja goedkoop sekali.[77]

Throughout this book, I will cite, translate, and contextualize passages that exhibit these linguistic vacillations. In selecting examples (at the cost of omitting many others), I aim to be historically illuminating rather than encyclopedic. What will be analyzed is what helps us understand Sino-Malay print culture, its rise to prominence, and the miscellaneous experiences it has documented "from within." The highlighted translingual practices, phraseology, humor, and other linguistic devices serve to illustrate and instantiate Chinese-Indonesian conceptions of self, others, and life under colonialism inasmuch as these can be reconstructed from their publications.

Chapter Outline

This book focuses on the years between 1911 and 1949 but does not take a strictly chronological approach. Instead, it is divided into five thematic chapters, dealing successively with the ways vernacular Malay was acquired, studied, appropriated, enriched, and hybridized by Chinese print entrepreneurs. Such an organization affords some observations on social and linguistic shifts occurring decade by decade, yet in view of the quantity and diversity of texts, any systematic attempt to do so would require corpus-linguistic techniques rather than close-reading.[78]

The multiple linguistic competencies of Indonesia's Chinese communities form the core of chapter 1. In Java, Makassar, and parts of Sumatra, Hokkien eventually ceased to be a first language, yet continued to share a space with Malay, Javanese, other Indonesian languages, Mandarin, other Sinitic languages, Dutch, or a combination of these. These languages also impacted on each other. All Chinese varieties introduced into the archipelago underwent considerable influence from Malay, while Malay adopted numerous words from Hokkien. The Malay and Javanese spoken by Peranakans also converged.[79] This sociolinguistic landscape inadvertently brings to mind the observation that "languages, like families, grow through marriage, and marriages are best when they involve different families."[80] But even within families, linguistic identity was varied, gendered, and shaped by educational opportunities. From the 1910s, Chinese children could theoretically receive schooling in one of their heritage languages (Hokkien, Hakka, Cantonese, or Teochew), the language of Chinese nationalism (Mandarin), the language of the colonizer (Dutch, and also occasionally English), or the lingua franca of the colony (Malay).

Although most Chinese were quick to adopt Malay, they often remained part of a distinct cultural world or were treated as such by others. Paradoxically, the Malay language eventually enabled them to reconnect with their Chinese roots, particularly through translations of Chinese literature and news coverage about China.[81] Malay proficiency also granted them economic advantages over more recent immigrants, known as *Singkeh* (new guests). Dutch sources consistently portrayed these China-born newcomers in uncharitable ways, with their linguistic otherness providing ample fodder for bigotry. In one description from 1860, we read that "the difference between foreign and local Chinese is only detectable from the [latter's] more stout physique and fluent tongue, in contrast to the skinny, bony, staccato-cackling newcomers or Singkehs."[82] The undernourishment of Chinese laborers intersected with other outward characteristics, such as their perceived linguistic deficiencies and lack of cultural capital. Like many other migrants, they were "racialized by language and languaged by race."[83]

If contemporaneous sources are anything to go by, many Sumatrans regarded their Malay as superior to that of Java, while people from Java were hardly impressed by the Sumatran variety. Yet the ultimate verdict on good and bad language came from European scholars and administrators, as is addressed in chapter 2. As colonizers, they had the epistemic privilege "of inventing the classification and being part of it,"[84] thus transfiguring local modes of thought, power, and hierarchy. Their canonical dictionaries, authorized grammars, Bible translations, and standard orthography solidified the hegemonic use of Malay and assigned regionalisms, plurilingualism, and other instances of vernacular language to the margins. But Chinese and other urban communities were not without agency to challenge such prescriptive regimes and replace them with their own. Not only did the majority reject the artificial Malay promoted by colonial authorities and indigenous elites, they produced alternative knowledge on and in their own preferred variety.

Chinese entrepreneurs in particular managed to secure a prime spot in the Malay printing industry, as is discussed in chapter 3. While Malay had long functioned as a print language under Dutch editorship, they transformed it into a carrier of popular culture, fashion, cultural revivalism, and political debate.[85] In doing so, they allowed unparalleled numbers of Indonesians-in-the-making to think about themselves in relation to the wider world. No less importantly, they enhanced the great tradition of Malay satire. The first secularized and profit-driven Malay newspapers emerged in the 1850s. Their popularity depended in part on the serialized stories they published, some of which were translated Chinese tales. The consumption of original and translated Malay fiction can be epitomized, to again quote from Virginia Woolf's critique of elitist literary values, as "people reading for the love of reading, slowly and unprofessionally, and judging with great sympathy and yet with great severity."[86] Political contestation entered the stage much later than fictional light reading,[87] displaying a reverse developmental trajectory from the western European public sphere. The Indies press remained under strict European censorship until regulations were slackened in 1906, only to be tightened again in 1914 in the wake of vigorous outbursts of criticism against the colonial government. Emboldened by pan-Chinese nationalism, growing numbers of Sino-Malay journalists made their grievances heard from the 1910s. Periodicals edited by indigenous Indonesians also emerged around this time and left an equally deep imprint on the colony's press landscape, in particular through the writings of left-wing intelligentsia.[88]

The Malay printing industry diversified during the 1910s, when it came to serve different political agendas. The colonial authorities continued to appropriate it as a controlling device and catalyst for "civilization." At the same time, growing numbers of indigenous progressives relied on periodicals to generate emancipatory change. Several Chinese-edited newspapers, too, were set up to serve political—rather than just commercial—interests. Among their numerous ambitions were short-lived plans to abandon the use of Malay and completely switch to Mandarin.[89] In practice, however, Malay proved ineradicable from Chinese print entrepreneurship. In terms of language as well as contents, the unruly Sino-Malay press stood in stark opposition to Dutch-edited publications, in particular those issued by the aforementioned Balai Poestaka and other government-sponsored bodies. One could argue that Batavia's *mission civilisatrice* was devised—with a few notable exceptions—to manicure Indonesia's cultural orientation (as the Balai Poestaka continued to do in postindependence times) and mentally keep the indigenous masses inside the village. While much of its moralistic literature was obsessed—not unlike the works of some Chinese authors—with the clash between tradition and modernity, Balai Poestaka persistently excluded writings and perspectives from Chinese, Medanese, British Malayan, and Islamic authors.[90] For anything to do with sex and violence, Malay-literate readers were best served by the Chinese-dominated vernacular press.

Most city-dwellers were quick to embrace the technological, educational, and employment opportunities afforded by colonial modernity. However, modern lifestyles hardly meant the end of conservative attitudes, many of which in fact came to be reinforced by them. As chapter 4 highlights, language again offers a window into these everyday-life contestations. Vernacular Malay became a language in which everything could be said, translated, and contested. It launched Indonesia's middle classes into a novel world of ideas and things.[91] The Dutch word *modern* was certainly a positive epithet for products and institutions, signifying a welcome break from all things *kolot* (old-fashioned) and *koeno* (out-of-date). Yet different rules applied to human beings. Whereas the modern man was at least portrayed as educated and technologically savvy, the modern girl tended to cause moral panic about the breakdown of traditions and the degradation of values. She became the tragic antihero of Westernization (*kebaratan*) and its hazards to chastity and propriety, as portrayed in Sino-Malay novels, short stories, theater plays, and newspapers alike, displaying clear parallels with other colonial settings.[92] Such sentiments stimulated alternative formulations of modernity inspired by China, although few would have termed them as such. As a consequence, cultural loyalties began to intersect with consumption patterns, with "pro-Chinese" commodities competing against European ones in the realms of attire, medicine, and food.

Unsurprisingly, linguistic heterogeneity produced and perpetuated inequality, as chapter 5 demonstrates. While the linguistic esthetics of Dutch and High Malay were informed by classical literary conventions and notions of purism, most Chinese espoused more pragmatic attitudes to language, adopting a colloquial variety that matched their commercial, emancipatory, and communal purposes, and that was enjoyed by other urban Malay-speaking communities. Although there was little consensus about the preferable type of Malay, satirical pieces make it abundantly clear that scorn and ridicule befell those who "talked funny." This included people whose Malay was deemed too Chinese, too Javanese, or too European. The deliberate use of faulty spelling became a clever satirical device, enabling authors to denigrate their enemies simply by surrounding their names with errors. In more amicable contexts, ethnicity could be inscribed through pronouns and other linguistic features. These practices come to the fore most prominently in advertisements, cartoons, and jokes sections, which were awash with regionalisms, colloquial expressions, and other phenomena from the lower ranks of the sociolinguistic spectrum (fig. I.1). In this regard, it would be remiss not to call attention to the high fecundity of jokes, innuendos, and ever insightful volleys of swearing abounding in Sino-Malay texts, which are also analyzed in this final chapter.

Amidst its copious injustices, the late colonial period occasioned a flourishing of Sino-Malay printing that postcolonialism foreclosed. After Indonesia proclaimed its independence in 1945, as this book's epilogue lays out, Chinese writers slowly assimilated into the nation's literary mainstream. Chinese-run newspapers faced Indonesianization of their titles, contents, and editorial boards. Homogeneity was also achieved through Indonesia's official orthography of 1947. The Sino-Malay tradition had shown itself defiant of top-down standardization throughout the colonial period, yet its distinct linguistic character proved helpless in the face of nation-building. The vernacular idiom of Sino-Malay texts—versatile and interlaced with European and Hokkien words—had become largely inseparable from standard Indonesian by the 1960s, at least in written form.[93] Although Chinese-Indonesian literary productions never completely died out, not even after the official ban on Chinese culture from 1966 to 1998, their thematic and linguistic diversity became ever more slender in this period.

More than anything, the steady dissolution of the Sino-Malay literary and journalistic tradition reveals the success and pervasiveness of Indonesian unitarism. Its raisons d'être—communal access to information, cultural education,

FIGURE I.1. Advertisement for baby powder in colloquial Chinese-Malay (*Keng Po*, 1935), featuring numerous words from Dutch and Hokkien

and, eventually, political organization—evaporated after independence, when conformity became the new objective. Many authors espoused the sentiment that, in an independent Indonesia, it was their nationalistic duty to write in the standardized language. The prominent journalist and teacher Nio Joe Lan, for example, wrote optimistically that Indonesia's hard-fought sovereignty obviated the special status historically imposed on its Chinese minority. In his opinion, Sino-Malay literature could be discontinued, to be cherished only as a beautiful remnant of bygone times.[94] One could argue, then, that Indonesia's postcolonial state successfully brought to completion a long-lasting project of Dutch colonialism: the homogenization of the Malay language.[95] That is not to say that the archipelago's numerous Chinese-Indonesian language varieties vanished without a trace. Ouster from the visible realm eventually pushed them underground, where they have persisted as spoken languages and continue to bear histories of in-betweenness. That, however, is another topic of study.

1
CONNECTED LANGUAGE HISTORIES

Chinese and Malay were in contact long before European colonialism and have remained so long afterward. This chapter reconstructs the plurilingual landscape of the Indies Chinese, along with its tensions and loyalty conflicts. To do so, it first traces episodes of language contact preceding the late colonial situation. In the first section, it follows words to designate, respectively, the different communities, languages, and language politics informing Chinese-Indonesian linguistic experiences and cultural productions. What terms were available to designate local-born Chinese, people born in China, and indigenous Southeast Asians? Where did they originate from? Which were considered pejorative? Addressing such questions unveils a complex hierarchy in which linguistic proficiency intersected with social mobility. From the early twentieth century, this plurilingual landscape was further complicated by the sudden entry of Mandarin as the proud vehicle of pan-Chinese chauvinism. As an important addition to half-forgotten Hokkien, insouciant Malay, and imperfect Dutch, Mandarin forced the colonial administration to reassess its entire education system. Up to the Japanese occupation in 1942, Chinese children could theoretically receive education in Dutch, Malay, Mandarin, or the provincial Sinitic variety of their ancestors. Such language choices shaped political allegiances and cultural identities. They were fiercely debated in schoolbooks, newspapers, phrasebooks, and other printed media.

From the mid-first millennium CE, China's imperial accounts chronicle the arrival of insular Southeast Asian embassies laden with luxurious ware. Most Chinese men traveling in the opposite direction did so as pilgrims en route to

India. These early cosmopolitans were among the first Chinese to pick up Malay. The Buddhist monk Yi Jing (635–713), for example, is known to have studied Sanskrit in Sumatra, presumably through Malay as the language of instruction. A reference to a resident Chinese expert (*juru cina*) in an 860 Old Javanese inscription indicates that people from China also occasionally settled down in the archipelago by that time.[1] Conversely, we may assume that Malay speakers were among the foreign merchants who set up shop in Guangzhou and other ports of coastal southern China during the Tang dynasty (618–907). During the trade-friendly Song dynasty (960–1279), Quanzhou grew into China's main trade hub with Southeast Asia. From the late eleventh century, Chinese men were permitted to stay abroad for long periods of time, enabling them to gain a stronger foothold in the lucrative commerce with Southeast Asia—or the "South Seas" (*lamyang*), as it was known to the Chinese—and the Indian Ocean. While China remained dependent on foreign shipping to export its products, Quanzhou and the wider Fujian area developed a sophisticated maritime tradition of its own.[2] Fujian and its people—better known in Southeast Asia under the local pronunciation "Hokkien" (Ml: *Hokkian*, Hk: *Hok-kiàn*)—became inextricably linked to the Malay-speaking world.

It is likely that Malay served as the lingua franca during these early interactions. As we learn from the early twelfth-century *Pingzhou Table Talks*, Chinese was not understood anywhere in the Malay kingdom of Sriwijaya.[3] Instead, newcomers had to learn their host's language, even though most preferred to eventually return to China. We may assume, for example, that the fourteenth-century Chinese community of East Java spoke both Malay and Javanese.[4] In the second half of the fourteenth century, when the xenophobic Ming dynasty rose to power, sojourning became illegal. Yet the ship had sailed—proverbially and literally—and Fujian-born merchants continued, now illegally, to participate in the Southeast Asia trade. The fifteenth-century Ming emissary Ma Huan described a Chinese community in Java with origins from Guangzhou and Zhangzhou, some of whom were Muslim.[5] Around the same time we find the world's earliest evidence of the institutionalized study of Malay in the form of a Chinese-Malay wordlist. This document already contains a number of Sinitic loanwords, demonstrating the extent of Chinese influence in maritime Southeast Asia.[6]

As Southeast Asia's first European settlers quickly realized, the success of empire-building was contingent on the presence of Chinese sojourners, merchants, laborers, shopkeepers, agriculturalists, artisans, and cooks. In Spanish-controlled Manila, Dutch-controlled Batavia, and other newly established trade hubs, they were housed in special districts and governed by their own leaders, following a pre-European practice across the region. At the head of a Chinese community stood the so-called captain (Ml: *kapitan*, Hk: *kap-pit-tan*).[7] Yet this coexistence was an uneasy one. The irremediable European fear of being outperformed reached its bloody apex in the Chinese massacres of Manila (1603, 1639) and Batavia (1740). In the aftermath, the Vereenigde Oostindische Compagnie (Dutch East India Company; VOC) imposed severe restrictions on Chinese mobility through a system known as the district and pass system (D: *wijken- en passenstelsel*), which was only fully abolished in 1916 in the heat of anticolonial mobilization. Many sought to circumvent these discriminatory policies by minimizing their visual markers of Chineseness, adopting Islam, and assimilating into the indigenous mainstream.[8]

From the latter half of the nineteenth century, Southeast Asia's demographics were fundamentally affected by events in China. In the wake of the crushed Taiping Rebellion (1850–64), many outlawed societies from the southern provinces sought refuge in Malaya, the Indies, and elsewhere. They were joined there by thousands of poverty-stricken manual laborers from the same regions. Indentured labor grew exponentially after the Second Opium War (1856–60), when the war-battered Qing government was forced to help resolve Europe's demand for agricultural labor after the abolition of slavery.[9] At the point of British bayonets, China also legalized the profitable opium trade. This drug quickly flooded Java and became the backbone of the island's Chinese economy, up to the introduction of a state monopoly in the 1890s.[10] This period was furthermore characterized by colonial expansion, anti-imperialist resentment, and technological advancements in printing, transportation, and communication. These developments culminated in a heightened Chinese self-consciousness, in the Netherlands Indies and elsewhere.[11] But to understand the literary and journalistic writing that emerged as a result in the early twentieth century, we must first appreciate the plurilingual roots of the Sino-Malay print culture.

What's in a Name?

As clarified in the introduction, the term "Chinese-Indonesians" is a teleological shorthand. This section calls attention to the complex late colonial terminology and its correlations with race, ethnicity, and gender. Sojourning between China and Southeast Asia long remained a male affair, with women facing legal and cultural restrictions to travel abroad. Yet despite its border control, the Qing government had little influence over outgoing travelers, even though they could face harsh punishment upon returning. This is described in the late eighteenth-century *Annals of Batavia*, which contains a vignette about a man from China who illegally brought his wife to Batavia in 1699. The arrival in that city of a "real" Chinese lady drew so much local spectacle that the port authorities back in China got scent of it and sentenced to death several assistants who facilitated the couple's short-lived adventure (but not the husband and wife).[12] The French explorer François Leguat (1637–1735), who stayed in Batavia a couple of years earlier, commented that "there were but three women born in China at Batavia when I was there, so that the Chineses were at first oblig'd to marry Javans, but their families have so encreas'd since that now they have enough daughters for their sons."[13] The number of China-born women residing in Java remained minimal throughout the colonial period. The semilegendary allure of the *putri cina* (Chinese princess) or *gundik cina* (Chinese concubine) in Indonesian storytelling traditions is testimony to her extreme rarity.[14]

In view of these restrictions, unions between Chinese men and indigenous women became the norm. Interethnic marriage had become common in the port cities of Southeast Asia and the wider Indian Ocean world. To better understand the language of Sino-Malay texts, it is therefore important to first elaborate on the relevant racial vocabulary they contain. The default Malay word for local-born children of foreign ancestry—typically with indigenous mothers—was *peranakan*. This word carried connotations of hybridity and was also used for crossbred animals. Etymologically, it referred to a place of birth. Hence, *peranakan* could also denote a womb, although Sino-Malay medical texts tended to use the Hokkien loan *tjoekiong* in this meaning. *Peranakan tjina* (local-born Chinese) referred to the descendants of Chinese men and Southeast Asian women.[15] It conveyed undertones of acculturation to the motherland and local know-how, as opposed to people born in China. The more recent term *Indo Tionghoa* (D: *Indo-Chineezen*) partly overlapped with *peranakan*, yet carried stronger multiracial connotations.[16] Both labels were used self-referentially but carried no distinct legal status. Children of interracial marriages were typically registered according to their father's (assigned) race. Their consequent absence in the population census makes it difficult to estimate their exact numbers.

The late colonial nomenclature for race was highly gendered. Peranakan Chinese men were referred to with the honorific *baba* (Hk: *bā-bā*).[17] By the twentieth century, a Baba was always of Chinese ancestry, whereas the term Peranakan could also designate Eurasians and mixed-race Arabs. But when the context was sufficiently clear, Babas simply referred to themselves as Peranakans (*kaoem peranakan*) without further specifications. Peranakan Chinese women were known as *njonja* (madam; Hk: *niû-á*), a Creole Portuguese word also used for European, Eurasian, and Arabic women. In the Straits Settlements, the term Baba-Nyonya became equivalent to Peranakan Chinese. Unmarried Peranakan Chinese, Arabic, European, and Eurasian girls were referred to as *nona*, *non*, or *noni* (young lady), whereas Eurasian men were known as *sinjo* (Sir), *serani* (Christian), or *Blanda idjo* (green Dutchman). Predictably, these ethnic designations were time specific. During the heydays of the VOC, Peranakans were seen by the Dutch authorities as distinct from the real Chinese and therefore subject to their own headmen and taxation rules.[18] Later Dutch sources used *hiergeboren Chinezen* (local-born Chinese) synonymously with *peranakan*. Technically, however, the former also encompassed the Indies-born children of China-born immigrants, akin to the usage of "Straits Chinese" or "Straits-born Chinese" in British Malaya.

Some Chinese-descended individuals rejected all the above designations. As the Fujian-born traveler Wang Dahai recounted in the late eighteenth century, a certain class of people imitated Java's natives and called themselves *Selam* (Hk: *Sit-lam*).[19] These men married into local families, no longer identified as Chinese, and gradually assimilated into the indigenous mainstream. They nevertheless left a significant cultural imprint on port cities like Batavia. The Javanese traveler Raden Mas Arya Candranegara from Demak observed in 1865 that Batavia's inhabitants "spoke Malay with a Chinese intonation." Raden Arya Sastradarma from Solo remarked in 1870 that "their manners have become like those of the Chinese.... They also sit and talk in the same way as the Chinese do. They sit on chairs or low benches; they eat on tables."[20] At the same time, constant waves of immigration enabled Batavia's Chinatowns to flourish. Over time, a unique Chinese-influenced culture took shape, characterized by performing arts such as *lenong, gambang kromong, tandjidor, tjokek, sipatmo,* and *barongsai*. The nineteenth-century Batavian dialect likewise contained numerous Hokkien loanwords unattested in other Malay varieties.[21]

The words *peranakan* and *baba* acquired new salience when greater numbers of immigrants arrived in the Indies. Designations for people born in China included *totok* (pure-blooded) and the Hokkien loan *singkeh* (newcomer), which were used contrastively to *peranakan* (mixed-blooded) and *laukeh* (old-hand). The element *keh*—as seen in *singkeh* and *laukeh*—originally denoted a guest. The Indies Chinese used it (Hk: *kheh*, Ml: *khe*) to designate Hakka people and the Dutch to address Chinese shopkeepers.[22] Interestingly, the colony's European population displayed a similar *singkeh-laukeh* dichotomy: sojourners (D: *trekkers*, Ml: *orang baroe*) versus settlers (D: *blijvers*, Ml: *orang lama*). In addition to racial purity, the terms *totok* and *orang baroe* connoted inexperience and unfamiliarity with the Indies. They could be applied to Chinese, Arabs, and Europeans alike. Late colonial sources—both Dutch and Sino-Malay—tell us repeatedly that Singkehs and/or Totoks worked hard, organized their lives along clan lines, held on to customs from China, ate Chinese dishes using chopsticks, dressed humbly, and spoke Sinitic languages alongside some rudimentary Malay, whereas Peranakans had adjusted more to life in Southeast Asia.

Needless to say, such distinctions were far from clear-cut. Totok families could peranakanize over time, whereas Peranakans could totokize as part of the early twentieth-century reformist movement. If anything, Peranakanness was fluid, context-dependent, and shaped by physical characteristics as well as cultural markers.[23] Linguistic proficiency was an inconclusive yardstick to determine who belonged to this group: the Peranakans of Java, Medan, Makassar, Singapore, Penang, Kelantan, Phuket, and other regions all identified as such, yet displayed vastly different linguistic abilities. In the eyes of some people, Peranakanness could be achieved through cultural orientation and local rootedness, rather than racial admixture and family origins.[24] Even so, poorly concealed Totok-Peranakan animosity prevailed throughout the first half of the twentieth century. Sino-Malay novels such as Tan Boen Soan's *Baba Fantasie* (1939) describe widespread fears among Peranakans of losing out to their frugal and hardworking Totok competitors. Newspaper articles, such as a 1930 op-ed in *Hoakiao*, corroborate these anxieties:

Totok people can work from six in the morning to ten in the evening, but can Peranakans do the same? Totoks can live on dried fish and some vegetables, sleep on a board, and reduce other expenses, while among the Peranakan—as far as we have observed—only a tiny minority is able to emulate this behavior.	Bangsa totok bisa bekerdja dari pagi djam 6 sampe malem djam 10, tapi apatah pranakan bisa toeroet ini? Kaoem totok bisa makan sama ikan kering dan sedikit sajoer tidoer diatas salembar papan dan laen-laen penarikan ongkos, sedeng kaoem pranakan—sabegitoe djaoe kita saksiken—tjoema brapa glintir sadja jang bisa toeroet ini toeladan.[25]

An even broader palette of terms existed to designate Chineseness in general. The most common Malay word was *tjina* (Chinese). Historically neutral, it had gradually obtained offensive connotations, so that *tionghoa* became the preferred term after the Chinese Revolution. As early as 1913, the Medan-based novelist Oeij Kim Tjoan complained about the offensive use of *tjina* in Malay newspapers. By the 1930s, the Chinese had almost universally rejected the term.[26] Non-Chinese speakers of Malay habitually resorted to such slurs as *tjina babi* (Chinese pork butcher), *tjina goenoeng* (Chinese from the mountains), *tjina koentjir* (pigtailed Chinese), *tjina loleng* (Chinese who can't say the R), *tjina mindring* (Chinese loan shark), and the exclamations *Tjina mati!* or *Tjina mampoes!* (Dead Chinese!). As was the case with "Chinaman" in English, such lexical choices were anything but innocent. Snapshots of the grievances caused by ill-chosen vocabulary abound in the Sino-Malay press. In 1939, *Sin Po* published a photograph taken near Blitar of a sign reading "Chinese and Singkehs are not allowed to enter the premises of Klepon." The picture's caption read: "The Dutchmen of the Klepon Plot contrived to put up this sign that insults the Chinese; the plot belongs to the Trading Association Amsterdam. Better hurry and pull the sign out, because the 'Chinese

FIGURE 1.1. Anti-Chinese sign using the pejorative terms *Tjina* and *Singkek* (*Sin Po* 826 [1939]: 9).

and Singkehs' are sick and tired of being insulted, regardless of who is doing it!" (fig. 1.1). This particular trading firm was embroiled in a long series of conflicts with Chinese businessmen and private financiers, yet its use of ethnic slurs was understandably seen as an intolerable new low.[27]

Chinese-Indonesians used several additional names to refer to themselves. Since many of China's southern communities still identified with the Tang dynasty, a well-attested designation in the Indies and elsewhere in Southeast Asia was *tenglang* or its Hakka-derived equivalent *tong-njin* (Tang person). Meanwhile, the Chinese mainland was known as *Tengswa* or *Tongsan* (Tang Mountain). The Hokkien appellation *entjek* (uncle) had acquired honorific connotations across the Malay world and was widely used to address Chinese males.[28] Less common was the Hokkien word *hoa djin* (Chinese person).[29] The coinage *tjoeng kwo jen* (Chinese person) gained popularity among Mandarin speakers in the early twentieth century. From the 1910s, the aforementioned word *tionghoa* (China, Chinese) and the etymologically connected *hoakiao* (overseas Chinese) found wide acceptance. Sino-Malay newspapers regularly reported on the *hoakiao* of Malaya, the Philippines, Australia, San Francisco, and Mexico, in addition to the local *hoakiao-totok* and *hoakiao-peranakan*. The words *Binkok* (the Chinese Republic), *kiaopao* (countryman living abroad), *tiongkok* (China; lit. the Middle Kingdom), *tjouwkok* (homeland), and *tongpao* (compatriot) gained popularity from the mid-1920s, especially in nationalist circles.[30] All of these were Hokkien pronunciations of popular terms used in China.

Less pleasant names also circulated in print. In view of the observation that "word histories often tell us about how people were discriminated against in terms of class, caste, or race,"[31] ethnic slurs carry considerable analytical value. An article published in the *Kabar Slalu* (Frequent News; Singapore 1924) is highly informative in this regard, as it lists many of the sensitive words prevalent around that time. It complains about the usage of *orang macao* (Cantonese), *orang puteh* (white European), *orang kling* (Tamil), and *orang srani* (Eurasian).[32] The author furthermore objects to the Cantonese slurs *fan phor* (native woman) and *sap yat tim* (not-quite-Chinese; lit. eleven o'clock), both of which were used derogatorily against Peranakans.[33] In the Indies and elsewhere in Southeast Asia, the Hokkien-derived word *hoana* was used for indigenous people. Semantically, it leveraged between foreigner, barbarian, and native. Etymologically, it was connected with the idiom *djip hoan*, which conveyed the idea of "going native" or aligning oneself with non-Chinese people. Indeed, both terms served as disciplinary tropes against Peranakans out of touch with their Chinese roots. In the reformist discourse, indigenization appears to have been as equally dreaded as Westernization. As the following Hokkien-saturated poems illustrate, moralistic writings from this movement associated indigenous people with impoliteness (first example) and outdated customs (second example):

The natives tend to be very reckless.	Hoana adatnja terlaloe bopan,
They speak with haughtiness and candor.	Kaloe bitjara sombong berdepan,
Shouldn't we prefer to be civilized	Apa kita tida maoe sopan,
As we've aspired since long times past?	Jang kita tjari sedari kapan.
(*Poem of Advice for Young People*)	(*Sair Nasehat Orang Moeda*)
And the 28th of the Chinese ailments Is that the women greet others by crouching and raising their hands with the palms together.	Lagi penjakitnja orang tionghoa jang ka 28, Jaitoe djongkok menjembah di berboeat kaoem prempoean,

Crouching and raising one's hands in the native fashion is inappropriate. Staying upright and clasping one's hands in front of the chest is what real Chinese do. (*The Ailments of the Chinese Nation*)	Djongkok menjembah sebagi adat hwana itoe em hoo pan, Kiongtjioe tjoekoep berdiri, itoe ada adat Tionghoa soenggoewan. (*Penjakitnja Rahajat Tiongkok*)[34]

Such ethno-specific terms afford deeper insights into stratified societies. To use them considerately is a sign of sympathy, especially in the printed domain where revision is possible. In this regard, the Sino-Malay press was overwhelmingly progressive. The Dutch term *inlander* (native), which carried strong pejorative connotations, is almost absent in their writings. From the mid-1920s, its Malay counterparts *priboemi*, *boemipoetra*, and *anak negri* were substituted with *Indonesier* (Indonesian). This was clearly done out of solidarity with indigenous nationalists.[35] For the same reason, the toponym *Hindia* (the Indies) increasingly made place for *Indonesia*. As the journalist and author Kwee Tek Hoay wrote in the late 1930s, the words *Indonesia* and *Indonesier* were detested by the Dutch authorities, who associated them with "left-wing groups, nationalists, or revolutionaries."[36] The indigenous press adopted similar editorial policies. In 1927, the journalist Parada Harahap (1899–1959) insisted on the usage of *Indonesia* instead of *Hindia Belanda* (the Netherlands Indies), *Hindoestan* instead of *Britsch Indie* (British India), *Voor-Indier* (Indian) instead of *Keling* (Tamil), and *buitengewesten* (outer districts) instead of *buitenbezittingen* (outer possessions).[37] Even the Dutch occasionally saw themselves forced to revise their linguistic habits. Historically, the colonial government addressed its perceived subjects by their race in official correspondence: "to the native" (D: *aan den Inlander*, Ml: *kapada orang Djawa*) and "to the Chinese" (D: *aan den Chinees*, Ml: *kapada orang Tjina*). To little surprise, both groups found this habit dehumanizing, and it was eventually abandoned in 1916.[38]

The term "creole" was carefully avoided by Chinese-Indonesians, even though it features extensively in the wider literature about them.[39] Deeply rooted in Iberian colonialism, this versatile word originally designated peoples, cultures, languages, and cuisines that blended European and "tropical" elements. Recent scholars have proposed broader understandings, taking it outside the trans-Atlantic context.[40] In colonial-era Southeast Asia, however, its semantics were neatly demarcated. The Philippine equivalent *criollo* referred to local-born Spaniards. The Dutch usage of *creool* was colony specific, denoting local-born Europeans (including Eurasians) in the Netherlands Indies, Afro-Europeans in the Netherlands Antilles, and African-descended townspeople in Suriname. It had a similar usage in the Sino-Malay literature. One author lists the creoles (*bangsa creol*) amongst the inhabitants of Suriname. Another informs us that the mother of the French artist Paul Gauguin was of creole ancestry (*toeroenan creole*).[41] Yet the word was never to my knowledge used for self-designation in the Chinese-Indonesian context. In all likelihood, authors realized the negative connotations (impurity, promiscuity, and decadence) the term conveyed at the time, refraining from its usage.[42]

Cumulatively, these terminological subtleties fueled practices of selfing and othering that became central to Sino-Malay print culture. Vertically imposed labels vied with self-identifications, while words associated with national pride competed with pejorative slurs. Between Malay, Dutch, Hokkien, Mandarin, and other languages was a space where people drew from all resources available to them, impulsively, imperfectly, and creatively. This forms a recurrent motif throughout this book.

A Very Peculiar Intonation

Having adumbrated the broader contours of language contact, two specific linguistic varieties warrant further attention: the Hokkien of the archipelago's first Chinese settlers, and the Malay many came to adopt over time. They were often used side by side. Additional languages also played a role, depending on a speaker's regional provenance, time period, social status, gender, and educational background. In some Sino-Malay publications from Central Java, such as the writings of the Solo-based journalist and linguist Tjoa Tjoe Kwan (1865–1905), chunks of romanized Malay were interspersed with Sinographic characters and words written in the Javanese script. This typographic extravaganza reflected technological advancements as well as new reading practices, in which individual consumers received metalinguistic information—such as punctuation, clarificatory notes, or the specific characters belonging to Chinese words and names—that had been irrelevant in preexisting modes of text recitation.[43] Yet in the eyes of many, plurilingualism also led to linguistic deterioration. The Singaporean author Chia Cheng Sit, writing in 1899, described the linguistic (in)competencies of the Indies Chinese as follows:

> [They] generally are able in many instances to speak Chinese, although their intonation of Chinese words is very peculiar, suggesting to one that the Chinese language is not natural to them. It would seem that the frequent use of the Malay or Javanese languages renders it awkward, even for the descendants of Chinese, to speak accurately the language of their ancestors. . . . The average Chinaman speaks Malay with all

the blemishes that characterize the attempts of the average Baba in the utterance of Chinese words.⁴⁴

Dutch assessments were equally censorious. One colonial official contended that "many [Chinese in Java] continue to prefer Malay at a later age, or at least pervade their Chinese with so many Malay words, that it must at first be incomprehensible to the Singkeh. Their pronunciation is also detestably bad." A fellow Dutchman claimed that "a Java-born Chinese, a Baba, does not know more Chinese words than are sufficient, mixed with Malay, to change it into an argot that neither the real Chinese, nor the European can understand."⁴⁵ In a number of Sino-Malay writings, plurilingualism was likewise associated with nonfluency. The short story "Poetra Fortuna" (Prince Fortuna), for example, contains a scene in which a certain Mr. Oh wants to cross the River Tjiliwoeng. He inquires whether there is a bridge, yet with multiple languages competing in his head—Javanese, Hokkien, and Dutch—he forgets the correct Malay word. Incapable of repressing his plurilingualism, we even see him shifting between languages for the mundane word "to say" (Hk: *kóng*, Ml: *bilang*):

"Is there no *tertek* here?" asked Mr. Oh.	"Sini 'ndah ada tertek?" toean Oh menanja.
"No, Sir," the boy answered. "What's a *tertek*, Sir?"	"Kaga ada, tjek." Si katjoeng menjaoet.
"How do people here say *tertek*? I can't remember. The Hokkien say *kio*, the Dutch say *brug*."	"Tertek itoe apa, tjek?"
	"Tertek itoe sini apa bilangnja? Saja 'ndah inget. Hokkian kong *kio*, Blanda bilang *brug*."
"Oh, *djembatan*, Sir, *djembatan*! Unfortunately, Sir, there is no *djembatan* here."	"Oh, djembatan, tjek, djembatan! Menjesel, tjek, djembatan di sini kaga ada."⁴⁶

Mr. Oh's confusion represents a well-known paradox among people with migrant roots: having access to multiple languages, yet struggling to use them in ways acceptable to "native speakers."⁴⁷ Most Totoks were fluent in one or more Sinitic varieties, yet their Malay was rudimentary. Many Peranakan, by contrast, were fluent speakers of Malay, Javanese, or other regional languages, often knew some Dutch, but were not typically proficient in Chinese. Due to the obvious commercial advantages of plurilingualism, shop owners were renowned polyglots. A 1915 Dutch-Malay-Javanese-Sundanese phrasebook informs its readers matter-of-factly: "If the owner of the *toko* is a Chinese, one will always be able to converse in Malay."⁴⁸ It is no surprise that jobseekers in the commercial sector listed their languages among their chief skills. This continued even after Indonesia's independence. A 1949 advertisement in *Sin Po*, written in Low Malay but containing several Dutch and English words, provides a case in point:

A CHINESE PERSON	SAORANG TIONGHOA
Aged over forty, looking for employment as traveling salesman, assistant manager, manager, etc. Speaks Hokkien, Teochew, Mandarin, English, and Malay well. Has knowledge of agricultural produce, sundries, cigars, cigarettes, etc. Has previously done business in Java, Sumatra, Riau, West and South Borneo, Sulawesi, Singapore, Malaya, Penang, and Bangka.	Oemoer 40 lebih tjari kerdja travelling salesman, assistent manager, manager etc. Bitjara Hokkian, Tiotjioe, Mandarin, English, Melajoe dengen baek. Faham hasil boemi, klontong, cigars, cigarettes etc. Perna koeliling dagang Java, Sumatra, Riouw, West and South Borneo, Celebes, Singapore, Malaya, Penang, djoega Banka.[49]

The Sinitic variety known in Southeast Asia as Hokkien long occupied a central position in the Chinese-Indonesian linguistic landscape. Hokkien is closely related though not mutually intelligible with Teochew and Hainanese, and more distantly with a number of other Sinitic varieties spoken in Fujian.[50] The two main Hokkien dialects correspond to the prefectures of Zhangzhou (Hk: *Chiang-chiu*, Ml: *Tjiangtjioe*) and Quanzhou (Hk: *Choân-chiu*, Ml: *Tjoantjioe*). Most varieties spoken in and around Xiamen (Hk: *Ē-mûiⁿ*, Ml: *Emoei*), Taiwan, and Southeast Asia constitute intermediate dialects with varying inclinations toward Zhangzhounese and Quanzhounese. As Zhangzhou was the chief Fujianese trading port during the late Ming and early Qing dynasties, we may assume that Southeast Asia's first Chinese communities were speakers of that dialect.[51]

Over time, certain Hokkien words acquired new usages in Southeast Asia. A well-known example is *thó-khò·* (Ml: *toko*), which originally referred to an underground brick storeroom and later to any robust place where goods are stored. It became the default word for a store in the Netherlands Indies and for a big commercial house or European-style firm in the Straits Settlements. Another example is *kong-si* (Ml: *kongsi*), a form of financial partnership or semitransparent business association, which in the Indies also became an honorific term corresponding to the rank of lieutenant.[52] The term *kong-koán* referred to a type of hotel in Fujian, but came to denote the building of the Chinese Council—and hence the institution itself—in Java. Other Hokkien terms specific to the Netherlands Indies include *jī-kak* (district secretary; Ml: *djikak*), *ku-lî-keng* (coolie quarters; Ml: *koelikeng*), *ló-tia* (district warden; Ml: *lootia*), and *tún* (guilder; lit. shield). Naturally, Indies Hokkien also adopted numerous Malay, Javanese, and Dutch words, some of which became barely recognizable as such.[53]

Needless to say, Hokkien was not the only Sinitic variety that made its way into the archipelago. Other sizable ethno-linguistic communities were the Hakkas (*Khe*), Cantonese (*Kongfoe, Kwitang*), Teochews (*Tiotjioe*), Hainanese (*Haylam*), and Fuqingese (*Hoktjia*). In the Netherlands Indies, *hoklo* (lit. Fujian person) was used for Teochews, the Hakka term *poenti* (lit. native person) for Cantonese, and *orang macao* (Macao person) for both Cantonese and Hakkas. Every speech group traditionally monopolized a number of professional specializations. As the well-known saying went: "Hakka build a city, Cantonese prosper, Teochew and Hokkien control."[54] In places like Bangka off Sumatra's east coast and Taiping in Malaya, all these Chinese varieties could be heard concurrently, so that different groups often had to resort to Low Malay to communicate with each other. The establishment in the second half of the nineteenth century of a Sinology Department at Leiden University, where all Sinitic varieties spoken in the Indies were studied, is a direct result of this remarkable linguistic diversity and the administrative difficulties it presented.[55] From the 1890s, we also see a number of commercially published wordlists and phrasebooks—typically in English—of the Sinitic languages encountered in the Malay-speaking world.

Malay is another key language of the Chinese-Indonesian sociolinguistic kaleidoscope. It was and remains Southeast Asia's chief lingua franca, picked up as a matter of course by the region's earliest visitors. In Java, it featured alongside Javanese as a language of classical epigraphy, Islamic manuscripts, and epistolary correspondence. Europeans drew upon Malay for missionary work and education. The resultant "barbarous dialect of Malay, confounded and confused by the introduction of Portuguese and Dutch"—as it was uncharitably dismissed by Java's interim ruler Thomas Stamford Raffles (1781–1826)—also entered Dutch usage to communicate with the courtly elites of Central Java.[56] This contact variety was popularly referred to as Low Malay (*Melajoe Rendah*), a term used interchangeably with Bazaar Malay (*Melajoe Pasar*) and Batavian Malay (*Melajoe Betawi*). Low Malay in fact designated a variety of overlapping phenomena. It could refer to a type of pidginized foreigner talk, habitually resorted to by not-so-fluent Europeans, Chinese, Arabs, and indigenous people. It was also used more broadly for any type of Malay that violated the grammatical principles of High Malay. Finally, it referred to Service Malay (*dienst-Maleisch*), an administrative language employed by the Dutch authorities in the domains of legal affairs, education, most missionary work, and the non-European press.[57]

Over time, the Low Malay of Java grew to be the preferred oral and literary vehicle of many urban Chinese, Arabs, Indians, and Eurasians. It differed considerably from the Malay of Sumatra, Borneo, and other islands. Hence, in the 1915 novel *Njai Aisah* (Mistress Aisah) by Tan Boen Kim, we encounter the sentence: "From the way the woman spoke, it was obvious she wasn't a person from Java; based on a few words she uttered in High Malay, it became clear that this mistress was from South Sumatra."[58] This quote corroborates that people living in Java, regardless of their ethnicity, spoke a different kind of Malay from Sumatrans. Java's Low Malay is perhaps best characterized in Bakhtinian terms as "heteroglossic":

> A complex interaction of utterances, discourses, speech-genres, "languages" which—far from being unitary, far from circling around generally accepted centers of authority—formed a continuum of mostly spoken forms, in a number of not very clearly defined domains and a great amount of variation. A slippery continuum, that is, a continuous switching between codes and styles. In the Indies, linguistic differences were great no doubt but they were not felt to be unsurmountable; nobody was able to give an exact definition of how the system worked, and yet most people managed to maintain themselves in it. Somehow differences did not really matter. Somehow things worked to the satisfaction of all of those involved.[59]

In view of its heterogeneity by time, location, ethnicity, class, gender, and education, a grammatical description of Java Malay would require the length of another book.[60] A few examples suffice. Some speakers used *kedjapa* (doing what?), whereas others preferred *ngapain* in the same meaning; some used *tra* (no, not), whereas others used *'ndah*, *'ngga*, or *kaga*; some used *pegimana* (how) and others *begimana* or *gimana*. Words characteristic for Java included *belon* (not yet), *kowe* (you), *maksi* (although), *misi* (still), *saben* (every), *semingkin* (increasingly), *serenta* (as soon as), *setaoe* (who knows?), and the transitive suffixes -*in* and -*ken*. Some other features often ascribed to Java Malay are in fact attested in colloquial Malay more generally, including the words *bilang* (to say), *bikin* (to do, to make), *kaloe* (if), *kasi* (to give), *pigi* (to go), and *sama* (with). The Malay of western, central, and eastern Java displayed local differences as well. In the eyes of Kwee Tek Hoay, the usage of forms like *tjobak* (to try) and *tanjak* (to ask) instead of the more mainstream *tjoba* and *tanja* "was the defect of second-rate journalists from West Java."[61] Some Hokkien loans also entered general use in Low Malay, including a number of pronouns. Common words such as *en* (and), *merk* (trademark), and *zonder* (without) reflect Dutch influence.

Typologically the Malay of Chinese speakers did not differ greatly from that of other urban communities. If anything, "Chinese-Malay" (*Melajoe Tionghoa*) was a political rather than linguistically motivated epithet.[62] It did have its idiosyncrasies. What set it apart from the colloquial Malay of other groups was chiefly translingual. Some Sino-Malay texts are so pervaded with Hokkienisms that they are incomprehensible for the uninitiated, puzzling present-day Indonesians and Indonesianists alike. In addition, Chinese speakers of Malay were renowned for their code-mixing with and lexical borrowing from Javanese and Dutch, although this was also done by Java's other ethnicities.[63] The linguistic landscape of Chinese-Indonesians furthermore featured the imperfect Malay of Totoks, which drew continuous scorn in the printed media.[64] The line of thinking was clear: knowledge of Malay and Dutch marked legitimacy in the rapidly modernizing colony, whereas unproficiency implied the opposite. The mocking of Singkeh speech was not confined to the borders of the Netherlands Indies. An ethnic Malay writer for the newspaper *Saudara* (Sibling; Penang, 1928), for example, criticized the commercial shrewdness of Chinese shopkeepers in one breath with their speech. Both, the argument seemed to be, undermined traditional Malay values. In an imaginary dialog, a Malay customer eventually adopts the Chinese idiom in order to get a better price:

He would reply: "You're stupid, you don't know anything about merchandise," and when we get agitated and walk away, after two or three steps, he'll call us back: "Hey, friend, please come! If you pay 1.5 ringgit it's fine." Eventually we answer: "Ah, just give it to me buddy, let's have it. If you don't give it that's fine too."	Jawabnya pula: Lu bodoh lu tak tahu balang, bila kita hati sudah panas langsung jalan, dua tiga langkah kita sudah angkat kaki, langsung dia panggil balik: Hai kawan-ah, mali lululah! Lu kasi 1 linggit tengah tak apalah, kata kita pula: ah lu kasi itu macak, kasilah! Lu tak kasi tak apa.[65]

From the early twentieth century, pan-Chinese chauvinism and political mobilization further impacted on this already complex linguistic landscape. A watershed moment in Chinese-Indonesian history was the founding in 1900 of the Tiong Hoa Hwee Koan (Chinese Association; THHK), which dedicated itself to promoting and facilitating Chinese culture in the Indies, including the teaching of Mandarin and even English.[66] In response, as discussed below, the colonial government finally made it easier for Chinese people to learn Dutch.

Cultivating Proficiencies

A clever cartoon can reveal more historical complexities than a thousand words. In 1926, the editors of *Hoakiao* published precisely that. Titled "Onderwijs T.H., di Djawa" (Chinese education, in Java), the cartoon in question is barely legible due to its low print quality, yet it contains a wealth of information. It shows an old-school pupil—barefoot, wearing a Chinese-style queue and a traditional frogged shirt—reciting in Hokkien the first two lines of a classical poem, followed by a flippant personal addition in Malay:

If jade is not cut, nothing can be made of it	Giok poet tok, poet sing khie Djin poet hak, poet tie gie
If people don't study, they will not know righteousness	Babahnja ngorok, singkehnja mimpie
The Peranakans snore, the Singkehs dream	Ngobrolnja ay-kok, maar ta' brani mati.
They babble about patriotism, but won't risk their life.	
	Bestuur T.H.H.K., Boekaklah matamoe! Pikirlah dosamoe!
Managers of the THHK, open your eyes! Reflect on your sins! Think of your posterity!	Ingetlah anak-tjoetjoemoe![67]

To his left sits the confident product of modernity, a Westernized Chinese student wearing a suit and shoes. He recites some Mandarin words and their Malay translations, followed by a mixture of colloquial Javanese and Malay:

tiān = heaven, dì = earth	Thie-en = langit, tie-ie = boemie
shuǐ = water, tǔ = land	soe-ieh = aijer, thoe-oeh = tanah
Imminent bankruptcy is fine by me	ngemben paleet ta'lakonie
Gallivanting beats going to school.	baikan ngelentjeer daripada tjekolah.
Pupils of the THHK, be careful!!! Think carefully about your future lives.	Moerid T.H.H.K., Awas!!! Pikir betoel penghidoepan-moe di kamoedian harie.

In this clever comparison between traditional Hokkien and modern Mandarin education, the cartoonist ended up criticizing both. The former was guilty of producing woefully depoliticized students, numbed by useless rote learning and out of touch with China's revolutionary politics. The latter, however, had spawned a generation of superficial dandies devoid of traditional virtues. They spoke bad Malay—the word *sekolah* (school) in the cartoon is pronounced *tjekolah*—and were thus equally unlikely to become valuable assets to society. Having juxtaposed the two systems and their representatives, a rhetorical question presented itself: "Which one is smarter? Are you well-informed, compatriots?" (Pinter mana? Thong-pauw sedarkah?). At the time the cartoon was published, neither type of education was deemed fully fit for purpose. Dutch or Malay-medium schools were likewise bedeviled with issues of cultural loyalty.[68]

Tensions of this sort reflected broader sociolinguistic questions. Historically, Java's Peranakans derived their social capital from their Malay proficiency. A somewhat different situation unfolded in Malaya and parts of Sumatra and Borneo, where ethnic Malays functioned as the native reference points. In those regions, Peranakans often retained fluency in Hokkien and/or other Sinitic languages. Yet even in the most polyglot havens, such as Singapore, one could encounter advocates of Malay as the Peranakan's only true language. They may have known other languages, but as one journalist put it, only in Malay could the educated (*si Panday*) fully communicate with the uneducated (*si Bebal*) without having to "punch water in a tray, only to splash his own face."[69] Whereas Malay was picked up colloquially, Dutch and Chinese had to be cultivated through expensive education. Even the board meetings of Batavia's Chinese Council (*Kong Koan*) were increasingly held in Malay, rather than Hokkien, by the mid-1910s.[70] It is no surprise, then, that the specter of language loss loomed bleakly on the horizon. As one journalist for *Hoakiao* reminded his readers in 1929, some fellow minorities in the Indies had already preceded them into linguistic orphanage:

It's true that we live in the Malay lands, so that we must utilize that language, but don't we realize that the Europeans, Arabs, and Jews have now totally switched to Malay?	Betoel kita tinggal di tanah Melajoe, maka kita moesti goenaken bahasa terseboet tapi inget apa bangsa Blanda, Arab dan Jahoedi lantas pake bahasa Melajoe semoea-moeanja?[71]

The author certainly had a flair for the melodramatic. His Europeans were most likely Eurasians, his Arabs were Peranakans of Hadhrami origins, and his Jews members of Surabaya's Baghdadi community. If anything, the trope of cultural uprooting echoes the resinicization discourse. In the same way that Dutch had gained ground among the Eurasians, the Chinese were encouraged by their spokespeople to prioritize Chinese. They had to sacrifice competing languages in the process, or so it was argued. The use of Dutch in particular became associated with the wrong type of modernity. Consistent with their pro-Chinese politics, *Sin Po*'s editors loathed what they perceived to be linguistic self-alienation. In mockery of Dutch-obsessed yet unproficient Peranakans, they deliberately misspelled the colonizer's language as *Gollans* rather than *Hollandsch*:

In the same way that countless Chinese are unable these days to speak even the tiniest bit of Chinese,	Seperti djoega sekarang banjak sekali Tjina jang tida mampoe bahasa Tionghoa barang sedikit, begitoelah

once upon a time many Eurasians did not understand a single word of Dutch. They spoke Portuguese or Malay, just like today's "modern" Baba Chinese speak Dutch and the traditional Baba speak Malay, Javanese, Sundanese, or whatever other indigenous languages you can think of.	doeloe sekali si Blanda-indo banjak jang tida mengarti sepata bahasa Blanda. Marika bitjara bahasa Portugeesch atawa bahasa Melajoe, precies seperti sekarang Tjina baba "modern" bitjara Gollans dan baba kolot bitjara Melajoe, Djawa, Soenda atawa setaoe bahasa anak negri jang mana lagi.[72]

Chinese education started to modernize in the pre-Revolution years. From 1895, political reformers led by Kang Youwei (1858–1927) and Liang Qichao (1873–1929) campaigned to strengthen China's national pride, resist European imperialism, implement Confucianism as the state religion, and emulate the Japanese school system. Assisted by a robust Chinese-language press, this revolutionary wind soon blew through Southeast Asia.[73] Through his 1897 *Hikajat Khonghoetjoe* (Life Story of Confucius), the scholar Lie Kim Hok, of whom more will be said later, drew from Confucianism to raise political awareness in the Indies. In Singapore, Confucian revivalism was patronized by powerful community leaders like Lim Boon Keng (1868–1957).[74] China started experimenting with girls' education in the late 1890s, and communities in the South Seas soon followed suit. The first overseas school for Chinese girls was established in Makassar in 1899, soon to be followed by another one in Singapore.[75] Five years later, the first school for indigenous girls was opened in Bandung by the better remembered educator Dewi Sartika (1884–1947). In both cases, girls' education was designed to cultivate domestic skills and agreeable personalities, yet the fact that it existed in the first place counted as progress.

Amidst this tidal wave of revolutionism, the THHK established schools all over the Indies. They drew intellectual support from Kang Youwei and his peers, logistical support from reformists based in Singapore, China, Japan, and even the United States, financial support from local businessmen, and moral support from a generation of enlightened young people.[76] China's Qing government belatedly tried to capitalize on these developments. From 1906 to 1911, the prestigious Khay Lam Hak Tong (Kainan School) in Nanjing opened its doors for Chinese pupils from overseas.[77] From 1907, Indonesia's once divided Chinese communities collectively established chambers of commerce (*siang hwee*) and reading clubs (*soe po sia*) oriented toward the "motherland."[78] The newspaper *Sin Po*, founded in 1910, displayed close links to the THHK. It encouraged Totoks and Peranakans alike to consider themselves part of China, study its culture, and stay away from Indonesian politics. The stereotype of Chinese people as inward-looking and politically aloof suddenly dashed on the rocks of reality. At the same time, true unity proved difficult to achieve. Simmering tensions between chauvinistic Totoks, indecisive Peranakans, and a heavy-handed Dutch government combusted into Chinese-on-Chinese riots in a number of cities. At the same time, the activism of Indies Chinese precipitated the emergence of indigenous mass organizations, most notably the Sarekat Islam (Islamic Union) in 1912. This anti-Chinese trade union was arguably the forerunner of pan-Indonesian nationalism.[79]

THHK's most lasting mark on Indonesia's linguistic landscape was its unwavering support for Mandarin, taught through the medium of Malay.[80] Mandarin had historically been the link-language of Chinese officials, although its literary idiom could also be read out in regional pronunciations. Mandarin proficiency quickly became an axiom of pan-Chinese reformism, following centuries of communicative barriers between different provinces. More than a decade before it was declared the national language of the Republic of China, this new linguistic standard had made impressive headway in the Indies. In British Malaya, it was likewise seen as a solution to the long-standing rivalry between competing speech communities.[81] THHK improved the level of spoken and written Mandarin through the aforementioned reading clubs, language trainings, and no fewer than four Chinese newspapers from 1909.[82] From 1921, *Sin Po* also appeared in Chinese, in spite—or, perhaps, for the sake—of its Peranakan-majority readership. Mandarin was considered prestigious enough to compete with Dutch, English, and Malay as a vehicle of progress. Another advantage was its aforementioned ability to bridge intergroup rivalries. The editors of *Sin Po* retrospectively summarized this sentiment as follows:

The THHK board of those days, because they realized that the association's primary goal was to tighten the bonds between the Chinese regardless of their provincial or village-level differences, deemed that the educational institution they wanted to establish could not teach Hokkien, Hakka, or Cantonese, but had to teach a neutral Chinese dialect.	Bestuurleden T.H.H.K. Batavia di itoe masa, kerna insjaf bahoea perkoempoelannja poenja toedjoean jang teroetama ada boeat meragemken orang Tionghoa zonder kenal perbedahan provincie atawa kampoeng, anggep dalem itoe pergoeroean jang marika hendak diriken tida boleh diadjar dialect Hokkian, Khe atawa Kongfoe hanja moesti dialect Tionghoa jang neutraal.[83]

Sino-Malay periodicals used different names for this popular language. Spoken Mandarin was known as *dialect Peking* (the Beijing dialect), *kwan hwa* (official speech), *kuoyü* (national language), or simply *bahasa Tionghoa* (the Chinese language). Its correct pronunciation was referred to as *tjeng-im* or *tjia-im*, as opposed to other spoken varieties of Chinese (*tengwah*). Classical or literary Chinese was known as *hanboen* or *toelisan lama* (old writings).⁸⁴ This was the most common type of written Chinese before the introduction in China and Southeast Asia of vernacular written Mandarin (*pai hwa*). Those not enrolled in THHK education could learn Mandarin through short courses (*Kuo Yu Pan*) or commercially printed phrasebooks. Such publications were advertised in uncompromisingly chauvinistic terms, such as "Are Overseas Chinese still sympathetic toward China?"⁸⁵

The success of Mandarin-medium education broke the hegemony of Hokkien schools.⁸⁶ As the cartoon at the beginning of this section illustrated, reformists had little positive to say about these old-fashioned institutions. Their inefficiency was wittily summarized in "Moesti Rajahken Lebih Rameh" (More People Ought to Celebrate). Published in 1929 in *Sin Po*, this short story centered on a traditional gentleman and recounted that "from his early days, uncle Kim Koen had been educated in a Chinese school, where the first thing he learned was *tjoewat* [punishment]."⁸⁷ Prior to the THHK, the educational prospects were indeed quite dire. Only a small minority had access to European-style schools, typically under the direction of missionaries. For most Chinese boys the options were limited to costly tutors, family or temple schools, traditional private schools (*soesiok*), or collectively funded free schools (*gie o*), all of which emphasized rote learning (*taktjeh*).⁸⁸ The education of girls received scant attention prior to the twentieth century, making knowledge of Hokkien and other Sinitic languages a male prerogative. While some Chinese schools were better organized than others, the THHK managed to rapidly put the majority out of business through their modern education. The linguistic focus increasingly shifted to Mandarin, whereas "vernacular languages from different regions of origin" were relegated to extracurricular activities.⁸⁹

The position of European languages remained a matter of controversy. The Netherlands Indies authorities had confined Dutch education to a rather careful selection of privileged children, baulking at the prospect of seeing a pidgin emerge (South Africa was often used as a cautionary tale). Dutch proficiency thus became a strong marker of class and power. Important administrative proceedings took place in this language, leaving those unfamiliar with it reliant on Malay summaries of the topics discussed.⁹⁰ THHK circumvented these exclusionary practices by introducing English across its schools. They had valid reasons to do so. Not only could English provide the next generation with access to Singapore, Penang, and other parts of the British Empire, affordable English teachers were easier to recruit.⁹¹ English and Mandarin thus came to symbolize a world beyond Dutch Empire. As we read in a 1911 issue of *Sin Po*, "even in Medan and Deli (a territory still counted as a Dutch colony) people should not hope to secure a fitting livelihood if they cannot speak Chinese and English."[92]

Shocked at THHK's dismissal of Dutch and even more at the prospect of colonial subjects loyal to the British Crown, the Dutch authorities rushed to establish a government-sponsored alternative in 1909, the Hollandsch-Chineesche School (Dutch-Chinese School). This was the first type of European education widely available to the Indies Chinese. The Hollandsch-Chineesche School charged higher tuition fees in exchange for better job opportunities, making it especially popular among the Peranakans.[93] The fruits of this policy soon became apparent. In 1928, the first cohort of Dutch-educated Peranakans founded a pro-government association named Chung Hwa Hui (Chinese Union). Despite its sluggish institutionalization, Dutch education became a countervailing force of Chinese nationalism. It fomented fierce intra-Chinese polemics on political, cultural, and linguistic loyalties. Nationalistic writers were prone to put the blame on Chung Hwa Hui, but also on Westernized Peranakans more generally. The editors of the *Swara Publiek* (Voice of the Public; Surabaya, 1925) illustrate these tensions compellingly. In a colloquial idiom deliberately peppered with Hokkien (*ho-lan-wa*, "to speak Dutch") and Dutch, they castigate Chinese-educated Peranakans for their lack of nationalism. Their excessive use of Dutch expressions like *voorgoed* (permanently), *te pas en te onpas* (again and again), and *He, wat lief!* (Hey, that's so cute!) must be seen as a satirical device:

[these] young men—after they complete their education in China—immediately run back to Indonesia to stay there permanently! They're also incapable of having a Totok Chinese girl as a wife; since they've become so accustomed to the life of real Chinese they ought to be well-equipped to live with a Totok Chinese girl. Instead, they look for partners that are proficient in Dutch, ladies who can chirp again and again: "Hey, that's so cute!"	pamoeda-pamoeda jang sasoedah troesken peladjarannja di Tiongkok ngiprit ka Indonesia lagi aken diam disitoe "voorgoed"! Djoega marika tida dong-dong satoe nona Tionghoa totok seperti istri, lantaran soeda tjotjok benar sama pengidoepan Tionghoa toelen, hingga melingken bisa hidoep sama nona Tionghoa totok. Marika sebaliknja mentjari pasangan, jang pande "ho-lan-wa" dan njonja jang bisa "te pas en te onpas" bisa mengotje: "He, wat lief!"[94]

The above diatribe, like the aforementioned cartoon, emanated from the bitter realization that neither Mandarin, Malay, Dutch, nor any regional Sinitic variety sufficed as the unifying language of Chinese education. THHK lost much of its allure by the 1920s, prompting many Totok parents to reembrace education in Hokkien, Hakka, Cantonese, or Teochew.⁹⁵ Similar "dialect schools" persevered in British Malaya. With Mandarin now firmly part of the equation, the competition between Chinese varieties returned with a vengeance. Matters were further complicated by the fact that several schools claimed to teach Mandarin, yet secretly used a regional variety.⁹⁶ This conundrum elicited these reflections from a *Hoakiao* editor:

Which one should we teach? Where do we want to use it? In Batavia, and generally in West Java, one finds more Hakkas, in Central and East Java more Hokkiens! Mandarin is only used among ex-pupils of Chinese schools! Should we teach four to five Chinese languages? Every Chinese dialect would obviously compete for the right to be called the "Chinese" language!	Jang mana kita moesti adjar? Dimana kita maoe goenaken? Di Batavia, oemoemnja West Java orang dapetken lebi banjak bangsa Hokka [*sic*!], di midden dan Oost Java bangsa Hokkian! Tjia-im melingken bisa dipake diantara ex moerid haktong! Apa orang moesti adjar itoe ampat-lima bahasa Tionghoa? Saben dialect Tionghoa tentoe kangkangin hak ia ada bahasa "Tionghoa"!⁹⁷

Eventually, a fragile equilibrium emerged. Malay, Mandarin, and other Chinese languages coexisted among the pro-China factions, Westernized elites embraced Dutch, and the majority of Peranakans continued to speak Malay and/or regional Indonesian languages. Hokkien remained important throughout the late colonial period. Some Chinese classics, like Laozi's *Kitab Too Tik King* (The Way and Its Power), were (re)published in their Chinese characters, Hokkien romanization, Mandarin romanization, and Malay translation, in that order.⁹⁸ Sino-Malay journalism was punctuated with Hokkien rather than Mandarin loanwords, as were many Malay dictionaries compiled by Chinese lexicographers.⁹⁹ Some of their Hokkien vocabulary had itself recently been borrowed from Japanese.¹⁰⁰ Neologisms promoted by THHK—such as *siansing* (gentleman), *hoedjin* (lady), and the days of the Chinese calendar—likewise only found wide acceptance in their Hokkien pronunciation. Even the names of eminent people were occasionally (re)romanized in Netherlands Indies Hokkien: Kang Youwei became "Khong Yoe Wi" and Lim Boon Keng became "Lim Boen Keng." In the realm of political terminology, Hokkien and Mandarin featured side by side. One article from *Nan Sing* (Voice of the South; Semarang, 1930) contains the Hokkien words *theehwee* (semiformal gathering) and *koksiahwee* (national assembly) alongside the Mandarin term *waichiaopu* (minister of foreign affairs), while using Mandarin *kuo min tang* (Nationalist Party) and its Hokkien equivalent *kok bin tong* interchangeably.[101] In the 1920s and 1930s, some Sino-Malay newspapers adopted Mandarin names, as opposed to Hokkien or Malay ones.[102] The actual content, however, was invariably in Low Malay.

From the 1920s, the widespread optimism that Mandarin would soon establish itself as the universal Chinese language made way for frustration at the low levels of fluency attested in the Indies. In coping with this problem and its debilitating impact on pan-Chinese nationalism, the editors of *Sin Po* again mobilized the trope of language attrition. One wonders whether they saw the irony of conveying their purist ideals in a mixture of Malay, Hokkien (*djip hoan*, "to go native"), and English:

If nothing is done about this, no shortage of Chinese children will one day go native or become half-baked. For that reason, let the work start right now! Don't talk about it, do it!	Kaloe ini dibiarken sadja, boekan sedikit anak anak Tionghoa satoe tempo djip hoan atawa djadi kapalang tanggoeng. Dari itoe, bekerdjalah moelai sekarang! Don't talk about [*sic*!], do it![103]

This chapter's investigation of Chinese-Indonesian plurilingualism thus ends in a stalemate. The issue of language loyalty remained unresolved throughout the colonial period. Mandarin was briefly instated as the sole medium of Chinese education during Indonesia's Japanese occupation from 1942 to 1945 and had to give some way to standard Indonesian in the period afterward.[104] The position of other Sinitic languages has dwindled ever since.

2
ON GOOD, BAD, AND UGLY MALAY

Whenever perceived outsiders encroach upon a language, notions of purity and authenticity soon take root.¹ Plurilingualism, then, provoked a variety of responses in the Netherlands Indies. This chapter examines how the Malay spoken, written, and described by people of Chinese ancestry resonated across the public sphere, from society's elites down to the grassroots. It illustrates how print entrepreneurs outraged colonial language hierarchies through their contents, but especially through the linguistic style they adopted. To examine how a community talks about their language—their metalinguistic discourse—normally involves fieldwork and in-depth interviews.² This is impossible for extinct languages, and yet some key research questions remain identical. How did people look at their language? How did others perceive it, and how did the speech community respond to such external judgments? What was the role of the written word in these exchanges? A wealth of Sino-Malay and other sources offers insights into these questions. This chapter first calls attention to a confluence of scholarly traditions—including Hokkien dialectology, Sinographic transcription systems, and European-influenced linguistics—that shaped the ways Chinese-Indonesians talked about language. Next, it dismantles the received wisdom that Java's Malay was inferior to that of Sumatra, highlighting strategies to talk back against these prevailing hierarchies. Finally, it underscores the importance of spelling to colonial language attitudes. Chinese writers never felt the need to impose a homogenized orthography but had several ideas on the correct way to spell words. Consequently, they found fault with the authoritative Malay orthography, as it failed to reflect the colloquial pronunciation of Java's cities.³

As the distance between literary and colloquial language had remained vast throughout the colonial period, the Malay of Chinese authors seldom drew praise from Dutch and indigenous intelligentsia. Its avid borrowing from and code-mixing with Javanese and Hokkien rendered it deficient in the eyes of orientalist scholars, whose preoccupations with language purity echoed contemporaneous ideas in Europe. Dutch newspaper editors and Bible translators were more sympathetic to vernacular Malay, as large readerships were at least as important to them as notions of correctness.[4] Indeed, Malay translations of novels and other books were frequently advertised with such epithets as *gampang* (easy) or *sederhana* (simple). Chinese print entrepreneurs insisted on using this vernacular language rather than the artificial Malay promoted by the colonial administration. Despite the low status of their language, they were influential enough to be noticed. In 1938, the linguist and missionary Samuel Jonathan Esser (1900–44) provides some insight into the quandary of Malay heterogeneity:

> The question has now become whether we must accept that, due to the influence of the powerful Chinese-Malay press, the language is bastardizing into an incomprehensible hybrid product. Many believe we must do so, since in their opinion the influence of this press is so great that it is anyhow impossible to row upstream. But when we take into account that it is urged from the side of the Chinese to abolish the default School Malay at the Malay-Chinese schools—as this language is incomprehensible to the Chinese and useless in practical life—and that the opinion is put forward from the side of the authorities that Chinese-Malay (which in the essence of the matter occurs in numerous local varieties), especially in Java, is so distant from the default Malay that it is in fact an entirely distinct language, the urgency becomes evident to arrive at clear proposals in this regard, to separate what does not belong together, and at the very least to ensure the systematic and scientific establishment and practical continuation of a good, modern Malay.[5]

The Dutch authorities seemed uncertain how to approach this Malay vernacular beyond belittlement and hegemonic ignorance. It received minimal attention from the academic establishment. The linguist Jacob Kats (1877–1945) was exceptional in including "Chinese-Malay" in his 1922 *Warna Sari Melajoe* (Anthology of Malay). Even earlier, Abraham Anthony Fokker (1862–1927) incorporated some Sino-Malay texts into his 1906 book on Malay epistolography, but only as negative examples: "In addition to letters in good Malay, which are assigned for imitation, letters composed in bad Chinese-Malay should thus also occur in a practical book on letter-writing."[6]

Institutionalized efforts to study language often interlock with prevailing power hierarchies. This chapter scrutinizes such dynamics in a late colonial context, yet they are the product of earlier developments. Both Malay and Hokkien were studied by the earliest European linguists operating in Southeast Asia. The protestant minister Justus Heurnius (1587–1652), arguably the first Dutch Sinologist, investigated them simultaneously.[7] Missionary zeal fueled European ventures to learn Malay and Chinese for the next centuries to come. Since China's southern harbors were off limits for missionaries until 1842, Southeast Asia became a key location to do so. The British missionary and lexicographer Walter Henry Medhurst (1796–1857) studied Hokkien in Malacca, Penang, and Batavia, alongside Malay and Javanese. His assistant Ko Tsching Dschang, a China-born Hakka who resided in Batavia and was posted in Leiden from 1830 to 1835, may have been Europe's first ethnic Chinese teacher.[8] We must recall here that Dutch Sinology owes its existence as an institutionalized field of knowledge-production to the Netherlands Indies.[9]

Malay proved less bothersome for Europeans to pick up than any of the Sinitic varieties, at least on a basic conversational level. As a preeminent lingua franca, it was relatively forgiving of pronunciations and grammatical structures induced by language contact. The relative accessibility of Malay—especially the pidginized "foreigner talk" used in trading entrepots—did its reputation no favors. No shortage of Western scholars dismissed it as a "lazy" language, undoubtedly by dint of its equatorial provenance. The Sinologist Gustaaf Schlegel (1840–1903), who had spent decades studying the Zhangzhou dialect of Hokkien, was hardly alone in linking the phonological peculiarities of Malay to racial stereotypes:

> This laziness of the tongue is very common among Malays and even among the dutch halfcaste or the creoles born in India [the Netherlands Indies]. I could never teach such a man to pronounce words like *kept, left, far,* etc.; he always pronounced them *kep, lef* and *fah* because he was too lazy to pronounce the final *t* and *r*.[10]

Such folkloristic attitudes to language may display universal characteristics, but colonialism certainly ossified them. No small number of Indies Chinese developed a linguistic inferiority complex, which persisted if not worsened in postcolonial times. Nio Joe Lan, for example, insisted modestly in his 1962 monograph on Sino-Malay literature that "the language is impoverished, yet the contents are full of things that could serve as study material for one purpose or the other." Around the same time, his colleague Gan Kok Liang (1928–2003) assured his readers that he had carefully changed all colonial-era spellings in his book into new ones, yet apologized for the "colloquial language and many other shortcomings" one might still find in it. In the words of Tjan Kwan Nio (1908–88), a woman writer of adventure novels reflecting on her own oeuvre: "the spelling is random, impressionistic, just following the sound of the words. The language was muddled, the composition disorganized. Is that what is called Chinese Malay? Is it unique? Antique? Or just terrific to be kept as a souvenir?"[11] Similar attitudes prevailed in Malaya.[12] Such metalinguistic comments were written retrospectively, at a time when Sino-Malay varieties had lost much ground and status. The situation was almost reversed in late colonial times. Under the paramountcy of Chinese print entrepreneurship, vernacular Malay counted as a self-confident carrier of knowledge and entertainment. It had brought forth brilliant lexicographic works and local histories, such as the *Riwajat Semarang* (Account of Semarang) published in 1933 by Liem Thian Joe. As mentioned previously, it was significantly more common for Chinese to study Malay than the other way around.[13]

From the seventeenth century onward, most Dutch observers distinguished between the "good" High Malay and "bad" Low Malay, a bifurcation also upheld by ethnic Malays. The former—it was claimed—was grammatically correct and used in classical literature, whereas the latter was corrupted by foreigners and regionally heterogeneous. Yet not all experts accepted this rigid distinction. As François Valentijn (1666–1727) wittily pointed out, "in that case Dutch would also be a bad language compared to German."[14] The Indies-bred linguist Herman Neubronner van der Tuuk (1824–94) rejected the idea that Low Malay equaled the speech of foreigners and High Malay that of "natives." In his own words: "one would then have to call the Dutch of a 'Hottentot' or Black African, etc. 'Low Dutch,' and the Dutch of a porter from Amsterdam 'High Dutch.'"[15] As this chapter illustrates, a number of Chinese-descended authors took yet another stance: they considered their Low Malay as superior to the High Malay of indigenous elites and European philologists. To the chagrin of language purists, they celebrated its lexical hybridity as a legitimate expression of everyday life. Uncharitable as the term Low Malay may have been, it was embraced and reclaimed by many.

Spelling, with its power to standardize, control, and expropriate, plays an important role in these contestations. At the turn of the twentieth century, it became a marker of elitist vis-à-vis vernacular language esthetics. Malay saw its first fixed spelling in 1901, when Charles Adriaan van Ophuijsen finalized his authoritative orthography. It was widely adopted by the colonial administration, nationalist elites, and authors from Sumatra, yet mostly ignored by private publishers based in Java.[16] Chinese print entrepreneurs almost universally stuck to their own spelling, which corresponded more closely to their Malay pronunciation. Spelling thus became crucial to distinguish the writings of Chinese journalists from those of indigenous nationalists, a situation that continued into the late 1940s. In postcolonial times, orthographic reform epitomized successive governments. The new spelling implemented in 1972 under President Suharto, for instance, drew this assessment from Benedict Anderson:

> The real motive behind it was to mark a decisive break between what was written under the dictatorship and everything written before it. One had

only to read the title of a book or pamphlet to know whether it was splendidly modern, or a derisory residue of Sukarnoism, constitutionalism, the revolution, or the colonial period. Any interest in old-orthography materials was automatically suspicious. The change was sufficiently great that youngsters could easily be persuaded that "old" printed materials were too hard to decipher, and so not to be bothered with.[17]

The situation has only become more complex. At present, Indonesia's pre-1947 spelling can be seen on display at numerous restaurants, shops, tourist attractions, and other sites with genuine or imaginary links to the past. Old-orthography materials carry a veneer of nostalgia, commercially driven or otherwise. To maintain historical authenticity, the renowned author Pramoedya Ananta Toer (1925–2006) insisted on keeping the original spelling of a number of late colonial stories republished in his 1981 *Antologi Sastra pra-Indonesia* (Anthology of Pre-Indonesian Literature). In addition, the old spelling can be seen throughout social media, typically in a playful fashion.

Beyond Linguistic Eurocentrism

In a one-page article from 1924, *Sin Po*'s editors pilloried Adriaan Herm Louis Badings (1840–1901) on account of his unidiomatic Malay. During the late nineteenth century, this lieutenant-colonel regularly published on the Malay of the Netherlands Indies military. Instead of pointing out his mistakes, the editors simply quoted several examples from his oeuvre. One gets the impression that *Sin Po*'s readers could intuitively grasp their awkwardness, making further commentary redundant. A short diatribe followed the anthology. How could someone associated with the KITLV, an institute allegedly specializing in Indonesian languages, produce such abominable Malay? Rather than *bahasa Malajoe* (Malay), it was baptized *bahasa Mal* (Crazy language), a clever pun on Dutch *mal* (crazy):

And this type of Crazy (Malay) language comes from a member of the Royal Institute for the Linguistics, Geography and Ethnology of the Netherlands Indies! Other than the Dutch chairmen of district courts, it would appear to us that not a soul in the Netherlands Indies (in all its vastness) uses this form of the "Malay" language.	Dan ini matjem "bahasa Mal(ajoe)" ada dari satoe lid dari Kon. Inst. V.d. Taal, Land- en Volkenkunde v. N.I.! Kita rasa salaennja voorzitter-voorzitter landraad bangsa Olanda, tiada laen manoesia di Hindia-Olanda (jang loewas) jang goenaken itoe matjem bahasa "Melajoe."[18]

To understand why a Sino-Malay newspaper would passionately deride the Malay of a European "expert," especially one who had passed away long since, we must delve into the conflicting ideas of what Malay was, or was supposed to be. To the Chinese print entrepreneurs of Batavia, Semarang, Surabaya, and other cities, most attempts of Dutch officials to use Malay in official communication were laughable on linguistic grounds alone. Yet in the eyes of European academics, the language of Chinese journalists, Eurasian clerks, and Batavia's porters offloading the trunks of their freshly arrived rulers hardly qualified as good Malay either. In the early 1930s, the Eurasian scholar Joseph Theodore Koks (1902–ca. 1970) characterized the spoken vernacular of Batavia as "the language in which everything that elevates itself above the most primitive life manages to be expressed and which everyone understands."[19] A decade earlier, the Dutch orientalist Philippus Samuel van Ronkel (1870–1954) cautioned against an Indies-wide "Batavianization" of Malay, alerting his readers that this low-status variety was spreading.[20] Similar judgments were made in the nineteenth century. The Malay contact variety of Java's other cities suffered an even lower reputation. Jan Pijnappel (1822–1901), Holland's first scholar to occupy a professorial chair in Malay, had little positive to say about this necessary evil (*noodzakelijk kwaad*):

> The study of the Malay language has no worse enemy than Low Malay and requires all possible efforts to defeat it; for although it has thrived for more than two centuries, that study remains a fragile seedling, which has had to endure many misfortunes, and for which one cannot yet with full certainty anticipate the speedy dawn of a sunny day; as her enemy is ever supported by the human proclivity to prefer convenience over effort.[21]

Pijnappel's condemnation illustrates the fissures between hegemonic prescriptions of grammaticality and grassroots notions of credibility. Opinions were not vastly different in British Malaya. In 1917, the orientalist Charles Otto Blagden (1864–1949) remarked on Baba Malay that "this jargon bears the same relation to the real Malay language as the Pidgin English of the China ports does to our own English."[22] In 1891, the British-American bishop William Fitzjames Oldham (1854–1937) characterized the situation in Singapore:

> In its purity Malay has been called the Italian of the East, but it suffers terribly at the lips of this polyglot people, each of whom brings to its pronunciation some native disability, and by the time the Chinaman has turns its r's into l's . . . the Malay heard commonly on the streets of Singapore is only a far-off and base-born relative of the beautiful idiomatic language whose name it bears. Indeed, there has grown up in the

island a distinct *patois* known as the "Baba Malay," so named from the Babas (Straits-born Chinese), who have mingled Chinese, English, and Malay words into an utterly amorphous conglomerate, the despair of the grammarian and an object of loathing contempt to the aristocratic Malay.[23]

Such assessments were commonplace in Europe, but also among the indigenous elites of Java, Sumatra, and Malaya. Across continents, purists shared their disdain for languages that were easily acquired, lexically hybrid, and grammatically influenced by non-native speakers. Such notions had been firmly thrust into the Dutch mindset since at least the French occupation of the Low Lands (1795–1813).[24] Even if multilingualism was encouraged, they saw the mixing of languages as detrimental, harnessing fresh memories of excessive French influence in their own tongue. Yet, as always, the scholars were not unequivocal. Discussions on the preferable Malay for a Bible translation—classical, demotic, or something in between—remained unresolved for centuries.[25] Opinions also differed on the legitimacy of language contact and lexical borrowing. The Sinologist Peter Adriaan van de Stadt (1876–1940) defended the existence of "bastard expressions" in the preface of his 1912 Hakka dictionary.[26] A decade later, his colleague Philippus Samuel van Ronkel dismissed the 1845 *Syair Baba Kong Sit* (Poem of Baba Kong Sit) as a "worthless poem" full of modern (Batavian and Dutch) words.[27]

The Chinese, rejoicing in the world's longest tradition of studying Malay, rarely arrived at similar conclusions. If anything, they were predominantly interested in the language as it was actually spoken. Along with other languages deemed relevant to China's foreign interests, Malay was taught from the fifteenth century at the College of All Foreigners. This imperial institution published the *Vocabulary Lists for Foreign Languages*, in which non-Chinese words and phrases were transcribed with homophonous characters. These lists are thus of interest to the languages that were described, but also to the phonological history of Chinese itself. The Malay glossary included in this compilation is the oldest extant proof of Malay lexicography (fig 2.1).[28]

Hokkien provided a phonological benchmark for the transcription of Malay. The *Sip Ngo Im* (Fifteen Initial Sounds), an 1818 rhyme dictionary published in Fujian, presumably helped Chinese writers to find characters for the sounds they heard.[29] The same was true for Javanese and Dutch words. As early as VOC times, the names of important Dutchmen were rendered with homophonous characters. To identify the people, places, and products mentioned by Chinese authors thus requires knowledge of literary Chinese, Malay, Javanese, Dutch, and Hokkien.[30] The vast majority of loanwords in Indies Hokkien were transcriptions

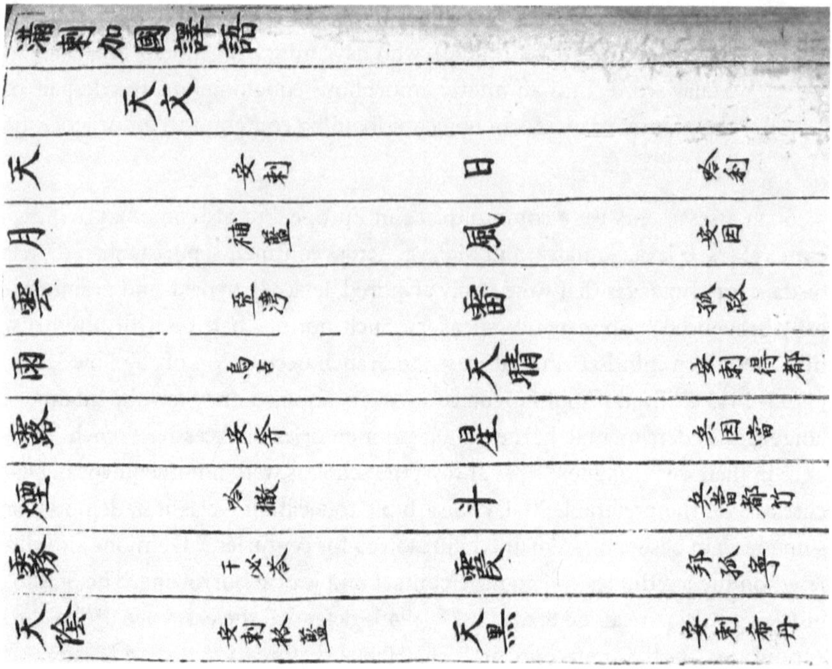

FIGURE 2.1. Page from the first known Malay wordlist (SOAS MS 48363)

of colonial institutions, ranks, and administrative terms. Needless to say, they "have given modern historians a lot of headaches."[31] The name of Java's anticolonial leader Pangeran Diponegoro (1785–1855), for example, was written in the characters corresponding to *Pang-ki-lân Lī-pò-lėk-gô-lô*, whereas the Dutch general de Kock (1779–1845) was spelled as *Jîn-tek-lah Lėk-kok*.[32] Bookkeeping contained additional lexicographic puzzles, such as *úi-hān-bùt-làt-tek* (road tax; D: *wegenbelasting*) and *hān-the-kong-pṅg-nî* (trade company; D: *handelscompagnie*).[33]

This system greatly assisted Hokkien-speakers to learn Malay. A key publication was the 1877 *New Words for Communicating with Foreigners*, which appeared in Singapore by the hands of Lim Kong Chuan.[34] I have not been able to locate any copies of this book, but the appearance in 1883 of a revised version under the name *Phrasebook for Chinese and Foreigners* attests to its popularity.[35] Lim's way of transcribing Malay words is of great linguistic interest and resourcefulness. Each dictionary entry is followed by Chinese characters that, when read out in Hokkien, sound like the envisaged Malay gloss. To transcribe syllables for which no default Sinographic characters existed, Lim resorted to tone marks and symbols indicating alternative pronunciations.[36] A circle signified that a character had to be read out in the colloquial pronunciation, a triangle in the Quanzhou dialect, and an apostrophe in the Zhangzhou dialect. On one page, for example, the Chinese word for "right now" (Ml: *ini kutika*) was transcribed with characters reading *î nî* (Zhangzhounese; otherwise: *jí^n*) *kū* (coll.; otherwise: *kiū*) *ti ka* (Quanzhounese; otherwise: *ke*), as is shown in figure 2.2 (left column, second line).[37]

More Malay scholarship appeared in the same period. In 1878, the scholar Lim Tjay Tat published a dictionary titled *Ferry and Bridge of the General Language*, which targeted Hokkien-speaking Singkehs. This self-study book on Batavian Malay contains numerous locally specific words, titles, and toponyms. It juxtaposes Hokkien entries and their Malay glosses, both in Sinographic transcription and Indies-style romanization.[38] Speakers of other Sinitic varieties published their own phrasebooks from the 1910s, including the 1912 *Malay–Cantonese Glossary* and the 1916 *Standard Hakka Glossary of the Malay Language*.[39] Due to phonological factors as well as individual preferences, their compilers often used different characters to represent the same Malay syllables. In the *Hakka Glossary of the Malay Language*, the Malay sentences *lu tidak tau adat* (You have no manners) and *lu mau potong sama orang* (You want to cut somebody down) could be satisfactorily transcribed with the characters reading out as *lû tî-thàt tá-vû hâ-thàt* and *lû mo po-tông sâm-mâ ô-liang*.[40] Such profane sentences, even though they made up a minor part of the examples, would be relatively hard to find in contemporaneous European-edited materials.

Chinese writers also published Western-style Malay grammars. Lie Kim Hok stands out in this regard. He was a product of European education—with Sundanese, Malay, and Dutch as his languages of instruction—in addition to the traditional Hokkien school system. Later in life, he became a Confucian revivalist linked to the THHK movement. Seen by many as the father of Sino-Malay literature, Lie Kim Hok also wrote a pioneering grammar of Batavian Malay.[41] We may assume that this 116-page monograph, first published in 1884, provided a boost in the self-confidence of Batavia's speech community—both Chinese and non-Chinese—whose Malay was habitually disregarded by Holland's Sumatra-obsessed philologists. Lie's grammar abounds in now obsolete linguistic terminology. His calques and original creations reflect an astute ability to describe new concepts without having to rely on loanwords, which added to his fame.[42] The same creativity can be seen in his successor Kwee Tek Hoay, who likewise coined novel terms to analyze the grammatical phenomena he observed in Malay.[43]

Lie Kim Hok had a British Malayan counterpart in the interpreter Lim Hiong Seng. In 1887, this Singaporean Teochew scholar published *A Manual of the Malay Colloquial* with the aim to describe the Straits vernacular as used by Babas rather than ethnic Malays.[44] Written in English, the 247-page phrasebook

甚 廢 時 候	際 遍
亞 把 梁	任萬実加 整
節 氣	現 刻
務 申	移 舊 瀾 知 加
新 年	立 刻
碼 溫 咯	移 瀾 裙 盃
元 旦	淡 前
加 拋 撈 碼 溫	流 咯
大 日 子	過 後
夏 利 勿 杀	須 撐 撈 汪
昔 時 即普時也	預 先
流 咯 加 撈	立 迷 跨 咯

FIGURE 2.2. Page from Lim Kong Chuan's *Phrasebook for Chinese and Foreigners* (Singapore, 1883)

contains numerous commercial and legal terms that prevailed at the time, such as *chŭrmin mata* (spectacles), *surat muatan* (ship's manifest), and *lawyer kompŭnni* (attorney-general). In contrast to contemporaneous European scholarship on High Malay, most examples from Lim's *Malay Colloquial* were rooted in the mundane experiences of urban Babas. Judging from some of its example sentences, the author appears to have been involved in missionary activities:

Christian people worship the true God | The God that created the heaven and the earth | The Chinese worship idols, Europeans say they are no use, they are only wood and stone.⁴⁵	Orang *Christian* sŭmbayang Tuhan Allah yang bŭttol | Itu Allah yang mŭnjadikan langet sama bumi | Orang China sŭmbayang dato*h*, orang pute bilang ta*h*da gunna nya, chuma kayu sama batu saja.

Additional works on Malay were written by a number of less celebrated linguists, whose publications have not been preserved. I have not been able to find any of the Malay teaching materials from the Solo-based print entrepreneur Tjoa Tjoe Kwan, nor the *Kitab Peladjaran Bahasa Melajoe Tionghoa* (Chinese-Malay Schoolbook) used in THHK schools.⁴⁶ Two other books on vernacular Malay—*Kitab Lograt Melajoe Tionghoa* (Malay–Chinese Dictionary) and *Kitab Peladjaran bahasa Melajoe Tionghoa* (Malay–Chinese Learning Book)—appeared in the 1930s at the hands of the Nanjing-based scholar Lu Pao Ru and have also been lost. Both were mentioned in Lu's *Correspondentie Dagang* (Business Correspondence), a 1935 compilation of Malay business letters intended for Chinese-educated readers.⁴⁷ In addition, several Mandarin–Malay dictionaries and phrasebooks were published in the early twentieth century by lexicographers from China, with the double aim of reconnecting the Indies Chinese with their ancestral heritage and familiarizing newcomers with the Malay language.⁴⁸

A small number of Sino-Malay linguistic studies deals with Hokkien. The aforementioned Tjoa Tjoe Kwan was a key figure in this arena. A renowned polyglot, he published several books in addition to a Javanese and a Sino-Malay newspaper. His 1897 *Penjoeratan pada Menjataken Hoeroef Tjina jang Beroepa Gambar* (Treatise to Clarify Chinese Letters that are Shaped like Drawings) traces the pictographic origins of a number of Sinographic characters, and his 1904 *Tjiap Kian Siang Tam* (Common Conversations for Meetings) contains numerous polite phrases, questions, and answers.⁴⁹ These short conversations are written in romanized Hokkien, followed by their Chinese characters, Malay translations, and occasionally their Javanese equivalents (in the Javanese and the Latin script). As such, the book is a key example of Chinese-Indonesian plurilingualism.

Knowledge of English also spread to the Netherlands Indies, including in THHK and Hollandsch-Chineesche School circles. Chinese lexicographers published a number of English dictionaries, such as the *English–Malay Dictionary* by Song Chong Sin (1921), the *English & Malay Dictionary* by "Kwee" (1929), and *The Standard English–Malay Dictionary* by Pouw Peng Hong (1931). These publications are often ignored in scholarship on Malay lexicography, presumably because few copies have ended up in public libraries. This is a pity, as they provide valuable insights into its language history. In a number of instances, their compilers reckoned that English words were best explained through their Hokkien equivalents. One dictionary translates "vagabond" as *kongtjoejasia*, the Hokkien term for a spoiled dandy or playboy. Another glosses "censor" as "the minister assigned to deal with criticism or debates concerning state affairs" before adding the Hokkien-derived synonym *gie-soe*.⁵⁰ For most relatively novel concepts, the dictionaries provide Malay glosses that were also used in Sino-Malay books and newspapers (see table 2).

Much scholarship on language came from print entrepreneurs allied with *Sin Po*. In 1923, Kwik Khing Djoen published a dictionary containing, as the subtitle read, "all foreign words that have become broadly used in Malay newspapers; as required by the readers of *Sin Po*."⁵¹ This *Kitab Vortaro*, which took its title from Malay *kitab* (book) and Esperanto *vortaro* (dictionary), can perhaps be considered as the earliest Malay dictionary of foreign words, including borrowings from Arabic, German, English, French, Greek, Dutch, Javanese, Latin, Portuguese, Sanskrit, Spanish, and Chinese. One imagines a warm reception of this handy resource, as Sino-Malay newspapers were notorious for their indulgence of arcane exoticisms, yet in reality it contains only a small fraction of the innumerable foreign words obtaining in the vernacular Malay of Chinese writers.

TABLE 2 Some English words and their Malay translations

ENGLISH	SONG (1921)	KWEE (1929)	POUW (1931)
colonize	doedoekin tanah djadjahan	—	memboeka negri baroe, doedoekin tanah asing (sebagi djadjahan)
freedom	kamerdikaän	kamerdika'an	kabebasan, kamerdikaän
independent	merdika, tiada terprenta	merdika	merdika, bebas
modern	matjem baroe	matjem baroe	baroe, boeatan baroeh, model atau kaloearan jang baroeh
politics	politiek, atoeran memberesin negri	—	ilmoe siasat negri, pengetaoean tentang hal pemerentahan negri, oeroesan government
progressive	madjoe	madjoe	jang bermadjoe atau berdjalan teroes, jang bertamba djadi lebi baik
youth	tempo masi moeda, anak moeda	di waktoe moeda	kamoedahan, anak moeda

From 1940, readers of *Sin Po* took matters in their own hands and submitted several lists of speculative Hokkien loanwords in Low Malay. Unfortunately, these inventories are difficult to interpret, as the words are neither glossed nor linked to Sinographic characters. They nevertheless testify to a preoccupation with the origins of everyday language. This interactive metalinguistic discourse sharply contrasted with the prescriptivism of Dutch and indigenous elites.

A Language Nobody Understands

The grit and grime of Java's cities birthed a type of Malay that was destined to lack elite approval. Advised by Malay men of education, Dutch administrators looked to neighboring Sumatra, especially the Residency of Riau and Dependencies (Residentie Riouw en Onderhoorigheden), for a variety that could serve as the colony's standard. Many espoused the half-truth that the purest Malay hailed from this region, just as the purest Dutch was allegedly spoken in Haarlem. The Riau island of Penyengat was indeed a center of classical literature, akin to Aceh in early modern times. It boasted a thriving printing industry in Jawi, the Arabic-derived script of Malay. Through their preoccupation with Riau, the colonial government could expand its ownership of the Malay language, conveniently locating its epicenter away from Java.[52] Some Dutchmen likened the prestigious Malay spoken in Riau to Latin, a language of civilizing potential. As the aforementioned Abraham Anthony Fokker asserted, "if Ethiopians had learned to use the language of Cicero, could not the vastly superior Javanese, Buginese, etc. learn Riau Malay?"[53] Eventually, however, European linguists and Bible translators realized that the spoken language of Riau was anything but the untouched philological relic they envisioned it to be. It showed the same signs of language contact as Malay varieties elsewhere. By the nineteenth century, the highly esteemed idiom of classical Malay literature was not natively spoken anywhere. Those who persisted to use it in writing required tremendous creativity to discuss novel concepts.

From the early twentieth century, the Indies administration promoted a Riau-inspired type of romanized Malay engineered to become a vehicle of modern usage and education.[54] This variety was known interchangeably as School Malay, Ophuijsen Malay, or Balai Poestaka Malay. Most teachers were recruited from Sumatra's populous Minangkabau area, which was not quite Riau but generally deemed close enough. From the 1920s into independence, this elevated Malay standardization had also been adopted and expanded by Indonesian language planners. They echoed their Dutch predecessors by speaking of it as a fragile flower or a vulnerable child in need of careful nurturing. A statement made in

1955 by the Padang-born writer Zuber Usman (1916–76) exemplifies this enduring mindset:

> The Malay language, if it is likened to a young girl ... has now taken the shape of an adolescent princess. We hope and anticipate that when the time has come our language will become a queen, honored and loved among the languages of the world!⁵⁵

In retrospect, the colloquial Malay of Chinese and other urban communities lacked four crucial things: elite patronage, literary cachet, an orthography, and a prescriptive grammar. Advocates of High Malay nevertheless saw its popularity as a threat. Among the Malay intellectuals, this view had already established itself in the nineteenth century. The writer Abdullah bin Abdul al Kadir or "Munsyi Abdullah" (1796–1854), himself a South Indian Peranakan, was a prominent critic of the Malay of foreigners. So was the poet-scholar Raja Ali Haji bin Raja Haji Ahmad (1808–73), who explicitly linked linguistic impurity to invasive peoples even though he was himself of Bugis extraction.⁵⁶ Undoubtedly to the chagrin of both, many Europeans and Singkehs indeed resorted to a Malay pidgin in their interactions with the archipelago's populations. The scholars found their views vindicated by Europe's own academic elite. Both van Ophuijsen and the influential missionary-lexicographer Hillebrandus Cornelius Klinkert (1829–1913) approached the Malay of Riau as the norm. Ethnic Minangkabau writers from West Sumatra likewise preferred it over Java's variety.⁵⁷ At the same time, there was little doubt that few Indies Chinese could fully understand High Malay. As Kwee Tek Hoay pointed out in 1935:

| When people examine Ophuijsen's Malay dictionary, the Malay–Dutch dictionaries by Klinkert, and others, they would definitely encounter thousands of Malay words that would be equally alien for writers of Low Malay as the words of "Eskimos" or "Hottentots." | Kapan orang preksa kitab logat Melajoe dari Ophuijzen [sic!] atawa boekoe-boekoe woordenboek Melajoe-Olanda dari Klinkert dan laen-laen lagi, nistjaja bisa diketemoein riboean perkata'an Melajoe jang bagi penoelis-penoelis Melajoe Rendah ada sama djoega asingnja seperti perkata'an-perkata'an Eskimo atawa Hottentot!⁵⁸ |

Perhaps without fully realizing it, print entrepreneurs had introduced their own written norm. Their texts prioritized accessibility and popular tastes over decorum and belletristic refinement. Few would have claimed that "their" Malay possessed high literary attainments. Unfamiliarity among the Chinese communities of the Indies and British Malaya with High Malay was by no means exaggerated.[59] As early as the 1890s, the *Surat Khabar Peranakan* (Peranakan Newspaper; Singapore, 1894) had deigned to publish some articles in this literary variety. A group of Babas immediately rushed to their office and complained that they could not understand it. The board decided to leave the matter to its readers—who overwhelmingly preferred Low Malay—and published the deliberations in its next issue:

We had printed those news pieces in correct Malay because some Babas and Europeans said that the Malay of *Surat Khabar Peranakan* was wrong; that its Malay was incorrect. Now the readers of this newspaper get to choose: the Malay we use in everyday life or correct Malay are both fine. Even many Europeans find it better if people would speak correct Malay, but they do not know that the majority of Babas and Chinese cannot understand it.	Kita chapkan itu khabar chara Malayu betol sebab ada Baba Baba dan Orang Puteh kata, yang Malayu "Surat Khabar Peranakan" ada salah dan Malayu-nya tada betol. Skarang masing masing yang membacha ini surat khabar, boleh pileh, Malayu yang kita kluar hari-hari punya baik atau Malayu betol baik. Banyak orang Puteh pun ada piker, kalu dia-orang boleh chakap Malayu betol ada banyak baik, tetapi dia-orang tada tau yang kabanyakan orang Baba Baba dan Orang China taboleh mengerti.[60]

In the Netherlands Indies, too, many Sino-Malay authors had internalized the elitist assertion that their language was inferior. In defense, they pointed out that their Malay (as opposed to Riau Malay) was not taught in primary schools, condemning it to stay impoverished. As a journalist for *Keng Po* wrote in 1935:

We have no hope, as long as the Chinese people here cannot receive Malay education at primary schools. The Chinese-Malay language is forced to remain impoverished, because the readers of our newspapers and books have never known more than two thousand words. A language cannot become perfect it if is not learned by the masses through schooling.	Kita tida mempoenjai harepan, sabegitoe lama orang Tionghoa di sini tida dapat peladjaran bahasa Melajoe di sekola rendah. Bahasa Melajoe-Tionghoa terpaksa tinggal miskin, lantaran pembatja dari koran-koran dan boekoe-boekoe kita selamanja tida kenal lebih dari 2000 perkata'an. Satoe bahasa tida bisa mendjadi sampoerna, bila tida dipeladjarin oleh rahajat dalem sekola.[61]

From the mid-1920s, the idea that the Malay used by Chinese was of a bad type increasingly made its way into the public sphere. Indigenous journalists were prone to ridicule it through mixed-vegetable metaphors: a chop suey language (*bahasa tjaptjay*), a ratatouille language (*bahasa ratjetoe*), a hotchpotch language (*bahasa hutspot*), a steamed-vegetables language (*bahasa gado-gado*), or a fruit-and-vegetable salad language (*bahasa roedjak*).[62] But equal numbers of Chinese writers, inspired by their pioneer Lie Kim Hok, stood up for this type of hybrid Malay, especially from the 1930s. As a journalist for *Sin Po* riposted, chop suey can be quite delicious for those who know how to appreciate it:

We should not forget the contributions of the late Lie Kim Hok, who in his pioneering efforts has created the Malay-Chinese language. This is what "Hok" has very aptly called Chinese in the "Malay" dialect. It's a chop suey language—said "Hok"—but delightful for those who happen to be fond of chop suey!	Kita tida boleh loepaken djasa-djasanja almarhoem Lie Kim Hok jang sebagi pionier telah tjiptaken bahasa Tionghoa-Melajoe. Jang oleh "Hok" dengan djitoe sekali dinamaken bahasa *Tionghoa* dengan dialect "Melajoe." Satoe bahasa tjaptjay—kata "Hok"—tapi sedep bagi jang memang soeka tjaptjay![63]

Distinguished by their unparalleled plurilingualism, Chinese wordsmiths occasionally drew praise for their expressive power. *Sin Po* proudly reported that the Sultan of Bulungan in northern Borneo had his government regulations translated into Malay by a Batavian Chinese, whose language was laudably clear.[64] Kwee Tek Hoay pointed out that the success of the opera troupe Dardanella was due to its adoption of Java Malay rather than Sumatran or Straits Malay.[65] Others insisted that the frequent exposure of Sino-Malay writers to European, Chinese, and indigenous languages increased the popularity of their literary products. A 1939 contribution to *Sin Po*, for instance, contrasts the idiom of the Chinese favorably to the stilted High Malay. The author's use of the Dutch particle *toch* followed by *persoonlijk* (personally) reveals his intimacy with that language and also serves as a clever confirmation of his point:

Even though Low Malay has incorporated influences from Chinese, Dutch, or English, I personally still find that this language makes for more pleasant reading than ... High Malay! The	Maski bahasa Melajoe Rendah kamasoekan pengaroe Tionghoa, Blanda atawa Inggris, toch persoonlijk saja anggep jang ini bahasa lebih enak dibatja dari ... Melajoe Tinggi! Bahasa Melajoe Tinggi semingkin

more ground High Malay gains, the more it will eventually be pushed out by Low Malay.

kasananja semingkin terdesek oleh bahasa Melajoe Rendah.[66]

Such views were not limited to Chinese authors. In the mid-1930s, the Sumatran author Sutan Takdir Alisjahbana (1908–94) justified the aforementioned bugbear of Batavianization as a natural and desirable outcome of Malay language development. To him, the Malay of Java's Chinese deserved the same recognition as Afrikaans had (allegedly) acquired in Dutch circles.[67] Alisjahbana applauded the lively prose of Sino-Malay journalists on everyday topics such as football, arguing that their style merited emulation by indigenous writers. Praise in the opposite direction, however, was less common. Few people in Java appear to have been enamored with the idiom of their Sumatran neighbors. The 1924 *Pantoen Tjapgome* (The Quatrain of the Spring Lantern Festival), for example, recounted that certain genres of popular theater failed to attract Chinese fans. The poem's realistic depiction of Batavia's Lantern Festival (*goansiauw*) makes it a valuable resource on cultural life in the city. A major inconvenience, according to its author Tjiong Soen Liang, were people's difficulties understanding the Sumatran Malay used in performances of *Dermoeloek* and *wajang Senggol*:

The two genres discussed before Were mostly performed by indigenous people. They regularly caused some problems Because the singing was in Sumatran Malay.	Ini doea permaenan jang terseboet Banjak dikeloearken oleh orang Boemipoetra Maennja sering-sering ada sedikit riboet Sebab menjanjinja pake Melajoe Sumatra.[68]

The Malay promoted by the Indies government was likewise rejected by many. As the journalist Kwee Tek Hoay observed, "its characteristics differ vastly from what we in Batavia are used to speak on a daily basis, since it originates from Riau."[69] In his popular 1938 novel *Drama di Boven Digoel* (Drama in Boven Digoel), set in the colony's notorious internment camp for communists and nationalists, he had one of the story's protagonists proclaim these words:

What's the purpose of using a foreign language which by and large does not correspond to our usage? . . . the style and rules of Riau Malay are no good to portray one's thoughts in a Western	Apakah goenanja dipake bahasa jang asing dan sabagian besar tida tjotjok dengen kabiasa'an kita? . . . styl dan atoerannja Melajoe Riouw tida bisa dipake boeat loekisken pikiran setjara atoeran Barat

fashion, which requires clarity and conciseness. With its stubborn insistence to impose these outdated paradigms, the Dutch Government annoys all those who are unable to understand the questions on tax return forms and other official documents, to the extent that they have to read the Dutch if they want to understand the matter, because the Malay is in such an abominable shape.	jang sifatnja terang dan ringkes. Pemerintah Belanda, jang masih berkoekoeh hendak pake teroes itoe atoeran koeno, membikin djengkelnja samoea orang jang tida bisa mengarti pertanja'an-pertanja'an jang ada dalem soerat aangifte padjek dan laen-laen soerat officieel, hingga kaloe maoe mengarti terang orang moesti batja bahasa Belandanja, kerna jang dalem bahasa Melajoe tida karoean djoentroengannja.[70]

Kwee Tek Hoay was not alone in his conviction that Riau Malay was unable to meet the demands of modern times. In fact, this exact point was made twice during the "First Conference of the Indonesian Language," also in 1938, by the celebrated Indonesian nationalist Soewardi Soerjaningrat (1889–1959) and by Takdir Alisjahbana.[71] Nevertheless, most Chinese writers probably considered themselves unsupported in their attempts to elevate the status of "their" Low Malay. These fictionalized grievances resonated in journalism. One *Sin Po* article, also published in 1938, made short shrift of High Malay. The author's use of the English phrase "last of all," for which perfectly suitable Malay equivalents existed, added to his defiance of top-down prescriptivism:

We just want to mention here that the kind of Malay Chinese people are forced to learn has in fact no teaching value. For the sake of High (?) Malay, people are forced to misunderstand what is readily understandable; forced to swirl around in dead corners where more straightforward ways should prevail. And last of all, people are forced to deal with the headache of constantly having to adhere to a spelling that is *extremely* unpopular in usage!	Kita tjoema maoe oendjoek di sini, bahoea itoe matjem bahasa Melajoe jang orang Tionghoa disoeroe peladjarin, sabetoelnja tida ada harganja aken dipeladjarken. Sebab dengan Melajoe Tinggi (?) orang disoeroe tida mengarti pada apa jang moestinja soeda dimengarti, disoeroe memoeter moeter ka podjok jang boentoe dimana moestinja ada djalanan jang lebih langsoeng. Dan last of all, orang disoeroe kapala poesing boeat meloeloe jakin pada edjahan-edjahan jang *terlaloe* tida oemoem dipake![72]

The aforementioned journalist Parada Harahap provided Chinese writers with additional reasons to dislike High Malay. This talented autodidact from Sumatra often belittled the idiom of Chinese journalists, who were quick to reply with equal acrimony.[73] With unabashed bravado, one *Sin Po* journalist compared Parada's Malay to that of a "Hottentot." Earlier in this chapter we saw Herman Neubronner van der Tuuk and Kwee Tek Hoay making similar allusions. The pejorative term "Hottentot" referred to South Africa's indigenous Khoekhoe people, whose language was notoriously incomprehensible to the Dutch. In a rather crude way, the author thus appropriated elements from the colonial master narrative to arrive at his own realities. He argued that Parada's Malay could impossibly be called "High" in view of its African-like unintelligibility, implying, moreover, that the Dutch linguist Jacob Kats would have agreed with him:

Pestering other people is a piece of cake, but correcting one's own mistakes is . . . tricky! Parada's Malay would be more appropriately classified as "Hottentot Malay," and I think it is so revolting that it could cause the Malay expert J. Kats to vomit!	Menjelah laen orang memang kliwat *hampang*, tapi memperbaekin kakliroean sendiri ada . . . soesa! Bahasa Melajoenja Parada oepamanja lebih soeroep dinamaken *Melajoe-Hottentot* dan saja kira bisa bikin achli bahasa Melajoe J. Kats moentah-oeger lantaran saking bleneknja![74]

The above examples reveal that the metalinguistic discourse of Malay became more complex over time. Simplistic dichotomies between High and Low Malay, Sumatra and Java Malay, and native and Chinese Malay gradually decreased in relevance. *Liekimhoksch*, the erudite and oft-imitated style of Lie Kim Hok, was respected for being orderly and free from unnecessary foreign borrowings. Gouw Peng Liang (1869–1928) was remembered as one of Lie's few successors who possessed an equally beautiful prose. The works of Tjoe Bou San (1891–1925) were enjoyed for their masterful use of colloquial language. The Malay of Tan Hong Boen, a versatile novelist, journalist, biographer, and *wayang*-author better known under his pen-name Im Yang Tjoe, was so impressive that one commentator solemnly declared they would soon obviate the Sermon on the Mount.[75] Njoo Cheong Seng, whose works still appeal to contemporary readers, was widely acclaimed for his expressive virtuosity. Kwee Tek Hoay, under the pseudonym "Goenasastra," wrote dozens of brilliant pages educating prospective authors about Malay grammar, punctuation, and spelling. He was less generous to those who violated his guidelines. In the pages of his periodical *Moestika Romans* (Jewel of Novels), he attacked an indigenous women's journal from Sulawesi for the sin of abbreviating the relative particle *jang* as "jg." Next thing, he grumbled, they will write the sentence "The amount of coolies who died from mosquito-transmitted malaria is uncountable" as "Kl2 jg mt krn dmm mlra jg dtlri ol njmk djmlja td trhtg."[76]

Such deregionalized and de-ethnicized language norms have prevailed in Indonesia ever since. They arguably helped standard Malay to establish itself as a unifying language. Neither literary grace nor vernacular esthetics were the prerogative of one specific group of people. Even the idiom of Indonesia's nationalist movement was not immune to (self-)criticism.[77] Amidst this linguistic complexity, orthographic choices became political acts. Writers keen to represent the spoken language of Java's cities would continue to write *malem* (evening), *kaloe* (if), *laen* (other), and *pake* (to use), as this was precisely what these words sounded like at the time. Those imbibed with notions of linguistic correctness, however, would spell them as *malam*, *kalau*, *lain*, and *pakai*, corresponding to a hypercorrect, Sumatran, and/or nationalistic usage. The importance of spelling and its impact on Sino-Malay print culture will be discussed next.

The Orthographical Babel

In March 1947, Indonesia's Republican government introduced a revised orthography of the Indonesian language—the term "Malay" had by then become obsolete—and issued a number of clarifications on the implemented changes.[78] At first sight, surprisingly little had changed compared to the Van Ophuijsen Spelling System of 1901. In the Republican spelling system—better known as the Soewandi Spelling System, after Indonesia's second minister of education—the digraph <oe> was to be written as <u> and the two distinct sounds previously (albeit inconsistently) spelled as <e> and <é> merged into just <e>. A great deal more changed for Chinese authors and journalists, most of whom had rejected the van Ophuijsen spelling to begin with. That is not to say that their writings were orthographically chaotic, as was often implied by others. Lie Kim Hok was known for his meticulously consistent spelling. The style of Gouw Peng Liang likewise inspired many journalists. In 1924, his junior colleague Kwee Tek Hoay appraised his Malay as follows:

His orthography or spelling is currently widely disseminated and used almost everywhere in Indonesia, and we believe it will eventually overthrow and obliterate the Riau Malay or Ophuijsen Malay	iapoenja edjaan atawa spellan sekarang soedah mendjalar dan terpake ampir di seloeroeh Indonesia, dan kita pertjaja achirnja bakal kalahken dan moesnaken sama sekali itoe bahasa Melajoe

| language that is presently still protected by the government. | Riouw atawa Melajoe Ophuijsen jang sekarang masih dilindoengken oleh gouvernement.[79] |

This invites us to examine the role of competing orthographies in Sino-Malay print culture and in Chinese-Indonesian language history more broadly. The history of Malay featured a coexistence of scripts and spelling systems (polygraphia and polyorthographia). Combined with a long plurilingual tradition, this yielded a complex and confounding orthographic "Babel."[80] The translingual nature of Sino-Malay texts makes it difficult to fully comprehend them even with knowledge of the individual constituent languages. In the absence of corresponding characters, many Hokkien words and phrases elude even native speakers of that language, since they are written in an inconsistent Indies-style romanization. Most contemporary Indonesian readers likewise struggle with the spelling and translingual subtleties of these sources.

It will come as no surprise that Indonesia's first Chinese writers used a Sinographic system. In addition, many acquired knowledge of the local Javanese, Balinese, or Makassarese syllabaries, making them truly "polygraphic."[81] In the absence of institutionalized education, knowledge of written Chinese proved hard to retain, so that the majority of Chinese in nineteenth-century Java, for example, had become most comfortable with the Javanese script.[82] For Malay, many Chinese originally used the aforementioned Jawi script, which they knew as *hoeroef Arab* (Arabic letters). The Peranakans of Batavia were involved in a vibrant Jawi manuscript tradition, which contained remarkably little Chinese influence.[83] While orally recited poetry (*sair*) and heroic and/or romantic tales (*hikajat*) had long remained a Jawi monopoly, the demand for romanized fiction grew steadily in the late nineteenth century.[84] The adoption of romanized Malay, specifically among the Chinese and other townspeople, was largely fueled by practical considerations: mass printing depended on letterpress technology and knowledge of the Latin alphabet facilitated upward mobility.[85] Even so, a number of Sino-Malay newspapers—such as *Li Po* (Rational Newspaper; Batavia, 1919), *Perobahan* (Change; Padang, 1921), and *Radio* (Radio; Padang, 1932)—contained occasional Jawi fragments.

As romanized Malay gained popularity, the question of how to correctly spell it grew more pertinent. Users of Low Malay evidently had ideas about spelling, yet none of these were strictly enforced.[86] Only a privileged minority had access to European education. The majority of aspiring writers must have picked up matters of spelling, punctuation, diacritics, capitalization, and formatting through exposure and practice. Such visual markers had previously been irrelevant, as Malay manuscripts were read collectively. Typographically printed texts, by contrast, became mass commodities, encouraging nonsequential reading and alternation between text and image.[87] Lie Kim Hok's grammar of Batavian Malay was highly respected for its structural and orthographic consistency, but quickly became obsolete. A number of Sino-Malay literary journals, such as Kwee Tek Hoay's *Moestika Romans*, contained rubrics on the craft of modern writing, spelling, and journalism. Alternatively, one could purchase commercial guidebooks for journalists, which were regularly advertised in Sino-Malay publications (see fig. 2.3). Equally popular were books with templates for romanized Malay application letters (Ml: *rekest*, D: *request*).[88] Among the numerous topics suitable for correspondence with the colonial government, we find requests to open a factory or carry a firearm, applications for the legal status of "European," and pleas to be admitted to a European rather than non-European prison.

The ubiquity of lexical borrowing and code-mixing involving Hokkien, Dutch, Javanese, and/or Sundanese precluded the development of a Sino-Malay romanization that could satisfy all parties. The role of Hokkien and other Sinitic languages made matters particularly complicated. The tones of Chinese words were rarely marked, and aspiration was not always accurately transcribed. The phonology of local languages—in particular Javanese—furthermore affected their romanization. The sounds /c^h/ and /k^h/ were transcribed as <dj> and <g> in Central and East Java, precisely as Javanese speakers would have perceived them. There were multiple ways to romanize Chinese names, depending on a person's ancestral origins in China and current location in the Indies. This provided colonial administrators with a conundrum. In order to combat fraud and tax avoidance, some urged Chinese businessmen to keep their financial records in romanized Malay or Dutch, while others maintained that Sinographic characters were essential to navigate the quagmire of inconsistently transcribed names and, hence, unidentifiable individuals.[89]

Despite the absence of a universally accepted orthography, many Sino-Malay publications offered apologies for any misspellings they might contain. This was particularly common in the Straits Settlements. Two examples of such disclaimers—excerpted respectively from *Sam Ha Lam Tong* (Three Expeditions against the Southern Tang, 1931) and *Hwi-kiam Ji-chap Si-kiap* (The Twenty-four Heroes, 1936)—are given below:

If the spelling of this writing is wrongly printed, I do hope that our comrades and readers will not be too upset about it.	Kalu ehja-an (spelling) surat-nya ada tersilap chap, sahya harap, sklian sobat-sobat-anday dan pembacha-pembacha jangan-lah jadi kechik hati.

Tanda-tanda Batjaän dalem Correspondentie.
尺牘內用標點符號

Tiap-tiap roentoenan perkataän djangan sekali meloepaken memboeboe tanda-tanda pembatjaän, seperti: **koma** (,), **titik** (.) dan laen-laen sebaginja seperti di bawa ini, soepaja orang jang batja gampang mengarti.

KOMA (,). Sepata omongan (brenti sebentar sadja). 讀號
TITIK-KOMA (;). Pengomongan ada sedikit laen maksoednja (brenti lebi lamaän). 分號
TITIK-DOEWA (:) Hendak mengartiken jang baroe di kata itoe (brenti lebi lamaän). 冒號
TITIK (.). Penoetoep sebagian omongan (brenti). 句號
TANDA MENANJA (?). Menanja atawa minta keterangan segala roepa 疑問號
TANDA SEROEAN (!). Bertreak, panggil orang kaget dan heran atawa mengerasken soewara. 感歎號
PENJAMBOENG (-). samboeng perkataän.
PEMBENTANG (—). brenti lama, soewara tiada poetoesken. 延折號
GOEMPITAN ( ) menoetoep soewatoe ingetan atawa kasi mengarti perkataän jang tadi di seboet. 注號
TANDA MEMOENGOET („,—") britaoe jang di dalem soewatoe soerat ada mengambil perkataän orang lain 引號
TANDA POETOES (....) njataken omongan ada poetoes-poetoes atawa omongan tida di teroesken. 刪節號

FIGURE 2.3. Explanation taken from Lu Pao Ru's *Business Correspondence* (Batavia, 1935, 18) of the proper usage of punctuation marks in vernacular Malay

In case of inconsistent spellings and wrongly printed word arrangements, it is hoped that the readers will not be upset.	Jikalu Surat Spelling terlepas dan atoran perkata-an tersilap chap, harap yang menbacha jangan-lah menjadi kechik hati.[90]

To understand what counted as a misspelling, we must highlight a number of conventions in romanized Malay. Known in the Netherlands Indies as *hoeroef Olanda* (Dutch letters) or *hoeroef Latijn* (Latin letters), the Dutch-style romanization came with various idiosyncrasies. Most striking to the contemporary eye are the graphs <ch>, <dj>, <j>, <nj>, <oe>, <sj>, and <tj>, corresponding to <kh>, <j>, <y>, <ny>, <u>, <sy>, and <c> in modern Indonesian. The letter <e> signified two distinct sounds: the schwa /ə/ and the mid-front unrounded vowel /e/. In most instances, readers would intuitively know the correct pronunciation. In cases of potential doubt, the former was sometimes transcribed as <ê> or <ĕ> and the latter as <è> or <é>.[91] Some of the words written with a schwa in Dutch-edited publications exhibited an <a> in Sino-Malay writings, for example, *dari* (from), *maski* (even though), and *samoea* (all) (vs. *dĕri*, *mĕski*, and *sĕmoea*). Chronological heterogeneity complicated matters further. Over time, European and Chinese writers no longer felt the need to spell intervocalic approximants: *toewan* (Sir), *ija* (s/he), *gowa* (cave), and *sakejan* (as much as this) increasingly became *toean*, *ia*, *goa*, and *sakean*. Lie Kim Hok's transcription of Malay vowels resembled the conventions of his European teachers: *malam* (night), *dapat* (to get), *lain* (other), and *baik* (good) rather than *malĕm*, *dapĕt*, *laén*, and *baék* used by Chinese authors of later decades.[92] For identical vowels separated by a syllable boundary, he consistently used the diaresis (two dots placed over a letter). Yet, while he would write *keadaän* (circumstances), other authors wrote *keadahan*, *keada'an*, or even *keada-an*. The general unpopularity of this diacritic may have been technical, as it could not be printed over capital letters.[93]

Many writers from Java, including Sino-Malay writers, added a final <h> to words ending in a vowel. Conversely, they tended to omit the /h/ in positions where—at least according to the logic of classical Malay—it did belong; for example, *abis* (all gone; *habis*), *oetang* (debt; *hoetang*), *bersi* (clean; *bersih*), and *soeda* (already; *soedah*). We may assume that the /h/ was phonologically inconspicuous, especially since words ending in /ah/, /eh/, /ih/, /oh/, and /oeh/ frequently rhymed with those ending in /a/, /e/, /i/, /o/, and /oe/ in Sino-Malay poems.[94] Nevertheless, some authors took issue with the habit. To add a gratuitous word-final /h/, according to Kwee Tek Hoay, "is completely meaningless, except to demonstrate the author's stupidity regarding the straightforward principles of Malay composition."[95] In another article, he conjured up some awkward situations arising from the inconsistent use of this letter: one could be misunderstood as writing about a penis (*boetoe*) rather than a necessity (*boetoeh*), or about blood (*darah*) rather than a girl (*dara*), or about unskilled labor (*boeroeh*) rather than hunting (*boeroe*).[96]

Graphic, orthographic, and typographic practices also carried socioeconomic relevance. A 1926 advertisement assured that Kho Tjeng Bie's printing house was "equipped with all sorts of Chinese letters and a complete set of Arabic letters."[97] As it would seem, commercial interests could hardly be overstated. The Signs Press, owned by Singapore-based missionaries, deliberately wrote their publications in the Indies romanization to tap into the vast markets of Java and Sumatra. Conversely, Malay educational materials from the Indies were sometimes reprinted in the Straits orthography for usage in British Malaya.[98] In other cases, people were expected to simply understand different writing systems. Some North Sumatran newspapers such as *Pewarta Deli* (Deli Messenger; Medan, 1910) contained occasional pieces written in the Straits style of Malaya, to which the region was in many ways better connected than Batavia.[99] A 1935 Mandarin–Malay dictionary published in Semarang (predictably) used the Indies romanization throughout the book, yet contained a foreword by Lim Boon Keng that was kept in its original Straits romanization.[100] Sino-Malay novels from the Netherlands Indies entered Singaporean markets in considerable numbers in their original spelling. Singaporean newspapers furthermore contained advertisements of imports from Java, which exhibited an inconsistent middle ground between the spellings of British Malaya and the Netherlands Indies. The result, as seen in an example from 1924, was presumably a bit confusing to everyone:

Products from Java. We have just received from Java all sorts of dried sweets packaged in bottles and other sorts of products, including ... and many other products, all made in Java and Sumatra; please Sirs, Ladies, and Uncles, come visit our store.	Barang-barang Java. Kita bahru trima dari Java rupah² manisan kering terisi didalam botol dan laen² rupah barang² sepertie, ... dan banyak lagi laen² barang, semoeahnja bikin[an] dari Java dan Sumatra, silahkan tuan² njonya² en intjek² datang di kita punya kede.[101]

Colonial-era advertisements were relatively free from the strictures of editorial review. In the Netherlands Indies, they exhibited low levels of fidelity to the Van Ophuijsen Spelling System, even in government-edited journals. These dynamics were reversed in postindependence times. Up to late 1949, the board of *Sin Po* rigidly held on to their own spelling, while many advertisers had already switched to the Soewandi Spelling System of 1947. Reports from Aneta (Indonesia's largest news agency) and communiqués from the Indonesian government likewise appeared in the standard orthography. Takdir Alisjahbana, who had previously lauded the expressive Malay idiom of Chinese journalists, opined in 1948 that convergence to standard Indonesian constituted its ultimate enrichment. Much of this had already happened, he argued, leaving its spelling the final bastion of heterogeneity.[102] Without any notification, *Sin Po* eventually adopted the Soewandi spelling on December 11, 1949, making it one of the last printed media outlets to do so. It was a symbolic step. By accepting its official orthography, *Sin Po* accepted the Indonesian nation-state. Only the names of Chinese people and institutions were occasionally still printed in a nonstandard spelling. As the irony of history had it, the only other publishing house to disregard Indonesia's new orthography for so long was its long-time competitor Balai Poestaka.

3
PRINTING, PULP, AND POPULARITY

Amidst all the linguistic diversity of the Netherlands Indies press, only vernacular Malay could fully satisfy the tastes of the colony's urban masses. Having entered the media landscape discreetly, Malay eventually became a print language par excellence. The resultant print culture required a radically different prose from that of the scribes, poets, and ecclesiastics of earlier times. Society shifted from chirographic literacy—that is, literacy based on manuscripts—to print literacy.[1] New linguistic conventions, introduced through periodicals and later novels, profoundly affected people's lexical and stylistic choices.[2] Indeed, industrialized printing caused nothing short of a mental revolution, with language at its core. It changed the very character of Malay texts and introduced individualized practices of reading. The interdependence of mass media and vernacular language, then, sits at the core of this chapter. It first situates the emergence of the Sino-Malay press in the broader constellation of popular printing in Asia, which took shape in the mid-nineteenth century. It then examines the interplay between print entrepreneurs, audiences, and linguistic styles. Finally, it highlights the importance of the vernacular in articulating society's effusions on violence, sex, and other explicit themes.

Entrepreneurialism stood at the cradle of all these developments. Only under European-introduced mechanized printing could texts turn into widely available commodities.[3] It thus comes as no surprise that the printing press became a worthwhile investment. In the mid-nineteenth century, when novel machines entered Java's markets and press regulations slackened, Chinese businessmen ventured into these uncharted territories. Tirto Adhi Soerjo (1880–1918), one of Java's leading anticolonial intellectuals and co-founder of the notable indigenous mass organization Sarekat Islam, saw them as pioneers in this profitable enterprise. As he wrote in 1909:

> The progress (*kamadjoean*) of the Chinese people in the Indies is not because of the education they received in schools, as their schooling is still far from perfect; their progress has for the greatest part been derived from the Malay press. It is generally known that the Chinese greatly value newspapers; people who can only barely read—yes, even people who cannot read at all have subscribed to newspapers, requesting others to read them out—pay close attention to the contents of the newspapers, so that right now, and even ten years ago, the Malay press has proven valuable.[4]

As Tirto Adhi Soerjo aptly observed, romanized Malay was read despite rather than due to European education. Many picked it up through self-study and private tutoring, away from the straitjackets of highbrow esthetics and top-down standardization. Reminiscent of earlier manuscript traditions, the collective reading of Malay newspapers enabled even illiterate people to access their contents.[5] In that sense, Malay printing brought the people of Java together. The very act of emancipating a language from the colloquial domain to that of non-governmental printing upset the prevailing power hierarchies, even under a government that had long realized the administrative utility of Low Malay. The Malay-speaking world was, of course, not alone in these developments. One century before Tirto Adhi Soerjo alerted his fellow proto-Indonesians to the benefits of mass printing, a strikingly similar remark was made by the India-born scholar and traveler Mirza Abu Taleb Khan (1752–1806):

> The other aspect of the newspaper is that it gives news from all the cities in England as well as throughout Europe and also the price of things, facts about everything from the smallest to the biggest. It also gives news about opera and the theatre, its performers and details, and dates of the performances; also it gives announcements of the aristocracy's social events, their births, deaths and marriages. The biggest benefit of the newspaper is that any request or job, or anything one wants, can be publicized.[6]

This early nineteenth-century observation resonated across Asia. Munsyi Abdullah assured his readers in 1831 that printing guaranteed "firstly, correct words without mistakes; secondly, quick results; thirdly, clear letters that are easy to read; fourthly, a cheap price." Across the Bay of Bengal, an 1832 Marathi textbook insisted that "this age is unrivalled (*uttam*) in its ability to enable the spread of knowledge through these means."[7] Asia's first modern newspapers—that is, newspapers that were printed, dated, appeared regularly, and contained a variety of news items—were relatively unpopular government gazettes, educative missionary mouthpieces, and commercial news sheets intended for mercantile elites. This changed gradually over the course of the nineteenth century, as the newspapers, their contents, and the people involved in their production became more professional.

The Malay press took shape at the crossroads of intra-Asian connections and technological advancements. From the late nineteenth century, when the first Chinese-owned printing houses (*kantor tjitak*) became operational, we can also speak of a Sino-Malay press. Its entrepreneurialism lay in its diversity. Many of its protagonists were simultaneously engaged in journalism, translation, newspaper editing, fiction writing, and the printing and publication of books. Their popularity depended in part on the serialized fiction they published, which could be translations, reworkings, or original creations. As mentioned previously, Sino-Malay genres were intimately connected. Most authors wrote for newspapers to supplement their meager earnings. At the same time, many journalists generated extra income by publishing sensationalized books of the juiciest news items they had reported on. These so-called *tjerita jang betoel soedah terdjadi* (stories that really happened) blurred the lines between fiction and nonfiction. It was not uncommon for such accounts to also appear in poetry form.[8] Some of the most successful Sino-Malay novels revolved around murders, robberies, adultery, violence, prostitution, and other forms of crime and vice. Such semifiction stood at the ideological opposite of the edifying literature promoted by the Balai Poestaka and other government-sponsored institutions. In opposition to governmental and missionary readings, print entrepreneurs fully embraced society's popular and often vulgar tastes.[9]

As a result, the Sino-Malay print culture enjoyed a broad appeal across the public realm. Tales from China had already been made digestible to the urban masses by itinerant storytellers (*toekang dongeng*, *toekang tjerita*), in glove puppetry (*potehi*), Cantonese theater (*wajang Makauw*), *gambang kromong* music, and other performance genres enjoyed across ethnic boundaries.[10] Literary fiction was thus closely intertwined with other forms of popular culture, and migrations between different platforms became a crucial and lucrative part of Chinese cultural entrepreneurship.[11] These economic opportunities also came with knowledge and enforcement of copyright laws. In many Sino-Malay publications, a copyright statement adorns the first page. The *Boekoe*

Sair "Park" (Poetry Book on the Park), published in Batavia in 1920, provides an example:

Poetry books that do not come with a signature like the one below should be regarded as stolen books. If anyone copies or circulates poetry books closely resembling this one, the publisher of this poetry book will take them to the district court.	Boekoe sair, jang tiada disertakan tanda tangan seperti dibawa ini, dianggep sebagi boekoe-boekoe tjoeriän. Djika siapa jang tiroe atawa siarken, boekoe sair jang seroepa ini, penerbitnja ini boekoe sair, nanti toentoet dihadepan pengadilan negri.[12]

The Enfant Terrible Awakens

How long will it take before Java's people, "once the usage of the printing press will have become as familiar to them as eating rice and dried meat," substitute their admiration for the Dutch government to criticism? Thus wondered a Dutch commentator in 1867.[13] In a plea directed to Governor-General Pieter Mijer (1812–81), the anonymous whistleblower warned of the dangers of press liberalization. The Press Act passed under Mijer's administration, he feared, left the nascent Malay-language press—whose relation to the "real" press was "like an infant to an adult man"—ill-prepared for the responsibilities that came with freedom of expression.[14] Others were less worried. The Dutch minister Wolter Robert van Hoëvell (1812–79) assured his readers that "the Javanese do not read," so that the emergence of critical voices could be safely dismissed.[15] The Malay press, which emerged in 1855 under Dutch editorship, was indeed embryonic from a Dutch perspective, yet it arose concurrently with equivalents elsewhere in Asia.[16]

More than half a century after its humble beginnings, the Malay press had yet to shake off its childlike image. Then again, young people were increasingly seen as the engine of progress (*kemadjoean*), and progress remained a buzzword throughout the 1920s. One poem, published in *Sin Po* in 1924, praised the transformative power of the youth. Even its language was immature: a colloquial type of Malay playfully interlaced with German and French phrases:

Not yet mature Youth has no virtue, but she's a …	Belon mateng Jugend hat keine Tugend, aber sie ist eine …
The white press sees the Eastern press As not yet mature and still green	Pers poeti pandang pers Timoer Belon mateng dan masi idjo

Not yet dry, nor tarnished by the sun	Belon kering, koerang di djemoer
Prone to sleep-talk during the day	Siang-siang soeka mengigo
The Eastern press still smells of milk	Pers Timoer masi baoe soesoe
Its logic is abracadabra	Logica-nja abracadabra
The white press is surely different	Pers poeti laen tentoe
For its logic is hocus-pocus	Hocuspocus ia poenja logica
The Eastern press is like a child	Pers Timoer seperti anak-anak
The white press like an elder	Pers poeti seperti orang toea
One is prone to jump around	Jang satoe soeka berdjingkrak
The other prone to sigh	Jang laen soeka mengela
The white press is called white	Pers poeti diseboet poeti
Because its hair has turned pale	Sebab ramboetnja soeda bloehoek
Its heart, unpredictable as it may be	Maski hatinja belon pasti
Can turn black as a cooking pot	Bisa djadi item prioek
The Eastern press is a child indeed	Pers Timoer betoel anak-anak
An enfant terrible, nothing less	Enfant terrible tidalah sala
Not to be threatened, nor intimidated	Soesa diantjem, soesa digertak
When stared down, it will laugh.	Kaloe didelikin, ia tertawa.[17]

The raucous Sino-Malay press grew from a modest sapling, planted in the nursery of local manuscript production and global industrialized printing. Strong distribution networks and a keenness to read paved the way for print entrepreneurship. The desire, especially among Chinese men, to follow the latest news pushed readers into the pages of the newspaper. But preindustrial modes of reading also played a role, in particular the aforementioned Jawi manuscript tradition. From at least the late eighteenth century, popular manuscripts could be borrowed from private collections or district libraries (*taman batjaan*) in Batavia and elsewhere.[18] Manuscripts of translated Chinese fiction were predominantly in Javanese.[19] For reasons that are not entirely clear, Malay translations of Chinese literature occur almost exclusively in print rather than chirography.[20] Although the circulation of manuscripts was dwarfed by that of printed materials, it nevertheless shaped people's relation with the written word, including their literary preferences and collective modes of reading.

The Malay printing industry long remained under European control. The introduction in the Indies of typographic "letterpress" printing was largely due to the efforts of missionaries, who had also founded some of the world's earliest

Malay periodicals and newspapers.[21] Prior to that, Malay printing had been a by-product of European printing. The *Samarangsch Advertentie-blad* (Semarang Advertiser) had started a short-lived experiment of adding appendices in Jawi in 1851, apparently to no great interest.[22] Eduard Fuhri, a progressive Netherlands-born printer famous for his support to the colony's impoverished Eurasians, proved instrumental to the formation of the Malay press.[23] He established the world's first completely Malay newspaper in December 1855, the *Soerat Kabar Bahasa Melaijoe* (Malay Newspaper) of Surabaya. No specimens of this newspaper are known to me, but Fuhri placed this advertisement in contemporaneous Dutch newspapers:

This newspaper, written with Dutch letters in the Malay language, provides the news for people in the Indies who read and speak Malay, not only of all the things that happen in Java, and the regions beyond Java, but also of the war in Europe and the one in China involving the people that are rebelling against the Chinese emperor, and additional affairs that have taken place in other countries, so that everyone has taken a liking to this newspaper from the start; in it, all manner of news items related to trade and shipping can be placed.... All news items may be submitted in Dutch, but one guilder must be paid as a fee to have it translated into Malay.	Ini soerat kabar, njang di toelis dengan aksara Wolanda di dalem bahasa Melaijoe, kasie kabar kapada orang-orang di tanah India ini njang batja dan bitjara bahasa Melaijoe, tida sadja darie segala perkara njang djadi di tanah Djawa, dan di negri di loewar tanah Djawa djoega darie perkara prang di Europa dan di negrie Tjiena sama orang njang melawan Radja Tjiena, dan lagie darie perkara njang soeda djadi di lain-lain negrie, maka itoe soerat kabar darie moelaienja soeda mendjadiekan kasoeka-anja orang; dan di dalamnja djoega boleh di tarook segala kabaran darie perkara dagang dan belaijaran.... Segala kabaran boleh di masoekan di dalam bahasa Wolanda, tetapi moesti baijar satoe roepia recepis, harga salinnanja di dalam bahasa Melajoe.[24]

Fuhri's communiqué suggests a diverse readership, from followers of the Crimean War to those affected by the Taiping Rebellion. It marks a sharp contrast with the contemporaneous Javanese *Bromartani* (The Proclaimer; Solo, 1855), which was chiefly intended for the local gentry.[25] The Malay press became the first in Southeast Asia to transcend ethnic and geographical boundaries. It diversified with the publication in 1858 of *Soerat Chabar Batawie* (Batavia Newspaper).

This short-lived weekly was neatly divided into two columns, one providing text in romanized Malay, and the other the precise same word arrangements in the Jawi script.[26] We can safely assume that such European-edited newspapers had Chinese readers. *Selompret Melajoe*, for example, contained Hokkienized announcements of ritual processions (*gia kangpe*), puppetry plays (*dho king ngah*), and fireworks (*howee sahee*). Most non-Chinese readers would presumably not have been familiar with these terms.

A transborder circuit of Islamic texts proliferated around the same time. Munsyi Abdullah's collaboration with European missionaries yielded a large distribution network of lithographic printing.[27] Singapore, with its relatively lax press laws, became a regional hub of Jawi literature from the 1840s and reached its peak in the 1880s and 1890s. Indonesia's first printed book outside the European sphere was published in 1853 in Surabaya.[28] In the late 1860s, Jawi printing spread to Sri Lanka's Muslim community, who also published in Tamil.[29] From 1876, the Penang-based company Jawi Peranakan (The Muslim-Indian Peranakan) likewise published in Malay and Tamil, including a Jawi periodical of the same name.[30] Wherever it established itself, Malay printing thus featured protagonists who were firmly ingrained in local milieus, yet simultaneously possessed ancestral ties to broader Asian networks. They were almost without exception plurilingual.

The Sino-Malay print culture was also influenced by developments in China, from where materials regularly found their way into the Indies.[31] On occasion, books printed or handwritten in China were copied by local scholars and ended up in private collections. Such circuits often managed to evade European control. News sheets on the latest events in China, for example, circulated in Java's medium-sized towns.[32] The Chinese also understood the benefits of more localized newspapers. In 1852, the aforementioned *Samarangsch Advertentie-blad* published a Chinese appendix, which proved considerably more popular than the quickly abandoned Malay and Javanese equivalents that originally followed it (fig. 3.1). This recurring lithographed page can be seen as Indonesia's first Chinese newspaper.[33] Lie Kim Hok purchased a printing press in 1885. One year later, Tjoa Tjoan Lok from Surabaya took over the financially troubled *Bintang Timor* (Star of the East). These two events marked the beginnings of the autonomous Sino-Malay press.[34] The aforementioned Tjoa Tjoe Kwan was the first print entrepreneur to dedicate a newspaper, *Ik Po* (Translation Newspaper; Solo, 1903), to society's growing pro-China factions. Not unlike the Malay-Tamil publishers of the late nineteenth century, this polyglot simultaneously published a newspaper in another language: the Javanese *Darmo Kondo* (Virtuous News; Solo, 1904). Modern Chinese-language newspapers also found their way into the Indonesian public sphere; Chinese imports from 1890 and local productions from 1908.[35]

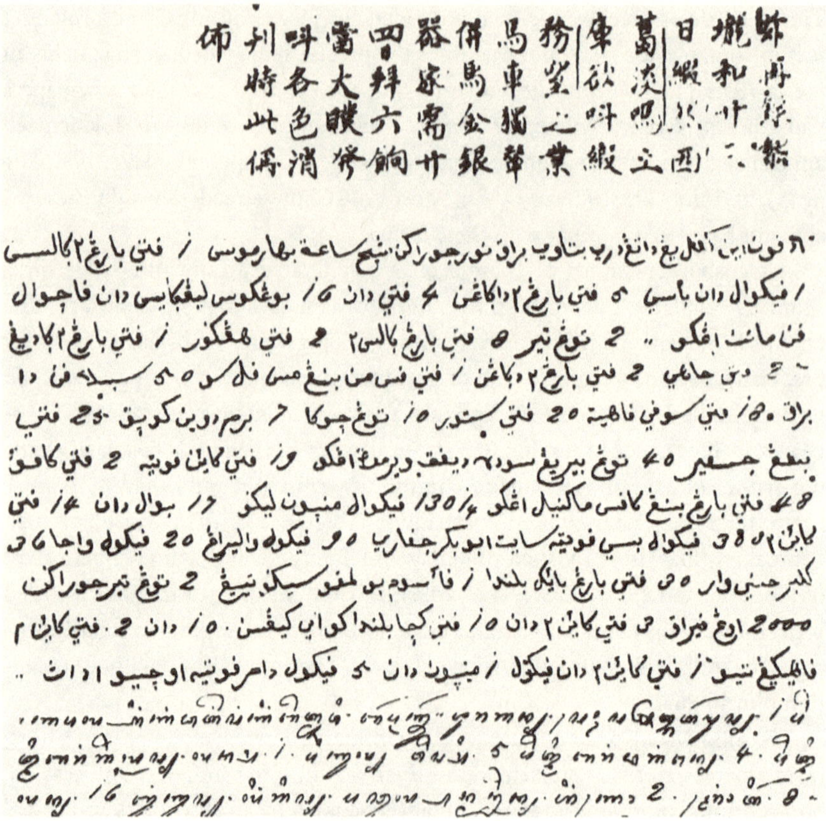

FIGURE 3.1. Appendix to the *Samarangsch Advertentie-blad* (July 16, 1852) in Chinese, Jawi-Malay, and Javanese

Similar developments unfolded in the Straits Settlements, albeit slightly later. The majority of Baba Malay newspapers appeared in the 1920s and 1930s.[36] As was the case in the Netherlands Indies, these periodicals served commercial, political, and cultural needs. The editors of the *Bintang Pranakan* (Star of the Peranakan; Singapore, 1930), in their first issue, justified the establishment of their newspaper along the following lines: It was first and foremost published in honor of the British Crown, under which the Babas had professedly been able to fare so well. Secondly, it would give a voice to the Baba community in Singapore, including their grievances and anxieties. Finally, a vernacular Malay newspaper was important because not all the Babas were proficient in English. In the characteristic Baba Malay idiom of the Straits, saturated with English and Hokkien, the editors launched their newspaper as follows:

Congratulations! Today we send our greetings to all Peranakans in the land of British Malaya, especially the Nyonyas and Babas and also to the Sirs and Lords. At this moment we think the time has come for the Straits-born Chinese to have a newspaper like the *Bintang Pranakan*, appearing every Saturday.

Kionghi! Ini hari kita kasi slamat kapada sklian Pranakan dalam negri British Malaya, istimewa (especially) Nyonya-nyonya dan Baba-baba dan kapada Inchek dan Tuan-tuan juga. Di ini ketika kita pikir tempu-nya sudah chukop yang Pranakan-Tionghua (Straits-born Chinese) mesti ada satu surat-kabar sperti ini "Bintang Pranakan" terkluar pada tiap-tiap Hari Anam.[37]

Singapore's printing houses were perfectly situated to maintain connections across the Straits of Malacca.[38] A number of Sino-Malay books from Singapore were evidently intended for the Netherlands Indies market. One example is *Mr. Tjoepeek Lie's Family Instructions*, published in 1896 and translated into Malay by the aforementioned Lim Tjay Tat. This publication is a short didactic work in literary Chinese, followed by translations in Hokkien and Malay, both in the Indies rather than Straits romanization (fig. 3.2).[39] The *Shaer Almarhoem Beginda Sultan Abubakar di Negri Johor* (Poem of His Late Majesty Sultan Abubakar of Johor),

FIGURE 3.2. A page from Lim Tjay Tat's *Mr. Tjoepeek Lie's Family Instructions* (Singapore, 1896, 9)

FIGURE 3.3. Advertisement for cognac specifically marketed to Chinese customers (*Sin Po*, 1929)

written in High Malay by the Sumatra-born Na Tian Piet, came out in the same year and was likewise printed in Singapore using an Indies-style romanization.

Links were also forged across different ethnicities. Whereas the Baba Malay press of British Malaya remained distinct from the Jawi press, print entrepreneurs in the Netherlands Indies were rarely averse to occasionally publishing the works of authors from other groups.[40] Editorial boards, too, remained relatively heterogeneous. In the 1910s, several Sino-Malay newspapers had a Eurasian editor on their board. The newspaper *Kiao Seng* (Voice of the Chinese Overseas; Batavia, 1931) mentioned with some affection a man named A. Mohammed among its staff, "our Indonesian helper" (*pembantoe kita Indonesier*), who contributed articles on the vicissitudes of the colony's indigenous populations. The fact that he specifically wrote about "indigenous" matters, however, confirms that the Malay print culture of the Indies was not truly cross-ethnic. In the realm of advertising, targeted audiences were product-dependent. A 1929 promotion for Jules Robin cognac portrayed two recognizably Chinese men standing at the entrance of a Chinese-style residence and greeting each other in the Chinese fashion on the occasion of Chinese New Year, with an indigenous Indonesian carrying a box of the advertised beverage (fig. 3.3). Considerably more inclusive was a 1930 advertisement for Ho Ho Biscuits, which depicted a Chinese, a European, and a Javanese boy relishing with equal joy this Singaporean snack that "will be distributed for free" at Batavia's Pasar Gambir fair (fig. 3.4).[41] With its emphasis on visuality and consumption, advertising was best suited to overstep ethno-religious boundaries, in both the Netherlands Indies and British Malaya.

Upon Roast Pig in Patois

In 1897, the editors of the irredeemably pro-English *Straits Chinese Magazine* thought it amusing to publish an occasional story in vernacular Malay. As its readership consisted of Western-educated Babas and Nyonyas, the magazine was filled to the brim with the King's English. Nevertheless, the editors realized that Baba Malay was the language most of their readers had grown up speaking. While the printed use of Malay was self-evident for Java's Peranakans, their Singaporean counterparts sounded almost apologetic when they first resorted to it:

> Believing that the popularity of this magazine will not suffer if occasionally an original article or a translation of an interesting article appears in it in Romanised Malay, this Malay translation of one of Charles Lamb's Essays which greatly amused the audience at the last Anniversary meeting of the Chinese Christian Association, it is now contributed in the

FIGURE 3.4. Advertisement for biscuits promoted to an ethnically diverse clientele (*Bintang Timoer*, Batavia, 1930)

hope that many of its Straits Chinese readers will find it not the least interesting item in this issue of the magazine.[42]

This disclaimer was followed by the Malay translation of Charles Lamb's "Upon Roast Pig," a staple for anyone educated in the British system. It had been a tremendous exercise in creativity to translate Lamb's notorious wit, yet doing so drew instant praise.[43] Amidst a community hungry for the fruits of global authors, the ability to translate foreign literature into Malay became a sine qua non for aspiring writers. The decision to do so in vernacular rather than High Malay raised some eyebrows. The Singaporean author Chia Cheng Sit was among the first to insinuate that the reliance on "Malay *patois*" was chiefly driven by the desire to sell many copies.⁴⁴ This was probably accurate, yet one may also envision linguistic reasons to opt for vernacular Malay. Most colloquialisms, nuances, and subtleties would have clashed with the literary conventions of High Malay. Only the vernacular had the expressive power to simultaneously convey popular stories, articulate cultural change, and retell society's best jokes. Almost half a century later, an article by Liem Thian Joe published in *Sin Po*—which incidentally also celebrates the divine succulence of roast pig—illustrates this point. We can only appreciate its humor by examining the Malay original, in which the word "essay" is written almost identically as the Hokkien term *eesay* (expertise), creating a witty play on words:

The "suckling pig" or "roasted pig dish" of the Chinese restaurants is very famous, because it is an entire pig made into a meal that is completely cooked, tender, fragrant, well-seasoned, and tasty. (Charles Lamb has even written an essay about his expertise . . . roast pig!)	Restaurant Tionghoa poenja peenvarken atawa sioti-djiak ada terkenal betoel, sebab satoe babi jang masi oetoe telah dibikin djadi saroepa santapan jang mateng seanteronja, empoek, wangi, sedep dan enak. (Charles Lamb sampe toelis essay tentang eesaynja . . . panggang babi!)⁴⁵

Chinese print entrepreneurs successfully tapped into the demands of the public sphere for translated stories. Malay translations of Chinese popular fiction entered the Indies from the 1880s. They were published even by newspapers that did not specifically target Chinese readers.⁴⁶ The earliest translated stories were China's classics and semiclassics, fantastic novels, and love ballads. Such tales of a glorious past were vital for a community struggling to secure its future. Yet China's rapidly modernizing literature, written in vernacular Mandarin, was followed with equal attention. Translations of detective novels and especially cloak-and-dagger stories enjoyed vast popularity from the mid-1920s.⁴⁷ Great liberties were taken to render the arcane Chinese source texts into understandable Malay.⁴⁸ European novels—including the works of Jules Verne, Alexandre Dumas, and Daniel Defoe—were also translated into vernacular Malay from the 1890s, yet their quantity was only one third of the Chinese works. The anonymous translators of European fiction may have been either Peranakan Chinese or Eurasians; nothing in their Malay reveals their background. A comparable industry of translated European works never took shape in British Malaya, presumably because Straits Babas had greater access to English.⁴⁹

At this point it must be reiterated that Sino-Malay publications were anything but linguistically uniform. The language of serialized stories was better edited than that of hastily written commercial books.⁵⁰ The idiom of translated European fiction was generally closer to High Malay than that of Chinese works, reflecting the educational differences of their translators. Many books in the latter category exhibited lexical and grammatical influence from Chinese.⁵¹ Authors from Sumatra were popularly perceived to use a better kind of Malay than their colleagues from Java. The style of Kwee Thiam Tjing and the unknown novelist writing under the pseudonym Bianglala (Rainbow), for example, carried a distinct East Javanese flavor and must have been difficult to understand for readers from other regions. Presumably, this made them all the more popular locally. Many Chinese poets also enriched their Malay with local languages, indicating that regional affinities outweighed ethnic differences.⁵² The accessible Betawi-flavored stories of Gouw Peng Liang and Kwee Tek Hoay were as equally enjoyed as those of the Eurasian authors Ferdinand Wiggers, Herman Kommer, and Gijsbert Francis.⁵³ Their Batavian idiom also spread to Chinese-run newspapers in Sumatra, Pontianak, and Makassar, as many of the editors in those places were Peranakans from West Java.⁵⁴ It was a completely different Malay from that of the Straits Settlements. In fact, in a 1924 contribution to *Sin Po*, several Singaporean Malay sentences were quoted simply for the readers' entertainment. As the accompanying texts read:

Singapore Malay (which of course uses the English spelling) is funny to read for us people here, so below we cite some items from a newspaper that appears in the Straits, named "Kabar Slalu."	Bahasa Melajoe Singapoer (jang tentoe sadja pake spellan Inggris) boeat kita orang disini loetjoe boeat dibatja, maka di bawah ini kita petik bebrapa toelisan dari soeratkabar jang terbit di Straits, jaitoe "Kabar Slalu."⁵⁵

Java's idiosyncratic Malay must have been equally confounding to readers from the Straits Settlements. Some of Singapore's pioneering Sino-Malay authors—such as Lim Hock Chee and the aforementioned Na Tian Piet—had Sumatran origins.⁵⁶ One can imagine that the dialectal differences were slightly less vast for them, making them perfect intermediaries. The works of Java-based authors, by contrast, reveled in Dutch, Batavian, Sundanese, and Javanese words, defying the ability of Malayan readers to fully understand them. These interdialectal tensions were summarized in the bilingual introduction of *Renchana Piatu* (Orphaned Narrations), a Singaporean anthology published in 1916:

A book of Malay poems in the Romanized Malay of the Straits colloquial language like this	Satu buku shair melayu dalam Bahasa Melayu Romanized dengan lagu perchakapan tanah Enggris

"Renchana Piatu" has never existed, though several other similar works have already been compiled and published by the Dutch-born Babas in Batavia in a language only appreciative and comprehensible to themselves.	macham ini "Renchana Piatu" belom perna boleh dapat di jumpa, sunggupun banyak lain lain karangan sama sperti ini telah ada di chapkan oleh Baba Baba tanah Blanda di negri Betawi dalam bahasa lagu yang dia-orang sendiri berkenan dan mengerti.[57]

Yet despite their purported incomprehensibility, novels from the Indies started to enter the Singaporean markets in larger quantities from the 1920s. We can read in the *Kabar Uchapan Baru* (Recently Announced News; Singapore, 1926) of 1926 that "new stories from Batavia have arrived" (chrita baru dari Betawi suda datang), in the *Bintang Pranakan* of 1930 that "Java Romanised story books [*sic!*]" are being sold, and in the *Story Teller* of 1934 that books "in the romanized Malay language of Java" (dalam Bahasa Java Romanised Malay) can be ordered alongside locally authored ones. Nio Joe Lan proudly reported that these books gained popularity on the island despite their different orthography.[58] Regardless of all elitist pronouncements about their linguistic deficiencies, Java's Sino-Malay print culture found acceptance abroad. The aforementioned suspicion of Chia Cheng Sit thus proved correct: only in their own patois were the urban masses willing to enter the world of reading. They were even curious about the patois of their neighbors. Others made similar observations. In 1915, the prominent Eurasian journalist Johan Frederik Hendrik August Later (1881–1948) describes the situation in Semarang:

> In the first place we must remark that the Malay in which most newspapers are written has much in common with Bazaar Malay, and that those newspapers will probably be read the most. Which is very sad. From a linguistic perspective, the Malay papers should be written in proper Malay, paying close attention to the suffixes and prefixes, the passive construction, and whatever else needs to be taken into account with Malay. Yet one of the editors of the newspapers from Semarang explained, and he would know, that most readers will not understand it. And if some purely indigenous newspapers were to write in a more proper language, they would only be able to do so for readers of a certain erudition.[59]

By the 1930s, Indonesia's indigenous literati had arrived at comparable verdicts. In a 1938 radio broadcast, Armijn Pané explained why the language of Sino-Malay publications so rarely attained the authoritative standards set by the

Balai Poestaka. He did not speak of good or bad Malay, as so many had done before him. Rather, he blamed time pressure and the lack of schooling. The Malay of Chinese authors was vibrant, he concluded, but not erudite:

> Out of a hundred pieces that we receive, we can normally only publish two. As we have said before, the Sino-Malay book publishers have to publish books every month, and for that reason they are of course regularly compelled to release whatever books they happen to have. The language they use, which is the language in daily use among the Chinese, is therefore very much alive. Of course, that comes with dangers. The language they use is not learned, not fostered in a school; as the Dutch say, not "cultivated." Fruit-bearing trees abandoned to grow in the forest will of course still produce fruits, but their yield could have been higher. It would be more profitable if they were taken good care of. Such is the case also for Sino-Malay books.[60]

Chinese authors from the Indies were the first to admit that their Malay was of the nonintellectual variety. Publications from British Malaya, too, inevitably came with disclaimers apologizing for their shallow (*chetek, chaytek*) language, adding repentantly that this would make it easier to understand for Babas who could not read English. Such admissions had become conventionalized across the Malay-speaking world. In the *Sair Oeij Tambah Sia* (Poem of Oeij Tambah Sia), published in 1922 in Batavia, the author Tjoa Boan Soeij apologized in rhyme for his deficient Malay. He thus interwove his bad-language disclaimer with the broader text, as had become common practice in popular poetry:

To all the readers, don't take offense	Sekalian pembatjalah djangan goesar
At my writing a poem in Bazaar Malay	Mengarang sair melajoe pasar
In case its words contain vulgarities	Djika perkatahan ada jang kasar
I profoundly hope for your forgiveness.	Minta maäf harepan besar.[61]

We see a similar apology in Kwee Tek Hoay's 1936 translation of *Rubaiyat of Omar Khayyam*. This work of poetry, published in English by Edward FitzGerald (1809–83) and ultimately attributed to the Persian scholar Omar Khayyam (1048–1131), was immensely popular among Europe's cultured classes. While he had elsewhere defended Low Malay, Kwee repentantly stated that the beauty of the European source text could only be rendered imperfectly in this impoverished language:

With regard to our translation, as is usual with works like this, it would be commonplace to find	Tentang kita poenja salinan, seperti biasanja pakerdjaän samatjem ini, soedah djamaknja terdapet tjatjat-

imperfections that cannot be avoided, and which will definitely be tolerated by anyone who has ever translated Western poetry into the impoverished Low Malay language.	tjatjat jang tida bisa disingkirken, dan jang soedah tentoe sampe dimengarti oleh siapa jang perna menjalin sair-sairan Barat ka dalam bahasa Melajoe Rendah jang miskin.[62]

Besides authors, typesetters (*letter zetter*) also frequently initiated communication with their readers. From the safe harbor of anonymity, they provided cynical commentary on the printed materials they presided over.[63] Some felt fully entitled to insert their personal opinions about the story and its characters. In the Malay rendition of the Sundanese tale *Pandji Woeloeng*, when the crooked minister Andakasoera fabricated a battlefield victory, the typesetter interrupted: "Was your fight with a mosquito or with a corpse, my courageous minister Andakasoera?" About a notorious playboy who could purportedly attach himself to women so skillfully that they forgot all their previous loves, one typesetter deadpanned: "Maybe he's using glue, that's why he's so good at attaching himself." In the Malay translation of *Dji Touw Bwe* (The Story of the Plumtree Flowers Twice), after a paramour proclaimed that his soul would rejoice if his beloved was to find happiness in the arms of another man, the typesetter inserted wryly: "Wow! That's how much you love her? This must be what true love looks like, if only it weren't a lie." In the translation of *La Revanche de Baccarat*, after an equally melodramatic profession of everlasting love, the typesetter added: "not even if the sun changes into a football!" A sobbing detainee in *Sat Tjoe Po* (Divine Retribution for Killing the Son) was castigated with "Hey, you're behaving like a woman, the moment you enter prison you already start to cry?" Somebody's failure to find a wife that was both pretty and of noble birth was greeted with a sarcastic: "How unfortunate indeed." A bereaved mother—bemoaning the irreversible end of her lineage—was admonished with the words: "Perhaps only one person out of a thousand would unconditionally love a stepchild." A villain's pretense to cleverness in the novel *Nio Thian Laj* (Liang Tianlai) was sardonically dismissed as "clever at being a miscreant."[64]

These communicative exchanges were linguistically embedded. Only the vernacular could convey the intimacy required for tongue-in-cheek textual commentary. Editorial apologies for linguistic shortcomings must be seen as additional strands of this performative discourse. In reality, almost all print entrepreneurs agreed that Low Malay was the best option to capture larger audiences by dint of its humor, accessibility, and translingual potential. It was precisely its lexical versatility that bridged the local and the cosmopolitan, guiding readers through the maelstrom of colonial modernity. The emphasis in many Sino-Malay works on violence and sex, then, carried greater significance than a simple desire for pulp fiction. It was a grassroots inquiry into previously unthinkable social relations and ideological constructs, all expressed through a vibrant new language.

True and Not-So-True Happenings

Translated fiction remained popular throughout the colonial period, yet an equally lucrative market opened up for stories based on more relatable people, locations, and events. From the early twentieth century, authors of Chinese, Eurasian, and indigenous ancestry started to produce sensationalized, realistic Malay literature.[65] Some of their most popular stories straddled society's moral fence: interracial love, crime and vice, supernatural tales, and ideological battles between traditionalists (*kaoem kolot*) and modernists (*kaoem moeda*).[66] Predictably, the colony's conservative spokespeople were unfavorably disposed to what they considered perverse books (Ml: *boekoe tjaboel*, D: *Schundliteratur*).[67] The fact is, though, that pulp fiction was only a fraction of the Sino-Malay oeuvre. Contrary to conventional wisdom, some novels were highly politicized and introduced sensitive issues to the public sphere. A number of Indies Chinese authors, for example, wrote fiction on Japan's military invasions against China. Kwee Tek Hoay, Liem Khing Hoo, and Njoo Cheong Seng published books about Boven Digoel, the notorious internment camp mentioned previously.[68] In addition, we find a broad array of nonfiction, including bibliographies, religious publications, instruction manuals, cookbooks, medical treatises, books about Chinese history and culture, and books about Javanese history and culture.

This multiplicity of genres gave rise to an even greater linguistic diversity. Western-educated Peranakans wrote in a Europeanized Malay, which was frequently mocked and scrutinized by their contemporaries.[69] Some of them were extremely well read in European literature. Lie Kim Hok, for example, was said to be an avid reader of Plato, Goethe, Shakespeare, William Makepeace Thackeray, Jean de La Fontaine, Émile Zola, Hendrik Tollens, Paulus Adriaans Daum, Charles Darwin, Camille Flammarion, and even Ludwig Büchner. Other popular European thinkers included Anthony Christiaan Winand Staring, Arthur Schopenhauer, Baruch Spinoza, Henry Wadsworth Longfellow, John Keats, Joost van den Vondel, Lord Byron, and Petrus Augustus de Génestet.[70] As pointed out previously, reworkings of Chinese stories displayed various linguistic idiosyncrasies. It is open for question whether these reflected word-for-word translations, a colloquial type of Malay in use among Singkehs, or both.

Classical Malay esthetics influenced Sino-Malay poetry above all else. Traditional ABAB quatrains (*pantoen*) and continuous AAAA poems (*sjair, sair*) were popular among Peranakans in the Indies as well as Malaya, featuring ubiquitously in their books and newspapers. Initially, the recitation of poetry was a purely oral practice accompanied by musical ensembles.[71] Even printed poems reveled in onomatopoeia and representations of specific accents, requiring capable performers to recite them. Given the popularity of the genre, it comes as no surprise that the oldest known printed book in romanized Malay was a long poem: the *Sair Kadatangan Sri Maharadja Siam di Betawi* (Poem on the Arrival of the Thai King in Batavia), commemorating King Chulalongkorn's trip to the capital in May 1871.[72] Equally important is Lie Kim Hok's *Siti Akbari* (1884), a reworking of the classical Malay *Syair Abdul Muluk* (Poem of Abdul Muluk), which was seen by many as the cynosure of Sino-Malay literature. From that time on, valuable insights into life in the colony have been preserved in poetry. It is through the Sino-Malay *sair* that we have insiders' perspectives on such wide-ranging concerns as the translation of Chinese books into Malay, the dynamics of late nineteenth-century opium farming, the robbery of the Java Bank in 1902, the establishment of the THHK, and the sensational murder of the Eurasian prostitute Fientje de Feniks.[73]

Another linguistically intriguing genre were the immensely popular martial arts stories (*tjerita silat*). They entered the Netherlands Indies in the early twentieth century and reached their zenith in the 1920s and 1930s. Most stories were translated from or inspired by Chinese fiction.[74] While martial arts also featured in many historical novels, the newest genre specifically revolved around "heroes who had opted out of society and relied solely on their own strength to confront the society whose workings escaped them."[75] This particular theme made *silat* novels extremely popular in late colonial (and postindependence) Indonesia. Famous pugilists (*djago silat*) were highly respected in Chinese and indigenous circles alike.[76] Besides the universal attraction of fighting injustice, these stories also gained popularity on account of Indonesia's homegrown martial arts traditions.[77] Sometimes, the term *silat* was used to designate the martial arts of indigenous people, whereas styles from China were referred to as *boegee, koenthauw*, or *koansoet*. However, after centuries of cross-fertilization, it had become impossible to enforce clear-cut distinctions between the two.

Print entrepreneurs saw various opportunities to benefit from the popularity of martial arts. Courses in traditional *silat* as well as modern styles quickly found their way into advertisements sections, along with commercially printed instruction books. The Republic of China's national system of martial arts, institutionalized in 1928, was referred to in Sino-Malay writings as *kok-soet* (national arts) and was typically described in admirable terms. Japanese jiu-jitsu entered the newspapers from the early 1940s. It was known among Indies Chinese as *djioe-soet*: the Hokkien pronunciation of its characters. And, with all the cinemas, public parks, night markets, and other new spaces modernity provided, the necessity of self-defense for women also increased. Accompanied by a photograph of a woman defending herself against a man, *Sin Po* gave its female readers tips on escaping unwanted male attention:

With the system of Chinese martial arts, persistent men who for instance want to grope around in the cinema can easily be taught a lesson. Smack his head by moving the palm of your hand forward, while pushing him to the back with the other hand, holding his shoulder. This will make him plunge forward!	Dengen systeem koenthauw Tionghoa, lelaki tjeriwis jang oepama maoe ngeraba di bioscoop gampang dibikin mati koetoenja. Geplak kapalanja dengen telapakan tangan ka depan dan dengen laen tangan berbareng dorong ia ka blakang dengen pegang poendaknja. Lantaran ia aken kanjoeknjoek![78]

The martial world came with a language of its own. Aficionados of *silat* novels acquired an impressive vocabulary from literary Chinese in its Hokkien pronunciation. They had to learn the names of various stock characters inhabiting this mystical universe.[79] They also needed to familiarize themselves with the personalities, institutions, and fighting practices specific to ancient China, real and imagined.[80] Following Chinese understandings of martial arts, styles were divided into hard ones (*ngekoen*) focusing on external power (*gwakang*) and exercises to strengthen the body (*ngekang*), and soft ones (*soeikoen*) prioritizing internal power (*lweekang, laykang*) and exercises to improve the body's flexibility (*noeikang*). The countless punches, kicks, supernatural attacks, and other combat techniques also came with specific names.[81] Some serialized stories even featured illustrated exercises, which the aspiring pugilist could use to practice at home. To illustrate the use of this jargon in context, one fighting scene will suffice. In the translated story *Kang Ouw Djie Sie Hiap* (24 Knight-Errants Roaming over Rivers and Lakes), a female warrior attacks her enemy with the punching technique *go-eng-kok-touw* (Hungry Hawk Catches a Rabbit). Her enemy dodges the attack and grabs her wrist using a move named *thian-ong-tho-thak* (Heaven King Upholds a Pagoda). He stabs her waist with his hand using the *ya-tjee-tam-hay* (Demon Searches the Sea). Forced to drop to the floor, the female fighter tries to sweep his leg using the *kong-hong-sauw-iap* (Fierce Wind Sweeps the Leaves). However, he quickly jumps into the air to avoid the attack and counters with a *go-houw-pok-sit* (Hungry Tiger Catches Its

Prey). The female fighter rolls away, "kicking her enemy against his penis," before attempting to finish the job with the *hie-tjiak-teng-tjie* (Cheerful Sparrow Goes up the Branch).[82] The fight continues for several more pages.

For locally authored *silat* books, it was a sound marketing strategy to celebrate the accomplishments of their prizefighters. One of Java's best promoted martial artists was the China-born Louw Djeng Tie (1855–1921)—nicknamed Garoeda Mas dari Tjabang Siao Liem (the Golden Eagle from the Shaolin Branch)—who had opened a martial arts school in the town of Parakan. His reputation remains strong until the present day. As a 1930 advertisement marketed his book:

| Master Louw is a martial arts teacher belonging to the Elite of Indonesia, who rarely finds his equal and has never been defeated by anyone. He has killed a master from Shandong, beaten up a tiger, competed against the "Champion" Bhe Kang Pin of Major Bhe Biauw Tjwan in Semarang, defeated a group of gangsters, brought to fall martial arts teacher The Soei, injured four soldiers on a train, almost fought with members of the Sarekat Islam, etc., etc. Most recently, martial arts teacher Tan Tik Sioe Sian witnessed his skills and praised him very highly. | Louw Kao-soe ada satoe goeroe silat Tjabang Atas di Indonesia jang djarang ada bandingan dan belon perna di pertjoendangin oleh siapa djoega. Ia boenoeh kao-soe dari Shantong, poekoel matjan, bertanding pada Bhe Kang Pin "Djago" dari Majoor Bhe Biauw Tjwan di Semarang, kalahken kawanan badjingan, roeboehken goeroe silat The Soei, meloekain 4 soldadoe diatas kreta-api, ampir bertempoer pada leden "sarekat islam," enz., enz. Paling belakang soehoe Tan Tik Sioe Sian soeda saksiken ia poenja kepandean dan memoedji tinggi sekali.[83] |

A quite different portion of Sino-Malay texts—also allegedly based on true stories—focused on sex scandals, especially from the 1910s onwards. For the first time in Indonesia's public sphere, these social issues received intense scrutiny in a broadly accessible language. Yet the ultimate message was a moralizing one: indecent behavior would inevitably lead to the death of the responsible femme fatale and the downfall of everyone on her path.[84] The encroachment of Western values indeed prompted numerous print entrepreneurs to contrast the pure, innocent East with the polluted, indecent West. European and North American women, many of whom had never set foot in the Indies, were framed as collectively responsible for society's sexual liberalization.[85] Here in particular, textuality was often complemented by visuality, especially after the wider availability of photography in the 1920s. A 1942 issue of *Sin Po*, for example, contains seemingly random photographs of American couples engaged in passionate kissing. As we learn from the captions, the editors mocked the women—using Dutch and Hokkien words—as being *offensief* (offensive) and *lauwdjiat* (exciting):

If women get to be offensive...	Kaloe prampoean boleh offensief...
1. At the University of North Carolina, on November 8 (Sadie Hawkins Day), women have the right to kiss men. The men are grabbed and cannot do anything back!	1. Di University of North Carolina pada 8 Nov. (Sadie Hawkins Day) kaoem prampoean dapet hak boeat tjioem lelaki. Lelaki diredjeng dan tida bisa membales!
2. A surprise attack, like the Japanese in Hawaii...	2. Serangan mendadak, kaja Djepang di Hawaii...
3. The attacked person eventually resists.	3. Jang diserang achirnja melawan.
4. How exciting! The man is jumped against, so that he falls on his back, and then gets kissed by the student girl.	4. Paling lauwdjiat! Lelaki diterdjang sampe djato terlentang dan teroes ditjioemin oleh non student.[86]

Vernacular Malay, more than any other language, equipped the public sphere with the words to discuss sex in its many guises. This discourse was dominated by scandals and extramarital affairs. An illicit female sexual partner was known as *goendik*, *kendak*, *madoe*, *njai*, or *selir*, all originally denoting a mistress or concubine. The Hokkien words *djinge* (second-rank concubine) and *see-ie* (concubine) conveyed the same meaning, as did the Malay euphemisms *bini moeda* (young wife) and *daon moeda* (young leaf). They were distinct from prostitutes, known interchangeably as *djalang*, *djobong*, *lonte*, *moler*, or *soendel*, in addition to a range of euphemisms.[87] Chinese prostitutes were also designated with the Hokkien terms *tjabo* (girl) and *Macao-po* (woman from Macau). Girls who were "modern" in their interactions with men attracted such derogatory labels as *genit* (flirtatious), *konde litjin* (slippery hair bun), *pipi aloes* (smooth cheeks), and *sweetheart*. In the latter case, the use of English rhetorically situated them in the immoral West. Male libertines were referred to as *bandot* (billygoat), *baron* (baron), *boeaja* (crocodile), *boeaja darat* (monitor lizard), or *setan bantal* (devil-of-the-pillows), whereas *idoeng belang* (striped nose) and *idoeng poeti* (white nose) could be used for all genders. A number of sexually loaded terms were ethnically specific. The archetypical Chinese playboy was known as *gong-kongtjoe* (crazy gentleman), *koetjiah* (turtle), *kongtjoejasia* (rich dandy), *phaykia* (lascivious person), or *tjabouw-tay-ong* (king of girls). He would often receive the nickname *Hoa Tjoe Ling*, after a notorious playboy figure in Hokkien folklore.[88]

Some authors also published nonfictional readings on sex, inspired by contemporaneous European sexology.[89] The first Sino-Malay example known to me is the 1913 *Boekoe Wet dan Rasia tentang Perhoeboengan antara Prampoean dan Lelaki* (Book of Laws and Secrets on the Interaction between Women and Men), which discusses such issues as genitals, pregnancy, venereal diseases, masturbation, and impotence. A later publication, titled *Nasehat en Recepten boewat Orang Mendjadi Waras en Koewat* (Tips and Recipes to Become Healthy and Strong), is filled with remedies for sexually transmitted diseases, recipes for aphrodisiacs, and solutions for other reproduction-related conditions.[90] Advertisements furthermore list the titles *Kitab "Adji Asmaragama"* (Book of "Charms for Sexual Relations"), *Boekoe Orang Prampoean* (Book of Women), and *Ilmoe Bersetoeboeh* (Knowledge of Sexual Intercourse), of which apparently no copies have been preserved. Vernacular Malay provided ample terms for the act of sex, including *berdjina* (to fornicate), *berhoeboengan* (to have interactions), *bersetoeboeh* (to have sexual intercourse), *bertidoer* (to sleep), *bertjintahan* (to make love), *menikah* (to marry), and *plesiran* (to have pleasure). It also drew from other languages. The word *mogor* (whoring) was taken from Sundanese and *patjoetjeng* (masturbation) from Hokkien, in which it originally referred to the act of firing a pistol. Rape was also commonly mentioned in Sino-Malay pulp fiction. In the 1920 *Sair Tan Keng Siang* (Poem of Tan Keng Siang), for example, a gruesome scene was recounted in rhyme:

Lady Antji and Lady Rebo were raped by the bandits	Njonja Antji dan Njonja Rebo rampok perkosa
Everything they wore was ripped off their bodies	Barang dibadan'nja dirampas paksa
Their mouths were closed so they could not scream	Moeloetnja ditoetoep mendjerit soesa
Their bodies were trembling out of fear.	Badan'nja gemeter takoet merasa.[91]

Across the realm of popular entertainment, a translingual, Chinese-dominated print culture reformulated society's thoughts on the everyday. Sino-Malay newspapers must be seen as the forerunners of Indonesia's postindependence press, and Sino-Malay novels as the antecedents of its modern literature.[92] Judged from their unmatched popularity, even the most uncouth publications on violence, crime, and sex helped people come to terms with the fast-changing world around them. Through an unapologetically hybrid language, the urban populations accessed and expressed these experiences in a way that made local sense. As the vernacular press matured, and as Chinese print entrepreneurs secured loyal audiences and stable markets, their Malay slowly gained legitimacy. Although still widely perceived as inferior to High Malay, its popularity made up for its lack of recognition. Its penchant for the vulgar, the humoristic, and even the invective made it indispensable to the vibrant yet stratified society from which it had risen.

4
COMPETING EXPRESSIONS OF MODERNITY

Indonesia's last decades of colonial rule coincided with the global rise of capitalism and visual mass culture. Print entrepreneurs led the way into this new era and its reconfigurations of race, class, and gender. At the same time, they spearheaded a fiery antidiscourse, openly doubting the benefits of modernity under the conditions of colonialism.[1] The press became the frontline for this ideological clash, with vernacular Malay once again arising as the language to articulate society's shifting values. It served as a tool for deparochialization, upward mobility, commercial success, and mass entertainment. As a result, its lexicon was continually expanded to express all that was novel, advanced, and global. This put print entrepreneurs at the forefront of modern lifestyles and concomitant processes of soul-searching. Their access to Dutch and English represented status and education, whereas Hokkien continued to inscribe ancestral pride. The associated translingual negotiations form the mainstay of this chapter.

In three specific arenas, the linguistic underpinnings of colonial modernity came to the fore in full complexity: attire, medicine, and cuisine. These seemingly disparate strands all conveyed deeply interpersonal expressions of identity. Dress, medicinal knowledge, food, and the language to discuss them epitomized changing ideas of body politics, ingestion, and consumption. In the domain of dress, competing Chinese, indigenous, and Western styles literally fashioned people's outward appearance and made their cultural orientation visible. Medical knowledge likewise vacillated between respected traditions and rationalized innovations, with increasing numbers of Chinese doctors receiving their training in the Netherlands. Cross-pollination between East Asian, Southeast Asian, and European elements took place most intimately in the culinary domain. The Peranakan cuisine was mixed in the truest sense of the word, yet existed amidst racially differentiated foodways. Even what people ate influenced how they perceived society and talked about it. Modernity's cultural battles, then, were fought at the crossroads of political identification and commercial resourcefulness.

The susceptibility of Malay to incorporate loanwords, combined with its ability to form neologisms, informed the ways modernity was negotiated in the public sphere. The language had long demanded and received lexical contributions from speech communities in contact. Print entrepreneurs expanded its vocabulary unaided by official institutions. Whereas the *Bintang Hindia* (Star of the Indies; Amsterdam, 1902)—a government-sponsored periodical overflowing with literary pretensions and "appropriate" readings—promoted awkward neologisms such as *kareta toep-toep* (puff-puff cart) for car, Sino-Malay newspapers simply adopted the Dutch word *automobiel* or its Straits equivalent *motoka* (motorcar).[2] Such designations reveal linguistic spontaneity rather than top-down direction. The cinema became a *gambar hidoep* (living picture) and the gramophone a *machine bitjara* (talking machine), while the Great Depression of the 1930s yielded *harga malaise* (malaise prices). This constant reconciliation between the traditional, the modern, and the hybrid meant tapping into multiple linguistic resources. The vernacular Malay of the Netherlands Indies used the Dutch words *batterij* (battery) and *plaat* (gramophone record), but in the Straits Settlements they became *obat elektrik* (electric medicine) and *piring nyanyi* (singing plate). Chinese authors were not alone in drawing liberally from Javanese, Dutch, and other European languages to fill the lexico-semantic gaps of Malay, but they uniquely added Hokkien to the mix. This was a travesty to at least some Dutch thinkers, who preferred Indonesia's peoples to remain uncorrupted by external influences, stick to their traditional cultures, wear regional clothes, write in their native languages, ban the radio and gramophone, and shy away from foreign loanwords. This unrealistic worldview was as persistent as it was destined to fail.[3]

Many Western concepts received a lukewarm treatment in the Sino-Malay press, yet eventually entered society under a localized guise.[4] The topic of feminism in particular sent tickles of unease, although its emancipatory potential did not go unnoticed. As early as the 1880s—long before the Western media wrote in awe about "the little Javanese feminist" Kartini—Lie Kim Hok advocated for more gender equality in his Malay publications.[5] Progressive newspapers became the platform for such insights to flourish. In China, the first women's periodical saw the light in 1898.[6] The Netherlands Indies followed suit seven years later, when the *Tiong Hoa Wi Sien Po* (Chinese Reformist Newspaper; Bogor, 1905) was established by forward-thinking Peranakan women.[7] This event marked the beginning of Indonesia's woman's press. Most Sino-Malay periodicals responded positively to girls' education, their participation in various sports, employment rights, and freedom (*kamerdikahan*).

However, such endorsements invariably came with reminders about the dangers of mixed-gender encounters. One author maligned Chinese festivals where one could meet "playboys wandering about in droves at those kinds of 'parties' who 'accidentally' grab, bump, or worse." Girls were vulnerable, a second author diagnosed, due to "their natural predisposition, interactions with good-for-nothing guys, faintheartedness, being overly romantic, and several other causes." Modern dancing styles, as a third author put it poetically, equaled "fornicating without taking one's trousers off" (berdjina zonder boeka tjelana).⁸ Such interactions and observations were phrased in the language of contamination, best expressed through European loanwords. In a 1939 *Sin Po* article discussing the theories of the British educational psychologist Meyrick Booth (b. 1883), modern values were blamed for the dwindling numbers of marriages. The English words *individualistic, non-racial, egocentric,* and *feminism* in the following paragraph represented precisely the type of foreign influence the author would rather see curbed:

The education system in England (or more accurately: in the West) is now under the influence of an individualistic and nonracial philosophy. Its only objective is to make pupils succeed in life on an individual base. And now a problematic situation has arisen in which individual interests clash severely with the interests of society. Yet, their understanding of modern life is so egocentric that this severe clash goes unnoticed, is considered to be nonexistent, because the interests of society are deprived of spokespeople capable of making their voices heard. We regard it favorable that all of this is taken into account by modern Chinese people, because among the Chinese people that are heavily contaminated by Western attitudes, feminism is also starting to sprout.

Systeem onderwijs di Engeland (lebih betoel dibilang di Barat) sekarang ada kena pengaroehnja philosophie jang individualistic dan non-racial. Iapoenja toedjoean tjoema boeat bikin moerid-moerid berhasil dalem penghidoepan setjara satoe-satoe orang. Dan sekarang djadi timboel soeal jang soeker dalem mana kapentingan satoe-satoe orang djadi kabentrok heibat sama kapentingannja shiahwee. Tapi, pemandangannja penghidoepan modern ada begitoe egocentric hingga itoe bentrokan heibat tida dirasaken, dipandang seperti tida ada, lantaran kapentingannja shiahwee tida poenja wakil-wakil boeat kasi denger soearanja. Ini semoea kita anggep ada baek djoega diperhatiken oleh orang Tionghoa modern kerna antara orang Tionghoa jang banjak katoelaran anggepan-anggepan Barat feminism djoega moelai bersemi.⁹

Chinese (and indigenous) journalists avidly spurned what they perceived to be slavish mimicry of European values. Their scorn fell, in equal measure, upon Westernized Asians and masculinized women. One 1928 op-ed in *Sin Po*, for example, attacks modern women for keeping their hair short and smoking tobacco. It follows the well-attested strategy of first encouraging women to advance (*madjoe*) and then dictating the conditions under which this must take place:

Women have to progress, be smart, be free, etc., but they should not imitate men; this would be as silly as men imitating women, for example by wearing a skirt, applying face powder, breastfeeding (sic!) a baby, twisting their hair into a chignon, wearing high heels, and so on. If there is such a man, we would obviously haste to send him to a mental institution.	Orang prampoean haroes madjoe, pinter, merdika enz., tapi boekan moestinja iaorang maen adjokin orang lelaki; ini sama geelonja kaloe oepama orang lelaki pergi adjokin orang prampoean, jalah oepama pake rok, pake poepoer, soesoein [sic!] anak, pake konde, pake spatoe tjang tinggi dan sebaginja. Kaloe ada orang lelaki begitoe, kita tentoe boeroe-boeroe kirim ia ka roemah gila.[10]

In this interplay of accepting, rejecting, and localizing external discourses, sarcastic translingual puns became rhetorical tools. Newspaper editors would facetiously refer to a homeless person as a *straat-gentleman*, from the Dutch word *straat* (street). One critic accused his enemies of *ay-kantong* (loving their pockets) and being *djiat-nama* (enthusiastic about fame), two nonce words modeled after the well-known Hokkienisms *aykok* (loving one's nation) and *djiatsim* (enthusiastic).[11] Detractors of THHK referred to the imperfect Mandarin of its students as *Tjap Tjay Im* (mixed-vegetable pronunciation), a pun on *tjaptay* (mixed vegetables) and *tjeng-im* (correct pronunciation).[12] An author for *Sin Po* coined the term "Fox-Trot-Lek"—the detested habit of dancing the foxtrot during celebrations of *Im Lek* (Lunar New Year) and *Jang Lek* (Solar New Year)—which he complained had been introduced by youngsters for whom Western dance had become the "spice of life" (sambel dari penghidoepan). Here, the mixture of Hokkien for respectable tradition and English for invasive novelty is difficult to miss. The worst language of all, however, was the pidginized Dutch seen in the accompanying cartoon: "Een beetje tjepetan, djifrou!" ("A little faster, Miss!")[13]

Outward Appearances

The aforementioned story "Moesti Rajahken Lebih Rameh" from 1929 describes in perfect detail a Chinese gentleman from Batavia and his sartorial preferences.

On festive occasions, uncle Kim Koen could be spotted donning his *kinsin* (close-fitting jacket), *kopia* (skull cap), and *beng-eh* (Ming-style shoes). The traditional septuagenarian rejected the *hollankow* (Dutch trousers) and *djas* (coat) that had come into vogue among his contemporaries. On normal days, however, he had made some attempts to modernize his ways:

But even though uncle Kim Koen was a conservative, he no longer wore a frogged coat with frontal pockets and loose-fitting trousers. He had to drift along with the flow of time, after all, and exchanged them long ago for a Western-style coat and trousers, albeit still oversized-looking.	Tapi 'ntjek Kim Koen maski kaoem kolot, ia tida pake lagi badjoe twiekim kantong titouw dan tjelana komprang. Ia toch moesti toeroet anjoet djoega dalem aliran djeman, dan soeda sakean lama toekar pake djas dan tjelana Barat maski dengan oekoeran jang kaliatan grombongan.[14]

We have just been treated to a description of someone hopelessly disconnected from the buzz of modernity. Yet not much earlier, uncle Kim Koen's style would have been the norm rather than the exception among Java's Chinese men. This beckons the interrelated questions of what the Chinese were wearing, why they were wearing it, how it changed, and why it changed. Needless to say, they wore a wide range of different clothes depending on the occasion, but their public attire is of chief interest here. Dress informed their cultural identification and therefore their relation to others. Sino-Malay fiction speaks volumes about the importance of clothes, tonsure, and other visual markers of identity. Kwee Seng Tjoan's novel *Tjerita Anak Prampoean di Bikin Sebagi Parit Mas* (The Story of the Daughter Turned into a Golden Goose) from 1917, for instance, contains a detailed description of sartorial dynamics. Set in 1902 Batavia, the account abounds with Hokkien words to illustrate the peculiarities of traditional Chinese dress:

At that time, the long shirt and close-fitting jacket with a skull cap and Ming-style shoes were still worn by many Chinese, because at that time, less than five percent of the Chinese had gotten rid of their head embellishment (queue); meanwhile, among the women, the loose-fitting long blouse was still greatly enjoyed by Chinese ladies and girls, yet there	Pada itoe masa badjoe Thengsha dan Kinsin bersama Kopia Batok dan Kasoet Beng-eh masi terpake oleh banjak orang Tiong Hoa, kerna pada waktoe itoe blon ada lima percent di antara orang-orang Tiong Hoa, jang telah boeang ia poenja periasan kepala (Thauwtjang), sedeng pada fihak prampoean badjoe koeroeng masi amat di soekai oleh Tiong Hoa

were also ladies and girls of Chinese descent who wanted to change these old principles, and started wearing lace-trimmed blouses; because at that time, as the readers will have learned, the Tiong Hoa Hwee Koan Society had already been established, and yet a short blouse with lace was something none of the Chinese women in Batavia dared to wear as they do today. The lace blouse has now become an item of dress that all Chinese ladies and girls need to have at their disposal to wear at any party venue.

Hoedjin dan Siotjia, tetapi ada djoega Njonja-Njonja dan Nona Nona bangsa Tiong Hoa, jang ingin roba platoeran koeno, telah berpake badjoe Pekie, kerna pada itoe waktoe, sebagimana pembatja telah mendapet taoe, Perhimpoenan Tiong Hoa Hwe Koan soeda di diriken, aken tetapi badjoe kebaja pendek pake renda ampir tida saorang prampoean Tiong Hoa di kota Betawi brani pake seperti pada waktoe sekarang. Badjoe kebaja renda soeda mendjadi seroepa pakean, jang semoea Tiong Hoa Hoedjin dan Siotjia perloe sediaken boeat di pake aken pegi di mana-mana medan pesta.[15]

For the Chinese of late colonial Southeast Asia, clothing and hairstyle stood at the center of a heated ideological battle for political loyalty and cultural orientation. As Kwee Seng Tjoan's novel illustrates, socioreligious organizations like the THHK tried to push people sartorially toward the Republic of China. But the roots of Chinese-Indonesian dressing practices go back much earlier. During the Ming dynasty, it was fashion for men to wear their hair in a bun (Hk: *kè*, Ml: *konde*) on top of their head. Chinese traders keen to evade the fiscal burdens placed upon them by the VOC often cut off their hair. The Qing dynasty imposed a novel hairstyle on its male subjects from the first half of the seventeenth century. This Manchu-style queue (Hk: *thâu-chang*, Ml: *thauwtjang*) involved shaving one's forehead and braiding the remaining hair at the back of the head. Failure to observe these unpopular regulations could result in punishment by decapitation. As the old adage went, "keep your hair, lose your head; keep your head, lose your hair" (Liû hoat put liû thâu, liû thâu put liû hoat).[16] Even in Southeast Asia—at safe distance from the decapitating blade—the queue persisted as a symbol of ancestral connections to China, even though some refused to cultivate it.[17] This hairstyle had long burdened Chinese men in the Indies with the obstinate slur *tjina koentjir* (pigtailed Chinese).

Items of dress were likewise influenced by Qing prescriptions. For men, they included a long upper-body garment (Hk: *tn̂g-sa*ⁿ, Ml: *thengsha*) and a cylindrical skull cap (Hk: *oá*ⁿ*-bō*, Ml: *kopia batok*). These outward affinities with the fatherland coalesced with the racialized sartorial regime of the Netherlands

Indies, in which Chinese and indigenous people were expected not to wear European clothes unless they adopted Christianity. The aim of such policies was clear. After generations of racial *métissage*, skin color had become insufficient to distinguish between those registered as Europeans, Chinese, and indigenous people.[18] Predictably, colonial dress regulations were defied from time to time. In the 1850s, Batavia's legendary playboy Oeij Tambah Sia could be seen wearing "a hat from fine silk velvet, his shirt of equally neat cut; with these clothes he looked extremely handsome, making him stand out like a flower among the Chinese bachelors in Batavia."[19] In 1872 a law was passed barring non-Europeans from wearing costumes associated with ethnicities other than their own, such as Western jackets and trousers for Chinese or Javanese people. This policy stood in sharp contrast with that of Singapore, where upper-class Babas were regularly photographed in European attire around the same period.[20]

As was the case in colonies worldwide, European attire streamlined racial hierarchies and simultaneously provoked struggles for emancipation. The fetish of wearing European clothes became a recurrent theme in vernacular Malay literature.[21] In 1889, the Semarang-based businessman Oei Tiong Ham (1866–1924) was the first ethnic Chinese who, in the words of the local authorities, "had been given permission to show himself in public places without a queue and in European clothes."[22] The prominence of a wealthy entrepreneur in the movement to wear Western clothes reveals an element of class in addition to race. In his wake, growing numbers of men started to reject their obligatory markers of Chineseness. Emboldened by Japan's military victory over Russia, they cut off their queues. They associated this hairstyle with subservience to the Manchus (*orang Boan*), who ruled China under the Qing dynasty. After the Chinese Revolution in 1911, Java's movement to get rid of the queue (*gerakan boeat hapoesken thauwtjang*) was eventually also embraced by conservatives.[23] Only after this watershed moment did the Netherlands Indies government abandon its legislation requiring Chinese men to adhere to the dress of imperial China.

Prior to the Chinese Revolution, the queue-cutting issue had sparked fierce debates. Sun Yat-sen got rid of his own queue as early as 1896; Southeast Asia's modernists gradually followed suit, but it would take some time before his example was broadly adopted in China.[24] The Sino-Malay *Boekoe Sair Kabaikannja Orang jang Hendak Melepas Thauw-tjang* (Poem about the Advantages of Cutting the Pigtail), written in 1905 by the Batavian Tjia Ki Siang, reported:

Now people understand better	Orang sekarang lebi mengarti
They consider what has to be done	Di timbang betoel jang telah misti
Look at the Japanese, they give proof	Liatken Djepang jang mendjadi boekti
If you cut the pigtail you won't die.	Lepasken Thauw-tjang traboleh mati.[25]

The sudden renunciation of so powerful a symbol of Chineseness, however, raised concerns. "Babas who have cut off their queue think that *they* have reformed—have become elevated, perhaps as elevated as Europeans," observed a Singaporean commentator wryly. "But in that case, why do we Babas wear white shoes, European footwear, and trousers?" retorted another author, arguing that the time had come to move beyond outdated sartorial loyalties.[26] They led to a peculiar paradox: while Singkeh men—oriented toward China and up-to-date on its political developments—cut off their queue and modernized their attire, part of the Baba community continued to fashion themselves after the defeated Qing dynasty to preserve their Chinese identity.[27]

The regulations in the Indies to wear Chinese clothes chiefly befell men, who enjoyed greater freedom to move into the public domain. Chinese women generally adopted a more indigenous style, as did Eurasian and European women.[28] Only the bridal gown (*toakhie*) was thoroughly Chinese and was retained by Peranakans even after it had disappeared in China.[29] In everyday life, Peranakan women wore a *badjoe koeroeng*, a tunic-like garment equally popular among indigenous women. A slight adaptation was the knee-length *badjoe pandjang*, which was loose-fitting and open at the front.[30] Both costumes were worn in combination with a hip-wrapper (*kaen sarong*). What distinguished the Nyonya's costume from that of an indigenous lady came with a price tag: brightly colored fabrics, intricate embroidery, beaded slippers, clasp-fastened waist belts (*angkin*), sophisticated lace trimmings, gold brocades, silks, and other Chinese-inspired adornments.[31] At the same time, Peranakans spearheaded the transborder trade in *batik* (Hk: *bâ-tèk*), Java's traditional wax-resist dyed cloths. Fabrics from the island's north coast—in particular the textile centers of Pekalongan, Lasem, Cirebon, and Tuban—became extremely popular throughout the Netherlands Indies and British Malaya.[32] Northern Java was famous for its chinoiserie-derived motifs, sometimes known as "auntie batik" (*batik entjim*).[33] This hybrid vestiary heritage is frequently exhibited by the Peranakan museums of Indonesia, Malaysia, and Singapore.

Global commerce opened new sartorial frontiers. Western fashion continued to represent wealth and status. Jackets, trousers, and shoes fulfilled this function in the male domain, in the Indies and elsewhere. Yet the route toward modernity developed into multiple branches and directions. A Cantonese-style short-sleeved blouse worn with trousers (*samfu, baju Shanghai*) quickly won the hearts of Singapore's Chinese women from 1890.[34] At the beginning of the twentieth century, Surabaya's Chinese women wore a blouse that opened on the right side (*pèhki*) combined with a pleated skirt (*hoakoen*). The city's Chinese men donned a frogged coat, rather than the bland dress of their Batavian counterparts. When this new, Surabayan fashion had finally conquered Batavia, the Nyonyas of the former city had already moved on to the next thing: a short blouse with lace trimmings. This European-inspired garment also quickly gained ground in the Straits Settlements.³⁵

Besides the commercial fashion industry, the establishment of girls' education also inspired new modes of dress. In the early twentieth century, girls' schools in China banned Western dress in favor of uniforms acceptable by local standards.³⁶ Similar developments took place in Southeast Asia. The aforementioned THHK promoted a Chinese-inspired uniform for girls known as *badjoe sioki*, which was worn in combination with a petticoat (*koen*). The aforementioned *pèhki* and *hoakoen* were also briefly in vogue among school girls.³⁷ In the Straits Settlements, the *samfu* became the garment of choice for female pupils at Chinese schools.³⁸ Medan soon followed suit. According to Oeij Kim Tjoan, in his tongue-in-cheek account of the city's history, this light-blue, two-foot blouse immediately freed women from the clutches of conservatism. In the following soliloquy, he positively contrasted the progressive Chinese girls wearing this garment to unsophisticated indigenous women:

Hey! Modernists of the Chinese nation! Follow our example: don't take a girl as a wife who still enjoys wearing long blouses, just like an indigenous woman; don't aspire marrying someone who still belongs to the traditionalists, who likes to chew betel and gamble. What's the use of all of that? Just look! Medan already has many Chinese women who wear the "Shanghai garment"! This dress looks very sweet to our eyes, and indeed appears sweeter than sugared honey.	Hai! Kaoem Moeda bangsa Tionghoa! Toeroetlah toeladan kami: djanganlah maoe berestri dengen satoe gadis, jang masi soeka pakai kabaja pandjang, sebagi "Hoana poo," djanganlah maoe mempoenjai estri orang jang masi masoek golongan kaoem Toewa, jang soeka makan siri dan soeka berdjoedi. Apa goenanja itoe semoewa? Liatlah! Di Medan soeda banjak orang prempoean Tionghoa, jang memakai badjoe Shanghai! Manis betoel pakaian itoe bagi mata kami, sahingga rasanja terlebi manis lagi dari madoe goela.³⁹

The petite bourgeoisie benefited optimally from these competing promises of modernity. It was not uncommon for Chinese shop owners to simultaneously advertise European fashion, Chinese attire, royal Manchurian bridal gowns, burial sheets (*sioe ie*), and doorway couplets (*toeilian*). Novel creations also proved popular.⁴⁰ In 1912, the *Ho Po* (Peaceful Newspaper; Sukabumi, 1904) contained advertisements of panama hats in the Chinese republican (*Binkok*) fashion, promoting the preferred models of Sun Yat-sen and Yuan Shikai. As an alternative, the store also offered "black sturdy hats of the flat model, which are very popular among Chinese officers here in the Indies, for 7.50 guilders."[41] A 1924 Singaporean advertisement described in detail the latest products imported from Java. Besides several food items and batik from Pekalongan, it offered the newest models of lace-trimmed chemises. As the advertisement clarified in order to stave off any interdialectal misunderstandings, "people from Java call them *kutang*" (Orang tana Jawa bilang Kutang). This trendy Europeanized creation was promoted unrelentingly: "If you love your wife and daughters, please kindly visit our store and have a look at the lace blouses from Java."[42] Many advertisements were plurilingual (Chinese and Malay) and stressed that their products came from Shanghai, one of Asia's booming fashion capitals.

China's traditional female garb (*qípáo*) had been subjected to a successful promotion campaign under the new republic. In redesigned form, it offered a homemade alternative to European fashion. Known in Malaya as *cheongsam*, this tight-fitting one-piece dress quickly became popular due to its ubiquity in Chinese movies. It conquered the Indies under the name "Shanghai-dress" or *chang-ie*, with several models being designed locally from the 1930s.[43] In a fascinating twist of history, this anti-European turn in Chinese fashion was spearheaded by Oei Hui Lan (1899–1992), the daughter of Oei Tiong Ham who had earlier insisted on his right to wear European clothes.[44] This move away from European attire shows interesting parallels among Java's Arab population. A 1932 advertisement in the newspaper *Al-Jaum* (The Day; Surabaya, 1931) contained a Malay poem that was clearly intended to elicit pan-Asian solidarity:

Oh, Asian siblings	Hae soedarakoe kaoem Azia
Wear Persian-style skull-caps	Pakelah kopiah model Perzia
Of the Ballon brand, cheap and sublime	Tjap Ballon moerah dan moelia
To replace the tarbush from Italy.	Boeat gantinja tarboos di Italia.[45]

Once again, retailers benefited maximally from these shifting political affinities and the need to express them outwardly.

Such encouragements to dress Asian hardly convinced everyone. Many upper-class Peranakans remained steadfast in their predilections for European clothes, now untrammeled by legal restrictions against wearing them. A photograph from the affluent Kwee family from Ciledug (West Java) shows the young sons "meticulously dressed in three-piece Western-style jackets. They wear neatly pressed trousers just over their knee with socks at knee length, have shiny leather-shoes, a pocket-watch, a bowtie, and carry a large khaki tropical hat."[46] As a commercial phenomenon, European attire provided new modes of self-validation through the mimicry of society's higher ranks. The "Chinese dandy" could be spotted in the latest fashion from France, wearing a watch and other accoutrements. He smoked cigarettes, consumed imported alcohol, and used perfumes and peppermints.[47] Advertisements provide meticulous insights into the ways modernity was marketed. In one example, a brand of British tonic wine was promoted—in vernacular Malay—through the visual representation of a Chinese man wearing a European suit, drinking the beverage, and drawing the admiring gaze of a large group of friends in similar attire (fig. 4.1).

FIGURE 4.1. Advertisement for tonic wine depicting a Westernized type of modernity (*Sin Po*, 1939)

Critics of Western modernity passionately ridiculed those who dressed European. Predictably, much of this discourse was gendered. While men could participate in various facets of modernity, women faced a bombardment of public scorn the moment they appeared too fashionably dressed or Western-educated.[48] Some Sino-Malay authors had the habit of dismissing European(ized) clothes in one breath with speaking Dutch and looking down on those who could not. In their minds, cultural uprooting manifested itself sartorially as well as linguistically. There is perhaps no pithier illustration of this mindset than a sentence from Injo Bian Hien's 1931 novel *Nasib* (Fate):

Nowadays Lin-nio has adopted modern habits and always walks around in a skirt and on high heels, and whenever she has a conversation she always speaks in Dutch; she is no longer keen to interact with indigenous women of West Javanese origins.	Sekarang Lin-nio jang mempoenjai kabiasahan modern dan selaloe berdjalan sama rok dan sepatoe tjang tinggi dan saban bitjara selaloe oetjapken bahasa blanda, soeda merasa poewas dengan bergaoelan sama prampoean-prampoean Boemi-poetra jang berasal dari Djawa Koelon.[49]

Even men could face such condemnations, albeit to a lesser degree. The archetype of a mendacious Chinese dandy donning European clothes persisted into the 1930s. It was brilliantly brought to life in Pat Taij Tjoe's *Sair Perdjaka* (Poem of the Bachelor), which cautioned against the dangers of playboys. The work itself follows the same format as other Sino-Malay pulp fiction: a chance meeting between two strangers, excessive flirting, sex before marriage, an unplanned pregnancy, a murder, and eventually a suicide. What concerns us here is the way the poem's male antihero was depicted:

A first-class felt hat covered his head Crockett & Jones shoes enveloped his feet In stylishness, he took defeat from no one Despite his lack of any abilities whatsoever.	Topi Vilt klas satoe menangkring diatas kepala Sepatoe Crokett Jones menempat di kakinja Pakean plente pada orang laen ia tida maoe mengala Maski djoega tida soeatoe apa mendjadi kepandeannja.[50]

As time progressed, sartorial conservatism gradually lost its grip on popular opinion. Girls increasingly relegated their convenient sarong and long blouse to the bedroom and reentered the path of progress in European clothes and hairstyles—"bobbed" and "single"—whenever they encountered like-minded spirits. Even the Sino-Malay press occasionally proved itself supportive. Writing in 1930, one journalist for *Hoakiao* contended that the hopelessly old-fashioned long blouse had reached its expiry date. To thicken the cosmopolitan veneer of his opinions, he invoked the Dutch words *liefst* (preferably) and *oude doos* (the days of yore):

the bulwark of the "long blouse," preferably with many colors, has fallen too; and so today we may make the "long blouse" into a cult object, a symbol indicating that its wearer comes from the "days of yore"—that is, "bygone times"—and that her intelligence can be measured accordingly.	bentengan dari "kebaja pandjang" dan liefst jang berwarna-warna, djoega soedah mengalah, hingga "kebaja pandjang" sekarang boleh diboeat djimat dan mendjadi symbool, jang pemakenja ada dari "oude doos" alias "djaman koeno," jang pengetaoeannja bisa dioekoer dari sitoe.[51]

The above citations testify that the sartorial choices of Chinese men and women were informed by competing types of modernity, in the Indies and elsewhere. Dress had long served exclusionary and discriminatory purposes, yet eventually allowed the middle classes to be seen in ways they preferred (and could afford). A crucial part of these negotiations took place on the pages of novels, newspapers, and advertisements.

From *Sinse* to *Dokter*

Health and medicine caused similar frictions between Chinese, Southeast Asian, and Western ideas. Administrative efforts in the Netherlands Indies to modernize healthcare had left traditional practices somewhat marginalized. Yet while modern science relegated non-Western medicine to the realm of folklore, innumerable colonized people lacked access to or trust in Western doctors, ensuring its survival.[52] Like their indigenous peers, Chinese medical practitioners straddled the boundaries of tradition and modernity. The Dutch-educated *dokter* faced competition from traditional healers known as *sinse*, a word derived from the Hokkien term for teacher. The *sinse* was a physician (*iseng*), but also an expert in medicine and pharmacy. In that sense, he was the equivalent of the Javanese *doekoen*, the Malay *pawang*, and the Arabic *thabib*. China's pharmacists had long been equally familiar with the medicinal herbs of Southeast Asia as with those of their own backyard. Indeed, their traditional materia medica included numerous products from the South Seas.⁵³ Prior to the twentieth century, local, Chinese, and European healing practices coexisted and influenced each other.⁵⁴ Amidst the colony's competing narratives of modernity, however, this diversity gradually became a source of tension.

The *sinse* is a recurring character in colonial-era accounts. As the historical vignette has it, the women's rights activist Raden Adjeng Kartini (1879–1904) once fell severely ill during her childhood. When no Western-educated doctor could cure her, a *sinse* eventually burned a piece of talismanic paper (*kertas hoe*) and fed the ashes to the ailing child, leading to her full recovery.⁵⁵ Similar anecdotes of miraculous healing can be read throughout Indonesia's history. Even the staid Dutchmen of the VOC frequently praised the quality of Batavia's Chinese doctors and hospitals. As early as the 1630s, the VOC employed a handsomely compensated Chinese physician.⁵⁶ The German botanist Georg Eberhard Rumphius (1628–1702) made extensive use of the knowledge of unnamed Chinese and indigenous consultants in his publications on the archipelago's useful plants.⁵⁷ The Dutch Governor-General Joan van Hoorn (1653–1711) was treated by the Batavian Chinese doctor Tjoe Bi Tia, whom he had commissioned in 1709 to accompany him on a trip to the Netherlands. The family of Governor-General Mattheus de Haan (1663–1729) likewise received healthcare from a Chinese physician, identified in the *Annals of Batavia* as the wife of Lieutenant Lim Somko.⁵⁸

Dutch attitudes toward Chinese medical practitioners turned ambivalent in the next two centuries. Several eyebrows were raised, for example, at the importance the *sinse* attributed to pulse diagnosis (*bongme*). However, while his theoretical knowledge was occasionally belittled, the *sinse*'s experience rarely presented grounds for doubt.⁵⁹ Certain Chinese practices, such as the medicinal use of peppermint (*poko*), were adopted by European doctors throughout the Netherlands Indies. The expertise of Chinese doctors in treating syphilis was likewise renowned among Europeans.⁶⁰ The *sinse*'s profound impact on society is linguistically substantiated. Several names for diseases—venereal or otherwise—were understood by their Hokkien names across the plebeian Malay-speaking world. The Arab readers of the aforementioned newspaper *Al-Jaum*, for example, were familiar with the term *laysiang* (tuberculosis).⁶¹

It would be no exaggeration to claim that print entrepreneurship aided the survival of traditional Chinese medicine. Many *sinse* initially kept their recipes a secret, but some eventually decided to publish them commercially.⁶² From the late nineteenth century, Sino-Malay medical treatises started to appear. Around 1890, Tjoa Tjoe Kwan finalized a Malay translation of a Chinese book containing a set of prescriptions to cholera.⁶³ Also in 1890, Yap Goan Ho's printing house published a Malay reworking of the *Tat Seng Pian* (Treatise on Successful Birth).

This Chinese work was advertised as "medicinal knowledge for the benefit of all men and women suffering from various illnesses." Another publication, of unknown authorship and year, was promoted as a "book of medicines for the plague that have proven very effective."[64] Numerous similar books must have circulated locally, yet only a few made their way into international libraries and academic publications.[65]

On the other end of the medical spectrum stood Western-educated doctors and pharmacists. Chinese students from the Indies disproportionately took up these disciplines. Lim Njat Fa (1871–1927), a Hakka from Muntok, was the first Indies Chinese to enroll in Leiden University in 1883. He was followed in 1909 by Yap Hong Tjoen (1885–1953), who was instrumental in establishing the Chung Hwa Hui, a Dutch student organization loosely connected to the aforementioned Chung Hwa Hui of the Indies. Sien Everdien Ongkiehong (1896–1960), who took up pharmacy from 1917 until 1925, was the first Chinese woman to study in the Netherlands.[66] Similar patterns unfolded around the same time in the Straits Settlements. In 1887, Lim Boon Keng became the first Malayan to study medicine in Edinburgh on a Queen's Scholarship. Lee Choo Neo, Malaya's first female doctor, graduated in 1919 in Singapore. She closely collaborated with Lim Boon Keng to improve girls' education.[67] These and other Western-educated doctors unleashed a heated debate to reform traditional Chinese medicine, if not do away with it entirely. The *dokter* was often accused of being only interested in seeking commercial gain.[68] Yet the *sinse* was equally prone to belittle his colleagues in the face of profit. In a bilingual advertisement (Chinese and Malay) published in 1932 in the Padang-based newspaper *Radio*, one author relays: "for a long time I have been seeing *sinse* and *dokter* who could not cure me, until I finally got treated in Padang; I called *sinse* Tjiang Soei Heng who treated me straight away, and after less than half a month my eyes were healed."[69]

The idiom in which some *sinse* published their recipes speaks volumes about the linguistic hybridity of Chinese-Indonesian medicine. This is best illustrated through a page from the aforementioned Malay reworking of the *Tat Seng Pian* (fig. 4.2). The text starts with a "prescription for a medicine" (*ijo twah obat*), a compound consisting of the Hokkien word for prescription (*iòh-toa^n*) and the Malay word for medicine (*obat*). The name of this medicine is *tîm hiang sàn*, a Hokkien term that translates as agarwood powder. Then, the actual instructions are given in literary Chinese, followed by their explanation in colloquial Malay. None of the explanations are word-for-word translations of the source texts. Instead, some consist of several additional pages. The Malay itself contains Dutch words, such as *poeijer* (powder) and *cholera*, alongside the Hokkienism *tio swah* (sudden stomach cramps). The latter term is "translated" into Malay as *salatri*, which is in fact a loanword from Sundanese. The book contains 192 such recipes.

IJo Twah obat nama »Tim Hiang San."

常用沉香散
香茹ニ兩薄荷ニ兩干葛五錢
藿香三兩山查二兩陳皮五錢
甘草四兩紫蘇三兩川朴五錢
羗扁豆五兩
水十盞煎五盞去渣存汁
攪活石粉一斤晒干研末
沉香枱香砂仁炒各二兩
研末和勻收貯

R. Di trangken obat Poeijer Tiem Hiang San aken goenanja boeat sekalian orang laki-laki dan prampoean jang mendapet sakit moenta berak (Cholera) atawa Tio Swah (Salatri), djikaloe orang maoe bli ini obat bole bawa dia poenja IJo Twah di roemah obat Tjina soeroe dia bikin obat begimana jang terseboet di dalem IJo Twah di atas, siapa-siapa jang hendak bikin obat itoe harep djangan sajang doeit atawa seboet mahal kerna bole dapet obat jang bagoes dan di pakenja djoega bole mendjadi mandjoer.

FIGURE 4.2. Medical prescription in Chinese and Malay against cholera or sudden stomach cramps, taken from the reworking of the *Treatise on Successful Birth* (1890, 61)

Another widely advertised treatise, published in 1912 in Telukbetung (South Sumatra), blends healing practices with Daoism. While written in vernacular Malay and only containing a few Chinese characters, this book carries the Hokkien title *Tong Thian Piet Hiauw*. It is devoted to the healing traditions of antiquity, which "can be used to control talismans, charms, or Daoist magic" (bisa digoenaken pengaroenja Isim, Hoehwat atawa Hwatsoet).[70] Alongside rather ambitious recipes to fend off predatory animals, "make oneself popular in social interaction" (membikin diri djadi disoeka dalem pergaoelan), and "make a corpse come to back life" (boeat idoepin mait), it addresses some of the world's more mundane problems. To get rid of excessive facial hair without a razor knife, the book recommends the aspiring *sinse*—in a mix of Malay and Hokkien—to "buy realgar and limestone, one tael of each, and two maces of camphor" (beli Tjiohong dan Tjio-hwee, masing-masing beratnja satoe tail, dan Tjiang-loo doea tjhi). When buying these ingredients, the book informs its readers, the proper characters need to be shown as listed in the appendix, otherwise the pharmacist will not understand.[71] This illustrates the aforementioned difficulties of representing the sounds of Hokkien in the Latin script, but it also reveals the existence of a plurilingual medical jargon.

In this regard, one authority on traditional medicine (Chinese and Javanese) cannot be left unmentioned: the illustrious hermit Tan Tik Sioe (1884–1929), also known as Rama-Moortie. Born in Surabaya and educated by the THHK, this mystic and martial artist was associated with numerous miracles during his lifetime, earning him the title of god (Ml: *Dewa*, Hk: *Sian*). As one Dutch newspaper reported in 1919, the "Yellow Prophet" had retreated into the mountains to preach a message of global brotherhood, proclaiming himself indifferent to the substantial fortune he inherited from his parents.[72] Java's Theosophical Society observed Tan Tik Sioe's curious juxtaposition of Daoist, Hindu, and Muslim influences with great interest. Yet not everyone was equally charmed by this late colonial messiah. In an anonymous diatribe titled "Kliwatan poenja Bodo" (Extravagant Stupidity), published in 1925 in *Hoakiao*, he was dismissed as a "low-quality god" (*Dewa-bangpak*) and a careless (*loo-tjoh*) one to boot.[73] A newspaper from Singapore criticized his insistence that Chinese women should wear Chinese clothes. It was furthermore suggested that he had only come to Singapore because his bubble in Java had burst.[74] The controversial figure reportedly passed away in Penang, after spending some time meditating in a cave.[75]

The linguistic character of Tan Tik Sioe's work reflects a now vanished tradition of medical writing, religion, philosophy, and poetry combined. He was equally literate in Chinese, Malay, and Javanese. A number of his books on Chinese and Javanese medicine survive in private collections. In light of their limited distribution, they have largely evaded the academic gaze. Some of his recipes have recently been reprinted in Indonesia, yet even these were never intended for broad circulation. Interspersed with philosophical musings in Malay and Javanese, most of his recipes are entirely in Chinese, following the usual model. Their Malay glosses are minimalistic and at times nebulous to noninsiders. Consider, for example, his "medicine for the nasal disease Nose Butterfly" (obat sakit hidoeng Phi Ijak), his "medicine for people who have been beaten half-dead (this medicine has saved many lives)" (obat orang terkenak poekool sampek ½ mati [Ini obat soeda banjak toeloeng djiwa]), or his "medicine for young children with spermatorrhea" (obat anak moeda dapet sakit Twitjing).[76]

As advertisements make abundantly clear, entrepreneurial Chinese healers were hardly alone in promoting their medical knowledge. In this regard, newspapers from Singapore show the greatest diversity. The advertisement sections of *Kabar Kawat Malayu* (Wired Malay News; Singapore, 1924) display T. M. Abdullah's Islamic medicine (*unanie*) alongside the Gujarati-owned Atank Nigrah pharmacy, followed on the next page by a quadrilingual (English, Tamil, Chinese, and Malay) advertisement of "The Universal Healing Institution." A 1928 issue of *Kabar Uchapan Baru* features an advertisement for a Tamil medicine that could "strengthen our body and cure a variety of diseases."[77] The previous issue, however, regrets the tragic death of a coolie who had consumed a Chinese decoction that as careful inspection revealed, consisted of musk, pearls, amber, frankincense, secretions from the Sichuan musk deer, scorpion, and centipede bodies.[78] In some 1930 issues of Singapore's *Bintang Pranakan*, the Indian doctor O. C. Mamoo advertised his treatment for cancer, diabetes, leprosy, and a series of other ailments. In others, the Ayurvedic medicine of his Sri Lankan colleague M. S. Waidyasurya promised to give "virile power even to the hopeless." Print entrepreneurship had indeed transformed traditional medicine into a global affair.

A wide assortment of potency drugs (*arak koeat, obat koeat, obat pouw*) also secured their spot in Sino-Malay and indigenous newspapers. One of the most successful brands, with the self-explanatory name *Si-Dojan* (The Enjoyer), was manufactured and distributed by the Batavia-based company Goan Hong. Interestingly, it was advertised in the Netherlands Indies "to be used especially by men; a fragrant oil intended for unequalled pleasure due to its potency."[79] In Singapore, however, the same product suddenly became "especially useful for women as it builds strength and reinvigorates the libido and body."[80] It was not exceptional to advertise the same product to different consumers, in different regions, through different promotion strategies. Germany's ubiquitous Sanatogen tonic promised to revitalize the body's nerves and brains in early twentieth-century China, ensured "victory over the decline of manly strength and vigour" in India (where it was advertised in women's journals), and became a food supplement claimed to bolster male virility in the Netherlands Indies.[81] By the 1920s, the Indies version of this product was also promoted—using the Dutch-based romanization of

Malay—in Singaporean newspapers. Other German hormone preparations, such as Neotestin for men and Venusin for women, also found their way into Malay advertisement sections.

Culinary Contestations

In a vitriolic op-ed published in 1936, one of *Sin Po*'s frequent contributors fulminated against Chinese girls attending Dutch schools. None of the things they learn, he insisted, had any practical value. They know how to cook European dishes, but end up unable to prepare *tong tjoe pia* (mooncakes) or *batjang* (sticky rice dumplings). Then again, their whole community consists of fake nationalists, who cannot even be bothered to buy authentic products from China. At home, these people indulge in bread, caviar, and jellied eels, rather than *tja haysiet* (= *hisiet*; stir-fried shark fins), *yan-o thung* (bird's nest soup), or *twadji* (= *tauwdji*; salted bean curd).[82] The author's complaints illustrate the racialized hierarchies of food under colonialism. The Chinese cuisine in particular suffers a long history of contempt by Europe's impromptu experts. For the Indies Chinese, the age-old question of what to eat thus became increasingly entangled with cultural loyalty, entrepreneurship, and language. In Sino-Malay print culture, writing about food automatically became food for thought.[83]

These culinary politics were aptly illustrated by a second *Sin Po* author, who insisted that "cooks who are good at preparing food are artists, and people who appreciate good food are art enthusiasts. How inappropriate to dismiss them with the words 'You're just like a pig.'" Continuing on a more cautionary note, he emphasized that "this should especially concern Chinese that are soiled with butter or filthy with cheese."[84] The author's ultimate argument, that traditional Asian food is superior to Europe's invasive dairy products, provides a pungent metaphor for anticolonial sentiments. As he pointed out, everyday Chinese products such as *kimtjiam* (tuberose flowers), *bokdjie* (edible fungus), *tauwhoe* (tofu), and *tauwge* (mung bean sprouts) have proven to be healthy, yet are barely considered edible by Westerners, not to speak of such delicacies as pork blood and *hisit* (shark fins). The connection between food and health was made by several other commentators. As the Semarang-based historian Liem Thian Joe put it pithily, "the Chinese eat while medicating and medicate while eating." *Jan-oh* (edible birds' nests) are not just a delicacy, they are a medicine to strengthen the body (*obat "pouw"*). Elsewhere he praised the medicinal properties of *ketjap* (soy sauce), informing his readers that plantation coolies receive two spoonfuls each day on account of its antimalarial efficacy.[85] With such a vast array of culinary heritage to take pride in, a *Sin Po* editor assured, there was truly no point in boycotting European food products just to showcase one's nationalism. After all,

Joannes Benedictus van Heutsz (1851–1924)—Holland's infamous warhorse turned governor-general—was allegedly a big fan of Chinese food:

Mr. Ping Djan Tio said that true nationalists, in his opinion, should not eat biscuits from [the Dutch company] Smabers and should not drink champagne, but he forgets that Dutch "nationalists" such as Van Heutsz were fond of chop suey and wheat noodles.	Toean Ping Djan Tio bilang, Nationalist toelen menoeroet iapoenja "anggepan" tida boleh makan koewe Smabers dan tida boleh minoem champagne, tapi ia loepa "Nationialist" Blanda sebagi Van Heutz dojan tjaptjay dan bahmi.[86]

Dutch elites gradually warmed up to Chinese food in the 1920s and 1930s, after doing so much earlier to (their customized versions of) indigenous fare. As a *Sin Po* journalist remarked in 1926, "numerous Asians are learning to eat cheese, but no fewer in number are Europeans who enjoy wheat noodles, egg foo young, and chop suey."[87] If the Chinese restaurants in Europe and America are anything to go by, another author argued, white people are starting to realize what the Chinese cuisine has to offer. These days they can even be spotted patronizing the Chinese restaurants of Pantjoran Street in Batavia.[88] Yet they were not always on their best behavior. An anonymous letter submitted to *Sin Po* describes how Europeans—sometimes in uniform—routinely visited Batavia's Chinese restaurants, ate until full, left without paying, and added insult to injury by abusing the dumbfounded restaurateurs verbally and physically.[89] Despite their alcohol-impaired table manners, Europeans had finally come to view the Chinese cuisine as real food. This curiosity was also reflected in contemporaneous cookbooks, such as a 1937 booklet published by the Semarang Association of Housewives. The delightful compilation contains nineteen local Chinese recipes, many of which were remarkably specialized.[90]

Europe's belated interest in Chinese food—especially compared to Chinese medical traditions—postdated centuries of culinary contact between China and the South Seas. The Chinese are generally credited for bringing tea, a number of leafy vegetables, several types of chives, and noodles (*mie*) to Southeast Asia.[91] Equally important was their introduction of soy products. Tofu (Hk: *tāu-hū*, Ml: *tahoe*) already features on a tenth-century Javanese copperplate inscription alongside other delicacies.[92] Another arena of fusion is that of multicolored, bite-size rice cakes (Hk: *kóe*, Ml: *kwee*), which combine Chinese pastry techniques with Southeast Asian ingredients such as coconut, pandan leaves, and palm sugar. Chinese-introduced cooking techniques included *tja* (stir-frying), *tim* (stewing in a covered pot), and *goreng angsio* (braising in soy sauce). In the Malay dialect of Batavia, including that of non-Chinese speakers, several porcine terms also go back to Hokkien.⁹³ This mix of traditions produced a unique Hokkien-Malay culinary jargon, inspiring ample poetic musings such as the following Singaporean *sair*:

Firm tofu, fried and mixed with Chinese chives	Tawkua goreng ber-champor kuchye
Dried shrimps cooked with bok choy	Udang kring di masak pekchye
Chinese cabbage made into soupy chop suey	Kobi China di bikin kua chap chye
Everything else is completely unnecessary.	Lain smua long-chong-em-sye.⁹⁴

Soy sauce was a key ingredient in the Chinese-Indonesian cuisine. This condiment became known as *ketjap* across the Malay-speaking world, a word initially denoting a "sauce made by boiling down fish, prawns or meat till a rich syrup (*petis*) is formed."⁹⁵ Its name reflects the Hokkien term for a type of brine made of pickled fish or shell-fish (*kê-chiap*). Java's original *ketjap* was indeed closer to *hie-louw* (fish sauce; Ml: *ketjap ikan*), whereas the later version had come to resemble *tao-yoe* (soy sauce).⁹⁶ In Java, numerous *ketjap* factories competed with each other. As Liem Thian Joe informs us in 1940, Semarang—a city of only 217,796 souls—boasts twenty *ketjap* factories. He adds in an insightful slice of local history that Batavia's Gang Ketjap (Ketjap Alley) was once a center of production, but has recently degraded into a "nest of Japanese whores and public women of other nationalities."⁹⁷ Newspaper advertisements reveal that the prestigious *ketjap benteng*, a product from the town of Tangerang near Batavia, was the most popular commercially available type. It was exported to Singapore by Lim & Company, where it was known as *kechup benteng* or *ketchap Batavia*.⁹⁸ The popularity of Batavian *ketjap* stands confirmed by an advertisement in the North Sumatran *Tjin Po* (Virtuous Newspaper; Medan, 1924). The ethno-specific appellations *Siangseng* (Chinese Sir), *Toean* (European Sir), *Njonja* (Chinese/European Madam), and *Enche* (Mr.) indicate that the product was deliberately promoted across different communities:

Beware! Beware! Don't get it wrong. Batavian *ketjap* of the brand Mata Hari. Importers: Tan Poen Hin & Co. This *ketjap* is famous along Sumatra's east coast and the Straits Settlements and has received praise from *Siangsengs*, *Toeans*, *Njonjas* and *Enches*.	Awas! Awas! Djangan silap. Ketjap Batavia tjap Mata Hari. Importeurs: Tan Poen Hin & Co. Ini KETJAP soedah terkenal baik di Sumatra Oostkust dan Straits Settlements dan soedah dapat poedjian dari Siangseng-Siangseng, Toean-Toean, Njonja-Njonja dan Enche-Enche.

Enduring connections across the South China Sea resulted in hybrid food practices. The Peranakan cuisine in particular shows deep influences from Southeast Asia's local traditions, including the use of coconut milk, seeds of the *Pangium edule* plant (*kloewak*), and numerous other flavoring ingredients.[99] Regional differences often outweighed ethnic boundaries. The two-volume *Boekoe Masakan Betawi* (Batavian Cookbook) compiled in 1915 by Lie Tek Long, for example, delves into the "cuisine of Batavian and Peranakan ladies" and includes "all kinds of cooking styles: European, Javanese, and Malay" according to its subtitle.[100] Historically, many Peranakans followed indigenous people in eating with their right hand, while Westernized families preferred European cutlery and Singkehs chopsticks. In some families, men retained Chinese ways of eating and women local ways.[101] Dietary practices were also influenced by the revival of ancient traditions from China. In the mid-1930s, several Sino-Malay cookbooks promoting *tjia tjai* (vegetarianism) entered the markets.[102]

This culinary heritage was by no means static. Multiple cuisines featured side by side in Peranakan women's magazines. European dishes became boastworthy novelties in the Nyonya's gastronomic repertoire. Popular examples included rissoles, macaroni with ham and cheese, *huzarensla* (Olivier salad), *kaasstengels* (dried cheese sticks), and *colombijn* (a Dutch round cake).[103] The *Fu Nu Tsa Chih* (Women's Journal; Malang, 1933) displayed on the same page a recipe for Hokkien-style *ang sioe hie* (snapper braised in soy sauce) and Dutch *sprits* (biscuits).[104] Some of the most popular Chinese dishes were recently introduced by Singkeh cooks. The name of a celebrated crab omelet, *foe jong hai*, betrays Cantonese influence. *Koe loe joek* (sweet-and-sour pork), meanwhile, was a 1937 introduction by Shanghainese refugees from Japan's military expansion. In a cruel twist of history, their restaurants became popular Japanese dining spots after the latter conquered Indonesia in 1942.[105] The refreshing Shanghai-style shaved ice (*ijs Shanghai*), also introduced in the late 1930s, may have been brought to the Indies by the same cooks.

Where people dined also mattered. While upmarket Western-style restaurants sprawled across the cities of the Netherlands Indies, they hardly affected the popularity of no-nonsense roadside food stalls (*waroeng*) that catered to local needs from time immemorial.[106] Throughout the archipelago, Chinese-owned eating houses featured alongside indigenous ones. Dutch-authored descriptions of these food establishments were incomplete without some derogatory remark about their perceived lack of hygiene. One short story published in 1926, "Batavia...De Stad der Schaduwen" (Batavia...the City of Shadows), deserves explicit mention in this regard, not for its sensationalist, condescending portrayal of the city's impoverished underbelly, but for its inclusion of unique night photos of these eating places.[107] As can be seen (fig. 4.3), the portrayed establishment looks

FIGURE 4.3 . A late-night eatery in Batavia. Photograph taken from the story "Batavia . . . the City of Shadows" (Hulsman 1926, 4)

almost identical to today's makeshift food stalls. The original caption translates as: "in a dirty, small food stall, some people sit, until very deep in the night." Such persistent allusions to poor hygiene prompted many Chinese entrepreneurs to advertise their restaurants in Dutch newspapers as "under European supervision."

Retailers and traders benefited from the colony's competing food narratives, as they had done in the realm of attire.[108] A crucial addition to the colony's stockpile of imports was Gourmet-Powder, also traded under the names *ve-tsin* and *aji-no-moto*. Known today as monosodium glutamate, this flavor enhancer was invented in Japan. It adopted an aggressive marketing strategy from the 1910s, quickly turning itself into a cupboard necessity across the world's East and Southeast Asian cuisines. To the Indies Chinese readership it was promoted as an unquestionable requirement for *mi-zoä* (salted wheat vermicelli), *baso pangsit* (wonton meatball soup), and *batjang* (sticky rice dumplings). The following 1924 advertisement specifically targeted women, invoking gendered expectations that resisted modernity's every permutation:

Those who can cook tasty as well as cheap dishes will obviously be loved and cherished by their husband. Not everyone can buy tasty and expensive food, nor is every girl skilled at cooking, so that they should always have Gourmet-Powder at their disposal to help them through their distress, because it can make all dishes tastier and more savory.	Jang bisa masak makanan enak serta moerah, tentoe moesti ditjinta dan disajang betoel-betoel oleh sang laki. Tida samoea orang bisa beli makanan enak-enak dan mahal-mahal, djoega tida sekalian nona-nona pinter masak, maka itoe perloe selaloe sedia Gourmet-Powder boeat menoeloeng dalem kasesakan, sebab ia bisa bikin segala makanan lebih enak dan lebih goeri.[109]

Several overlapping processes are at play here. Commercially available mass products—which quickly customized themselves to gender and ethnicity—bolstered the narrative of modernity by sprinkling instant convenience on life's distress. They did so in ways that appealed to the specific challenges of the time: busier schedules, economic precarity, and a desire to preserve a sense of cultural rootedness. In fashion and medical practices, too, reinvented notions of Chineseness offered a counterforce to Western modernity. Once again, vernacular Malay set the stage to articulate these intimate modes of self-styling and self-identification.

5
THE HUMORISTIC AND THE INVECTIVE

The true power of vernacular Malay resided in its endless possibilities for humor and playfulness, away from the wrath of colonial administrators, language purists, and elitist intelligentsia. As the previous chapters have shown, Chinese print entrepreneurs consciously prioritized the colloquial over the official, the translingual over the homogeneous, and the subversive over the hegemonic. By knitting together contents and style, they had become the paladins of word-juggling. It comes as little surprise that people with overlapping cultural and linguistic identities were able to maximize the capacities of language. This chapter zooms in on these practices through three complementary prisms. First, it highlights how Malay could be used to inscribe ethnic, cultural, or regional difference. Next, it focuses on personal pronouns and their significance in expressing cultural affinity and (im)politeness. Finally, it presents a typology of irreverent language as used in Sino-Malay publications.

Along with their Eurasian, Arab, and indigenous colleagues, Chinese wordsmiths provided entertainment for the masses. Their lowbrow cultural offerings and ungoverned language practices regularly challenged prevalent power hierarchies. In that sense, the following characterizations of linguistic hierarchies in Malaysia and Egypt would be equally apt for Indonesia:

> Translingual punning and an irreverent disregard for language norms: these are absolutely central features of Malaysian sociolinguistic life, indices of the effortless heteroglossic play that exists and proliferates in the undercurrents of hegemonic languages deployed by states and other authorities.

Many of the comedic dialogues depicted in political cartoons and vaudeville repeatedly contrasted the mispronunciations of foreigners—who often played unsympathetic or villainous roles—with the "correct" pronunciation of affable Egyptian characters.[1]

Sino-Malay print culture features a vast array of imitating, lampooning, punning, swearing, and other manifestations of translingual creativity. These strategies served multiple purposes. They could be utilized to contest colonial conditions, but by putting uneducated speakers "back in their place," they also often perpetuated them. As a result, written representations of how one spoke became indicators of character and mentality.[2] In this regard, the most inventive language could be found in cartoons, comics, advertisements, and jokes sections—known as *laloetjoean* in the Netherlands Indies and *klaka-an* in the Straits Settlements—rather than the more serious prose of journalists and novelists. Despite their prominence in the vernacular press, Chinese print entrepreneurs never monopolized this satirical and otherwise subversive Malay discourse.[3] Needless to add, the vast majority of subject matter remained in the sphere of orality. Popular performance genres—such Batavia's *lenong* and Penang's *boria*—abounded in humoristic representations of Europeans, Chinese, and other groups identifiable by their "funny accents."[4] Comical songs provided another venue to push the limits of the Malay language, mix it with those of others, and contribute to the entertainment of many. However, as most of these texts were not printed, we can only guess at their contents and compare them with mediatized representations of more recent times.[5]

Such practices drew from a number of linguistic devices. From George Bernard Shaw's *Pygmalion* to José Rizal's *Noli me Tángere* and from America's blackface minstrelsy to South Africa's early theatre, written or performed manifestations of nonstandard speech have long been contrived to mark regional, ethnoracial, and/or class difference. Kwee Thiam Tjing was a famed expert in this art. In his *Indonesia dalem Api dan Bara* (Indonesia in Flames and Cinders), he masterfully portrayed the speech of the Chinese, Javanese, Madurese, Dutch, and Japanese of East Java during the tumultuous 1940s.[6] The author is best seen as the product of a long and productive tradition. Like writers from other communities, Sino-Malay novelists, journalists, and playwrights continuously generated puns, double entendres, and willful ambiguity. They mocked with equal alacrity the deficient Malay of speakers born in China, the Netherlands, or rural Java. Another major target was the artificially Europeanized Malay of Asians desperate to showcase their Western education. In a 1911 article in *Sin Po*, for instance, a certain Kim To caricatures the prose of his fellow journalist "Butatuli" for its redundant use of foreign words. It is one of the many examples of journalists scrutinizing each other's Low Malay, which, while lacking a universally adopted standard, certainly had its own esthetics. The complementarity of narrative content and linguistic style—a laughable brew of Dutch, German, and French—is clearly deliberate:

Oh, our detractors would immediately assign the title of "Doctor in the Humanities" to the writer Butatuli upon examining his articles that are replete with all sorts of foreign languages, and even notes from the Honorable Editor providing clarification. We almost want to say this title is "the will of God."	Oh, siapatah jang tida safakat dengen kami, aken lantas membri gelaran "doktor in de letterkunde" pada penoelis Butatuli, bila tilik karangannja jang disertaken roepa roepa bahasa asing, hingga dengen noot sianseng Redacteur soedah kasih *Anmerkung*. Ampir kami maoe bilang gelaran itoe *Dieu le veut*.[7]

These linguistic markers of ethnic, cultural, or educational background show up most prominently in the realm of pronouns, of which vernacular Malay had many. As with Malay varieties in general, the choice of first- and second-person singular pronouns ("I" and "you") revealed a speaker's cultural orientation (Chinese-oriented, Dutch-oriented, generic), degree of politeness (honorific, rude, neutral), or register (colloquial, formal, literary).[8] In addition, as will be discussed below, several forms of address ("Sir," "Madam," etc.) were used pronominally to clarify the relation between speech participants or targeted audiences. Irreverence was another topic of great linguistic diversity. Given the legal troubles one could encounter if the insults were too overt, this typically took place in a roundabout way. Invective-laden tirades are relatively rare in Sino-Malay print. We may call attention to a quip published in *Sin Po*'s joke section in 1949, which poked fun at the harsh pedagogical techniques of traditional fathers:

Outdated wisdom. Let us listen to uncle A Hong haranguing his child: You dog, shrimp-for-brains, buffalo-head, with your handwriting like duck feet, lazy as the devil, in short, you're considered the Black Sheep.	Ilmoe lama. Tjoba denger 'ntjek A Hong maki anaknja: asoe loe, otak oedang, kepala kebo, toelisan tjakar bebek, males seperti setan, ringkesnja dianggep Kambing Item.[9]

In most cases, however, irreverence was articulated more subtly, especially when it was directed at those in power. Here, Sino-Malay print entrepreneurs tended to show their progressive face. The jokes they published served, simultaneously, as coping mechanisms to manage life's grievances and as gateways to raise awareness about them. Under the innocuous guise of humor, journalists could tackle some of the very serious issues that affected them. One continued source of annoyance, as mentioned previously, were the racialized formulas used in governmental correspondence with Chinese and indigenous people. How would those Dutchmen like it, asked a certain P. S. Liu in the jokes section of *Hoakiao*, if we would give them a similar treatment?

GENTLEMAN...?
The Dutch are a people who take great pleasure in being called "gentleman" by Chinese and indigenous Indonesians, but they are reluctant to address those two groups with the same term; in fact many Dutchmen tend to write letters to Chinese people like this: To the "Chinese"... Imagine if we were to correspond with them like this: To "Dutchman" Billy Orangey. How would they feel if we were to do that, sour or sweet?

HEERRRR...?
Bangsa Blanda ada bangsa jang paling soeka di panggil "heer" oleh bangsa Tionghoa atau Boemipoetra, tapi tida maoe bahasaken pada itoe kadoea bangsa begitoe djoega, malahan banjak Blanda jang soeka toelis soerat kepada orang Tionghoa begini: Kapada "tjina"... Tjoba kaloe kita toelis padanja begini: Kapada "blanda" Billem (e) Orang (e). Apa jang ia nanti rasaken bila kita berboeat begitoe, asem atawa manis?[10]

Spelling is key here. In romanized Malay, deliberate acts of misspelling (cacography) could generate a range of comical effects. This is the case across a wide range of print languages. When young people in the Netherlands feel the need to mock the imperfect English of their parents or professors, *deej woed spel it laaik dis*. Indonesians might provincialize the names of politicians such as Fadli Zon and Fahri Hamzah as *Padeli Jon* and *Pahri Amjah*, typically when they are making fun of them. As for the above example, the raucously rolling /r/ in *heerrr* (gentleman) added a very indigenous touch to a European word, thereby burlesquing it. Spelling turned the "gentlemen" in question into a parochial wannabe, who could probably speak some Dutch but was unable to write in it, or the other way around. Perhaps he was "only" a local Eurasian? The concocted Dutch name *Billem (e) Orang (e)* had acquired the Javanese suffix *-e*, again indicating that it was pronounced in a heavily localized fashion. It is evidently a wordplay on Willem van Oranje (1533–84), the celebrated ancestor of the Dutch monarchy. As we will see, such linguistically encoded strategies of selfing and othering proliferate in Sino-Malay print culture.

Selfing and Othering

"A Typhoon from the West Rages across the East." So, at least, read the ominous title of a 1923 short story published in *Sin Po*.[11] Centering on a young couple about to join in matrimonial bliss, the author confected a flippant portrayal of Europeanized Peranakan society. Spoiled by their "Western upbringing that smells of butter" (Westersche opvoeding jang belepotan mentega), they denounced traditional delicacies like preserved radish (*tjaypo*) and insisted on holding a European-style wedding. The incense sticks (*hio*) quickly made way for bouquets of flowers and an orchestra obediently playing the Dutch national anthem. One of the invited guests—a millionaire's daughter donning Western clothes and twirling around the dance floor—proved incapable of eating with her hands. After trying in vain to find cutlery, she left the party on an empty stomach. Toasting their lifelong pursuit of happiness, the prospective bridegroom launched into a speech:

Mientje, now I want to exchange rings with you, which symbolizes that me and you are engaged, and I hope that you will do as required [when] you become my wife.	Mientje, sekarang ikke wil toekar ring sama jij, jang menandaken ikke dan jij al perloop, serta ikke harep jij wil doen sebagimana moestinja jij worden ikke poenja prouw.

The above sentence exhibits a Malay syntax overlaid with a patina of Dutch words. Such ways of speaking were associated with advanced stages of Westernization. It was even more scandalous—at least in the eyes of many a journalist—if this was done by women, supposedly the upholders of traditional values and family honor. Nevertheless, and to the shock of her conservative parents, the story's bride-to-be promptly returned with this string of words:

Of courrrrse, Joost, I later do like it must be as obligation husband and wife.	Tirrrrlik, Joost, ikke strakies berboeat sebagimana moet zijn as kewadjiban man en prouw.

Language is vital to these acts of self-styling, but also to their satirical portrayal. Even the names of the story's protagonists embody the clash between inherited values and Westernization. The father-in-law is introduced to the readers as Mr. Bebodor (clown) and his wife as Mrs. Selodor (a children's game), two unmistakably Betawi words. The young couple, by contrast, rejoice in names as Dutch as a windmill: Joost and Mientje. Their inauthenticity radiates from their mispronunciations, *perloop* for *verloofd* (engaged), *prouw* for *vrouw* (wife), and *tirrrrlik* for *natuurlijk* (of course). Such faux-European ways of speaking drew ample contempt. According to a 1926 *Sin Po* editorial, one among many to bemoan the loss of Chinese values, the "ugly habit" of speaking European languages reflects the vice of cultural immaturity. The adoption of foreign names, or so it was argued, stemmed from the same naïve mindset:

Also, the Chinese people here have to start making an effort to break the ugly habit of using foreign languages and names. We feel that the Chinese are no longer small children who are "proud" to have names of white people such as "Fientje," "Lotje," "Piet," etc.	Djoega orang Tionghoa disini moesti moelain berichtiar boeat boewang itoe kabiasahan djelek boeat goenaken bahasa dan nama asing. Kita rasa orang Tionghoa boekan anak ketjil lagi jang "bangga" mempoenjai nama bangsa koelit poeti sebagi "Fientje," "Lotje," "Piet" enz.¹²

While impeccable Dutch remained a prerogative of the elites, localized pidgin Dutch enlivened the streets and fueled the machinery of satire.¹³ The illustrated story "Lelakonnja 'Nir Petroes" (The Tale of Mr. Petroes) provides an illuminating example. Published in 1923 in *Sin Po*, the eponymous protagonist was characterized—in a half-Hokkien half-Malay idiom—as a person "interested in money, not in people, with a head smelling of butter" (khwa tjhi bo khwa lang dan kapala berlopotan mentega).¹⁴ This unpropitious mix of perversions made him look down on his Chinese seniors, cozy up to Europeans, and adopt the Dutch name "Nir Petroes" (D: *Meneer Petrus*). The story turned yet weirder when he extended his preferential treatment to humble Eurasian soldiers, disparagingly categorized as "thirteenth-class green Dutchmen" (Blanda idjo golongan klas 13). In an accompanying cartoon (fig. 5.1), the "European" inquires in broken Dutch: "Hi, Sir, where are you heading to?" Mispronouncing his friend's name Johan as Djohan, Petroes answers: "Morning, Mr. Johan, I just want to have a bit of fun and catch some air."

Such instances of translingual performance, credibly executed or otherwise, provided opportunities to express competing and shifting affinities. Print entrepreneurs fully realized this power. In fictional accounts, many authors infused their portrayals of people and events with non-Malay words as if to coat them with a layer of authenticity. In such cases, linguistic otherness was consciously achieved, rather than externally ascribed as in the previous examples. In the aforementioned story "Moesti Rajahken Lebih Rameh," uncle Kim Koen was deliberately framed as a traditional Singkeh. To do so convincingly, the author drew from an abundance of Hokkien words to characterize him—such as *bad djie lang* (literate person), *ngoliam* (to grumble), *taktjhelang* (scholar), and many more—even though perfectly suitable Malay words could have been used:

FIGURE 5.1. Illustration from "The Tale of Mr. Petroes" (*Sin Po* 33 [1923]), caricaturing a Chinese man (*right*) who is overly friendly to a Eurasian (*left*)

And to pride himself upon being a literate person, uncle Kim Koen also spent his spare time manufacturing Chinese gatepost couplets for his neighbors. At Chinese New Year, despite being poor, Kim Koen was quite unsatisfied if any of his neighbors failed to pay him a visit. He would grumble endlessly until the final day of the New Year celebration. But he was outlandishly happy with people who didn't forget to pay their respect at his home....

Dan boeat banggaken diri ada satoe bad djie lang, 'ntjek Kim Koen pwakangan bikinin djoega moei-twienja iapoenja tetangga-tetangga. Tiap-tiap Sintjhia 'ntjek Kim Koen kendati miskin tida senang betoel kaloe ada tetangga-tetangga jang tida perloein pergi tjari padanja. Ia ngoliam tida bisa soeda sampe sahabisnja Tjapgomeh. Tapi ia girang boekan patoet kaloe orang tida loepa dateng paytjhia padanja.... Ia kasi taoe jang ia ada satoe taktjhelang, sampe taoe

He would let them know that he was a scholar, and knew all about the sayings of Confucius. In the Four Books, he informed them, it was said that *"sin tjiong toei wan,"* and in his interpretation this book-phrase implied that people should celebrate abundantly with those who were about to draw their final breath. He had used these four characters innumerable times for inscriptions placed above the incense burner [in home altars], whenever his neighbors enlisted his help to write them.

dengen oedjar oedjar Nabi Khongtjoe. Dalem Soesi, ia kata ada dibilang, sin tjiong toei wan, dan ini tjeekoe sataoe bagimana ia artiken, bahoea orang moesti rajahken dengen satjoekoepnja sama apa jang hendak tarik napasnja pengabisan. Ini ampat letter tida taoenja ada jang paling sering ia goenaken boeat menoelis perkatahan di atas hiolouw, kaloe tetangganja minta toeloeng ia toelisin.[15]

The same tendency can be seen in journalism. Kwee Tek Hoay, in a comment on Gouw Peng Liang's alleged opposition to the Republic of China, pointed out that Java's local Chinese almost universally held pro-Qing sentiments before the ideals of the Revolution had reached them. As with the fictional account cited above, it would have been less credible for him to express this message without profusely enriching his Malay with Hokkien:

In the Sino-Malay press, almost nobody had an anti-Qing orientation; in fact, many praised that government which had shown great kindness to the overseas Chinese. One might say that at that time, all overseas Chinese were monarchists. When a dignitary visited or a holiday came up, people would raise the Dragon Flag. The birthday of the Emperor's Wife and the Guangxu Emperor were celebrated like holidays; people closed their schools and stores, even though the majority just closed their shop's windows as remains the case today.

Pers Tionghoa Melajoe ampir tida ada jang berhaloean anti-Tjhing Tiauw, malah semoea memoedji itoe pamerentah jang soedah oendjoek banjak boedi pada Hoakiauw. Boleh dibilang itoe koetika semoea Hoakiauw ada Monarchist. Kaloe dateng satoe Taydjin atawa hari besar, orang kiberken bendera Liongkie. Hari lahirnja Kokbo dan Keizer Kong Sie Koen dirajaken sabagi hari besar, orang toetoep haktong dan toko-toko, maski djoega kabanjakan tjoemah toetoep tiamtang sadja seperti djoega sekarang.[16]

The linguistic character of these descriptions—of an elderly Singkeh gentleman, and of pro-Qing sentiments in Java—conveys a shared sense of Chineseness (selfing). On the eclectic patchwork that was vernacular Malay, word choices often served as ethnolinguistic markers. Consider, for example, the use of *antjoa* (how, for what reason), *ginlan* (disgusted), and *tjialat* (tiresome), which made it hard to miss that someone came from a Hokkien background. People from West Java could in turn adorn their Low Malay with Sundanese words, such as *kasep* (handsome), *kedoehoeng* (remorse), and *wedoek* (invulnerable). Had they come from Central or East Java, they would have peppered their speech with Javanese words such as *klabakan* (to flounder), *klojongan* (to wander about), and *soengkan* (unwilling). Meanwhile, Betawi words such as *blongkotan* (unadulterated), *mendoesin* (to be aware), and *tjikoetan* (hiccups) gave people away as residents of the colony's capital. This was even more the case in oral communication, of which only a few fragments have survived.[17]

These translingual modes of selfing coexisted with deliberate representations of ungrammatical language (othering), such as the flawed Dutch of Mientje and Nir Petroes. Chinese-accented Malay, Javanese-accented Dutch, and other possible combinations signaled unproficiency and hence backwardness. The salient otherness of Singkehs, for example, rarely went unnoticed by more fluent speakers of Malay. In his 1927 *Kitab Pengetahuan Bahasa* (Book of Linguistics), the aforementioned scholar Raja Ali Haji observed: "An accent refers to people speaking languages that are not their own, thus mispronouncing the letters of other people's languages, such as ... Chinese people who attempt to say *orang* (person) in Malay but pronounce it as *onang*, or *udang* (shrimp) as *ulang*."[18] As a result, the not-yet-fluent Singkeh became a recurring stock character of Peranakan and European comedy.[19] At times he could verbalize his observations more pithily than anyone: "Olang Djawa patjot, Olang Tjina kompot, Olang Wolanda angkot" (Javanese people farm, Chinese people accumulate, Dutch people seize).[20] In the 1933 theater play *Hambanja Satoe Soedagar Radja Oewang* (The Servant of a Merchant Money King), the archetypical fresh-off-the-boat personage is immediately recognizable by his language. Greeted with laughter, or so one would imagine, he inadvertently substituted /r/ for /l/—a well-known Chinese shibboleth—and used the redundant Hokkien words *djang-koo* (to sing) and *tenglang* (Chinese):

And now I would like to sing a bit of an English song for you, but because I'm a Chinese, I'll just sing the do-re-mi. Please listen ... this is a goodbye song.	Nah sedikit-sedikit goea sekarang maoe kasih djang-koo lagoe ingglis, tapi sebab goea orang tenglang, djadi njanjiken doo, lee, mienja sadja. Dengellah ... ini ada lagoe selamaat belpisah.[21]

The accents of other ethnicities were prolifically made fun of as well. In his 1933 novel *Naga Poeti* (The White Dragon), Tjie Tek Goan parodied Japanese soldiers along with their speech. He nicknamed them *Kateto*, seemingly a pun on the anti-Japanese slur *kate* (midget). Since the story is set in China, the Japanese men in question would not have spoken Malay. Even so, their tendency to pronounce the /l/ as /r/ was apparently received wisdom among the book's readers. We can only imagine how the Malay of Japanese immigrants, many of whom were business rivals and political foes of the Chinese, was mimicked in oral communication. It is no surprise, then, to find Sino-Malay writers interweaving popular fiction with anti-Japanese rhetoric. This sentence, uttered by a Japanese villain, was clearly conceived to make him unlikable on linguistic as well as moral grounds:

"Neverrr mind!" said the Japanese Kateto. "This time we failed, next time I'll whack them some more!! League of Nations? Ah, I don't care about them!"	"Neverrr mind!" kata si Kateto Japan. "Sekari ini gagar, raen kari goea poekoer ragi!! Vorkenbond? Ah—goea tida perdoeli sama dia!"[22]

Chinese authors, along with many others writing in Malay, also mercilessly mocked the peculiar speech of Dutchmen—especially of the ill-tempered variety—with their trademark furor of interjections, lapses into foreigner talk, and unnatural constructions. The authors Kwee Tek Hoay and Tan Boen Soan were particularly gifted at reproducing this clumsy patois. The former, in his 1930 novel *Zonder Lentera* (Without a Lantern), represented the Malay of an angry Dutch police commissioner as follows:

"You don't need to inquire about my wife and children!" snapped de Stijf: "God dammit, you are so ill-mannered! Now get out of here!"	"Tida perloe kowe tjari taoe dari halnja saja poenja njonja dan anak!" membentak de Stijf: "God verdomme, kowe koerang adjar sekali! Lekas pigi dari sini!"[23]

On the opposite side of the law we encounter another cantankerous Hollander, aptly named Van Brommepot (McGrumbler). This specimen was portrayed as a notorious habitué of brothels in Tan Boen Soan's 1937 novel *Kembang Latar* (Prostitute). Predictably, his Malay was of the abominable kind so often associated with his nation. The following excerpt recounts his negotiations with a procuress over the price of an underage prostitute. While the relation between moral and linguistic decrepitude materializes subliminally, it is nevertheless hard to escape:

Van Brommepot became angry: "Why, goshdarnit, do you think I'm not aware of your deceit? Okay, I'll tip you two hundred guilders and the child fifty, and otherwise I'll file a report to the police that you've opened an illegal brothel, you old ... I know your tricks, eh, old bag! Anyway, here's your two hundred guilders and shut your trap, okay?"

Van Brommepot djadi goesar: "Wel, godverdikkie, apa kowe kira akoe tida taoe kowe poenja tipoe? Soeda, akoe persen kaoe ƒ200 dan itoe anak ƒ50- of akoe lantas rapport pada politie kowe boeka bordeel gelap, ouwe ... akoe taoe kaoe poenja akal, he, oudwijf! Enfin, hier heb je die ƒ 200- enne toetoep kowe poenja batjot ja!"[24]

As many Chinese writers would insist, the Malay of Dutchmen—even those from the higher strata of society—was of the basest sort, charged with impolite speech and cusswords.[25] Their excessive use of *poenja* in possessive constructions, the phrase-initial position of the demonstratives *ini* (this) and *itoe* (that), and the pronouns *goea* (I) and *loe* (you) were characteristic of Low Malay in general. Indeed, these particular features were also found among Chinese speakers. Somewhat more idiosyncratically, Europeans were known for their usage of the impolite Javanese second-person suffix *kowe* (or *kwee, kwé, koewe,* etc.).[26] Such pronominal choices will be discussed next.

What Are Your Pronouns?

The semiweekly *Oetoesan Borneo* (Borneo Messenger; Pontianak, 1927) was one of the few Sino-Malay periodicals from the western part of that island, making it a valuable source for historians and linguists alike. In the city of Pontianak, situated closer to British North Borneo than to Batavia, a homegrown type of Malay served to facilitate communication between its ethnic Malays, Chinese, Arabs, and several indigenous peoples. In 1928, the *Oetoesan Borneo* provided an insightful vista into this vernacular:

Sunday's claptrap. To be observed by those who wish to observe it.
Kwik: "Hello! Mr. Kwek! Did you have fun going out by taxi?"
Kwek: "Yes, Kwik! But you shouldn't think I just went to get some fresh air without anything in my pocket!

Omong kosong hari Minggoe. Perhatikanlah siapa jang maoe perhatikan.
Kwik: "Halo! Mester Kwek! Apa kaoe soedah poeas pelezier dengen taxi?"
Kwek: "Ja, Wik! Tapi entê djangan kira, ana tjoema makan angin sadja

Anyway... dude! Where is Kwak?..."

zonder wat in de zak! Maar... vent! Mana si Wak?..."

Kwak: "Ah, let's sit down first. Have a seat! Boooy, get us three glasses of lime soda!"

Kwak: "Ach, marilah doedoek doeloe. Tjo'a! Boooy, kasih djeroek soda 3 glas!"

Kwek: "What's up, Kwik? I heard you went to Kampoeng Loear?"

Kwek: "Apa kabar Wik? Goea dengar you ada pergi ka Kp. Loear?"[27]

This conversation affords a number of sociolinguistic observations. Kwik's language is unmarked. His usage of the pronoun *kaoe* (you; coll.) is the default in Pontianak Malay. Kwek must be of Arabic descent, as he uses the Arabic-derived pronouns *ana* (I) and *entê* (you). He later also uses *goea* (I)—ultimately derived from Hokkien but widespread in generic spoken Malay—and the English pronoun *you*. Other English loanwords in this short conversation are *mester* (mister) and *boy*. Kwak appears to be Chinese, as he uses the Teochew phrase *tjo'a* (have a seat). These pronominal choices speak volumes about the ethnicity of the speech participants and their relation to each other. As their use was highly intuitive, pronouns were rarely commented upon. Lie Kim Hok's 1891 *Batavian Malay*, for example, simply gives a juxtaposition:

To be used to substitute one's own name: *goewa, akoe, saja, hamba, kami, kita,* or *kita-orang*.... To substitute the name of the person one is addressing: *loe, koewe, kaoe* or *angkaoe, kamoe, kaoe-orang,* or *kamoe-orang*.... To substitute the name of the entity that is being discussed: *dija* or *ija, ija-orang* or *marika, ini* and *itoe*.

Jang dipake akan mengganti nama sendiri: *goewa, akoe, saja, hamba, kami, kita,* atawa *kita-orang*.... Akan ganti namanja orang, pada siapa orang bitjara: *loe, koewe, kaoe* atawa *angkaoe, kamoe, kaoe-orang* atawa *kamoe-orang*.... Akan mengganti namanja paada jang diomongkan: *dija* atawa *ija, ija-orang* atawa *marika, ini* dan *itoe*.[28]

All these pronouns were known to Java's Malay-speaking communities, but their usage was not identical. The formation of plural pronouns through the word *orang* (person) was distinctly vernacular and frowned upon by writers of High Malay. The pronoun *hamba* (I; hon.), conversely, was restricted to literary language.[29] Likewise, such pronouns as *angkaoe* or *engkau* (you), *kami* (we; excl.), and *mereka* or *marika* (they) were known and used by Chinese print entrepreneurs, but regarded as rather formal. Not mentioned by Lie Kim Hok but sporadically seen in twentieth-century Sino-Malay texts is the pronoun *beliau* (s/he; hon.), which was used when referring to people deemed worthy of respect.

Needless to say, excessive linguistic formality—through the use of pronouns or otherwise—violated the language esthetics of popular culture. This is illustrated in the aforementioned *Pantoen Tjapgome*. In one scene, the poem explicitly correlates a disappointing theater performance with the usage by its actors of literary rather than colloquial Malay pronouns:

But even though they performed a Chinese story	Tapi sedeng lelakonnja tjerita Tjina
With costumes like those of the Cantonese opera	Dengen pakeannja seperti wajang Makau
There was still something imperfect about it	Toch diliatnja tida djadi sampoerna
Because they were saying *hamba* and *engkau*.	Sebab mengomongnja: hamba dan engkau.[30]

It almost goes without saying that the audience would have preferred the Sino-Malay pronouns *goea* (I) and *loe* (you), which have entered numerous other Malay varieties. Other ways of addressing people included the pronominal use of their name or an ethno-specific form of address. *Baba* was used for Peranakan men, *toean* (Hk: *tōan*) for European or highly respected Chinese or Arab men, and *njonja* and *nona* for respectively married and unmarried Chinese, Arab, European, or Eurasian women. Specific forms of address for Chinese individuals included a series of Hokkien-derived kinship terms and honorifics.[31] When the ethnicity of the addressee was unspecified, one could always resort to *sobat* (friend).

The pronoun *goea* (I), also written as *goewa*, is derived from Hokkien *góa* in the same meaning.[32] Its second-person counterpart *loe* (you) goes back to Hokkien *lú*, which is a substandard form of *lí*.[33] The use of *goea* and *loe* was very widespread among the Indies Chinese, who had long considered it acceptable even to older interlocutors. Yet these pronouns were impolite against indigenous people. Lim Hiong Seng's *Manual of the Malay Colloquial* provides some context:

> *Gua* is a Chinese word, and is only used by the Babas among themselves. They do not use it in conversation with the other nationalities; with whom they use the word *saya*.
>
> *Lu* is a Chinese word, and is generally used by the Babas among themselves. It is better for Europeans to use *lu* than *angkau* to the Babas and Chinese of equal or inferior rank. But *lu* is never used in polite conversation.[34]

Several other Malay phrasebooks from the Straits Settlements remind their readers to restrict the usage *lu* to Chinese people.[35] These warnings were anything but redundant. With no shortage of bewilderment, Munsyi Abdullah recalls in his autobiography that his former employer Thomas Stamford Raffles once resorted to *lu* in a heated conflict with a number of Malay chiefs. In the Netherlands Indies, not-so-fluent Dutchmen regularly shocked their company by using *loe* or *kwé* to indigenous gentry.[36] People so addressed obviously took offense to these pronouns, which implied familiarity if not inferiority. In this arena, we can see additional examples of Chinese print entrepreneurs using their outlets to combat retrograde linguistic practices. A journalist for the *Ien Po* (Merciful Newspaper; Batavia, 1917) objected to the usage of *loe* in court, as it conveyed blatant disrespect to the Chinese or indigenous persons who stood accused. He asserted:

The word "loe" for an accused editor, even if he is of the Chinese or indigenous race, is inappropriate.	Perkata'an "loe" bagi saorang persakitan redacteur, kendatipoen bangsa Tiong Hoa atawa Boemipoetra ada koerang pantes.[37]

This complaint did not stand in isolation. Reporting on the 1931 Congress of Indonesian Journalists, an anonymous Chinese author voiced a similar concern. As he highlighted, the usage of *loe* was only appropriate when addressing people of extremely low social prestige:

When a journalist labeled as *Inlander* [native] is involved in a lawsuit, that journalist acquires the appellation *loe*, as if they're investigating a CRIMINAL or SMUGGLER.	Djikalau seorang Journalist jang bertjap Inlander dapet perkara maka si Journalist itoe dapet titel LOE, sebagi memeriksa kepada PENDJAHAT atau PENJAMOEN.[38]

Despite frequent claims to the contrary, polite language is well attested in Sino-Malay prose. Hokkien-derived pronouns could convey multiple layers of respect. A common first-person pronoun to converse with elders or superiors was *boanseng* (junior). Its second-person counterpart was *sianseng* (senior), which could be used to address respected men. Another honorific first-person pronoun was *owe*, also written as *owek, owee, oewee,* or *oweh*. In Hokkien, *ôe* is the polite way to answer to a call. In the Malay of the Indies Chinese, however, male speakers often used *owe* pronominally (I).[39] To some late colonial writers, this "*owe* language" embodied everything that was substandard, outdated, and parochial. It was clear that Chinese writers were not unequivocal on this matter. One 1930 article in *Sin Po* launched a full-scale attack on the colloquial Malay of Peranakans, its copious borrowings from Dutch, and its usage of *owe*. The pronoun's unfortunate similarity with the sound of vomiting had not gone unnoticed by the author. Once again, South Africa was invoked as a cautionary example of linguistic degeneration, echoing hegemonic Dutch tropes on language purity:

The Baba Chinese drunkards over here also might like to create their "special" language according to the South African model, and that special language will possibly sound as follows: "Wow, man, I totally didn't know." This worthless stuff is Malay with a Javanese accent rather than a "special" Indo language, and from this "language" no beautiful literature or distinct culture will ever emerge, because an "owek" culture can only make people throw up, because . . . [sound of retching]!	Kaoem mabok baba Tionghoa di sini djoega brangkali maoe terbitken bahasa "speciaal" menoeroet toeladan dari Afrika Selatan dan boleh djadi itoe bahasa speciaal boenjinja ada seperti brikoet: "Waah zek, owwekk mak tidak taoh." Ini met verlof ada bahasa Melajoe dengen accent Djawa dan boekan bahasa indo "speciaal" dan dari ini matjem "bahasa" tida aken terbit literatuur bagoes atawa cultuur sendiri sebab cultuur "owek" tjoema bisa bikin orang moenta oeger sebab . . . oweh.[40]

Pronouns could also give away someone's status as a newcomer to the colony. A Singkeh speaker of Hakka, for example, would sometimes use *ngai* (I) instead of *goea*. The second-person pronoun *li* rather than *loe* was a shibboleth of foreign rather than local Hokkien.[41] Such speakers could also use *lan* (instead of *goea*) for the first-person singular. So, in the aforementioned story "Poetra Fortuna," an employer addressed his employee with *li* and referred to himself with *lan*, indicating mainland Chinese or Straits origins. His employee used the localized pronoun *owe*, implying that he grew up in the Indies:

"What kind of financial loss, boss? I didn't suffer any loss." "Yes, but it's best if you just take [my money], because if not, my conscience would be distressed."	"Karoegian apa, tauwkee? Owe tida ada roegi apa-apa." "Ja, tapi baek li trima sadja, sebab kaloe 'nda, nanti lan poenja liangsim 'nda enak."[42]

The usage of *lan* as a singular pronoun was relatively uncommon. In Hokkien, *lán* tends to be plural (we; incl.).[43] Equally nonmainstream were the pronouns *gwan* (I; we) and *lin* (you), which are chiefly found in East Javanese periodicals.[44] To give just one example, the 1929 serialized story "Penghidoepannja Njonja

Millionnair" (Life of a Millionaire Lady) features both pronouns in the context of a friendly conversation:

I'm very happy to have met you, and I foresee that you will certainly make great fortune in the future. I hope you would like to pay me a visit at Ciherang, where I trust my family will be even happier to get to know you than I am myself.	Gwan ada amat girang bisa berdjoempa pada lin, dan gwan ramalken nistjaja lin ada mempoenjain peroentoengan jang besar di kamoedian hari. Gwan ingin lin soeka bikin perkoendjoengan pada gwan di Tjiherang, dimana gwan pertjaja jang gwan poenja familie nanti berasa girang boeat berkenalan pada lin lebih-lebih dari gwan sendiri.[45]

Pronouns from Dutch are also frequently attested. They carried a different set of sociolinguistic implications. While some Peranakans adopted all Dutch pronouns in their Malay, the first- and second-person equivalents *ik* (or *ikke*) and *jij* predominated.[46] In popular literature, these words were associated with insufferable devotees of all things Western. Their usage undoubtedly reflected a self-styling practice, yet they also provide another instance of print entrepreneurs fusing language with ideological cues. The 1937 novel *O, Prempoean!* (Oh, Women!) by Pouw Kioe An, which was based on a theater play, provides a case in point. Its antihero Corrie is a Westernized young mother described as "fun-loving and unwilling to take care of her household." She embarks on a fatal affair with Kong Ik, "who is well-acquainted with the freedoms of Westerners." Their ill-fated dalliance—of course she died at the end of the story—was initially restricted to "flirting and continuously displaying affection with words uttered in Dutch."[47] Pouw Kioe An left no opportunity unexploited to portray his archetypical femme fatale as a fluent speaker of Europeanized Malay. As in earlier examples, he imparted an unspoken yet inescapable correlation between moral and linguistic pollution:

Corrie lunged at the man, kissed Kong Ik passionately and said: "Oh, you don't know ... My love is bigger than Mount Gede, taller than Mount Semeru, so that I left my husband and children to be there for you."	Corrie toebroek itoe lelaki, tjioemin Kong Ik dengen bernafsoe seraja berkata: "Oh, jij tida taoe ... ikke poenja tjinta lebih besar dari goenoeng Gede, lebih tinggi dari goenoeng Smeroe, sampe tinggalken laki dan anak boeat bela jij."[48]

A very similar account is given in Yang-Lioe's 1937 novel *Pelita Penghidoepan* (The Lamp of Life), which narrates the scandalous affair of a young Chinese woman—incidentally also named Corry—with the well-heeled playboy Tan Tik Sing. When Tik Sing finally convinces Corry to leave her fiancé, it is almost redundant to point out that this unholy proposal is expressed entirely in Dutch-inflicted Malay, along with its trademark pronouns and expletives:

Damn it! That engagement may be canceled. I love you, we will get married. Just leave it to your siblings to cancel your engagement.	Verrek! Itoe pertoendangan boleh dipoetoesken. Ik tjinta jij, kita nanti menika. Jij poenja pertoendangan serahken sadja pada jij poenja soedara boeat poetoesken.⁴⁹

The Dutch pronoun *jij* had a polite equivalent *U* (you; hon.), which is occasionally encountered in Sino-Malay texts. It was sometimes confused with *Uw* (your; hon.). More so than in colloquial language, this pronoun was used in advertisements. A 1936 promotion of popular martial arts books, for example, addressed its targeted clientele with this loan-pronoun, merging linguistic creativity with commercial opportunism:

A nice offer	Satoe penawaran bagoes
If you send 0.70 guilders, you will receive through free home delivery: one volume of the book Three Generations of Chivalrous Men, ... If you send 3.65 guilders, we will send to your home: one volume of the book Three Generations of Chivalrous Men, ... so that you'll save more than 1.40 guilders.	Kaloe U kirim oewang f0.70, U aken trima franco di roemah: satoe djilid boekoe Sam Tay Kie Hiap, ... Kaloe U kirim oewang f3.65, kita aken kirim sampe di U poenja roemah: Satoe djilid boekoe Sam Tay Kie Hiap, ... hingga U djadi oentoeng f1.40 lebih.⁵⁰

Predictably, this deluge of Dutch pronouns triggered frustration among society's less Westernized individuals. Lee Soen Liang's short play "Njonja mantoe modern" (A Modern Mother-in-Law) contains a striking example. In a rather hilarious quarrel, the traditional mother-in-law figure Ms. Koe Nio lashes out against her prospective daughter-in-law Elsje. Both protagonists are symbolically named: as we have seen before, Asian names represented rigid conservatism and Western ones slick modernity. Elsje had indeed been inculcated with European subjects at school, yet despite her impressive educational record she proved farcically unable to prepare dinner. And, to add insult to injury, she littered her Malay with Dutch pronouns:

Elsje: "I don't know. I told you I can't cook. At school we never learned to cook; we only learn Dutch, English, philosophy."	Elsje: "Ik tida taoe. Ik soedah bilang ik tida bisa masak. Di Sekolahan kita blon perna bladjar masak; kita tjoema bladjar bahasa Blanda, Inggris, Philosofie."
Ms. Koe Nio (impatient): "What's with all this *ak-ak ik-ik*?! I don't understand what *ak-ik ak-ik* means. I can't speak Dutch. Just say *saya*, don't you *ik* me when you're talking to me! What's the use of learning all about philosophy when you can't even cook beef soup?"	Entjim Koe Nio (Tida sabar): "Apa itoe ak-ak ik-ik! Goea tida mengarti apa itoe ak-ik ak-ik. Goea tida bisa Olan-sprek. Bilang sadja 'Saya,' tida boleh ngomong sama goea pake ik-ikkan! Apa goenanja loe bladjar segala Pilo-sapi kaloe tida bisa masak Sop Sampi?"⁵¹

Ms. Koe Nio's angry rant is a treasure trove of linguistic creativity. She interprets the Dutch word *philosophie* (philosophy) as a derivation of Malay *sapi* (beef), prompting her to recommend the kitchen over the classroom. She substantiates her self-proclaimed inability to speak Dutch by calling it—in a thick Malay accent—*Olan-sprek* instead of *Hollandsch spreken*. She then creates the impromptu expression *pake ik-ikkan* (to use *ik* all the time). Linguistic markers of Dutchness, then, could be used for selfing, othering, and—in the above case—self-othering. The humorous effects of doing so were well understood by Chinese playwrights, yet by no means restricted to them. In the *Pembrita-India* (Indian Messenger; Padang, 1922), the mouthpiece of West Sumatra's Indian Peranakan community, one writer complained that "foreign orientals" on public transportation were charged more than indigenous people. Since he had to pay European prices, he jested, he had apparently achieved Europeanness. This epiphany was embellished with the Dutch pronoun *ik* and the particle *zeg*, demonstrating once more the co-constitutiveness of narrative content and linguistic style:

If an Indian, Arab, Chinese, etc. would enter a second-class train, that person would be charged a higher fee than our indigenous brothers. Why??? Well, in this regard I've definitely been transformed into a European!	Djikalau sekiranja seorang Keling, Arab, Tionghoa d.s.b. menoempang kereta api kelas doea maka orang itoe dipoengoet bajaran lebih daripada saudara kita Boemipoetra. Kenapa??? Och, disini ik soedah didjadikan European, zeg!⁵²

A Panorama of Irreverence

In 1939, amidst Japan's military incursions into China, a particularly sharp-edged diatribe appeared in the weekly *Kung Yen*. Like many other Chinese institutions, this newspaper had adopted a fiercely anti-Japanese stance.[53] To their chagrin, a small number of Malay newspapers exhibited Japanophile propensities. A prominent example was the *Tjaja Timoer* (Eastern Light; Batavia, 1936) of Parada Harahap. Few could have phrased these frustrations better than *Kung Yen*'s editor Tay Tong, who raised his pen to spurn the Japanese, the Dutch, and especially their indigenous supporters. It is a great illustration of the combative language so characteristic of Sino-Malay print culture. One prominent feature in the text is the aforementioned misspelling of words—such as *Wollanda* (Dutch; Ml: *Olanda*) and *rrrresident* (Resident)—to underscore that the newspaper's enemies were contemptible morally as well as linguistically:

The newspaper of Japan's slaves "Tjaja Timoer" (with only fifty subscribers) feels proud that Dutch newspapers occasionally quote its writings. . . . Being quoted by a "Dutch newspaper" seems to be an "honor" of extraordinary magnitude for servile people like Parada Harahap, as is the case for many people of his sort who feel proud to be . . . the domestic servants of the Governor-General or the toilet cleaners of the Resident! . . . What should we care about whether Jan from this or that newspaper, or the Bureau of Literature and their news overview, ever takes our "stuff" into account or not. Because we don't care! The political, social, etc. fate of our Chinese people does not depend on Jan, Piet, or Klaas, nor on other persons or other races, but on ourselves and our ancestral country.	Koran boedak Djepang "Tjaja Timoer" (dengen tjoema 50 abonné's) merasa bangga jang kadang-kadang koran Blanda petik iapoenja toelisan . . . Dipetik oleh "koran Wollanda" boeat manoesia bersifat boedak sebagi Parada Harahap roepanja ada "kahormatan" jang terlampau besarnja, seperti djoega banjak manoesia model dia merasa bangga djadi . . . djongos G.G. atawa djadi toekang bersiken kakoes rrrresident! . . . Apa kita ferdoeli pada Jan dari nieuwsblad ini of itoe, dan tentang Volkslectuur poenja overzicht, liat poen ini "barang" kitaorang belon perna. Sebab kaga ferdoeli! Kita bangsa Tionghoa poenja nasib politiek, sociaal enz. kaga bergantoeng pada Jan, Piet, of Klaas dan djoega kaga dari laen orang dan laen bangsa, tapi pada kita sendiri dan negeri laloehoer kita.[54]

From the early twentieth century, journalists writing in Low Malay had developed a commendable expertise in the art of vituperation. *Bin Seng* (Voice of the People; Batavia, 1922), a short-lived newspaper linked to *Sin Po*, regularly attacked more conservative Sino-Malay newspapers such as *Perniagaän* (Commerce; Batavia, 1902) and *Djawa-Tengah* (Central Java; Semarang, 1910). One editorial piece from 1922 accused both newspapers of *idiotisme* and promised to make short shrift of their respective boards, concluding with a poem:

Mr. Gouw Soeng Seng	Toean Gouw Soeng Seng
We're going to dry-fry you	Kita nanti gongseng
[and when we're done]	[dan nanti bikin]
Mr. Kwee Tee Tie	Toean Kwee Kee Tie
Will be left moaning.	Sampe merinti-rinti.[55]

The not-so-revolutionary Sino-Malay newspapers—with *Perniagaän* leading the way—were inclined to respond with equal acrimony. *Perniagaän* was the mouthpiece of Chinese officials who largely conformed to Dutch rule. In the heat of the anti-Japanese trade boycotts of 1923, a number of pro–*Sin Po* activists had smeared the building of their long-time rival with tar to punish them for their inactivity.[56] The latter immediately published an abuse-laden tirade titled "Tole, Abis Napas" (You Boys, All out of Breath). The usage of the colloquial Javanese word *tole* (boy) was deliberate and intended to belittle their detractors. *Perniagaän* condemned *Sin Po* for their childish actions, but also for their alleged inefficiency in achieving real progress. It is a prime example of putting somebody in their place using vernacular Malay:

First and foremost, regarding the boycott movement, *Sin Po* accuses us of snuffing out the fire of that movement, only because we don't want to yell like a bunch of alley dogs, which only dare to bark from underneath a building.... *Sin Po* still lacks the courage to articulate their position in the matter, not a word leaves their mouths, they only hide their heads in their hands. Hey, the actions of you boys [whippersnappers] are too lightweight, more lightweight than West Javanese tobacco!	Paling teroetama, perkara gerakan boycot, *Sinpo* toedoe kita bikin dingin apinja itoe gerakan, tjoema lantaran kita tida maoe bertreak setjara andjing kampoeng, jang tjoema brani menggonggong dari kolong bale.... *Sinpo* sampe sekarang tida brani njatain iapoenja haloean dalem hal itoe, tida kata ngak atawa ngoek tinggal oempetken tengkorak sadja. Ha, tole-tole [katjoen-entong] poenja actie terlaloe seboel, lebi seboel dari tembako [m]ole![57]

Such irreverent language was one of the driving forces of Sino-Malay print culture, inviting a closer look at the interconnected practices of coarseness, swearing, satire, and puns. Like any more-or-less functional society, swearing (*maki-maki*) was an integral part of daily life, and speakers of Malay had a well-stocked repository of insults (*tjatjian*) at their disposal. One of the most versatile swear words of those days was without a doubt *bangsat* (bedbug; Hk. *bák-sat*), a widespread Hokkien loan albeit almost never recognized as such. On account of its parasitic connotations, *bangsat* primarily came to denote a vagabond or morally despicable person. It was written as *mangsat* when pronounced by nonfluent Chinese interlocutors. This profanity also surfaced in Dutch newspapers, which frequently reported its usage against policemen or private individuals, after which the culprit was fined. It was not the only animal name used in swearing. The term *koenjoek* (macaque) was reserved for people deemed exceedingly stupid or ill-behaved, whereas *boeaja* (crocodile), *boeaja darat* (monitor lizard), and *koetjiah* (turtle) denoted womanizers and *bandot* (billy-goat) referred to lascivious old men. The word *badjing* (squirrel) yielded the derivation *badjingan*, which denoted quick-fingered, agile opportunists, rascals, and thieves. A number of other animal names were likewise used beyond their zoological sense.[58]

Naturally, not all swear words were taken from the animal kingdom. An assorted string of insults suggested mental incapability.[59] In addition, we find *anak sambel* (son of a bitch; lit. child of chili sauce), *anak setan* (child of Satan), *boesoek* (rotten), *djahanam* (lowlife), *ketjoe* (bandit), *toea bangka* (old sod), *toekang bantahan* (troublemaker), and *toekang sikoet* (swindler) in Sino-Malay texts. Words from other languages provided additional pejorative material. The Dutch exclamations *godverdomme* (goddammit), *onzin* (nonsense), *snert* (useless), and *verrek* (damn) quickly entered the language of those who knew Dutch or pretended to do so. In the latter case, the first expletive was pronounced as *hotperdom* and the last as *prèk*. A 1923 cartoon published in *Sin Po* depicts a low-ranked indigenous policeman littering his Malay with mispronounced Dutch exclamations and phrases from Javanese while trying to arrest a Sundanese-speaking prostitute (fig. 5.2). Such Dutch profanities coexisted with their Malay equivalents, such as *boeset* (damn), *mampoes loe* (drop dead), *poeki ajam* (chicken vagina), *persetan* (to the Devil), and *tai koetjing* (bullshit, lit. cat shit). Dutch loan-insults included *ezelskop* (donkey head), *idioot* (idiot), *schreeuwer* (loudmouth), while *anak kamtjekan* (worm-infected kid), *anak tjaptjay* (mongrel; lit. chop suey kid), and *botawlo* (idler) were Hokkien-inspired. Swear words of a more vulgar character—including those based on sex and genitals—were uncommon in print, presumably because editors might get in trouble for publishing them.[60] At times, they surface in unexpected places. In the classical Malay *Syair Siti Zubaidah* (Poem of Siti Zubaidah), for example, a quarrelsome Chinese supercargo is

FIGURE 5.2. Illustration from a short story in *Sin Po* (38 [1923]), depicting a Javanese policeman yelling mispronounced Dutch obscenities to a Sundanese prostitute

repeatedly cited as saying *funi cukung*, which I believe reflects the Hokkien phrase *phok lí chó-kong* (fuck your great-grandfather).[61]

Newspapers also facilitated more subtle ways of insulting people. Romanized Malay had the advantage over Jawi of being able to represent minor phonological nuances. As a result, it could easily mark "funny" Malay pronunciations. We have already called attention to speakers whose rolling /r/ gave away their provincial origins. Cacography often affected seemingly reputable words, whose meanings were then inflated: *gollans* or *olan* (D: *Hollands*) was not quite Dutch, an *intelektoewil* (D: *intellectueel*) not a genuine intellectual, *nongkoprasie* (D: *non-cooperatie*) a diluted form of noncooperation, an *ooropian* (D: *Europeaan*) a European-on-paper, a *mepro* or *djipro* (D: *mevrouw, juffrouw*) hardly the European ladies they hoped to pass for, an *oenipestet* (D: *universiteit*) rarely a top-ranked university, and *kongsikeweng* (D: *consequent*) anything but consistent. More orthographic mockery can be seen in a 1927 *Sin Po* article, which takes issue with people's cheap admiration for Western degrees. The Dutch word for Master of Laws (*meester in de rechten*) is again spelled with a rolling /r/, confirming that the holder of this title will never be a real European. The piece furthermore contains an untranslatable pun. The Dutch word *recht* can denote "law" as well as "right," so that someone with a law degree is caricatured as always being right in the eyes of the naïve public:

If some LL.M. takes the word, people are suddenly amazed by his title Master of Laws, and think he's a master of everything, and always "right" in his opinions. . . .	Kaloe satoe Mr. jang angkat bitjara, lantas orang kasima pada itoe gelaran meester in de rrrechten, dan kira ia ada meester dalem segala apa, dan selaloe "recht"

If somebody who isn't "highly educated" at an *oenipestet* says the same thing, people would certainly ridicule him, "other people know that too"; but if it's some doctor, or LL.M., or Dr., or B.A., or M.A. who says it, suddenly everyone is impressed and behaves differently.	dalem ia-poenja anggepan.... Kaloe orang tida "terpeladjar tinggi" di oenipestet kata begitoe, orang tentoe djengekin padanja "orang laen djoega taoe"; tapi kaloe satoe doctor, atawa Mr., atawa Dr., atawa B.A., atawa M.A. jang bilang itoe, lantas pada djadi kagoem dan djadi laen.[62]

It must be reiterated that translingual puns were made by all groups with proficiency in Low Malay. In 1946, the newly established *Malang Post* called attention to the deliberate butchering of Chinese names by Dutch journalists. Anything but innocent was their corruption of Soe Lie Piet (1904–88) into Loe Sie Piet, evidently a pun on *loe sipit* (you're slant-eyed).[63] Of a more harmless nature was a cartoon in *Sin Po* depicting three customers ordering hotchpotch (*snert*) in a Western restaurant. The waiter promptly yelled: "All three want hotchpotch!" (Tiga-tiga ... snert!), which could also be interpreted as "All three are useless!"[64] Other translingual puns required knowledge of Hokkien. In the aforementioned play *Hambanja Satoe Soedagar Radja Oewang*, the sentence "Phoa Sie is my secretary" could be interpreted as "My secretary is half dead" (Hk: *pòaⁿ-sí*), leading to an amusing deal of confusion about the good man's mortality. To further stir the translingual hornet's nest, the moderately offensive word for "dead" was taken from Dutch (*dood*) rather than Malay (*mati*):

Mr. To Bak King: "Oh, good heavens! Phoa Sie is my secretary." Swie Phoa Sie: "Why ... Hey! Sir you must be confused! I'm still alive, so why do you call me half dead? What's up with that?"	Thaukee To Bak King: "Aija Tjikoah! Phoa Sie akoe poenja djoeroe toelis." Swie Phoa Sie: "Eh ... Loh! Thaukee bengkali lingloeng, nih! La oewee kan masi idoep, kok dikatain setengah dood. Kenapa sih!"[65]

Hokkien puns also enabled writers to sneak in vulgarities that might otherwise get stuck in the mire of (self-)censorship. A 1914 editorial published in *Pewarta Soerabaia* (Surabaya Messenger) lambasted the Dutch media for their empty promises of a bright future under European leadership. Unimpressed, the anonymous writers vented their displeasure by faux-accidentally swapping two similar-sounding Hokkien words: "underway" (*kiâⁿ-kàu*) and "menstruating" (kiâⁿ-keng). Their likening of European colonialism to physical inconvenience presents us with another instance of Sino-Malay burlesque:

Yes, yes, the foundations for the prosperity of Europeans are felicitous, the fortune of Europeans is menstruating—oops, sorry readers—we wanted to say, their fortune is underway!	Ja, ja, dasar peroentoengan orang Europa moedjoer, orang Europa Djieoennja Kiaking, eh ma'af pembatja, kita maoe bilang Djieoennja Kiakauw!⁶⁶

We find another example in Kho An Kim's *Pendjara Fasis* (The Fascist Prison), which recounts the experiences of North Sumatra's Chinese during World War II. When the Japanese army conquered Medan in 1942, as the author recalls, local children got away with shouting *Pangsai!* (take a shit) instead of "Banzai!"⁶⁷ Again, the pun succeeded by virtue of its phonological proximity to a safe word. Accidental slips of the pen provided another prolific source of entertainment. Many journalists took pleasure in outwitting their colleagues, which involved ferreting through each other's work in search of clumsy literal translations from Dutch. In one instance, a mistranslation of the Dutch word *staat*—which can mean "status," "country," or "standing"—prompted a *Sin Po* editor to tease an inexperienced colleague by adding of pun of his own, involving an erection:

One Chinese-Malay newspaper had to translate "because of her marriage she shared her husband's status" but translated it as "because of her marriage, she shared her husband's ... country." Good thing they didn't translate: shared her husband's "standing up" (*staat*).	Satoe koran Tionghoa Melajoe moesti salin "door haar huwelyk volgt zij den staat van haar man" dan ia salin "sebab ia poenja nikahan, ia djadi moesti toeroet soeaminja poenja ... negri." Baeknja ia tida salin: toeroet soeaminja "berdiri" (staat).⁶⁸

Despite drawing from various languages, the examples in this chapter were distinctly localized. Chinese print entrepreneurs spearheaded—but were not alone in—a print culture that utilized vernacular language in its most creative form, fusing image and word, highlighting grassroots issues, and engaging with hegemonic narratives, either defiantly or complicity. They did so through lexical choices, particularly in the domain of pronouns, which conveyed neutral, pro-Chinese, or pro-European cultural orientations. They also ridiculed people's views by mocking their accents. Two types of Malay received the lion's share of scorn: the ungrammatical Malay of newly arrived and/or poorly socialized outsiders, and the artificial Malay of people keen to flaunt their Westernization.

A surefire method to disparage such individuals was to dwell in detail on the words they mispronounced. This could be done most easily in the Latin script, although the mock-substitution of /r/ for /l/ also took place in Jawi. Another option was to write contemptuous poems or short articles about one's enemies. And, if all else failed to get the point across, Sino-Malay also featured a panorama of potent profanities. This extensive range of linguistic phenomena is crucial to appreciate the expressive power of Malay as used and produced in the vernacular press.

Epilogue
AN IMPORTANT HISTORICAL MONUMENT

People with migratory backgrounds tend to reinvent themselves, sometimes minimally and sometimes dramatically. They adjust their cultural outlook, political orientation, linguistic proficiencies, religious observances, and everyday practices. Their migration can in turn profoundly affect the recipient society. The influence of Indonesia's Chinese communities, in all their diversity, is often assumed to have predominated in the economic sphere. The textual realm, then, reveals the proverbial other side of the coin. The significance of their written legacy was epitomized in 1960 in the left-leaning newspaper *Republik* (Jakarta, 1955):

> Although the Chinese culture has never exerted influences of the kind that gave rise to monumental buildings like the Borobudur, Prambanan and other temples, the writers and guests from China erected an important historical monument for Indonesia in the form of their writings about Indonesia. Seen from the perspective of history and culture, these writings of Chinese people about Indonesia in early times do not yield in importance to the temples of Borobudur, Prambanan, or Sewu.[1]

While the author had in mind some of the earliest descriptions of the archipelago, having flowed—one imagines—from the elegant ink brushes of China's ancient geographers and travelers, the above dollop of praise could have equally befitted a more recent manifestation of the written word: Sino-Malay printing. Some of its most prodigious representatives had arrived at similar conclusions.

Nio Joe Lan explicitly categorized the Sino-Malay literature as Indonesian rather than Chinese heritage in his 1962 monograph on the genre:

> In my opinion, we have to see it as the property of the Indonesian people, because they are the works of those who have become Indonesians, and because they are written in the Indonesian language, albeit not in beautiful Indonesian nor in official Indonesian. And what about the literary works of Peranakan Chinese authors who refused Indonesian citizenship and became Chinese citizens? I feel that their works, which are certainly smaller in number compared to the works of people who became Indonesian, should likewise be regarded as the property of the Indonesian people. After all, those works were written in Indonesian, albeit not the official type, and have been created on Indonesian soil. Whatever the case, the works of Peranakan-Chinese authors who have become Chinese cannot be considered part of the Chinese literature on account of the language and atmosphere of the stories, and their place of publication.[2]

The same point was made in a different way in 2016, more than half a century later, by the scholar Leo Suryadinata. In his momentous coedited volume on Indonesia's Chinese minority, he endorsed their literary heritage as follows:

> Some Peranakan authors prefer to highlight their Indonesian identity. The author Abdul Hadi WM, for example, has completely assimilated. Other Peranakan authors, however, held on to their Peranakan identity, including Kho Ping Hoo, Marga T, and Basuki Sudjatmiko. Their Peranakan identity is reflected in their work; sometimes clearly and sometimes vaguely. But this does not make their work "less Indonesian." They are true Indonesians, born and raised on the Garuda's soil, and their work reflects the diverse conditions of Indonesian society. From a literary point of view, the preservation in their work of their personal identity will only further enrich Indonesia's modern literature.[3]

The above excerpts, all three of them, read as pleas to accept Chinese cultural productions as a legitimate part of Indonesia's heritage and, by extension, Chinese-descended citizens as a legitimate part of the nation. Their murky path to acceptance raises broader questions about the dynamics of inclusion and exclusion. We may recall that some of the gatekeepers of "pure" Malay literature were equally marginal in terms of regional origins (Raja Ali) and race (Munsyi Abdullah), yet enjoyed elite approval during their lifetime and after. Their Islamic background undoubtedly aided their canonization, but there was probably more to it. Urban Java oozed hybridity, religious cross-pollination, cultural integration, and plurilingualism. The specific nature of this society, in combination with the economic, cultural, and linguistic capital of its Chinese print entrepreneurs, forged a viable, self-confident industry unconnected to royal courts and colonial offices. On account of its subversive power, this tradition was almost intrinsically at odds with the interests of ruling institutions. Ungovernability was, simultaneously, its lifeblood and its Achilles' heel.

In Indonesia and elsewhere, letterpress printing revolutionized the way political, social-economic, and cultural issues resonated across the public sphere. Language stood at the very core. Print entrepreneurs confidently stripped it of many literary embellishments and stylistic patterns, only to introduce their own conventions. In doing so, they created discourses that transgressed ethno-religious, regional, and class boundaries. After Chinese writers had adopted romanized Malay, they started to forge new realities in it, reverberating far beyond their own cities and communities. They set the stage for competing articulations of modernity, purposefully strip-mining the linguistic resources of Malay, Hokkien, Dutch, and other languages. Sino-Malay texts were also intermeshed with the language of visuality: illustrations, cartoons, photographs, and advertisements afforded by mechanized printing. Their texts deeply influenced the work of playwrights, musicians, and film producers. The popular, vulgar, sensational, and facetious amalgamated with critical interventions on language, traditions, power hierarchies, violence, race, sex, and emancipation. In this sense, print culture had a similar impact on language and society as radio, television, the Internet, and social media in later times: it captured and produced human perceptions of novelty and change.

It is not surprising that communities with expanded cultural horizons pioneered in these creative ventures. Few phenomena in life are as plurilingual as people aspiring to be modern, save for the cultural brokers supplying them with the prerequisite tools. The mediating force of in-between groups—some would call them "creoles," "mestizos," or "Peranakans"—has long been observed, yet the linguistic embedding of their brokerage seldom receives due attention. While many print entrepreneurs had privileged backgrounds, they patronized a language that was sufficiently popular to attract large readerships, sufficiently localized to address grassroots concerns, sufficiently hybrid to cut across demographic categories, sufficiently egalitarian to blur class distinctions, and sufficiently counterhegemonic to prevent elite cooptation. Their lowbrow cultural productions and versatile language attitudes incessantly defied hegemonic norms. By publishing in print languages, sometimes two or three at the same time, they improved the literacy of multiple communities and even managed to make the experience enjoyable. In this sense, no high-prestige European or Indonesian language could have assumed with equal success the function of so humble and unpretentious a patois as Low Malay.

This book has approached "ungoverned" Malay as a counterforce to the dictates of colonialism, the nation-state, and conventional wisdom. True meaning was made—or, rather, mass-produced—outside the elite realm, in advertisements and joke sections, in poems and diatribes. Vernacular Malay was crucial for Indonesia's public sphere to develop and for its middle classes to catch the pace of modernity. It caused an efflorescence of pleasure in reading and writing. Through the fluid, the profane, and the humoristic, the experiences of creators and consumers of texts radiated in all their complexity. Translingual puns, deliberate misspellings, crackling jokes, rapid-fire tirades, and many more instances of linguistic creativity reveal language at its most expressive. It was in outbursts of anger or sarcasm—two categories famously prone to overlap—that its power was stretched to the fullest. Lexical borrowing, code-mixing, and other expressions of hybridity became baubles of cosmopolitanism. The print culture of Chinese writers was indeed anchored in translingualism. Among themselves, they may have used a Hokkienized Malay incomprehensible to outsiders, yet they kicked the habit whenever they targeted broader readerships. Their plurilingual identity was mobilized and repressed, as the context demanded. It is hardly a surprise, then, that they almost universally rejected the rigid, elitist Malay promoted by the Netherlands Indies administration.

More generally, this book proposes that vernacular language is fundamental to understand the counterpull people faced—and continue to face—between modernity and tradition, progressivism and conservatism, cosmopolitanism and nationalism, Asia and the West. It propels the interplay of pushing and pulling, accepting and rejecting, ridiculing and fetishizing. Similar translingual practices to those described in the Netherlands Indies can be observed in contemporary Indonesia, or elsewhere; among Black or Hispanic Americans, for example, or Arab or Caribbean Europeans. To understand their modes of self-styling is to take issue with the cliché of impoverished languages, many of which turn out, upon closer inspection, to simply contradict the norms of ruling elites. In the same way that hip-hop artists have been repeatedly shown to possess equally large if not larger vocabularies than canonical literati, a token analysis of vernacular-language versus standard-language corpora may well put the kibosh on such poverty myths. If anything, the study of vernacular words, meanings, and messages offers glimpses into the knowledge produced and acquired by the so-called common people, in all their heterogeneity, who are by no means as commonly understood as the term would suggest.

For All Races Once Again

I will conclude with two sets of reflections: first on postcolonial attitudes towards Sino-Malay print culture and then on directions for further research. Amidst the kaleidoscope of Asian studies and institutionalized knowledge production, Sino-Malay books and periodicals occupy a nebulous position. They do not constitute a coherent corpus. Rather, they provide a storehouse of ideas, harboring a multiplicity of voices. Few were expropriated, cataloged, studied, and stored during colonial times. No self-respecting orientalist deigned to pay much attention to these sources, devoid as they perceived them to be of depth and authenticity. When the intellectual Armijn Pané complained in 1941 about the Dutch scholarly obsession with immutable research treasures—"the old culture is so mighty interesting, it is such a nice object of study"—he was clearly not talking about the Sino-Malay literature.[4] Yet Chinese-Indonesian writers should not be seen as subalterns in need of vindication or representation. Many of their periodicals contain the word for "voice." They were ready to be heard, expecting it, and relying on it. They could evidently speak, voluminously, and have written more about themselves than any group of outsiders.

Most Chinese authors wrote for the entire Malay-literate community and insisted that their works were intended for all races (*oentoek segala bangsa*). Yet however close their writings remained to the language, experiences, and cultural world of their readership, they gradually drifted away from the archipelago's nationalist project. Language-mixing and lexical borrowing—particularly of the variety involving Dutch and Chinese—contravened the interests of the nation-state. From the 1930s, standard Indonesian slowly gained ground as the language of the educated classes. The Japanese occupation of Indonesia (1942–45), during which European languages (except German) were banned, accelerated this process of homogenization. On the one hand, this stimulated the emancipation of standard Indonesian, which was finally given the space to express everything it needed to express in its own terms. On the other, it concluded an era in which the Malay language had escaped the straitjackets of those seeking to control it.

Asia's groundswell of decolonization and the ensuing projects of nation-building and transregional unity rendered linguistic diversity an impediment rather than enrichment. Nevertheless, some people kept high hopes for the future of vernacular Malay, in particular the variety adopted by the Chinese. One correspondent to the *Bangkok Post* recommended in 1949 to institutionalize "the type of simple Malay used by Chinese dealers" as the pan-Asian lingua franca. *Sin Po*'s aptly named satirist Tawon (Wasp) responded with flippancy to this short-lived proposition: "Well, well ... so the *Sin Po* style has silently helped to build an Asian Bloc."[5] It would indeed be incorrect to claim that Sino-Malay did not make it, whereas High Malay did. Chinese authors started to use Malay affixes in a more consistent way, while indigenous authors accepted a number of words and constructions historically associated with Low Malay, such as *bikin* (make, do), *bisa* (can), *dimengerti* (to be understood), *mendingan* (it would be better), and *toebroek* (to collide).[6] Yet convergence inevitably reduced diversity. Many Dutch and Hokkien words, such as *kouwkati* (egoistic), *poerstel* (proposal; D: *voorstel*), *siahwee* (society), *advertentie* (advertisement), and *djornalis* (journalist), gradually disappeared from the language, the latter four having been replaced by the neologisms *usul, masjarakat, iklan*, and *wartawan*.[7]

Most Chinese authors voluntarily standardized their writing by the late 1940s, at a time when Indonesia's national language was still widely perceived as artificial and restricted to the intellectual avant-garde.[8] They had been quick to do so. Indonesia's postindependence film industry experienced a considerable slowdown because so few people could fully understand its dialogs. Popular national-language theater likewise took a long time to flourish. It was confined up to the early 1960s to the region of North Sumatra, with its significant ethnic Malay population.[9] In their quick acceptance of the new standard, Chinese-Indonesian authors repeated a historical pattern. Just as their predecessors had adopted vernacular Malay prior to the masses, a new generation of authors embraced standard Indonesian before it became mainstream. Yet the circumstances were hardly the same. Adopting Malay had been a strategic but optional choice in colonial times, whereas the acceptance of standard Indonesian was a conscious expression of loyalty to the Indonesian state over China (both the Republic and the People's Republic) or the Netherlands. Writing in the 1960s, the author Gan Kok Liang, himself born in China, apologized for any shortcomings in his written Indonesian, which he asserted had to "fulfill the appropriate grammatical requirements as a moral responsibility to our national language."[10] Defiance against elitist language practices, of course, survived in various guises, but the Chinese no longer took the lead.

The (temporary) disappearance from the public sphere of vernacular language and translingual practices shows parallels across postcolonial societies. In Egypt they were framed as an assault on tradition, in Malaysia on the dominant ethnic group, and in Indonesia on national cohesion.[11] As soon as Chinese-Indonesians would develop a sense of national belonging, it was believed as early as the 1930s, their linguistic otherness would inevitably dissipate.[12] Under President Sukarno (1901–70), they were reimagined as one of Indonesia's ethnic communities (*suku*), theoretically almost on par with indigenous groups. In reality, however, they were continuously expected to prove their commitment to the nation-state. The call rang increasingly louder, for instance, to change their Chinese names into "Indonesian" ones, a policy that was reintroduced under

President Suharto.[13] Such antipluralist dogmas obviously generated resistance. The Badan Permusjawaratan Indonesia (Consultative Body for Indonesian Citizenship) or Baperki, founded in 1954, established Indonesian-medium schools that additionally offered Mandarin classes in an attempt to safeguard the group's plurilingual tradition. This left-wing organization also founded the Universitas Res Publica (Res Publica University) or Ureca, largely in response to anti-Chinese ethnic quotas on university enrollment. These nonassimilationist endeavors drew the ire of right-wing nationalists.[14] Both Baperki and Ureca were destroyed by anticommunists in 1965, foreshadowing a period of cultural cleansing that lasted over three decades. Suharto's New Order government drew to a tumultuous close in 1998, a year rife with anti-Chinese and other violence.[15] Eventually, all laws banning Chinese cultural expressions were abolished under the presidency of Abdurrahman Wahid (1999–2001), as many people recall with bittersweet tears. The question of where Indonesia's Chinese minority stood within the frame of the nation gained renewed relevance.

All nation-states face the task of dealing humanely with citizens of (partly) external origins, along with their indigenous communities. It has been argued in the case of Singapore that a synthesis of Chinese and Southeast Asian cultures lies at the core of the nation.[16] While such a discourse is less likely to take shape in Indonesia, Chinese culture has resurfaced abundantly after 1998, including— once again—in the form of a Chinese-Indonesian press.[17] If one takes heritage to be the residue of canonization, selection, and omission, present times have certainly been kinder than Suharto's New Order. Chinese holidays, cultural festivals, and museums are no longer forced underground. Their sudden ubiquity in public spaces has elicited mixed reactions, attesting to the perseverance of the outsider stigma flaring up with predictable regularity during times of unrest. Some people within the community find contemporary expressions of Chineseness sterile and unable to encompass the hybrid Peranakan culture.[18] Nevertheless, the contributions of Chinese-descended Indonesians to the fabric of the nation are increasingly taken into account, especially on a local level.[19] It is not insignificant that the National Library has recently included a large number of Sino-Malay novels in its online portal of digital Indonesian heritage.

In 1998, it became legal again to learn Chinese. Indonesia follows the global trend where Mandarin serves as the pan-Chinese language at the expense of Hokkien, Hakka, Cantonese, and Teochew.[20] Mandarin proficiency has introduced new translingual practices, somewhat reminiscent of the Hokkien-tinged Malay of late colonial times.[21] In view of China's global ascendancy and outward orientation, similar phenomena are likely to emerge throughout the postcolonial world. Another sign of continuity is the fact that republished Sino-Malay stories are enjoyed by people of various ethno-religious backgrounds.[22] To dismiss their ongoing recuperation as merely nostalgic is to overlook their relevance as instruments of identity-formation and stimuli for new cultural creations. We may call attention here to Remy Sylado's *Ca-Bau-Kan: Hanya Sebuah Dosa* (The Courtesan: Only a Sin), Indonesia's first historical novel about Peranakan life in colonial times. Reconstructed on the basis of archival sources, this popular book came out in 1999 and inspired a movie released in 2002.[23] As such, it represents a small step—among many other community-initiated efforts—to reinvent a viable Chinese-Indonesian culture, however negotiable and riddled with ambiguity. Such a culture, to mobilize a well-worn stereotype that nevertheless has some truth to it, will be distinctly Indonesian in its ability to involve different communities and incorporate external influences without losing its local character.

Different Fields, Different Yields

This monograph has foregrounded vernacular language as a crucible to investigate and instantiate experiences of colonial modernity, warts and all. Akin to Jews, Parsis, Eurasians, and similarly positioned communities in other contexts, the Chinese were destined to function as a buffer—culturally, economically, and linguistically—between European elites, indigenous masses, and a cosmopolitan urban bourgeoisie. Their activities were transregional and yet local, reflecting the group's own ambiguous place in society. With varying degrees of access to China, the Indies, and the West, Chinese print entrepreneurs manifested themselves as natural-born harbingers and interpreters of popular culture and modern lifestyles. They influenced the lives of middle-class families, many of which participated on some level in the colonial system, but were anything but happy about it. Ultimately, writers could only engineer changes that made sense to their larger audiences. Language, as I have insisted, was inherent to these negotiations.

What, then, can one gain from a close reading of vernacular texts printed in colonial times? What significance do these sources hold, and for which fields? What further contributions could be furnished in future scholarship? Foremost, the Sino-Malay print culture—and comparable material from other contexts—provides insights into lives that did not necessarily intersect with those of Europeans. In many cases, they tell a fuller, more textured story of the period in which they appeared. Claudine Salmon, probably the most prolific scholar of the material, offers some directions:

> The texts should not be approached from the standpoint of the literary critic, because the reader would probably be disappointed, but from that of a linguist or a historian. The language of the Baba is extremely

interesting, and the historian will find material on which to base an analysis of how an uprooted minority group recreates its own culture, how it lives out its links with its native country, how it takes possession of its history, and how it looks on the present.[24]

In doing so, one must fully take into account the sociolinguistic idiosyncrasies of colonized territories where the main print language was non-European. Texts produced in these Asian and African societies engage with everyday life through a framework that is neither fully colonial nor overtly nationalistic. This book's fleeting analogies with Swahili and various creole languages merit more substantial treatment in future research. Such language histories are considerably less studied than their Western counterparts, reflecting in part the durabilities of colonially rooted power imbalances. Chua Beng Huat characterizes this academic stalemate as follows:

> That many of these Southeast Asian texts are written in non-European languages may be one of the primary reasons for their exclusion, signifying a very colonial practice at work in the production of knowledge of postcoloniality.[25]

At the risk of peddling banalities, the academic study of these texts has the potential to "provincialize Europe."[26] This cannot be an individual effort, nor has it been the primary objective of this monograph. Nevertheless, I have found it almost impossible to examine Sino-Malay books, periodicals, poems, and other texts without constantly marveling at their significance outside my own field of expertise. With dazzling regularity, Chinese and indigenous journalists addressed the Sino-Japanese War, the rise of fascism in Europe, Tagore's ideas of Asianness, Gandhi's Swadeshi movement, Italy's occupation of Libya and Ethiopia, anti-colonial struggles across the world, the lynching of Black Americans, and other topics revealing a sharp eye for global injustices. By virtue of vernacular Malay, solidarities across the colonized world figured not only in the minds of Western-educated elites, but—perhaps more importantly—in middle-class households. This story is yet to be told.

The Sino-Malay press was the biggest vernacular press of the Indies, but it was not the only one. From the 1910s, Chinese, indigenous, and Arabic publications appeared side by side, influenced each other, and concurred on issues of shared concern. All these primary sources are of immense historical value, even though their poor accessibility might suggest otherwise. The first issues of *Sin Po* are notoriously difficult to find. The same is true for *Medan Prijaji* (Arena of the Gentry; Bandung, 1907–12), Indonesia's first outspokenly anticolonial periodical edited by Tirto Adhi Soerjo. Access to primary sources is a global concern.

In South Africa, no publicly available copies have survived of Gandhi's original *Indian Home Rule*, which galvanized Indian nationalism and inspired the global anticolonial movement.[27] Some of the most influential publications of the modern world, hence, are not public. The intellectual foundations of South-South solidarity, in which Indonesia played a pivotal role in the 1940s and 1950s, lie scattered in forgotten nooks and corners. Digitalization of and public access to these documents remains—for the most part—a distant dream, although the situation is certainly improving. And to complicate matters further, some primary sources are written in languages not generally known to academics.[28]

This book has illustrated how a community with migratory roots adopted the vernacular language of their new homeland, wrote newspapers and fiction in it, enriched it, made it more chaotic, and changed society in the process. Despite its many omissions, silences, and loose ends, I hope it provides some value for future scholars, who might derive completely different conclusions from the same material. I hope, furthermore, that some of the publications I have indicated as lost might yet show up in unexpected places, and that their value is appreciated. I feel unqualified to stray too far from the subject of language, but even in this field much can be done. Is it possible—amidst all its heterogeneity—to write a grammar of Java's late colonial Malay as used by its Chinese-descended community? As similar projects have been undertaken for European languages on the basis of vernacular texts, the answer should be positive.[29] Such an effort may prove an exercise in corpus linguistics, requiring a better digital infrastructure than has been available to me. How does this variety compare to other Malay varieties in past and present? What kinds of early films and audio recordings could help us reconstruct how it sounded?

Potential topics for further research are nigh inexhaustible. The Sino-Malay printed heritage offers a repository of popular entertainment, commercial opportunity, cultural contestation, political conflict, religious innovation, intellectual discourse, foodways, and many other aspects shaping the lives not just of urban Chinese, but of a broad range of Indonesians and global citizens in the making. These sources add a human dimension to the past in ways that colonial or nationalistic historiography often neglects. Contemporary researchers and other interested readers will find much of appeal on their pages. It is hoped that digitalization efforts will further augment the pleasure of reading them. Even the sarcasm, the swearing, the impoliteness, and the bigotry that some of the texts are rife with might generate some diversion, if only to recognize in them the selfsame human proclivities that shape our own existence.

Appendix

All words are from Hokkien, unless indicated otherwise: Cn (Cantonese), Ha (Hakka), Md (Mandarin), and Tc (Teochew). Attestations marked as S are specific to the Straits Settlements.

TABLE A.1 Chinese words in Sino-Malay

SINO-MALAY SPELLING	MODERN ORTHOGRAPHY	CHARACTERS	MEANING
aija	ai-ia	哎呀	Oh!
aikok (see aykok)			
anak kamtjekan	anak kam-chek-an	疳積	worm-infected kid
anak tjaptjay	anak chàp-chhài	雜菜	mongrel (lit. chop suey kid)
angmoh	âng-mô͘	紅毛	British (lit. red-haired)
ang moh kwan (S)	âng-mô͘ khoán	紅毛款	anglicized
Angke	Âng-khe	紅溪/洪溪	Red Creek
angkin	âng-kin	紅巾	clasp-fastened waist belt
angsio hie	âng-sio hî	紅燒魚	fish braised in soy sauce
antjoa	án-chóaⁿ	按怎	how, for what reason
ay-kok (see aykok)			
aykok	ài-kok	愛國	loving one's nation, patriotism
aytjiong	ài-chiòng	愛眾	loving the masses
baba seow (S)	baba siau	痟	crazy Baba
bad djie lang	bat-jī-lâng	捌字人	literate person
badjoe sioki	baju sió-ki	小裾	Chinese-inspired uniform for girls

(continued)

TABLE A1 *(continued)*

SINO-MALAY SPELLING	MODERN ORTHOGRAPHY	CHARACTERS	MEANING
badjoe twiekim	*baju* tùi-kim	對襟	frogged coat
bahmi	bah-mī	肉麵	wheat noodles
bakkoet	bah-kut	肉骨	pigs' bones
bami (see bahmi)			
ban swee	bān-sòe	萬歲	long live!
bandji	bān-jī	卍字	swastika
bangsat	bȧk-sat	木蝨	bedbug
barongsai	*barong*-sai	獅	Chinese-Indonesian lion dance
baso pangsit	bah-so pán-sit	肉搓扁食	wonton meatball soup
batjang	bah-chàng	肉粽	sticky rice dumplings
bayhok	bâi-hȯk	埋伏	ambush
beng-eh	bêng-ê	明鞋	Ming-style (shoes)
bengtjoe	bêng-chú	盟主	leader of an alliance
bihoen	bí-hún	米粉	rice vermicelli
Bin Seng	Bîn-seng	民聲	*Voice of the People*
Binkok	Bîn-kok	民國	Chinese Republic
boanseng	boán-seng	晚生	I (junior)
boegee	bú-gē	武藝	Chinese martial arts
boehiap	bú-hiȧp	武俠	knight-errant
boe-kie-djin	bú-kí-jîn	武舉人	military graduates of the Provincial Examinations
boenkhoa	bûn-koaⁿ	文官	civil official
bohokki	bô hok-khì	無福氣	unfortunate
bokdji	bȯk-jí	木耳	edible fungus
bokdjie (see bokdji)			
bongme	bong-mėh	摸脈	pulse diagnosis
bongsiat	bōng-siat	夢洩	nocturnal emissions
bopan	bô pān	無辦	reckless
botawlo	bô thâu-lō·	無頭路	idler (lit. no work)
chap chye (S, see tjaptjay)			
chang-ie	chǎngyī (Md)	氅衣	a tight-fitting one-piece dress
Chau Sing	Cháoshēng (Md)	潮聲	*Voice of the Tide*
cheongsam (S)	chèuhng sāam	長衫	a tight-fitting one-piece dress
china gerk (S)	*cina* khek	客	Chinese hillbilly
Chung Hsioh	Zhōngxué (Md)	中學	secondary school
Chung Hwa Hui	Zhōnghuá Huì (Md)	中華會	Chinese Union
daging samtjam	*daging* sam-chân	三層	pork belly
dho king ngah	tōa-khîm-á	大琴仔	puppetry play
djang-koo	chhiàng-ko	唱歌	to sing
Dji Touw Bwe	Jī Tō· Bôe	二度梅	*The Story of the Plumtree Flowers Twice*
djiatsim	jiȧt-sim	熱心	warm-hearted, enthusiastic
djieoen	jī-ūn	字運	fortune
djikak	jī-kak	二角	district secretary
Djilakeng	Jī-lȧk-keng	二六間	26 Buildings

SINO-MALAY SPELLING	MODERN ORTHOGRAPHY	CHARACTERS	MEANING
djin poet hak, poet tie gie	jîn put ha̍k, put ti gī	人不學, 不知義	if people don't study, they will not know righteousness
djinge	jī-ngé	二「㐧雅女」	second-rank concubine
djioe-soet	jiû-su̍t	柔術	jiu-jitsu
djip hoan	jip-hoan	入番	to go native
djoehi	jiû-hî	鰇魚	squid
eesay	ē-sái	會使	able to, expertise
em hoo pan	m̄ hó pān	毋好辦	inappropriate
Emoei	Ē-mûiⁿ	廈門	Xiamen (a city)
enche (S, see entjek)			
enghiong	eng-hiông	英雄	hero
engkoh	ńg-ko	俺哥	older brother
engkong	ńg-kong	俺公	grandfather
enso	ńg-só	俺嫂	sister-in-law
entjek	ńg-chek	俺叔	uncle
entjim	ńg-chím	俺嬸	auntie
fan phor	fāan pòh (Cn)	番婆	native woman
foe jong hai	fùh yùhng háaih (Cn)	芙蓉蟹	egg foo young (a crab omelet)
Fu Nu Tsa Chih	Fùnǚ Zázhì (Md)	婦女雜誌	Women's Journal
gahong	kha-hong	跤瘋	rheumatic pains in the leg
gia kangpe	giâ kang-pêⁿ	蜈蚣坪	a specific ritual procession
gie o	gī-o̍h	義學	free school
giehiap	gī-hia̍p	義俠	chivalrous knight
gie-lim-koen	gī-lîm-kun	御林軍	palace guards
gie-soe	gī-sú	御史	censor
ginkang (see khinkang)			
ginlan	gīn-lān	恨𣍐	disgusted
Giok Lek	Gio̍k Le̍k	玉歷	The Jade Guidebook
giok poet tok, poet sing khie	gio̍k put tok, put sêng khì	玉不琢，不成器	if jade is not cut, nothing can be made of it
goansiauw	gōan-siau	元宵	Lantern Festival
goea	góa	我	I
go-eng-kok-touw	gō eng khok thò	餓鷹攫兔	Hungry Hawk Catches a Rabbit
go-houw-pok-sit	gō hó pok sit	餓虎搏食	Hungry Tiger Catches Its Prey
gong-kongtjoe	gōng kong-chú	戇公子	playboy, womanizer (lit. crazy gentleman)
goreng angsio	goreng âng-sio	紅燒	to braise in soy sauce
gwakang	gōa-kang	外功	external power
gwan	góan	阮	I (uncommon)
haktong	ha̍k-tông	學堂	Chinese school
hanboen	hàn-bûn	漢文	literary Chinese
hay mo kee	hái bó-ke	海母雞	blubberlip snapper
Haylam	Hái-lâm	海南	Hainanese
haysom	hái-som	海參	sea cucumber

(continued)

TABLE A1 *(continued)*

SINO-MALAY SPELLING	MODERN ORTHOGRAPHY	CHARACTERS	MEANING
hebie	hê-bí	蝦米	dried shrimps
hie-louw	hî-lō·	魚露	fish sauce
hie-tjiak-teng-tjie	hí chhiak teng chi	喜雀登枝	Cheerful Sparrow Goes up the Branch
hio	hioⁿ	香	incense sticks
hioko	hioⁿ-ko·	香菇	shiitake
hiolouw	hioⁿ-lō·	香爐	incense burner
hisiet (see hisit)			
hisit	hî-sìt	魚翼	shark fins
Ho Po	Hô Pò	和報	*Peaceful Newspaper*
hoa djin	hôa-jîn	華人	Chinese person
Hoa Tjoe Ling	Hoa Chú Lêng	花子能	name of a famous playboy
Hoa Tok Po	Hoa Tòk Pò	華鐸報	*Hoa Tok Newspaper*
Hoa Woe Ho Pie	Huá Wū Hébì (Md)	華巫合璧	*Combining Chinese and Malay*
hoakiao	hôa-kiâu	華僑	overseas Chinese
hoakiauw (see hoakiao)			
hoakoen	hoa-kûn	花裙	pleated skirt
hoana	hoan-á	番仔	native person
hoana poo	hoan-á pô	番仔婆	native woman
hoedjin	hu-jîn	夫人	lady
hoehwat	hû-hoat	符法	charms
hoema	hû-má	駙馬	emperor's son-in-law
hohan	hó-hàn	好漢	brave man
Hokkian	Hok-kiàn	福建	Hokkien (Fujian)
hoklo	Hok-ló	福佬	Teochew (lit. Fujian person)
Hoktjia	Hok-chhiaⁿ	福清	Fuqingese
Hoktjioe	Hok-chiu	福州	Fuzhounese
ho-lan-wa	Hô-lân ōa	荷蘭話	Dutch (language)
hollankow	Hô-lân khò·	荷蘭褲	Dutch trousers
hong	hông	鳳	phoenix
hongho	hông-hō·	皇后	empress
honghwee	hong-hóe	風火	internal heat
hongtee	hông-tè	皇帝	emperor
hoo (S)	hû	符	talisman
hooboen	hô-bûn	和文	literary Japanese
howee sahee	hóe-sai	火屎	a kind of firework
hwatsoet	hoat-sùt	法術	Daoist magic
hweetjat	húi-chhát	匪賊	bandit
hwesio	hôe-sioⁿ	和尚	Buddhist monk
Hwi-kiam Ji-chap Si-kiap (S)	Hui-kiàm Jī-cháp Sì-kiap	飛劍二十四俠	*Flying Swords: The Twenty-four Heroes*
Ien Po	Iń Pò	恩報	*Merciful Newspaper*
ijo twah	iòh-toaⁿ	藥單	prescription
Ik Po	Èk Pò	譯報	*Translation Newspaper*
Im Lek	Im-lėk	陰曆	Lunar New Year
iseng	i-seng	醫生	physician
Jang Lek	Iâng-lėk	陽曆	Solar New Year

SINO-MALAY SPELLING	MODERN ORTHOGRAPHY	CHARACTERS	MEANING
jangbwee	iâng-bôe	瘍梅	buboes
jan-oh	iàn-o	燕窩	edible birds' nests
janswat	ián-soat	演說	speech
kamthjeng	kam-chhng	疳瘡	genital ulcers
kan hiong	kan-hiông	奸雄	master deceiver
Kang Ouw Djie Sie Hiap	Kang-ô· Jī-sì Hiáp	江湖二四俠	24 Knight-Errants Roaming over Rivers and Lakes
kang-ouw	kang-ô·	江湖	the martial arts world
kansin	kan-sîn	奸臣	corrupt official
kantong titouw	*kantong* ti-tō·	豬肚	frontal pockets
kao-soe (see kauwsoe)			
kauwkoen	kâu-kûn	猴拳	monkey kung fu
kauwsoe	kàu-su	教師	silat master
kauwtjoe	kàu-chú	教主	religious head
kaypang	kài-pang	丐幫	beggar's union
ke (see Khe)			
kek lim	kek-lîm	激淋	retention of urine
kekbeng	kek-bēng	革命	revolution
keng kie poet twie	keng-kî put tùi	經期不對	irregular menstruation
kertas hoe	*kertas* hû	符	talismanic paper
Khay Lam Hak Tong	Khài-lâm Hák-tông	開南學堂	Kainan School
Khe	Kheh	客	Hakka people
khikang	khì-kang	氣功	breath control
khinkang	khin-kang	輕功	the art of making the body light
khoabo	khòaⁿ-bô	看無	not noticing
khoahoe	koaⁿ-hú	官府	feudal official
khongkauw	khóng-kàu	孔教	Confucianism
Khongtjoe	Khóng-chú	孔子	Confucius
khwa tjhi bo khwa lang	khòaⁿ chîⁿ bô khòaⁿ lâng	看錢無看人	interested in money, not in people
kiakauw	kiâⁿ-kàu	行到	to be underway
kiaking	kiâⁿ-keng	行經	menstruating
kiamhiap	kiàm-hiáp	劍俠	chivalrous swordsman
Kiao Seng	Kiâu Seng	僑聲	*Voice of the Chinese Overseas*
kiaopao	kiâu-pau	僑胞	countryman living abroad
kiauwpauw (see kiaopao)			
kidjin	kí-jîn	舉人	Provincial Graduate (title)
kihong	khì-hong	去瘋	to remove rheumatic pains
kilin	kî-lîn	麒麟	dragon-headed ungulate of Chinese mythology
kim-ie-wie	kim-i-ūi	金衣衛	gold-clad guards
kimtan	kim-tan	金丹	alchemy
kinsin	kín-sin	緊身	close-fitting jacket
kintjam	kim-cham	金針	tuberose flowers
kio	kiô	橋	bridge
kioekin	kiù-kin	勾筋	cramps

(continued)

TABLE A1 *(continued)*

SINO-MALAY SPELLING	MODERN ORTHOGRAPHY	CHARACTERS	MEANING
kiok hoa	kiok-hoa	菊花	chrysanthemums
kionghi	kiong-hí	恭喜	congratulations
kiongtjioe	kióng-chhiú	拱手	to clasp the hands together
kisiang	khì-siang	去傷	to cure injuries
kisip	khì-sip	去濕	the treatment of dampness
ko (see engkoh)			
koansoet	koân-sùt	拳術	Chinese martial arts
koe loe joek	gū lōu yuhk (Cn)	咕嚕肉	sweet-and-sour pork
koelikeng	ku-lí-keng	苦力間	coolie quarters
koen	kûn	裙	petticoat
koenthauw	kûn-thâu	拳頭	Chinese martial arts
koetjai	kú-chhài	韭菜	Chinese chives
koetjiah	ku-chiaⁿ	龜精	womanizer (lit. turtle)
kok bin tong	kok-bîn-tóng	國民黨	Nationalist Party
kok-soet	kok-sùt	國術	China's national system of martial arts
kokbo	kok-bó	國母	empress dowager
koksiahwee	kok-siā-hōe	國社會	national assembly
kokthio	kok-tiōⁿ	國丈	emperor's father-in-law
kong	kóng	講	to say
kong-ek	kong-ek	公益	social organization
kong-hong-sauw-iap	kông hong sàu iáp	狂風掃葉	Fierce Wind Sweeps the Leaves
Kong Koan	Kong-koán	公館	building of the Chinese Council
Kong Sie Koen	Kong Sī Kun	光緒君	the Guangxu emperor
Kongfoe	Gwóng fú (Cn)	廣府	Cantonese
kongkou	kóng-kó·	講古	to chat
konglo	kong-lô	功勞	merit
kongsi	kong-si	公司	form of financial partnership
kongtauw	kòng-thâu	降頭	black magic
kongtjoejasia	kong-chú-iâ-sià	公子爺舍	rich dandy, playboy
koon-sah (S)	kûn-saⁿ	裙衫	a Chinese-inspired upper garment and skirt combination
kouwkati	kò·-ka-tī	顧家己	egoistic
kuchye (S, see koetjai)			
Kung Yen	Gōngyán (Md)	公言	*Public Declaration*
kuo min tang	Guómíndǎng (Md)	國民黨	Nationalist Party
Kuo Yu Pan	Guóyǔ Bān (Md)	國語班	Mandarin course
kuoyü	Guóyǔ (Md)	國語	Mandarin (lit. national language)
kwan hwa	Guānhuà (Md)	官話	official speech
kwee	kóe	粿	sweet rice cake
kweetiau	kóe-tiâu	粿條	flat rice noodles
Kwitang	Kúiⁿ-tang	廣東	Cantonese

SINO-MALAY SPELLING	MODERN ORTHOGRAPHY	CHARACTERS	MEANING
Lam Yang Hoen Bong Kwan	Lâm-iâng Hùn-bông Kóan	南洋訓蒙館	School of the South Seas
lamsin	lám-sin	荏身	weakness
lamyang	Lâm-iâng	南洋	Southeast Asia (lit. South Seas)
lan	lán	咱	I (uncommon)
laukeh	láu-kheh	老客	old-hand
lauwdjiat	lāu-jiȧt	鬧熱	exciting
laykang	lāi-kang	內功	internal power
laysiang	lāi-siang	內傷	tuberculosis
li	lí	你	you
Li Po	Lí Pò	理報	*Rational Newspaper*
Li Si Bin	Lí Sì-bîn	李世民	name of a Tang emperor
lian hoa	liân-hoa	蓮花	lotus
liangsim	liâng-sim	良心	conscience
liatwi	liȧt-ūi	列位	all of you
lihiap	lí-hiȧp	女俠	female warrior
lin	lín	恁	you (uncommon)
liong	liông	龍	dragon
liongkie	liông-kî	龍旗	Dragon Flag
liongkoet	liông-kut	龍骨	pigs' spine
lobak	lòh baahk (Cn)	蘿蔔	Chinese radish
loe	lú	汝	you
loeitay	lūi-tâi	擂臺	elevated fighting arena
long-chong-em-sye (S)	lóng-chóng m̄-sái	攏總母使	completely unnecessary
longkoen	long-kun	郎君	young man, husband
loohoedjin	ló-hu-jîn	老夫人	elderly lady
loosianseng	ló-sian-seng	老先生	elderly gentleman
lootia	ló-tia	老爹	district warden
loo-tjoh	ló-chhó	潦草	careless
lweekang	lōe-kang	內功	internal power
Macao-po	Má-káu-pô	馬狗婆	prostitute (lit. woman from Macau)
Makauw	Má-káu	馬狗	Macau
mie	mī	麵	noodles
misoa	mī-sòaⁿ	麵線	salted wheat vermicelli
mi-zoä (see misoa)			
mo foo long	mòuh fu lohng (Cn)	無褲襠	slur for Babas (lit. trousers without a crotch)
moei-twie	mûi-tùi	門對	Chinese gatepost couplets
Nan Sing	Nánshēng (Md)	南聲	*Voice of the South*
ngai	ngài (Ha)	厓	I (uncommon)
ngekang	ngē-kang	硬功	exercises to strengthen the body
ngekoen	ngē-kûn	硬拳	hard martial arts
Ngo Bie Yan	Ngó Bí lân	五美緣	*Romances of Five Beauties*
ngohiang	ngó-hiang	五香	five-spice powder
ngoliam	ngâu-liām	嗷念	to grumble

(continued)

TABLE A1 *(continued)*

SINO-MALAY SPELLING	MODERN ORTHOGRAPHY	CHARACTERS	MEANING
nikouw	nî-ko͘	尼姑	nun
Nio Thian Laj	Niô͘ Thian Lâi	梁天來	Liang Tianlai (name of a protagonist)
noeikang	núi-kang	軟功	exercises to improve the body's flexibility
obat "pouw"	obat pó͘	補	medicine to strengthen the body
oehauw	ū-hàu	有孝	to have filial piety
oen tong	ūn-tōng	運動	sports
oewee (see owe)			
ongya	ông-iâ	王爺	prince
orang Boan	orang Boán	滿	the Manchu people
oteng	o̍h-tn̂g	學堂	Chinese school
owe	ôe	喂	a polite way to answer to a call
owee (see owe)			
oweh (see owe)			
owek (see owe)			
pai hwa	báihuà (Md)	白話	vernacular Mandarin (lit. vernacular language)
pangsai	pàng-sái	放屎	to take a shit
pangtjoe	pang-chú	幫主	gang leader
pao hie	pau-hî	鮑魚	abalones
pat sian	pat-sian	八仙	the Eight Gods
pat-tin-touw	pat-tīn-tô͘	八陣圖	stone troops
Patekoan	Pat-tê-koàn	八茶罐	Eight Teapots
Patike	Phah-thih-ke	拍鐵街/打鐵街	Blacksmith St.
patjoetjeng	phah chhíu-chhèng	拍手銃	to masturbate (lit. to fire the pistol)
paytjhia	pài-chiaⁿ	拜正	to pay one's respect
pekchye (S)	pe̍h-chhài	白菜	bok choy (a vegetable)
pekie	pe̍h-ki	白裾	a white garment
pektai	pe̍h-tài	白帶	leucorrhea
phaykia	pháiⁿ-kiáⁿ	歹囝	lascivious person
phi ijak	phīⁿ-ia̍h	鼻蝶	nose butterfly (a disease)
phoa sie	pòaⁿ-sí	半死	half dead
pianswi	piàn-sūi	半遂	total paralysis
piauwkiok	piau-kio̍k	鏢局	escort bureau
piauwsoe	piau-su	鏢師	armed escort
pihi	píⁿ-hî	扁魚	dried flounder
Pinangsia	Pin-nn̂g-siā	檳榔社	Areca Village
poankoan	phoàn-koan	判官	judge
poenti	pún-thi (Ha)	本地	Cantonese (lit. native person)
poko	po̍k-hô	薄荷	peppermint
pookiam	pó-kiàm	寶劍	two-edged sword
potehi	pò͘-tē-hì	布袋戲	cloth-glove puppetry
pow-tee-hie (see potehi)			
pwakangan	poah-kang-an	撥工	spare time

SINO-MALAY SPELLING	MODERN ORTHOGRAPHY	CHARACTERS	MEANING
Sam Ha Lam Tong (S)	Sam Hā Lâm Tông	三下南唐	*Three Expeditions against the Southern Tang*
Sam Kok	Sam-kok	三國	*Romance of the Three Kingdoms*
Sam Tay Kie Hiap	Sam Tāi Kī Hiảp	三代奇俠	*Three Generations of Chivalrous Men*
samfu (S)	sāam fu (Cn)	衫褲	set of short-sleeved blouse and trousers
Sampan Liauw	Sam-pán-liâu	杉板寮	Sampan Shed
sap yat tim	sahp yāt dím (Cn)	十一點	not-quite-Chinese (slur for Peranakans; lit. eleven o'clock)
Sat Tjoe Po	Sat Chú Pò	殺子報	*Divine Retribution for Killing the Son*
saykong	sai-kong	師公	Daoist priest
see-ie	sè-î	細姨	concubine
sekhong	sek-hong	色瘋	venereal diseases
sengtjie	sèng-chí	聖旨	imperial edict
Sentiong	Sin-thióng	新塚/新冢	New Burying Ground
seteng	seⁿ-teng	生疔	small hard boils
she li lat	seⁿ-lí-lảt	生癧瘰	scrofula
sheswaja	seⁿ-soāiⁿ-á	生檨仔	syphilis
shetjheng	seⁿ-chhng	生瘡	venereal ulcers
siahwee	siā-hōe	社會	society
Sian	sian	仙	god
siang hwee	siang-hōe	商會	chamber of commerce
siangseng (see sianseng)			
sianhong	sian-hong	先鋒	vanguard, ranger
sianseng	sian-seng	先生	sir, gentleman
siansing (see sianseng)			
siauw soat	siáu-soat	小說	fiction
Siauwliem sie	Siàu-lîm-sī	少林寺	Shaolin Temple
siham	sī hām (Cn)	蟮蚶	cockles
Sin Po	Sin Pò	新報	*New Newspaper*
sin tjiong toei wan	sīn chiong tui oán	慎終追遠	care for the funeral rites of one's parents, honor the memory of one's ancestors
singke (see singkeh)			
singkeh	sin-kheh	新客	newcomer
singkek (see singkeh)			
sinkang	sîn-kang	神功	supernatural powers
sinse	sin-seⁿ	先生	Chinese doctor
sinseh (see sinse)			
sinsian	sîn-sian	神仙	immortal
sintjhia	sin-chiaⁿ	新正	Chinese New Year
sioe ie	siū-i	壽衣	burial sheet
sioetjai	siù-châi	秀才	scholar
sioti-djiak	sio-ti chiảh	燒豬食	roasted pig dish
siotjia	sió-chiá	小姐	young lady

(continued)

TABLE A1 (continued)

SINO-MALAY SPELLING	MODERN ORTHOGRAPHY	CHARACTERS	MEANING
sipatmo	sit-pat-moˑ	四八摸	a music style (lit. eighteen caresses)
soe po sia	su-pò-siā	書報社	reading club
Soeara Tsing Niën	*Suara Qīngnián* (Md)	青年	*Voice of the Youth*
soehoe	su-hū	師父	silat teacher
soeieh	shuǐ (Md)	水	water
soeikoen	súi-kûn	媠拳	soft martial arts
Soesie	*Sù-si*	四書	*The Four Books*
soe-siok	su-siók	私塾	traditional Chinese private school
song soe	song-sū	喪事	funeral
so-oen	soh-hún	索粉	cellophane noodles
swikee	súi-ke	水雞	edible frogs
tahoe	tāu-hū	豆腐	tofu
taktjeh	thàk-chheh	讀冊	to study
taktjhelang	thàk-chheh-lâng	讀冊人	scholar
tao-yoe	tāu-iû	豆油	soy sauce
Tat Seng Pian	*Tàt Seng Pian*	達生編	*Treatise on Successful Birth*
tauwdji	tāu-jí	豆乳	salted bean curd
tauwhoe (see tahoe)			
tauwkwa	tāu-koaⁿ	豆乾	firm tofu
tawkua (S, see tauwkwa)			
taydjin	tāi-jîn	大人	dignitary
tenglang	tn̂g-lâng	唐人	Chinese person
tengswa	tn̂g-soaⁿ	唐山	mainland China (lit. Tang Mountain)
tengwah	tn̂g-ōa	唐話	spoken Chinese
thauké	thâu-ke	頭家	business owner
thauwtjang	thâu-chang	頭鬃	queue
thayhouw	thài-hōˑ	太后	empress dowager
thaykam	thài-kàm	太監	eunuch
thaykoen	tāi-kun	大君	emperor
thaysoe	tāi-su	大師	silat grandmaster
thaytjoe	thài-chú	太子	prince
theehwee	tê-hōe	茶會	semiformal gathering
thengsha	tn̂g-saⁿ	長衫	long shirt
thian-ong-tho-thak	thian ong thok thah	天王托塔	Heaven King Upholds a Pagoda
thianpauw	thian-phàu	天泡	pus-filled ulcers
thien	tiān (Md)	天	heaven
thoeh	tǔ (Md)	土	earth
thunglang (see tenglang)			
tiamhiat	tiám-hiàt	點穴	to hit the body's pressure points
tiamtang	tiàm-thang	店窗	shop window
tiangseng	tiâng-seng	長生	longevity
tie	dì (Md)	地	earth
tihi	ti-hī	豬耳	pigs' ear
tiko	ti-ko	豬哥	male pig (insult)

SINO-MALAY SPELLING	MODERN ORTHOGRAPHY	CHARACTERS	MEANING
tim	tīm	燖	to stew in a covered pot
tio swah	tióh-soa	著痧	sudden stomach cramps
tiokie	thiàu-kî	跳棋	Chinese checkers
tiong gie	tiong-gī	忠義	man of honor
tiong hak	tiong-ha̍k	中學	secondary school
Tiong Hoa Hwee Koan	Tiong-hôa Hōe-koán	中華會館	Chinese Association
Tiong Hoa Wi Sien Po	Tiong-hôa Ûi-sin Pò	中華維新報	*Chinese Reformist Newspaper*
Tiong Kok (see tiongkok)			
tionghoa	Tiong-hôa	中華	China, Chinese
tiongkok	Tiong-kok	中國	China (lit. the Middle Kingdom)
tiooksiang	tióh-siang	著傷	injuries
Tiotjioe	Tiô-chiu	潮州	Teochew
titee	ti-tê	豬蹄	pigs' trotters
tithauw	ti-thâu	豬頭	pigs' head
titjheng	tī-chhng	痔瘡	hemorrhoids
titouw	ti-tō͘	豬肚	pigs' tripe
tja	chhá	炒	stir-frying
tjabo	cha-bó͘	查某	girl, prostitute
tjabouw (see tjabo)			
tjabouw-tay-ong	cha-bó͘ tāi-ông	查某大王	playboy (lit. king of girls)
tjap tjay (see tjaptjay)			
tjapgomeh	cha̍p-gō͘-mê	十五暝	the Spring Lantern Festival (the final day of the New Year celebration)
tjaplek	chiap-le̍k	接肋	soft loin (of pig)
tjaptjay	cha̍p-chhài	雜菜	chop suey (a vegetable dish; lit. mixed vegetables)
tjawan	chhâ-oán	茶碗	tea bowl
tjay-hoa-tjat	chhái-hoa-cha̍t	采花賊	serial rapist
tjaypo	chhài-pó͘	菜脯	preserved radish
tjeekoe	chheh-kù	冊句	book-phrase
tjek (see entjek)			
tjeng-im	chèng-im	正音	correct pronunciation (of Chinese)
tjenteng	chhin-teng	親丁	guard, hired thug
tjhi	chīⁿ	錢	a mace (weight unit)
tjhing tiauw	chheng-tiâu	清朝	Qing Dynasty
tjia tjai	chia̍h-chhài	食菜	vegetarianism
tjia-besiauw	chia̍h-bē-siau	食未消	indigestion
tjia-im	chiàⁿ-im	正音	correct pronunciation (of Chinese)
tjialat	chia̍h-la̍t	食力	tiresome, exhausting
tjiangkoen	chiang-kun	將軍	general
tjiang-loo	chiang-ló	樟腦	camphor
Tjiangtjioe	Chiang-chiu	漳州	Zhangzhou (a city)
tjiang-yoe	jiàngyóu (Md)	醬油	soy sauce

(continued)

TABLE A1 (continued)

SINO-MALAY SPELLING	MODERN ORTHOGRAPHY	CHARACTERS	MEANING
Tjiap Kian Siang Tam	Chiap-kian Siâng tâm	接見常談	*Common Conversations for Meetings*
tjikoah!	chhì-khòaⁿ	試看	an exclamation
Tjin Po	Chin Pò	貞報	*Virtuous Newspaper*
tjinkong	chìn-kòng	進貢	to pay tribute
tjinsoe	chìn-sū	進士	Advanced Scholar (title)
tjintong	chhin-tông	親堂	ancestral hall
tjioe tjhing	chiùⁿ-chheng	醬清	light soy sauce
tjioegi	chiù-gí	咒語	enchantment
tjio-hong	chioh-hông	石黃	realgar
tjio-hwee	chioh-hoe	石灰	limestone
tjo'a!	zŏ ā! (Tc)	坐啊	have a seat!
Tjoantjioe	Choân-chiu	泉州	Quanzhou (a city)
tjoe bo	chú-bó	主母	mistress
tjoekin	chhiú-kin	手巾	towel
tjoekiong	chú-kiong	子宮	womb, uterus
tjoeng kwo jen	Zhōngguó rén (Md)	中國人	Chinese person
tjoet goa	chhut-gōa	出外	to migrate
tjoewat	chhù-hoat	處罰	punishment
tjo-h'm-lang	chò-hm̂-lâng	做媒人	matchmaker
tjo-ho-sim	chò-hó-sim	做好心	charity
tjo-ho-soe	chò-hó-sū	做好事	wedding
tjokek	chhiòⁿ-khek	唱曲	a traditional music form
tjonggoan	chiōng-goân	狀元	person ranked first in the Palace Examination
tjouwkok	chó͘-kok	祖國	homeland
toakhie	tōa-ki	大裾	Manchu-style bridal gown
Toasebio	Tōa-sài-biō	大使廟	Ambassador Temple
toeilian	tùi-liân	對聯	doorway couplets
toen hoat	tūn-hoat	遁法	invisibility
toengtji	tóngzhì (Md)	同志	comrade
toenphoa	tún-pòaⁿ	盾半	1.5 guilders
tok	tok	毒	toxin
toko	*thó͘-khò͘*	土庫	store
tokouw	tō-ko͘	道姑	female Daoist
tokwie	tok-ûi	桌幃	altar cloth
Tong Gi Tjin Liong	Thong Gí Chin Liông	通语津梁	*Ferry and Bridge of the General Language*
Tong Thian	Tōng-thian	洞天	*Heavenly Cavern*
tong tjoe pia	tong-chhiu-piáⁿ	中秋餅	mooncakes
tongkoen	tông-kun	堂君	boss
tong-njin	thòng-ngìn (Ha)	唐人	Chinese person
tongpao	tông-pau	同胞	compatriot
tongsan	thòng-sân (Ha)	唐山	mainland China
tongtjoe	tông-chú	童子	pupil
Too Tik King	Tō-tek-keng	道德經	*The Way and its Power*
tosoe	tō-su	道師	male Daoist
towyu (S, see tao-yoe)			
toyang	tó-iâng	倒陽	impotence
twatji	tōa-chí	大姐	older sister

SINO-MALAY SPELLING	MODERN ORTHOGRAPHY	CHARACTERS	MEANING
twitjing	tūi-cheng	墜精	spermatorrhea
ve-tsin	vi-jīn (Shanghainese)	味精	monosodium glutamate
waichiaopu	wàijiāobù (Md)	外交部	minister of foreign affairs
wan-gwee	oân-gōe	員外	rich man
yan-o thung	iàn-o thng	燕窩湯	bird's nest soup
ya-tjee-tam-hay	iā chhe tham hái	夜叉探海	Demon Searches the Sea

Note: This table constitutes no attempt to provide a complete list. It contains only the Chinese words found in the Sino-Malay texts cited in this book's main text and endnotes. The majority of the Hokkien etyma are taken from the *Chinese–English Dictionary of the Vernacular or Spoken Language of Amoy* (Douglas 1899). Their transcription has been slightly updated to the modern Pe̍h-ōe-jī romanization. The glosses reflect early twentieth-century Indonesian usage, as I could determine from the context in Sino-Malay texts. The italics in the "modern orthography" column indicate Malay words or morphemes.

TABLE A.2 Words, names, and toponyms from Chinese varieties

MODERN ORTHOGRAPHY	CHARACTERS	MEANING
âng-mô͘-hoan	紅毛番	red-haired barbarians
bā-bā	峇峇	Baba (Ml: *baba*)
Bân-lâm-gú	閩南語	Southern Min
bâ-te̍k	峇澤/貓澤	batik (Ml: *batik*)
be̍k-sī	默氏	district warden (D: *wijkmeester*)
chiàⁿ kâu chó	正猴棗	bezoar stone of simian origin
chu-á	朱仔	secretary (see chu-kat-ta)
chu-kat-ta	朱葛礁	secretary (D: *sekretaris*)
hān-the-kong-pńg-nî	汗theh公本哖	trade company (D: *handelscompagnie*)
Heng-hòa	興化	Putianese
jiānghú (Md)	江湖	the universe of martial heroes
Jîn-tek-lah Le̍k-kok	仁得垃吻國	General de Kock (D: *Generaal de Kock*)
kâ-mê-ya (Ha)	加姆夜	shirt (Ml: *kemeja*)
kap-pit-tan	甲必丹	captain (Ml: *kapitan*)
kap-tōa	甲大	captain (see kap-pit-tan)
kè	髻	hair worn in a bun (Ml: *konde*)
kê-chiap	鮭汁	brine of pickled fish or shellfish (Ml: *kecap ikan*)
kheh	客	guest
kú-lû-puk (Ha)	古魯卜	prawn crackers (Ml: *kerupuk*)
lâng	儂	particle to form plural pronouns
Lán-nâng-ōe	咱人話	our people's language
liû hoat put liû thâu, liû thâu put liû hoat	留髮不留頭, 留頭不留髮	Keep your hair, lose your head; keep your head, lose your hair
ló-kun	老君	Indonesian traditional healer (Ml: *dukun*)
lú mo po-tông sâm-mâ ô-liang (Ha)	魯帽報當三馬阿令	You want to cut somebody down (Ml: *lu mau potong sama orang*)
lú tī-tha̍t tá-vū hâ-tha̍t (Ha)	魯知撻打烏哈撻	You have no manners (Ml: *lu tidak tau adat*)
lûi-tin-lân	雷珍蘭	lieutenant (D: *luitenant*)
lú-lâ (Ha)	魯拉	village head (Ml: *lurah*)
má-io	馬腰	major (D: *majoor*)
nâ-âu sán	嚨喉散	medicine for throat pain (Ml: *obat orang sakit leher*)

(continued)

TABLE A2 *(continued)*

MODERN ORTHOGRAPHY	CHARACTERS	MEANING
niû-á	娘仔	Madam (MI: nyonya)
oán-bō	碗帽	cylindrical skullcap
Pang-ki-lân Lī-pò-lėk-gô-lô	邦基蘭利報力敖勞	Pangeran Diponegoro
phok lí chó-kong	撲你祖公	fuck your great-grandfather
qípáo (Md)	旗袍	tight-fitting one-piece dress
se-kûng-mî-sî (Ha)	細公美西	supervisor (D: chef-commissie)
Sip Ngó Im	十五音	*Fifteen Initial Sounds*
Sit-lam	息垒	assimilated Chinese who converted to Islam (MI: Selam)
Tâi-oân-gú	臺灣語	the Taiwanese language
thian tiok hông	天竹黃	siliceous concretion from the nodal joints of bamboo
tîm hiang sàn	沉香散	agarwood powder
tōa bôe phiàn	大梅片	Sumatran camphor
tōan	緞	Sir (MI: tuan)
tún	盾	guilder (lit. shield)
úi-hān-bút-lát-tek	猥汗勿叻實竹	road tax (D: wegenbelasting)
vút-lî-thung-mát-su-kap-pî (Ha)	物里洞末士甲卑	Belitung Company (D: Billiton Maatschappij)
wǔxiá (Md)	武俠	martial heroes

Note: This table contains words, names, and toponyms from Indonesian Hokkien and other Chinese and localized Chinese varieties cited in this book, followed by their Sinographic characters.

TABLE A.3 Originals of cited Chinese names, works, and proverbs

ENGLISH	CHINESE
Anecdotes about the Sea Islands	Hǎidǎo Yìzhì (海島逸志)
Annals of Batavia	Kāi Ba Lìdài Shǐjì (開吧歷代史記)
Book of Medicines for the Plague that have Proven very Effective	Shíyàn Shǔyì Liáng Wàn (實驗鼠疫良萬)
Book of Rites	Lǐ Jì (禮記)
Brief Account of Island Barbarians	Dǎo Yí Zhì Lüè (島夷誌略)
Butterfly Lovers	Liáng Shānbó yǔ Zhù Yīngtái (梁山伯與祝英台)
The Chinese Magazine	Chá Shìsú Měiyuè Tǒngjì Zhuàn (察世俗每月統紀傳)
College of All Foreigners	Sì Yí Guǎn (四譯館)
The Complete Story of Hai Rui's Small Scarlet Robe	Hǎigōng Xiǎohóngpáo Quánzhuàn (海公小紅袍全專)
Hakka build a city, Cantonese prosper, Teochew and Hokkien control	Kè rén kāi bù, Guǎngfǔ rén wàng bù, Cháofú rén zhàn bù (客人開埠，廣府人旺埠，潮福人佔埠)
Malay-Cantonese Glossary	Mǎlāyǔ Yuè Yīnyì Yì (馬拉語粵音譯義)
Mingcheng School	Míngchéng Shūyuàn (明誠書院)
The Monthly Magazine	Tèxuǎn Cuòyào Měiyuè Jìzhuàn (特選撮要每月紀傳)
Mr. Tjoepeek Lie's Family Instructions	Zhū Bǎilú Xiānshēng Jiāxùn (朱柏廬先生家訓)
Overall Survey of the Ocean's Shores	Yíngyá Shènglǎn (瀛涯勝覽)
Phrasebook for Chinese and Foreigners	Huáyí Tōngyǔ (華夷通語)
The Picture of Tianbao	Tiānbào Tú (天豹圖)
Pingzhou Table Talks	Píngzhōu Kětán (萍洲可談)

ENGLISH	CHINESE
Precious Records of the Jade Register to Admonish the World	Yùlì Bǎochāo Quànshì Wén (玉歷寶鈔勸世文)
Standard Hakka Glossary of the Malay Language	Zhèng Kè Yīnyì Yì Mùláiyóuhuà (正客音譯義木來由話)
Vocabulary Lists for Foreign Languages	Gèguó Yì Yǔ (各國譯語)
Xue Rengui Clears the East	Xuē Rénguì Zhēng Dōng (薛仁貴征東)

Note: This table contains the original names and spellings of all translated Chinese names, works, and proverbs cited in this book.

Notes

INTRODUCTION

1. Oei 1939b, 9; Lee S. L. 1930, 40–41; Tjiong 1924, 19.
2. For a lively contemporaneous overview of these dynamics, see Kwee K. B. 1935, 197, 199.
3. Adam 1995; Herudjati 2008. See also Moriyama 2005 on the situation in West Java, Wirawan 2011 on Makassar, and Sunarti 2013 on West Sumatra.
4. Shiraishi 1990.
5. This point has been made in detail by L. H. Liu 1995. See also Giddens 1990 on modernity as an epistemic and cultural phenomenon and McHale 2004, Ikeya 2011, Lewis 2016, and Protschky and van den Berge 2018 on colonial and other modernities across Southeast Asia. Borthwick 1983, Rutnin 1993, and Wickramasinghe 2014 discuss the dilemmas of modernization in, respectively, China, Siam/Thailand, and Sri Lanka.
6. See Chow 1993 for a broader discussion of these inherent ambivalences.
7. Hoogervorst and Schulte Nordholt 2017.
8. Bakhtin 1984, 466.
9. Shih 2007, 2.
10. See Latif 2008 on the origins of Indonesia's public sphere and Habermas 1989 on western Europe. For public sphere conceptions outside Europe, see Naregal 2001 on India, McHale 2004 on Vietnam, Lean 2007 on China, and Hunter 2015 on Tanzania.
11. Reed 2004, 8. Also see Anderson 1991, Siegel 1997, and Errington 2008.
12. Farid and Razif (2008, 278) therefore speak of "print colonialism."
13. See Rea and Volland 2015 on processes of cultural entrepreneurship in late colonial China and Southeast Asia.
14. Wickramasinghe 2014, 151.
15. Sidharta 2004, Suryadinata 2015, and Suryadinata and Kwartanada 2016 provide detailed information on a selection of individual print entrepreneurs.
16. Salmon 1984; Sidharta 1992; Chandra 2015a. An insight into elite Peranakan life is given in Post 2019.
17. Estimations range between two and three million. See Suryadinata 2016a for an insightful article on the difficulties of quantifying Indonesia's Chinese minority.
18. See, for example, Siegel 1997, Coppel 2002, Sai and Hoon 2013, Suryadinata 2015, and Stenberg 2019.
19. Elson 2008 convincingly demonstrates the historiographical benefits of speaking of "Indonesians" in a preindependence setting.
20. The 1930 Netherlands Indies census shows that 60 percent of Chinese men and 20.7 percent of the women could read, but it fails to specify whether this was in Chinese and/or Malay (Departement van Economische Zaken 1935, 6, 13, 88).
21. See Somers-Heidhues 1996 and Kuiper 2017 for more information on the Chinese outside Java.
22. See Hofmeyr 2013 and Amrith 2013 on printing networks across the Indian Ocean and Reed 2004, Naregal 2001, Huffman 1997, and McHale 2004 on late colonial print culture in, respectively, China, India, Japan, and Vietnam.
23. A. Ong 1992, 2.

24. Godley 1981.

25. Shih 2007; Tan E. K. 2013; Bernards 2015; Hee 2019.

26. See Chandra 2015b and Stenberg 2017 on the shortcomings of labeling Indonesia's Chinese communities as uniformly Sinophone. Ang 2001 and Hau 2014 provide more background on the specific ways non-Sinophone Chinese people are racialized.

27. See Gee 2000–1 and Palmer 2007 on achieved and ascribed identities.

28. Chow 2013, 55, n. 12; Ang 2001, 36.

29. Woolf 1986, 71.

30. Coppel 2002, 194; Maier 2004, 274.

31. Coppel 2002, 195.

32. See Naregal 2001 and Mahadevan 2015 on the role of Parsis in India's popular entertainment and Sandrow 1996 on Yiddish theater.

33. Chatterjee 1993 and Naregal 2001 explore the role of bilingual intelligentsia in colonial India.

34. Chow 1993, 126.

35. Rafael 2016, 5.

36. Hoffman 1979, 65; Anderson 1991, 132–33; Grijns 1991, 58.

37. M. I. Cohen 2006; Keppy 2019.

38. Mahdi 2016.

39. I borrow this phrase from Errington (2008, 3), who explores the role of linguistics under colonialism.

40. Teeuw 1972; Maier 1991, 1993a; Jedamski 1992; Siegel 1997, 131–32, 134–35; Chandra 2006; Errington 2008, 142; Mahdi 2016; Kuitert 2020, 234–47.

41. Hoogervorst 2017.

42. "Kadang-kadang kita bertanja pada diri kita sendiri, apa perloenja koetipan dalam bahasa Perantjis, bahasa Djerman, bahasa Latin. Koetipan itoe kebanjakannja tidak diterdjemahkan, tidak poela diterangkan apa artinja" (Pané 1938, 77).

43. Jedamski 2014 provides more background on these competing factions in late colonial Malay printing.

44. Jedamski 1997, Plomp 2012, Lubis 2018, and Suryadi 2019 discuss the Medan literature in more detail. See also Sunarti 2015, 231–33 on criticism in West Sumatran newspapers on the Malay used in Java.

45. *Verslag Congres Budyåtåmå* 1909.

46. Hoffman 1995; Foulcher 2000; Maier 2004, 20–23.

47. Heryanto 1998, 99. Only *Harian Indonesia* (Indonesia Daily) was allowed to exist. This organ of government propaganda featured four pages in Chinese.

48. Laobing 2003, 10; Stenberg 2017, 640.

49. Only five monographs are known to me: Nio 1962, Kwee J. B. 1977, Salmon 1981, Chandra 2006, and Susanto 2015.

50. Jaap Erkelens (e-mail message to author, March 6, 2016); Ding C. M. 1978.

51. Coppel 2002 (repr. of 1977 essay), 60.

52. Salmon 1981. See Teeuw 1981, Maier 1993a, and Coppel 2002 on the impact of Claudine Salmon's work on the field of Malay literature.

53. Maier 1993a, 284.

54. Song G. 2017; Salmon and Sidharta 2018.

55. The Delpher website, which contains digitized newspapers from the Netherlands and its former colonies, has as yet ignored materials in Malay and other Indonesian languages.

56. Kwee K. B. 1935, 196.

57. For example, see L. W. Chan 2003 and Kuiper 2010.

58. Around two thousand of the books were digitized in 2004 under the Metamorfoze project undertaken by the National Library of the Netherlands. A considerable part consists of microfilms donated by Myra Sidharta from her personal collection.

59. *Sin Po* started as a weekly in 1910 and became a daily in 1913. The available yet incomplete issues of these two periodicals kept at the Leiden University Library were digitized in 2015 with funding from KITLV. An online portal is presently under construction. Due to stringent copyright laws, it is unlikely that the majority of this material will soon be made available outside the library's walls. A large number of *Sin Po* issues has also been made available through the Monash Collections Online at the time of finishing this book.

60. Suryadinata 1971, 10. As the author remarks on the basis of an interview with Tio Ie Soei, Sino-Malay newspapers normally avoided publishing their accurate circulation figures.

61. *Hoakiao* only made the headlines once, in May 1931, when its editors were forced to apologize after publishing an article that insulted Islam (Poeze 1988, 72–73). On Netherlands Indies press censorship concerning Sino-Malay newspapers, see Poeze 1994, lxviii, Maters 1998, 39–42, Yamamoto 2019, 227–55, and Kuitert 2020, 172–74.

62. See the volume edited by Herudjati (2008) for an isolated academic reappraisal of Chinese-Indonesian linguistic and literary practices from the late colonial period.

63. Suryadinata and Kwartanada 2016.

64. L. H. Liu 1995. The concept of "translanguaging" has been applied most successfully in the context of education (García and Li Wei 2014; Mazzaferro 2018).

65. Adhikari 1996; Blommaert 2008; Fahmy 2011.

66. I borrow this phrase from Lalla and D'Costa (1990, xiii) in their history of Jamaican Creole.

67. This idea is further explored in Chow 2014, 13.

68. Mohamad 2008, 311.

69. This point is elaborated on by Fabian (1990, 164) in the context of eastern Congo.

70. Appadurai 1986, 5.

71. Their British-educated peers in Singapore, meanwhile, where dismissed as *ang moh kwan* (Anglicized), *baba cherlop* (whitewashed Babas), and *baba orang putih itam* (dark-skinned Caucasian Babas) (F. Chia 1983, 83).

72. "Satoe tindakan baroe" 1926, 6.

73. I use the established term "foreign orientals," but some contemporaneous English sources display "non-indigenous orientals." Article 163 of the Indies Constitution, which made "foreign orientals" a legally distinct category positioned below "Europeans" and also separate from "indigenous" people, was introduced in 1925. This tripartite racial classification is widely misconceived to be of much older pedigree. That being said, a variety of regulations governing the taxation of ethnic Chinese, Arabs, and Indians and restricting their mobility, education, modes of dress, and property matters had been in place before 1925. See Wertheim 1997, Coppel 2002, 157–68, and Tjiook-Liem 2009 for more background.

74. "al mag hij de grofste koeli of de grootste boef zijn, terwijl zijn rasgenoot, doch [sic!] Nederlandsch onderdaan, met een lagere rechtspositie tevreden mag zijn, al heeft hij een academische titel van een Nederlandsche Universiteit" ("De gelijkstelling der Chineezen" 1940, 27). It was perceived an equally wry absurdity that the majority of Japanese citizens in the Netherlands Indies were prostitutes (Paulus 1917, 483).

75. Teekenpen 1926, 735.

76. Chow 2014, 8.

77. Teekenpen 1926, 735.

78. While the availability of a largely digitized corpus has proven tremendously helpful for me to evaluate the salience of specific topics and identify the texts in which they occur, I have not used computational tools beyond relatively straightforward multiple-file searches. Examining more complex processes, such as grammatical change, would require levels of preprocessing that far exceed the budgetary restraints and time limits of individual scholarship. First, the OCR would need to be optimized to about 97 percent

accuracy, which is difficult to achieve in the absence of specific language packs. Second, the metadata of thousands of files would need to be entered manually to enable search queries by time, place, and genre. Third, the orthography would have to be normalized to improve the searchability of inconsistently spelled words. Fourth, the entire corpus would need to be parsed and interlinearized to separate words from affixes and particles. Fifth, specific software would need to be developed to quantify and visualize word frequencies or syntactic patterns, for example through metadata-based n-gram tables.

79. See Oetomo 1987 on the linguistic nature of Peranakan speech in East Java and Kong 2005 and Jones 2009b on Chinese loanwords in Malay.

80. Chaudhary 2009, 51.

81. Kwartanada 2014. As Wieringa 2020 shows in detail, this resinicization discourse yielded some remarkable examples of acculturation in the form of Indonesian reworkings of Chinese texts.

82. "Het onderscheid tusschen uit- en inlandsche Chinezen is alleen op te merken, aan het meer gevleeschte ligchaam en de vloeijende tongval, tegen de magere, knookige, met hortende klanken kakelende nieuwelingen of Sinke's" (Hageman 1860, 19).

83. Chow 2014, 9. The retired military officer Jan Baptist Jozef van Doren (1791–1873), for example, characterized the linguistic situation of Java's Chinese as follows: "The Chinese language has nothing pleasant to it, it is cacophonous and deafening to the ear. When several Chinese are together, their conversation is so passionate and shrill that one would assume they are in a fierce argument" (De Chinesche taal heeft niets aangenaams, zij is wanluidend en verdoovend voor het gehoor. Wanneer verscheidene Chinezen bij elkander zijn, is hun gesprek zoo driftig en schel, dat men zou veronderstellen, dat zij in hevigen onderlingen twist zijn) (van Doren 1853, 43).

84. Mignolo 2009, 8. For studies on specific colonial settings, see Fabian 1990 on Congo, Cohn 1996 and Naregal 2001 on India, and Rafael 2016 on the Philippines.

85. Hoffman 1979; Mahdi 2016.

86. Woolf 1986, 80.

87. See McHale 2004, 15 for a similar observation on late colonial Vietnam.

88. Farid and Razif 2008; Jedamski 2014. See Yamamoto 2019 for more information on this period.

89. See Govaars-Tjia 1999, 216–17 on the unsuccessful attempts of the Batavia-based student association Chung Hsioh (Secondary School) to make Mandarin the daily language of all Indies Chinese.

90. Maier 2004, 305; Errington 2008, 142.

91. This point has been made in greater detail by Siegel 1997, 18.

92. Chin and Hoogervorst 2017. See Weinbaum et al. 2008, Lewis 2009, and Ikeya 2011 on the "modern girl" phenomenon in other late colonial contexts. For more background on gender and modernity in this period, see Finnane 2007 and Judge 2008 on China, Than 2014 on Burma, and George 2014 on Nigeria.

93. Suryadinata 2003, 90; Chandra 2006, 175. Kung fu novels managed to withstand cultural erasure by virtue of their broadly digestible stories. See Suryadinata 2013 for an overview of this genre. As he shows, the serialization of kung fu stories in newspapers was restricted in the late 1950s, yet the genre was allowed to continue as pocketbooks.

94. Nio 1962, 5, 165.

95. See Heryanto 1995, Bertrand 2003, and Samuel 2005 for more detailed studies.

1. CONNECTED LANGUAGE HISTORIES

1. The term is mentioned in the Kañcana Inscription (Kern 1881, 98). For more background, see Wang G. 1958 and Wheatley 1961.

2. Wang G, 1996; Chang 1998; Heng 2008; Schottenhammer 2015.

3. Heng 2008, 11–12.

4. This community is mentioned in the *Brief Account of Island Barbarians* (Rockhill 1915, 240).

5. As described in the *Overall Survey of the Ocean's Shores* (Mill 1970, 89).

6. Examples of Chinese loanwords in this list are *cawan* (tea bowl; Hk: *chhâ-oán*) and *lobak* (Chinese radish; Cn: *lòh baahk*). The earliest Portuguese vocabularies of Malay, too, contain Hokkien loans. See Salmon 2019 for an overview of Chinese–Malay language contact in this period.

7. Additional titles specific to the Netherlands Indies' administration were lieutenant (D: *luitenant*, Hk: *lûi-tin-lân*), major (D: *majoor*, Hk: *má-io*), and district warden (D: *wijkmeester*, Hk: *bėk-sĩ*).

8. See Lohanda 2005 on these emancipatory struggles and Lombard and Salmon 1993 for more information on Islam and Chineseness in the Netherlands Indies.

9. Pan 1990; Look Lai 1993; McKeown 2008; S. Chan 2018. Also see Frost 2005 on a detailed study of the Straits Chinese in Singapore.

10. This was particularly so since many other professions were legally confined to Europeans or indigenous groups. See Rush 1960, Derks 2012, and Kim 2020 on the history of opium in Java.

11. It is often assumed that this development started in the early twentieth century, but Salmon 1996 calls attention to important late nineteenth-century precedents.

12. Blussé and Nie 2018, 96.

13. Oliver 1708, 203.

14. See Sidharta 2007 on these legends.

15. As such, it runs parallel to Myanmar's *thauke kabya*, Cambodia's *kooncav cen*, Thailand's *lookjin*, and the Philippines' *chino mestizo*. The offspring of an Arab man and a non-Arab woman was often designated as *muwallad*.

16. In Dutch, *Indo* had been in use from the 1880s to designate Eurasians. Its full form was *Indo-Europeaan*, corresponding to Malay *Indo Belanda*. People of mixed Arabic and Indonesian origins were designated as *Indo Arab* (D: *Indo-Arabieren*).

17. Also written as *babah*, this word ultimately reflects the Hindustani term *bābā* (Sir). It is glossed as "a significant man and also his son" (een aanzienlijk man en ook diens zoon) in an early Betawi Malay dictionary (Batten 1868, 37) and is also used in this sense by the Malays of Sri Lanka. Along similar lines, the appellation for men of South Asian ancestry (Ml: *kodja*) goes back to Hindustani *khojā* (master).

18. The word was spelled interchangeably as *pernakan*, *pranakan*, *parnakan*, *parnakkan*, *parnacang*, etc. Most people so classified were Chinese Muslims with Arabic or Javanese names. This distinction also prevailed in Cape Town, which in VOC times housed a community of Chinese convicts, exiles, ship crew, and enslaved people from the Indies (Franken 1953, 75).

19. See the *Anecdotes about the Sea Islands* (Ong T. H. 1849, 33). The Malay word *Selam* goes back to Islam.

20. "Cara mlajeng mawi sajak cina" (Candranegara 1877, 50); "Cara-caranipun sampun kados Cina. . . . Lelenggahan utawi wicantenan inggih sami ugi kalih Cina sadaya tiyang. Bilih lelenggahan sami kursen utawi dhingklik; yen nedha, wonten ing meja" (*Cariyos ing Betawi* 1.16). The latter, unpublished, text was kindly provided by Willem van der Molen.

21. Leo 1975 and Kwa 2016 offer an overview of the Hokkien loanwords used by Chinese and non-Chinese speakers of Betawi. On the creolized Betawi culture, see Knörr 2014. Several of Batavia's late nineteenth-century neighborhoods had Hokkien names, such as *Angke* (Red Creek), *Djilakeng* (26 Buildings), *Patekoan* (Eight Teapots), *Patike* (Blacksmith St.), *Pinangsia* (Areca Village), *Sampan Liauw* (Sampan Shed), *Sentiong* (New Burying Ground), and *Toasebio* (Ambassador Temple).

22. See, for example, the Malay phrasebook by Badings (1883, 39). The *singkeh-laukeh* distinction was also made in other colonial contexts with Chinese minorities, such as Suriname (Tjon Sie Fat 2009, 49, n. 32). In the context of indentured labor, *laukeh* also referred to a former "coolie"—of any non-European ethnicity—who was sent back to his region of origin to recruit new workers.

23. Suryadinata (2005, 122) and Coppel (2002, 106–23) elaborate on the limitations of the Totok-Peranakan dichotomy. This distinction has lost additional relevance after the forced cultural assimilation under the Suharto government (1966–98) and optional resinicization afterwards (Sai 2006). See Rudolph 1998, 25–32 on partly similar discussions of Peranakanness in Singapore.

24. For example, *Sin Po* proudly reported on "yet another Chinese woman pilot": Ms. Lin Peng Hsieh, who was a "Singaporean Peranakan and her parents were born in Fuzhou (Fujian)" (Pranakan Singapore dan orang toea kelahiran Foochow [Hokkian]) ("Lagi Satoe Djoeroe Terbang Prampoean Tionghoa" 1932).

25. Lg. 1930.

26. Tan D. S. 1913, 28; Nio 1937, 40. For more background, see Coppel and Suryadinata 1978.

27. This particular history is described in Claver 2014. In response to this controversy, the Dutch government assured that no similar cases of signs forbidding Chinese people from entry were known to them ("Verboden toegang voor Chineezen" 1939).

28. Its counterparts in West Sumatra (*intjek*), Makassar (*intjé*), West Borneo (*entji*), and British Malaya (*enche'*) had acquired the broader meaning of "Mr.," whereas in the Philippines (*intsik*) and Thailand (*jeek*) the term developed into a derogatory slur for Chinese men.

29. Hoa Djin was also the pseudonym of the social activist Phoa Keng Hek (1857–1937) (Oi 2014, 166).

30. These terms were also used by Chinese-descended communities elsewhere. See, for example, Tjon Sie Fat (2009, 343–50) on the corresponding terminology in Suriname.

31. Keessen 2009, 125.

32. Siow 1924.

33. Babas could reciprocate such insults with *china gerk* (Chinese hillbilly), to which Hokkien-speaking Singkehs had the option to retort with *baba seow* (crazy Baba) and Cantonese-speakers with *mo foo long* (trousers without a crotch), mocking the localized dress of the Peranakan (F. Chia 1983, 16). Meanwhile, white Europeans were known in Straits Hokkien as *âng-mô-hoan* (red-haired barbarians). The usage of this rather unfavorable designation was even reported among Singapore's Chinese court interpreters when they referred to their British employers (R. N. Jackson 1965, 18–19). In Sino-Malay texts published in Java, the word *angmoh* chiefly referred to British people, although it historically denoted the Dutch as well.

34. Yap n.d., 44; Han 1923, 55.

35. See Liem 1933, 277 for a contemporaneous account and Tan B. H. 2009, 49 for a retrospective one. In administrative circles, the insensitive term *inlander* remained commonplace until 1940 (Poeze 1994, xlii–xliii).

36. "Golongan dari partij kiri, Nationalisten atawa revolutionairen" (Kwee T. H. 1938–41, 1:124).

37. *Bintang Timoer*, November 7, 1927, 1.

38. Liem 1933, 197.

39. See, for example, Skinner 1996, Ho 2006, Hung 2011, and Bernards 2015. At least one British author, John Crawfurd (1783–1868), referred to people of mixed Southeast Asian and Chinese ancestry as "creole Chinese" (Rudolph 1998, 33).

40. R. Cohen 2007, for example, applies "creole" to ethnic identities that emerge under unequal power relations, draw from a variety of cultures, create new traditions, or invest

existing traditions with new meanings. As usual, there is no scholarly agreement on its precise usage. It is impossible to give a complete overview of the relevant literature, but see Price 2001 and Stewart 2007.

41. Hwat San 1929; T. F. 1937, 5.

42. See Gyssels 2007 on these negative portrayals in general and Dharmowijono 2009, 363 on the Netherlands Indies context.

43. The same has been observed in Baba Malay print culture (Proudfoot 1994, 20).

44. Chia C. S. 1899, 11.

45. "blijven veelen in later leeftijd de voorkeur geven aan het Maleisch, doorspekken althans hun Chineesch met zooveel Maleische woorden, dat ze voor een sinkee in den aanvang onverstaanbaar moeten zijn. Hun uitspraak is daarbij verfoeilijk slecht" (Albrecht 1879, 241); "een op Java geboren Chinees, een *Babah*, kent niet meer Chineesche woorden dan voldoende zijn om, in het Maleisch gemengd, dit te veranderen in een argot dat noch de echte Chinees, noch de Europeaan begrijpt" (Dermout 1894, 13).

46. Pekdjit 1941, 1.

47. See Chow 2014 for an elaborate study on "foreign" versus "native" language practices in postcolonial contexts and Rafael 2016 on "motherless tongues."

48. "In de tokohouder een Chinees, dan zal men steeds Maleisch kunnen spreken" (v.d. Kop and Bezemer 1915, 199, n. 1).

49. "Saorang Tionghoa" 1949.

50. These include the varieties of Fuqing (Hk: *Hok-chhia^n*; Ml: *Hoktjia*), Fuzhou (Hk: *Hok-chiu*; Ml: *Hoktjioe*), and Putian (Hk: *Heng-hòa*); see Mian Yan 2006, 120–47. In China, Hokkien is better known as *Bân-lâm-gú* (Southern Min), in Taiwan as *Tâi-oân-gú* (Taiwanese), and in the Philippines as *Lán-nâng-ōe* (our people's language). See Lin 2015, 2 for a more detailed introduction.

51. See Jones 2009a on the earliest Hokkien dialects in the Malay-speaking world and Klöter 2011 on the Philippines. It must be kept in mind that Chinese letters, manuscripts, temple inscriptions, tombstones, and other written sources contain little information on the dialectal origins of its authors, as they used literary Chinese.

52. See Mills 1938 and Chien 2012 on *toko* and Liem 1933, 52, Wang T. P. 1994, and Salmon 2006, 175, n. 52 on *kongsi*. In the Malay of Malaysia and Singapore, *kongsi* has become the word for "sharing."

53. Examples of such linguistic puzzles include *kap-tōa* (captain) and *chu-á* (secretary), which are abbreviated forms of *kap-pit-tan* (Ml: *kapitan*) and *chu-kat-ta* (D: *secretaris*) (Liem 1933, 13, 51). See Wade 2007, Salmon 2009a, and Kuiper 2017, 1117–19 for more examples. Elsewhere in Southeast Asia, too, Hokkien adjusted to local conditions. See P. S. Ding 2016 on the Hokkien of Singapore and Myanmar.

54. Wen Zi Chuan 1979, 718. See Paulus 1917 and Kuiper 2017 on the different Chinese subgroups in the Netherlands Indies.

55. The exhaustive standard work on this particular history is Kuiper 2017. Similar enterprises followed suit in British Malaya from the 1870s (King 2009; Leow 2016).

56. Raffles 1814, 13; Maier 1993b, 44. Also see Carey 1992, 21–22 and Groeneboer 1993 on the early European adoption of Malay.

57. Hoffman 1979; Grijns 1991; Mahdi 2016.

58. "Dari lagoe bitjaranja prampoean itoe, njatalah ia boekan orang poelo Djawa, kerna dari bebrapa perkata'an Melajoe tinggi jang dioetjapken, menjataken jang ini njai ada orang Sumatra Salatan" (Tan B. K. 1915, 11).

59. Maier 1993b, 47–48.

60. Yet see Rafferty 1984, Oetomo 1991, Nothofer 2004, and Mahdi 2016 for descriptive studies.

61. "Djadi penjakitnja djornalis-djornalis bangpak di Djawa Koelon" (Kwee T. H. 1935c, 65).

62. This point was also made by Suryadinata 1971 and Salmon 1980. In Dutch sources, however, references to *Chineesch-Maleisch* as a separate linguistic entity can already be found in the 1880s (*De Locomotief*, October 7, 1882, 1).

63. Nio 1932; Rafferty 1984; Oetomo 1988.

64. As the Dutch author Michael Theophile Hubert Perelaer (1831–1901) deliberated in one of his novels: "But why should one attempt to accurately represent the Malay gibberish of the Chinese? This would be an impossible task due to the difficulty of that race to pronounce certain consonants, so that they substitute them for others, and their speech becomes almost incomprehensible" (Maar waarom te trachten het brabbelmaleisch van den Chinees weer te geven. Dat zou een onmogelijkheid probeeren zijn door de moeilijkheid, welke die landaard heeft om sommige medeklinkers uit te spreken, waardoor zij die door andere verwisselen, en hun spreken schier niet te volgen is) (Perelaer 1886, 43). Ever since the influx of new immigrants from China, European newspapers took pleasure in the publication of fake letters in broken Dutch, supposedly written by Chinese men. Examples can be seen in *Padangsch Nieuws- en Advertentie-blad*, November 13, 1860, 4; *Sumatra-courant*, July 20, 1872, 3; *Bataviaasch Handelsblad*, June 15, 1881, 5; and *Het Nieuws van den Dag*, February 2, 1886, 5.

65. Selapar bin Kenyang 1931.

66. See Nio 1939a and 1940, Tan B. H. 2009, and Kwartanada 2013 on the historical relevance of this organization.

67. *Hoakiao* 10, 1926, 1; the first two lines are from Confucius's *Book of Rites*.

68. See Govaars-Tjia 1999 on these tensions.

69. "Tepok ayer di dulang, terprichit muka sendiri" ("Masok terbilang" 1931).

70. Li Minghuan 2003, 219; Erkelens 2013, 36. It is telling that the Straits-educated imperial commissioner Wang Ronghe relied on an interpreter to communicate with Surabaya's local Chinese during his 1887 visit (Salmon 2009b, 45).

71. Lie T. T. 1929, 12.

72. The C. 1936, 221.

73. See Coppel 1981 and Salmon and Lombard 1997 on the Chinese reformist movement in the Netherlands Indies, Yen 1976 on British Malaya, and Borthwick 1983 on China.

74. Williams 1960, 54–63; Yen 1976; Sutrisno 2017.

75. Kwartanada 2017. See Bailey 2003 on girls' education in China.

76. Williams 1960, 66–95; Yen 1976, 47–48; Oi 2014, 96–98.

77. In addition, some local schools in the southern provinces opened their doors to students from outside China (Sai 2006, 151).

78. Paulus 1917; Williams 1960, 95–107; Tan B. H. 2009.

79. Shiraishi 1990. See Salmon 2009b, 54 on the Chinese riots in Surabaya.

80. Sai 2013; 2016, 386–87; Kwartanada 2018; Hoogervorst forthcoming.

81. The first Mandarin-medium school in Penang opened in 1904 (Godley 1981, 40). Yen 2003 and Sai 2013 illustrate the transborder networks in which this took place. One may assume that the success of Mandarin in the diaspora was accelerated by a sense of shame among its early reformists for their inability to read or speak Chinese (Yen 1976, 52).

82. Williams 1960, 108–9.

83. "Onderwijs Tionghoa di Indonesia" 1935.

84. Some Chinese schools offered *hanboen* (literary Chinese) alongside *hooboen* (literary Japanese) (*Hanboen dalem Holl. Chin. School* 1926).

85. "Apatah Hoakiauw masih berhati Tiong Hoa?" (*Ho Po* 1912). Hoogervorst forthcoming contextualizes these teaching materials.

86. Hokkien education can be traced back to the establishment of Batavia's Mingcheng School in 1775 (Blussé and Nie 2018, 178).

87. "Ntjek Kim Koen memang sedari masi ketjil ada masoek oteng dimana ia pertama diadjar 'tjoewat'" (Tong Ketik 1929).

88. See Albrecht 1879, Nio 1939a, and Govaars-Tjia 1999 on Chinese education in the Netherlands Indies. Education had long been a transborder affair. As early as 1849, Chinese businessmen based in Java donated money to Chinese schools in Singapore (Salmon 2000, 85; Kwartanada 2013, 30–31). Some Indies Chinese traveled to China to continue their education. The Surabayan Tjioe Ping Wie, for example, founded the Lam Yang Hoen Bong Kwan (School of the South Seas) in the 1870s after returning from China (Salmon and Lombard 1997, 387–88). In the early 1890s, Babas from the Straits Settlements opened an Anglo-Chinese School in Batavia, where Hokkien, Hakka, Cantonese, and Teochew were taught (Frost 2005, 58, n. 99).

89. "Bahasa omong dari masing masing kampoeng asalnja" (K. H. N. 1926). Also see Sai 2016, 385.

90. Liem 1933, 185. See Groeneboer 1993, 154–214 on the teaching of Dutch to indigenous Indonesians.

91. Oi 2014, 98–100.

92. "di Medan Deli sadja (satoe tempat jang masi teritoeng djadjahan Olanda) iaorang tiada oesa harep nanti bisa dapet pengidoepan jang pantes apabila iaorang tiada pande bahasa Tionghoa dan Inggris" (Nova Hino 1911, 442).

93. Liem 1933, 177; Groeneboer 1993, 357–65; Govaars-Tjia 1999.

94. *Swara Publiek* 417 (1929): 2.

95. Govaars-Tjia 1999, 171.

96. K. W. S. 1931. This point was also made by Sai (2006, 159; 2016, 384) and Kwartanada (2018, 44).

97. "Bahasa Tionghoa . . . !" 1929, 2.

98. Tan S. D. 1940.

99. Common examples include *aykok* (patriotism), *aytjiong* (loving the masses), *ban swee* (long live!), *khongkauw* (Confucianism), *kong-ek* (social organization), *oehauw* (filial piety), *siauw soat* (fiction), *song soe* (funeral arrangements), *tjoet goa* (to migrate), *tjo-h'm-lang* (matchmaker; Ml: *tjomblang*), *tjo-ho-sim* (charity), and *tjo-ho-soe* (wedding arrangements). See Hoogervorst forthcoming on the use of Hokkien in Chinese–Malay dictionaries.

100. In this case, the corresponding characters were transcribed in romanized Hokkien, e.g., *janswat* (speech), *kekbeng* (revolution), *kuoyü* (national language), *oen tong* (sports), *siahwee* (society), and *tiong hak* (secondary school). See Williams 1960, 62 on the role of THHK in promoting such words, L. H. Liu 1995 on novel concepts that entered the Chinese language through Japanese, and McHale 2004, 11 for similar examples in Vietnamese.

101. *Nan Sing* 36 (1930): 2.

102. Examples include *Chau Sing* (Voice of the Tide; Makassar, 1924), *Soeara Tsing Niën* (Voice of the Youth; Surabaya, 1928), *Nan Sing* (Voice of the South; Semarang, 1930), and *Kung Yen* (Public Declaration; Batavia, 1936).

103. "Hikajat Bahasa Blanda di Indonesie" 1926, 822.

104. See Horton 2020 on language policy during the Japanese occupation.

2. ON GOOD, BAD, AND UGLY MALAY

1. Maier (2004, 16) specifically makes this point with regard to Malay in the Netherlands Indies.

2. See, for example, Dorleijn and Nortier 2017 on the metalinguistic discourse of youth languages and their speakers.

3. Despite frequent claims to the contrary, the standard orthography of Indonesian likewise does not correspond one-to-one with its pronunciation, particularly when it

comes to loanwords. See Vikør 1988 and Fogg 2015 for a discussion on the standardization of Arabic-derived vocabulary.

4. See Groeneboer 1993 and Nothofer 2004 on the Malay of Bible translators and Mahdi 2016 on that of newspaper editors. These dynamics are also explored in Maier (2004, 18).

5. "De vraag is nu maar of men er zich bij neer moet leggen, dat door den invloed der machtige Chineesch-Maleische pers de taal verbastert tot een onbegrijpelijk, hybridisch product. Velen meenen van wel, omdat naar hun meening de invloed van deze pers zóó groot zou zijn dat men toch niet tegen den stroom op kan roeien. Maar wanneer men dan verneemt dat van Chineesche zijde wordt aangedrongen op afschaffing van het gebruikelijke school-Maleisch op de Maleisch-Chineesche scholen, omdat deze taal voor de Chineezen onbegrijpelijk en in het practische leven onbruikbaar is, en van gezaghebbende zijde de meening wordt geopperd dat het (uit den aard der zaak ook weer in tal van locale variëteiten voorkomende) Chineezen-Maleisch, speciaal op Java, zóó ver van het gewone Maleisch afstaat dat het eigenlijk een geheel aparte taal is, dan blijkt toch wel duidelijk de urgentie om in dit opzicht tot klare voorstellingen te komen, te scheiden wat niet bijeen behoort, en in elk geval te zorgen voor het systematisch en wetenschappelijk opbouwen en in de practijk doorzetten van een goed, modern Maleisch" (Esser 1938, 160).

6. "Naast brieven in goed Maleisch, die ter navolging worden opgegeven, dienen dus ook in 't slechte Chineezen-Maleisch gestelde brieven in een praktisch brievenboek voor te komen" (Fokker 1906, 1).

7. Kuiper 2005. In the same period, Spanish "friar linguists" described the Hokkien dialect of the Philippines (Klöter 2011).

8. He was also known as Kok Sin Tjong and Kuo Ch'eng-chang (Blussé 2014, 37–38; Kuiper 2017, 89). See Su 1996, Reed 2004, 31–32, Blussé 2014, 36, and Kuiper 2017, 161 on Medhurst's Southeast Asian years.

9. In the mid-nineteenth century, Leiden's Sinology Department was established with the aim to remedy the colonial government's ignorance of Chinese communities in the Indies, their languages, bookkeeping systems, and legal conflicts (Kuiper 2017).

10. Schlegel 1900, 16.

11. "Bahasanja miskin, tetapi isinja penuh dengan bahan² jang dapat didjadikan material studi untuk sesuatu maksud" (Nio 1962, 4); "bahasa lisan dan banjak kekurangan² lain" (Gan n.d., 179); "ejaannya awut-awutan, sekenanya saja, asal bunyi kata-kata. Bahasanya tidak karuan, susunan tidak teratur. Itulah yang dinamakan Melayu-Tiong Hoa? Unik? Antik? Atau hebat untuk di simpan sebagai kenangan?" (Tjan 1992, 163). The translation of the latter excerpt is from Coppel (2002, 206), who also discusses the Chinese-Indonesian linguistic inferiority complex.

12. Recently, a Malaysian Peranakan writer proclaimed that "Baba Malay is a corrupt form of the Malay language: it borrows liberally from Hokkien" (Khoo 1998, 9). Almost a century earlier, a Singaporean author (correctly) predicted that "soon there will be a literature to perpetuate this corrupt form of the Malay tongue" (Chia C. S. 1899, 12–13).

13. Honorable counterexamples include Mohamed Salleh bin Perang (1841–1915) of Johor (Sweeney 1980, 52) and presumably several indigenous wives of Chinese elites.

14. "dan is 't Neerduits, in opzicht van de zuivre Hoog-duytze, ook een quade Taal" (Valentyn 1726, 416). This sentence is difficult to accurately translate into English. *Nederduitsch* (Low German) was a common term for Dutch, whereas *Hoogduitsch* (High German) denoted the German prestige variety. Valentijn thus took issue with the use of "high" and "low" as adjectives of quality. The inaccuracy of these epithets was also elaborated on by Pijnappel 1865, van Wijk 1881, and others. During the "First Conference on the Indonesian Language" in 1938, the Sumatran author and dramatist Sanoesi Pané (1905–68) also rejected the High Malay/Riau Malay versus Low Malay/Bazaar Malay dichotomy ("Keputusan Kongres Bahasa Indonesia I" 1983, 208).

15. "dan zal men 't Hollandsch van een Hottentot of Kaffer, enz. *Laag-Hollandsch* moeten noemen, en 't Hollandsch van een Amsterdamschen kruijer *Hoog-Hollandsch*" (van der Tuuk 1864, 530). Instead, he differentiated between literary Malay, Malay dialects spoken natively (e.g., Batavian Malay), and pidgin Malay, which he consistently dismissed as gibberish (*brabbeltaal*) (van der Tuuk 1856, 172).

16. The Van Ophuijsen Spelling System was not implemented beyond the Netherlands Indies, yet see Leow 2016, 76–79 on its influence on orthographic standardization in British Malaya.

17. Anderson 2008, 52–53.

18. "Bahasa Melajoe" 1924, 473.

19. "de taal, waarin alles wat zich boven het allerprimitiefste leven verheft, zich uit weet te drukken en die iedereen verstaat" (Koks 1931, 114).

20. Van Ronkel 1918b, 658.

21. "De Maleische taalstudie heeft geen erger vijand dan het Laag-Maleisch en vereischt alle mogelijke inspanning om dien te overwinnen; want ofschoon reeds meer dan een tweetal eeuwen heugende, is die studie nog een teder plantje, dat met veel tegenspoeden te kampen heeft gehad, en waarvoor men nog niet met volle zekerheid kan vertrouwen op het spoedig aanbreken van een zonnigen dag; terwijl haar vijand altijd gesteund wordt door de menschelijke neiging om het gemak te verkiezen boven inspanning" (Pijnappel 1865, 158–59).

22. Blagden 1917–20, 97.

23. Oldham 1891, 211–12.

24. De Jonghe 1967; Groeneboer 1993, 100.

25. Groeneboer 1993.

26. These included *min-thap* (to ask for; Ml: *minta*) and *tó-lông* (to help; Ml: *toeloeng*) (van de Stadt 1912, i; Kuiper 2017, 678).

27. "vol moderne, zoowel Bataviasche als Hollandsche, woorden . . . waardeloos gedicht" (van Ronkel 1921, 87).

28. The Malay wordlist has been analyzed by Edwards and Blagden (1931). Other languages studied at the College of All Foreigners included Tibetan, Sanskrit, Persian, Shan, Uyghur, and Burmese (Hirth 1888). These wordlists were historically part of the Morrison Collection and are currently kept at the School of Oriental and African Studies in London. See Yong and Peng 2008 on the history of Chinese lexicography more generally.

29. See Kuiper 2017, 168 for more background. *Sip Ngo Im* was evidently known in the Indies. It was advertised by a Sino-Malay publisher as late as the 1930s. Copies have survived in one private collection and are currently kept at the Leiden University Library (Kuiper 2010).

30. Wade 2007, Salmon 2009a, and Blussé and Nie 2018 give numerous examples. See Cushman and Milner 1979 for similar observations in the Malay Peninsula.

31. Kuiper 2017, 257. For more examples, see Kang 2017, Kuiper 2017, and Blussé and Nie 2018.

32. Liem 1933, 96.

33. These words are taken from Vleming (1925, 48), who also gives additional examples.

34. Lim K. C. 1877. See Chen 1967, 55 and Uchida 2017, 141–42 for more background.

35. Lim K. C. 1883. This dictionary is currently kept at the National Library Board of Singapore, where it has received much public attention.

36. As Hokkien tones are phonologically connected to the syllable coda, tone marks offered an ingenious way to transcribe syllables that violate Chinese phonotactics. See Schlegel 1900, 11–15 on this system.

37. Lim K. C. 1883, 41.

38. Lim T. T. 1878. The book's method of transcribing non-Chinese syllables was carefully studied by Gustaaf Schlegel (1900) with the ultimate aim to learn how Chinese literati dealt with words from classical Indic texts.

39. See Hermawan 1994 on the *Standard Hakka Glossary of the Malay Language* and Wang X. 2012 on the *Malay–Cantonese Glossary*.

40. Hermawan 1994, 165, 167. Van de Stadt's aforementioned Hakka dictionary (1912) also contained loanwords that could be written in Chinese characters, for example *se-kûng-mî-sî* (supervisor; D: *chef-commissie*) and *vùt-lî-thung-màt-sṳ-kap-pî* (Belitung Company; D: *Billiton Maatschappij*). This is still done in modern Indonesian Hakka, e.g., *kâ-mê-ya* (shirt; Ml: *kemeja*), *kú-lû-puk* (prawn crackers; Ml: *kerupuk*), and *lû-lâ* (village head; Ml: *lurah*) (Hermawan 1994). These dynamics are also discussed in Kuiper 2017, 750–51.

41. Lie K. H. 1891. See Tio I. S. 1958, J. B. Kwee 1977, 54–66, and Coppel 2002, 256–78 on his role in Chinese cultural revivalism.

42. Examples include *nama paäda* (noun), *pengganti nama* (pronoun), *penerang* (adjective), *pemoela* (article), *nama bilangan* (numeral), *nama kerdja* (verb), *penerangan* (adverb), *pengoendjoek* (preposition), *pengoeboeng* (conjunction), and *oetjap seroe* (interjection). See Tio I. S. 1958, 111–24, Lombard 1972, and Liaw 2016 for more information on his linguistic terminology and Hidayatullah 2012 on the completely different system used by Raja Ali Haji.

43. These include, for example, *goerat-pendek* (short scratch) for "grave accent" <ò> and *tanda sikoe* (elbow sign) for "circumflex diacritic" <ô> (Kwee T. H. 1935b, 867–69).

44. Lim H. S. 1887. See Santa-Maria 1980 for a preliminary description.

45. Lim H. S. 1887, 125.

46. According to his granddaughter Anny Tan (1917–2007), Tjoa Tjoe Kwan published four different Malay teaching books (Blussé 2000, 70). The THHK schoolbook was advertised in *Sin Po*, November 17, 1923 (I owe this observation to Azmi Abubakar).

47. Lu 1935.

48. Hoogervorst forthcoming.

49. Tjoa T. K. 1897; 1904.

50. Pouw P. H. 1931, 580; Song C. S. 1921, 64.

51. "Sagala perkatahan-perkatahan asing jang soeda oemoem di goenaken di dalem soerat-soerat kabar Melayoe; di perloeken boewat pembatja-pembatja Sin Po" (Kwik 1923). See Samuel 2005, 154–55 and Leow 2016, 115 for more background.

52. A similar "philological displacement of the language's origin" took place in other colonies, for example in Swahili-speaking Africa (Errington 2008, 133). For more background on the importance of Riau's printing industry, see van der Putten 1997 and Leow 2016, 66–68.

53. "als Ethiopiërs de taal van Cicero leerden gebruiken, zouden dan de veel hooger staande Javanen, Boegineezen enz. geen Riouwsch Maleisch kunnen leeren?" (Fokker 1891, 87).

54. Teeuw 1972; Hoffman 1979; Drewes 1981; Grijns 1991; Maier 1993b; Jedamski 1997; Mahdi 2006.

55. "Bahasa Melaju, jang djika diibaratkan sebagai gadis ketjil . . . sekarang telah mendjelma mendjadi seorang puteri remadja. Kita mengharapkan dan menanti-nanti, bilakah saatnja bahasa kita mendjadi ratu jang dimuliakan dan ditjintai diantara bahasa[2] dunia!" (Usman 1955, 60).

56. See Hill 1955, 201–2 and Maier 2004, 17 on Munsyi Abdullah. Raja Ali's views on the topic can be read in his own work (1986–87, 197).

57. See Sunarti 2013, 231–33 on linguistic purism as advocated in late colonial newspapers from West Sumatra.

58. Kwee T. H. 1935a, 276.

59. Even writers who sporadically used High Malay felt the need to explain unfamiliar words in English or in Low Malay. So, in Singapore's *Kabar Slalu*, January 5, 1924, we find *stia* explained as "(hati betol; faith)," *stiawan* as "(turut dngan bnar; faithful)," *estimewa* as "(slebeh-lebeh; especially)," *maju* as "(untong; prosper)," and *uchap-an* as "(perminta-an; utterance)." Nevertheless, the wealthy Babas of the Straits felt little compulsion to adopt what they dismissed as jungle Malay (*Malayu hutan*)—that is, nonurban varieties associated with ethnic Malays—at the cost of their own vibrant dialect (Shellabear 1913, 52).

60. *Surat Khabar Peranakan*, April 3, 1894.
61. G. 1935, 43.
62. Alisjahbana 1934, 97; Kwee K. B. 1936, 91–92.
63. Pena Baek 1940.
64. *Sin Po Wekelijksche Editie* 961 (1941): 27.
65. Kwee T. H. 1934c, 773; Siegel 1997, 131–32; Keppy 2019, 218–19.
66. Tan K. G. 1939, 17.
67. Alisjahbana 1933–34, 174–75; 1934.
68. Tjiong 1924, 48.
69. "sifatnja berbeda djaoe dengen apa jang kita biasa omongken di Batavia satiap hari, kerna beratsal dari Riouw" (Kwee T. H. 1938–41, 2:322).
70. Kwee T. H. 1938–41, 2:322–23.
71. "Keputusan Kongres Bahasa Indonesia I" 1983, 210, 221.
72. Goerz 1938, 22.
73. See Lubis 2018, 95–99 for more background.
74. Tan K. G. 1939, 17.
75. See, respectively, J. B. Kwee 1977, 63 on Lie Kim Hok, Kwee T. H. 1928 on Gouw Peng Liang, Nio 1937, 42 on Tjoe Bou San, and Pena Baek 1940 on Tan Hong Boen. See also Sidharta 2004 on the life of the latter.
76. "Koeli-koeli jang mati karena demam malaria jang ditoelari oleh njamoek djoemlahnja tida terhitoeng" (Kwee T. H. 1934a, 982).
77. In a sparsely known article, the aforementioned Armijn Pané (1941, 27–30) panned the original text of Indonesia's national anthem. Many of the grammatical inconsistencies he called attention to indeed never made it into the final version.
78. "Perubahan Edjaan dengan Huruf Latin" 1953. See Alisjahbana 1948b and Vikør 1988 for more details on successive Malay orthographies.
79. Kwee T. H. 1928, 1685.
80. I borrow this term from Leow 2016 on Malaysia's language history. Also see Klöter (2005, 37–39), who examines polygraphia and polyorthographia in the context of Taiwanese Hokkien.
81. See Vleming 1925, 4 for a contemporaneous description.
82. The Central Javanese newspaper *Selompret Melajoe* (Malay Trumpet; Semarang, 1860) owed much of its popularity to the fact that it contained a serialized Javanese version of the story *Sam Kok* (The Three Kingdoms) (Liem 1933, 144). It is furthermore telling that the biography of the businessman Ko Ho Sing (1826–90)—one of Southeast Asia's first non-European biographies—was entirely written in Javanese. Incidentally, the latter was an avid reader of the *Selompret Melajoe* (van der Molen forthcoming).
83. Van der Tuuk 1886, 975; Salmon 1981, 16; Chambert-Loir and Kramadibrata 2013. The sizable collection of the late nineteenth-century Batavian librarian Muhammad Bakir, for example, contains no reworkings of Chinese tales (Maier 2004, 117). However, as shown by Gallop (2009) in a study on Malay manuscript art, the paucity of Chinese influence did not mean absence. The Jawi-Malay reworking of the didactic book *Precious Records of the Jade Register to Admonish the World* is another anomaly in its evidently Chinese provenance. Printed in Singapore in 1877, it was circulated in the Indies under

its Sino-Malay name *Giok Lek* (Salmon 2013c, 252–53). Malay poems set in a Chinese milieu—such as the *Sjair Baba Kong Sit* (Poem of Baba Kong Sit) and *Sjair Perkawinan Kapitan Tik Sing* (Poem of the Marriage of Kapitan Tik Seng)—may have been authored by Peranakans too, but this is not entirely certain (Salmon 1981, 17).

84. In 1890, for example, the poet Tan Teng Kie from Bekasi explicitly asked for a romanized version of a well-known Jawi poem circulated earlier that year (Salmon 1981, 16–17, 124, n. 11).

85. There were probably additional reasons. The colonial authorities promoted Latin over Arabic orthographies due to the latter's association with Islam (Hoffman 1979, 77; Groeneboer 1993, 176–79; Errington 2008, 142). However, as Sunarti (2013, 98) shows for West Sumatra, in some regions Jawi literacy prevailed well into the twentieth century. Fogg 2015 provides more background on the postindependence transition from Jawi to romanized Indonesian in Islamic circles, arguing that in this period, too, the former script was marginalized by the archipelago's political elites.

86. A similar situation existed with regard to the spelling of Jawi (Wilkinson 1985, 711–12).

87. See Proudfoot 1994, 20 for a similar argument on Baba Malay literature and Maier 1993a, 297 on the conscious usage of an exclamation mark in a Sino-Malay novel.

88. See Tan B. K. 1929 and Lu 1935 for examples of such publications.

89. These debates are described in Kuiper 2017, 762–64.

90. Wan B. S. 1931; Seow and Seow 1936.

91. Vernacular Malay indeed contained a small number of contrastive word pairs, such as *měnjěrět* (to slow down) vs. *měnjérét* (to drag), *běrsěroe* (to shout) vs. *běrséroe* (to form an alliance), and *sěntak* (to lash out) vs. *séntak* (to pull) (Lie K. H. 1891, 114). In British Malaya, especially in journals edited by missionaries, the schwa was written as <ŭ> or left out entirely.

92. See Kwee T. H. 1928, 1684–85 for more examples.

93. Mahdi 2012, 121. The contemporary spelling *keadaan* was less common, possibly because an intervocalic-glottalized <aa> could lead to confusion with a geminated <aa> in Dutch words such as *straat* (street) and *te laat* (too late). Lie Kim Hok also used the diaresis to make Chinese names better recognizable; the name *Liangïn* could only be *Liang-In*, not *Lian-Gin* or *Lia-Ngin*.

94. According to Batten (1868, 22), the /h/ was written but rarely pronounced in the Betawi dialect.

95. "Tida ada artinja apa-apa, katjoeali boeat boektiken kagoblokannja si penoelis dalem rangkean bahasa Melajoe poenja atoeran jang sederhana" (Kwee T. H. 1934b, 599). We may furthermore recall that copyists from Batavia exhibited the same habit when they wrote in Jawi (Voorhoeve 1964, 262 n. 1).

96. Kwee T. H. 1934d, 823.

97. "Ada sedia, roepa-roepa hoeroef Tionghoa dan hoeroef Arab jang compleet"; this advertisement was found in van der Burg 1926.

98. Ishak 1998, 68; Proudfoot 1994, 13.

99. Nio 1939b, 418–19.

100. Hwang 1935, 11.

101. *Kabar Kawat Malayu* 1924.

102. Alisjahbana 1948c, 100.

3. PRINTING, PULP, AND POPULARITY

1. See W. J. Ong 2012 on the different stages of literacy.

2. This point is made in detail by Anderson 1991, with a focus on newspapers.

3. Movable-type printing was not a European invention, yet its influence in preindustrialized societies was relatively limited. A somewhat different view is adopted by Pollock (2006, 558), who calls attention to India's massive circulation of manuscripts and inscriptions ("script-mercantilism") prior to European colonialism.

4. "Kamadjoean bangsa Tiong-hoa di Hindia boekan kerna pengadjaran jang didapet dalem sekolahan, kerna sekolahan oentoek marika itoe misi blon sampoerna, hanja kamadjoean marika itoe bagian jang terbesar soeda diambil oleh pers Melajoe. Oemoem soedahlah di ketahoei bahwa bangsa Tionghoa ada sanget hargakan soerat-soerat kabar, orang jang hanja tjoema bisa batja, ja sehingga jang tida bisa batja sekalipoen soeda berlangganan soerat kabar di soeroeh membatjakan dan diperhatikan betoel-betoel akan isi soerat kabar itoe, sehingga sekarang, ja sepoeloeh taoen jang soeda pers Melajoe soeda ada harga." Malay text quoted from Salmon (1980, 178). I have not been able to find the original article.

5. See Proudfoot 1994, 12 for a similar argument in the context of British Malaya.

6. Khadiv-Jam 1994, 199. A translation of the original Persian was kindly provided by Hossein Pourbagheri.

7. "pertama betul perkataannja dengan tiada bersalah, kedua lekas pekerdjaannja, ketiga terang hurufnja lagi senang membatjanja, keempat murah harganja" (Situmorang and Teeuw 1952, xxii). The Marathi example is taken from Naregal (2001, 155).

8. J. B. Kwee 1977, 13–14, 67–68; Chandra 2006, 69–70. Also see Siegel 1997, 25–26 and Maier 2004, 124 for more discussion.

9. Interestingly, Malay reworkings of stories already considered vulgar in their original setting often achieved the highest success (Maier 2004, 148–49).

10. See Liem 1933, 7 for a contemporaneous account on storytellers and Sie 1938 on *gambang kromong*. Stenberg 2015b provides more background on cloth-glove puppetry.

11. The transposition of fictional accounts to theater, for example, could become an author's financial salvation (Kwee T. H. 1930a, ii–iii; J. B. Kwee 1977, 67–68). Other stories were adapted to films, which was another Chinese-dominated industry (Setijadi and Barker 2010; Woodrich 2016).

12. Paradijs 1920. See J. B. Kwee 1977, 16 and Maier 2004, 143–44 for more background on copyright laws.

13. "wanneer eenmaal het gebruik maken van de drukpers hun zoo gemeenzaam zal zijn geworden als het eten van *nassi* en *dendeng*" (D. H. 1867, 132). Under the 1856 Netherlands Indies Press Act (*Drukpersregelement*), private publishing in languages other than Dutch had become easier (Kuitert 2020, 148–74). Before that time, printed materials in romanized Malay predominantly consisted of catechisms and other Christian literature.

14. "gelijk een zuigeling tot een volwassen man" (D. H. 1867, 139).

15. Van Hoëvell 1849, 110; Mahdi 2016, 118, 149.

16. The first Dutch newspaper appeared in 1744 in the Indies and in 1618 in the Netherlands (Termorshuizen 2001, 27). King Mongkut of Siam oversaw the establishment of the first Thai newspaper in 1858 as part of his broader policy to modernize society (Rutnin 1993), Sri Lanka's newspaper industry developed in 1860 in the train of technological modernization (Wickramasinghe 2014), and Japan's first quasi-modern newspapers emerged in 1868 (Huffman 1997). Throughout Asia, missionaries and other transregional brokers spearheaded these developments.

17. *Sin Po Wekelijksche Editie* 68 (1924): 266.

18. This mirrored a common practice in China and among Chinese communities elsewhere in Southeast Asia. See Iskandar 1981, Salmon 1981, 16, Behrend 1993, and van der Meij 2017, 107–9 for more information on Indonesian manuscript libraries.

19. Schlegel 1891; Liem 1939c; Salmon 2013a. A story titled *Li Si Bin*, written by Babah Tig Og and dated to 1859, is the oldest such manuscript in existence and goes back to the

Chinese story *Xue Rengui Clears the East* (Salmon 2013a, 241–42). The earliest printed Javanese translation of a Chinese story is *Sam Pik Eng Tae*, published in 1873 in Semarang and based on the *Butterfly Lovers* (Quinn 2013, 339).

20. The oldest known example is an 1882 translation of *The Complete Story of Hai Rui's Small Scarlet Robe* (Salmon 1976).

21. These included *Bintang Oetara* (Star of the North; Rotterdam, 1856) and *Selompret Melajoe*. See Adam 1995 for a detailed background study. The origins of Malay printing can be traced to biblical and lexicographical works, printed from the seventeenth century in the Netherlands and from the nineteenth century in Batavia and the Straits Settlements (Byrd 1970; Gallop 1990; Ishak 1998).

22. Salmon 2000, 86 n. 7.

23. See Termorshuizen 2001, 237–40 and Kuitert 2020, 54–56 for more background. In *De Oostpost* (The East Post; Surabaya, 1853), a Dutch newspaper he founded in 1853, we can already find examples of announcements in Low Malay.

24. For example, *Java-Bode*, March 15, 1856.

25. See Adam 1995, 16–19. *Bromartani* must be considered the first newspaper in any Indonesian language. It was first published by the Eurasian Carel Frederik Winter (1799–1859).

26. Adam 1995, 21.

27. The Jawi lithographic tradition can be traced to the 1840s (Gallop 1990, 97–98; Proudfoot 1994, 32–34; Proudfoot 1998; van der Putten 1997).

28. This was the Muslim devotional text *Sharaf al Ānām* (The Best of Mankind), written in Arabic with an interlinear rendering in Malay. It is currently kept at the Leiden University Library (Kaptein 1993).

29. The scholar Baba Ounus Saldin (1832–1906)—of Indonesian origins—printed numerous Malay and Tamil publications in the Arabic script. These included *Alamat Langkapuri* (News of Langkapuri; Colombo, 1869), the world's first Malay newspaper published outside the European orbit (Ricci 2013).

30. Birch 1969; Amrith 2013, 165–66.

31. Although China had a sophisticated woodblock print culture (xylography) dating from the Tang dynasty (Reed 2004), Chinese printing was uncommon in the Netherlands Indies and the Straits prior to the twentieth century. Industrialized Sinographic printing was introduced to Malacca in 1815 (Chen Mong Hock 1967, 1–6) and to Batavia in 1828 (Kuiper 2017, 475–77) under the auspices of European missionaries. In both cases, Southeast Asia served as a springboard to China, which was off-limits to Europeans prior to the First Opium War. The introduction of Western-style printing in China thus had important antecedents in the Malay-speaking world (Reed 2004).

32. When the geologist Joseph Beete Jukes (1811–69) visited the East Javanese town of Lumajang in 1847, the local court official Sumowijoyo revealed that the city's Chinese population was aware of the English cruelties of the First Opium War (Beete Jukes 1847, 51). None of these news sheets seem to have been preserved. See Salmon 2013b, 13–14 on Chinese books in Indonesian collections.

33. Salmon 2000, 79; Termorshuizen 2001, 361; Kuiper 2017, 14. It appeared in the same year as America's first Chinese newspaper, roughly contemporaneous to two pioneering Singaporean weeklies, and a decade earlier than the first modern newspaper in China (Salmon 2000, 79). Missionary periodicals appeared even earlier. Malacca's *The Chinese Magazine* was launched in 1815 and Batavia's *The Monthly Magazine* in 1823 (Su 1996, 58, 206).

34. See Adam 1995, 64–65 and Kuitert 2020, 210–18. As the authors demonstrate, Chinese writers had previously operated in the Malay press as editors, typesetters, advertisers, and subscribers. Some may have also run unofficial printshops from home (Kuitert 2020, 209–10).

35. Liem 1939b.

36. See Tan C. B. 1981, Huang Huimin 2004, and Salmon 2013d for an overview. The first Peranakan-owned newspaper was the *Straits Chinese Herald* (Singapore, 1894) published in English and Malay. It was followed in the same year by the *Bintang Timor* (Star of the East), not to be confused with the similarly named newspapers from Padang (1864), Surabaya (1868), and Penang (1900).

37. *Bintang Pranakan*, October 11, 1930.

38. Salmon 1986 provides a historical overview.

39. This book was also translated into Javanese under the title *Serat Tiyang Gegriya* (Book for People on Running their Homes and Households). See Wieringa 2020 on this versification written in Surabaya in 1878.

40. A locally authored Chinese book, for example, had been translated into Malay and Dutch and popularized by the Eurasian interpreter James William Young (1855–98) (Tshoa 1889). Conversely, the Eurasian author Herman Kommer (1873–1924) wrote stories set in a Chinese milieu and published by a Chinese printing house. See Tsuchiya 1991, Mahdi 2006, 92, and Hoogervorst 2021 for more examples.

41. See Hoogervorst and Schulte Nordholt 2017 for more examples of multiethnic advertising.

42. *Straits Chinese Magazine* 1 (1897): 158.

43. Some words, like "Abyssinia," "Court," and "insurance," proved too difficult to translate and were kept in English. A Malay equivalent was found for one unfamiliar word, but fearing that nobody would understand it, the English was given afterwards: "uzor (excuse)."

44. "Objectionable as is the spelling of words of this Malay *patois*, it has the merit of being intelligible to the very poorly educated Straits Chinese, of whom there is such a considerable number in this Colony. It may safely be said that no original work or translation intended principally for the Straits Chinese reading public has the slightest chance of being sold to the number of 500 copies unless it was written in this *patois*" (Chia C. S. 1899, 14).

45. Liem 1940b, 14.

46. See, for example, Wirawan 2011, 54 on the Sino-Malay press in Makassar and Salmon 1981, 2013c on Chinese translations in the Netherlands Indies. The Straits Settlements soon followed suit, with the first translated works appearing in 1889 (Tan C. B. 1981; Salmon 2013d).

47. Salmon 1981, 2013c; Chandra 2006. A contemporary account of the importance of classical Chinese tales is given in Kwee K. B. (1935, 203–4).

48. See Oey 2013 and Quinn 2013 for more information. Even though Chinese writers had a stronger concept of the original text compared to their indigenous colleagues, it is not always clear on which manuscript, printed publication, or orally transmitted version a Malay or Javanese translation of a Chinese work was based (Jedamski 2014).

49. One notable exception is the Baba Malay translation from 1913 of Anna Sewell's *Black Beauty* (*Si Hitam yang Chantek*). See Salmon 1981, 2013c and Jedamski 2014 on translated European stories in the Netherlands Indies.

50. This point was also made by Nio (1962, 23). See Jedamski 2014 for more background on Malay translations in the Netherlands Indies.

51. See Salmon and Lombard 1974 and Hoogervorst 2017 for examples.

52. These included Javanese, Sundanese, Minangkabau, Makassarese, and Lampung (Soenoto 1988).

53. See Tio I. S. 1958, 113 for a retrospective assessment.

54. Liem 1939a, 22; Nio 1939b, 409; J. B. Kwee 1977, 68. However, the characteristic Minangkabau-influenced Malay idiom seen in indigenous newspapers from West

Sumatra (Sunarti 2013) was also widely used in the Sino-Malay newspapers from that area, making the latter instantly recognizable from their language.

55. *Sin Po Wekelijksche Editie* 43 (1924): 684.
56. Salmon 2013d, 285–86.
57. Tan P. T. 1916, i.
58. Nio 1943, 172.
59. "In de eerste plaats moeten we opmerken dat het Maleisch, waarin de meeste kranten zijn geschreven, veel weg heeft van het pasar Maleisch en dat die kranten wel het meeste zullen worden gelezen. Wat heel treurig is. Uit een taalkundig oogpunt beschouwd moesten de Maleische bladen geschreven worden in behoorlijk Maleisch, waarbij goed wordt gelet op de achter- en voorvoegsels, op den lijdenden vorm en wat er al meer bij het Maleisch valt op te letten. Maar een der redacteuren van de Semarangsche bladen verklaarde, en hij kon het wel weten, dat de meeste lezers dat niet begrijpen. En wanneer eenige zuiver inlandsche bladen een behoorlijker taal schrijven, dan zullen zij dat alleen kunnen doen voor lezers van zekere ontwikkeling" (Later 1915, 1269).
60. "Dalam seratoes karangan jang kami terima, biasanja doea sadja jang dapat diterbitkan. Seperti soedah kita katakan tadi, penerbit boekoe-boekoe Melajoe-Tionghoa itoe tiap-tiap boelan haroes menerbitkan boekoe, karena itoe soedah tentoe kerap kali terpaksa mengeloearkan boekoe jang asal ada sadja. Bahasa jang dipakai, ialah bahasa jang dipakai orang Tionghoa sehari-hari, karena itoe hidoep-hidoep. Tentoe ada bahajanja. Bahasa jang dipakai itoe tidak diadjarkan, tidak dipoepoek dalam sesoeatoe sekolah, kata orang Belanda, tidak gecultiveerd. Pohon boeah-boeahan jang dibiarkan sadja toemboeh dihoetan memang djoega berboeah, tetapi hasilnja akan lebih banjak. Akan lebih mengoentoengkan, kalau dipelihara baik-baik. Demikian poela dengan boekoe-boekoe Tionghoa-Melajoe itoe" (Pané 1938, 80).
61. Tjoa B. S. 1922, 4.
62. Kwee T. H. 1936, ii.
63. Nio 1962, 18; J. B. Kwee 1977, 80.
64. "Beklai sama njamoek atau bangke mantrikoe Andakasoera jang gaga perkasa?" (Jap 1926, 39); "Brangkali ada gomnja, maka begitoe gampang bisa lengket!" (*Korbannja Setan Bantal* n.d., 2); "Hala! Tjinta sampe begitoe? Ini baroelah katjintaän jang benar, asal sadja tida djoesta" (Lie K. H. 1914, 134); "biarpoen sampe matahari mendjadi voetbal!" (Lie K. H. 1912, 215); "Loh, kok kaja orang prampoean sadja, baroe ditahan sadja soeda menangis-nangis?" (O. & Y. 1921, 295); "Betoel bohokki" (Lie I. E. 1918, 290); "Seriboe brangkali tjoema satoe orang jang sajang sagenap hati pada anak kwalonnja" (Lie S. G. 1915, 40); "Pinter bangsat" (Lie K. H. 1919, 62).
65. Nio 1962; Sykorsky 1980; Salmon 1981; Chandra 2006.
66. Watson 1974; Tsuchiya 1991; Maier 1993a; Siegel 1997; Worsley 2004; Chandra 2011a, 2016; Susanto 2015.
67. See Maier 1991 for more background. McHale (2004, 31) observes similar attitudes in late colonial Vietnam.
68. These three novels are discussed in detail by Chandra 2013. See Rieger 1992 on the Sino-Japanese war in Indonesian literature.
69. Kwee K. B. (1936, 105–6) and Nio (1937, 39; 1955b; 1961) provide contemporaneous assessments.
70. Tio I. S. 1958, 23; Nio 1962, 42.
71. Nio 1937; Salmon 1981, 26. For more detailed studies, see Tan C. B. 1981 and 2003; Sykorsky 1980, and F. Chia 1983.
72. Salmon 1981, 15.
73. See Salmon 1974 on the *Sair dari Adanja Boekoe Tjerita Tjina njang Soeda Disalin Bahasa Melajoe* (Poem on Translated Chinese Story Books into Malay), Salmon 1991 on

the *Boekoe Sair Binatang* (Poem of Animals), Chambert-Loir 1999 on the *Sair Java-Bank di Rampok* (Poem on the Java Bank Robbery), Salmon 1971 on the *Boekoe Sair Tionghwa-hwe-kwan* (Poem of the THHK), and Watson 1974 on the *Sair Nona Fientje de Feniks* (Poem of Fientje de Feniks).

74. From the early twentieth century, Chinese fiction about martial heroes (*wŭxiá*) and the universe they inhabited (*jiānghú*) yielded innumerable serialized novels and eventually films in the Sinophone world (M. B. Wan 2009; P. Liu 2011). In Sino-Malay texts, the two concepts were known under their Hokkien pronunciations: *boehiap* and *kang-ouw*.

75. Salmon 2013c, 266.

76. Liem (1933, 3, 27, 98) provides a contemporaneous Chinese-Indonesian account. Also see Suryadinata 2013 and Hoogervorst 2016.

77. For more background, see Lombard 1977 and Gartenberg 2000, 131–47.

78. *Sin Po Wekelijksche Editie* 950 (1941): 7.

79. Typical protagonists included the *boehiap* (knight-errant), *enghiong* (hero), *giehiap* (chivalrous knight), *hohan* (brave man), *kiamhiap* (chivalrous swordsman), *longkoen* (young man), and *tiong gie* (man of honor). Examples of enemies included the *hweetjat* (bandit), *kan hiong* (master deceiver), *kansin* (corrupt official), *pangtjoe* (gang leader), *tjay-hoa-tjat* (serial rapist), and *tjenteng* (guard). Other common persona were the *bengtjoe* (leader of an alliance), *hwesio* (Buddhist monk), *kauwsoe* (silat master), *kauwtjoe* (religious head), *lihiap* (female warrior), *nikouw* (nun), *saykong* (Daoist priest), *sianhong* (vanguard), *sinsian* (immortal), *soehoe* (silat teacher), *thaysoe* (silat grandmaster), *tjiangkoen* (general), *tokouw* (female Daoist), *tongtjoe* (pupil), and *tosoe* (male Daoist).

80. These personalities included the *boenkhoa* (civil official), *hoema* (emperor's son-in-law), *hongho* (empress), *hongtee* or *thaykoen* (emperor), *khoahoe* (feudal official), *kidjin* (Provincial Graduate), *kokthio* (emperor's father-in-law), *ongya* or *thaytjoe* (prince), *piauwsoe* (armed escort), *poankoan* (judge), *sioetjai* (scholar), *taydjin* (dignitary), *thayhouw* (empress dowager), *thaykam* (eunuch), *tjinsoe* (Advanced Scholar), *tjoe bo* (mistress), *tjonggoan* (person ranked first in the Palace Examination), and *wan-gwee* (rich man). Specific Chinese concepts included the *kaypang* (beggar's union), *konglo* (merit), *loeitay* (elevated fighting arena), *piauwkiok* (escort bureau), *pookiam* (two-edged sword), *sengtjie* (imperial edict), *Siauwliem sie* (Shaolin Temple), *tiokie* (Chinese checkers), and *tjinkong* (to pay tribute). In stories set in Chinese cities, one could further encounter *boe-kie-djin* (military graduates of the Provincial Examinations), *gie-lim-koen* (palace guards), *kim-ie-wie* (gold-clad guards), *pat-tin-touw* (stone troops), and the *tjintong* (ancestral hall).

81. Among the numerous strategies and techniques used by the fighters, we find *bayhok* (ambush), *ginkang* or *khinkang* (the art of making the body light), *kauwkoen* (monkey kung fu), *khikang* (breath control), *kimtan* (alchemy), *kongtauw* (black magic), *sinkang* (supernatural powers), *tiamhiat* (hitting the body's pressure points), *tiangseng* (longevity), *tjioegi* (enchantment), and *toen hoat* (invisibility).

82. "sembari menendang pada pelernja iapoenja moesoeh" (Yo 1939, 608–9).

83. Seen in *Hoakiao* 25 (1930).

84. Chandra 2011a.

85. Examples are given in Chin and Hoogervorst 2017.

86. *Sin Po Wekelijksche Editie* 987 (1942): 3–5.

87. For example *boenga raja* (hibiscus flower), *dewi keplesiran* (goddess of pleasure), *kembang latar* (reclined flower), *koepoe-koepoe malam* (night butterfly), *prampoean hina* (lowly woman), *prampoean perniaga'an* (commercial woman), or *toekang plesir* (pleasure worker).

88. Nio (1937, 232) identifies this character as a philanderer from *Ngo Bie Yan* (Romances of Five Beauties), yet that story contains no personage with that name. I assume the character Hoa Tjoe Ling originates from the 1814 novel *The Picture of Tianbao*. However,

since no early Malay translations of that book are known to me, the name was probably introduced through theater or storytelling rather than literature.

89. This happened almost simultaneously in other East and Southeast Asian contexts. See Ikeya 2018 on Burma and Chiang 2018 on China.

90. Butatuli and Hemeling 1913; T. P. B. n.d. I have briefly discussed these works elsewhere (Hoogervorst 2016, 293).

91. Paradijs 1920, 44–45.

92. Pramoedya Ananta Toer was among the few people who already made this argument in the 1960s. It should be pointed out that this observation only holds true for Indonesia. The antecedents of modern Malaysian and (Malay) Singaporean literature can be traced to the Jawi tradition rather than Baba Malay literature (Proudfoot 1994, 59). See Wahab Ali 2012 for a historical comparison between Indonesian and Malaysian novels.

4. COMPETING EXPRESSIONS OF MODERNITY

1. Hoogervorst and Schulte Nordholt 2017; Chin and Hoogervorst 2017.

2. See, for example, "Seorang Parisienne-tjina" 1903. More background on the newspaper *Bintang Hindia* is provided by Poeze (1986, 37–51).

3. In the words of one Dutch journalist, the Westernized Indonesian "is neither Dutch nor indigenous, neither fish nor fowl, but a product of the complicated society in the Indies. In one regard he is genuine, i.e., in the mimicry of what he sees others do and wear. The real Javanese is more worthy of our sympathy" (is noch Hollander noch inlander, noch vleesch noch visch, maar een product van de gecompliceerde samenleving in Indië. In één opzicht is hij echt, n.l. in het naäpen van wat hij anderen ziet doen en dragen. De echte Javaan is beter onze sympathie waard) (B. 1932). One of the fiercest critics of these essentialist views was Armijn Pané, who provides an insightful discussion on these clashing perspectives in the context of music (Pané 1941).

4. This was no different elsewhere in Asia. See Judge 2008, 60–83 on discussions of modernity in China.

5. See "Letters of a Javanese Princess" 1922 on Kartini and Woodrich 2017 on the proto-feminist writings of Lie Kim Hok.

6. Coppel 1997; Chandra 2015a; Kwartanada 2017; Zhu 2017.

7. Salmon 2013c, 259; Kwartanada 2017, 432. In the Straits, the discourse on women's rights largely took place in English.

8. "boeaja darat jang banjak mengglandangan di itoe matjem 'pesta' berlaga 'kasalahan' pegang, toebroek atawa laen-laen lagi" ("Kaboeroekan" 1926, 833); "Tabeat didalem dasar, tjampoeran pamoeda rosokan, lembek hati, terlaloe romantic, dan sakean banjak alesan lagi" (T. K. S. 1930, 22); "Balzaalschittering..." 1936, 26.

9. F. 1928, 474.

10. Lao Jen 1928, 403.

11. "Gila Hormat" 1928, 32.

12. Kwartanada 2018, 44.

13. "Fox-Trot-Lek" 1924, 699.

14. Tong Ketik 1929.

15. Kwee S. T. 1917, 59–60.

16. Cheng 1998, 125; Kwa 2009, 137.

17. Blussé and Nie 2018, 34.

18. A detailed study of these dynamics is provided in van der Meer forthcoming. On the legal situation in the Netherlands Indies, see Prins 1933 and Tjiook-Liem 2009, 228–29, 244–53, 450–54.

19. "Topi petjies dari bloedroe soetra jang aloes, badjoenja poen rapi sekali potongannja, dengen pakei ini pakeian ija djadi amat tjakep, sahingga sabagi kembangnja antara

anak-anak djedjaka Tjina di dalem kota Betawi'" ("Tambahsia" 2002, 31–32). A similar Chinese dandy was described in detail in a popular Dutch story titled "De dubbele moord" (The Double Murder) (Ritter 1855, 191–92; Hoogervorst 2021).

20. See Rudolph 1998, 211–12 on British Malaya and van der Meer forthcoming on the Netherlands Indies. From the 1860s, the British administration even tried to enforce European sartorial markers on Straits-born Chinese visiting China in an attempt to make them distinguishable from the local population (Sai 2019).

21. This has been considered in detail by Siegel (1997, 84–89). For more general background, see Bhabha 1994, Tarlo 1996, and Hulsbosch 2014.

22. "Diberi idzin aken zonder koentjir dan dengen pakean Europa boleh mengoendjoeken diri di tempat oemoem" (Liem 1933, 156). Obtaining written approval to do so was legally required for non-Europeans until 1905 (Liem 1933, 154). Incidentally, Oei Tiong Ham was also Java's first Chinese to obtain permission to settle outside Chinatown (Wellington Koo 1975, 20).

23. Liem 1933, 182. Note also that modernists did the same thing in China (Cheng 1998).

24. See Cheng 1998 and Finnane 2007, 77–82 on queue-cutting in China and Tejapira 1992 on the situation in Thailand. These debates overlapped with those on girls' education, opium consumption, and gambling (Rudolph 1998, 135–45; Sai 2019, 462–67).

25. Rieger 1996, 158–59.

26. "Baba-Baba yang sudah potong tauchang fikir *dia-orang* sudah tukar (reform)— sudah mnjadi tinggi, dan barangkali tinggi sperti orang Puteh" ("Baba" 1906, 5); "Kalau bgitu apa pasal kita Baba Baba pakai spatu puteh-kasut dan sluar orang puteh?" ("Fasal tauchang" 1906, 3).

27. See F. Chia 1983, 32–33 on this phenomenon in the Straits Settlements. One extreme case was the British-educated scholar Koh Hong Beng (1857–1928), who started growing a queue at a later age, moved to China to become a mandarin, and ended up considerably more traditional than most of his China-born contemporaries (Godley 1981, 40).

28. See Locher-Scholten 2000 on the sartorial practices of European women, P. Lee 2014, 160–289 on Peranakan women, and Hulsbosch 2014 and van der Meer forthcoming for more background on Netherlands Indies dress regimes in general.

29. Tan C. B. 1988, 299; Rudolph 1998, 222.

30. Kwa 2009, 141.

31. Mahmood 2004; P. Lee 2014; T. Lee 2016; Brinkgreve and Leijfeldt 2017. Chinese merchants furthermore imported needles, yarn, buttons, wooden clogs, silk fabrics, and flatirons into the archipelago (Lombard 2005, 318–19).

32. Duggan 2001; Kwa 2009, 158–59; P. Lee 2014, 104–20, 232–50; T. Lee 2016.

33. Chinese-inspired batik motifs include *bandji* (swastikas), *hong* (phoenixes), *kilin* (dragon-headed ungulates of Chinese mythology), *kiok hoa* (chrysanthemums), *lian hoa* (lotuses), *liong* (dragons), and *pat sian* (the Eight Gods) (Knight-Achjadi and Damais 2005; T. Lee 2016). Many of these motifs can also be seen on altar cloths (*tokwie*) and towels (*tjoekin*) (Knight-Achjadi and Damais 2005, 129–45; Brinkgreve and Leijfeldt 2017).

34. Rudolph 1998, 227.

35. Lee Choo Neo (1895–1947), Singapore's first female doctor and a role model for progressive women, famously adopted it in 1914 (P. Lee 2014, 18–19; T. Lee 2016, 194–95). In China too, the mid-1910s marked the height of Europeanized fashion. Song Qingling (1893–1981), the wife of Sun Yat-sen, donned a tailored jacket and skirt in her wedding picture (Finnane 2007, 143). Also see Tio T. H. 2007, 55 for a retrospective account and Kwa 2009, 148, 158 for an illustrated study of Chinese-Indonesian dress.

36. Bailey 2003, 334; Finnane 2007, 82–87.

37. Kwartanada 2017, 429; Kwa 2009, 141, 148.

38. Rudolph 1998, 237; T. Lee 2016, 92.

39. Tan D. S. 1913, 38–39.

40. A prominent example is the *koon-sah*, a Chinese-inspired upper garment and skirt combination that was invented locally in the Straits (T. Lee 2016, 222).

41. "Topi item kras model papak, jang amat disoeka oleh Officier-officier Tionghoa di Insulinde sini, a f 7.50."

42. "Jika Tuan² sayang Tuan² punia istri dan anak² prawan, bolehlah tolong selahkan datang kekedai kita dan merlihat Kebaya² itu dari Jawa" (*Kabar Kawat*, 1924).

43. Finnane 2007; P. Lee 2013, 8; Knight-Achjadi and Damais 2005, 111.

44. In the 1920s, Oei Hui Lan refashioned the Shanghai-style *qípáo* and berated designers in China for their infatuation with Western styles and fabrics (Wellington Koo 1943, 255–56; 1975, 181; Finnane 2007, 153).

45. These anti-Italian sentiments among Java's Muslim communities were partly in response to Italy's military aggression in Libya (Poeze 1988, xxxviii–xxxix).

46. Post 2019, 33.

47. Hoogervorst 2016, 296–300. See Bhabha 1994 on the phenomenon of mimicry.

48. See Hoogervorst 2016 on the male discourse of modernity among the Indies Chinese and Chandra 2011b and Chin and Hoogervorst 2017 on its vastly different female counterpart. The body politics of modern girls show remarkable parallels across Southeast Asia. See Roces 2005 on the Philippines, Ikeya 2008 and Than 2014 on Burma, and Lewis 2009 on Penang.

49. Injo 1931, 68.

50. Pat 1930, 1.

51. "Tanda djaman" 1930, 4–5.

52. This pattern holds across numerous colonial settings. See Vaughan 1991 and George 2014 on colonial-era health practices in Africa and Chakrabarti 2014 and Widmer and Lipphart 2016 on medicine under imperialism generally. Pols 2018 provides a detailed study on colonial medicine from the viewpoint of Indonesian physicians.

53. Examples of Southeast Asian products include Sumatran camphor (*tōa bôe phiàn*), bezoar stones of simian origin (*chiàⁿ kâu chó*), and the siliceous concretion from the nodal joints of bamboo (*thian tiok hông*) (Vorderman 1889, 599, 631, 634). Interestingly, the thirteenth-century Java Sea wreck contains medical goods from China as well as the Indian Ocean (Respess and Niziolek 2016), indicating a convergence of medical practices as early as late medieval times.

54. An 1845 Malay *Kitab Mujarabat* (Book of Remedies), for instance, contains knowledge of acupressure and other Chinese practices alongside Arabic medicine (Wieringa 2007, 195–97).

55. "Raden Adjeng Kartini dan Bangsa Tionghoa" 1930.

56. De Haan 1922, 508. The doctor was nicknamed "Loccon," which is the Hokkien pronunciation (*ló-kun*) of Malay *dukun*. See Lombard 2005, 323–25 and Salmon and Sidharta 2007, 167–72 for more information on Chinese doctors in early modern Indonesia.

57. Yoo 2018.

58. See Blussé 1990, Salmon and Sidharta 2007, 170, and Blussé and Nie 2018, 86–87 on the former and de Haan 1922, 508 and Blussé and Nie 2018, 90 on the latter.

59. In his description of Batavia's Chinese apothecaries, the Dutch doctor Pieter Bleeker (1819–78) wondered why European observers had dedicated such a great part of their studies to the indigenous medicinal traditions, but none to those of the Chinese (Bleeker 1844, 257–58).

60. Vorderman 1889, 625–26; Hesselink 2011, 45. Several additional examples may be mentioned. An 1855 Dutch report praised a secret Chinese method to extract teeth painlessly, whereas an 1865 government decision led to the appointment of a Chinese vaccinator in Batavia (Hesselink 2011, 28, 29). In the 1880s, several European scholars tried to

analyze a mysterious "medicine for throat pain" (Ml: *obat orang sakit leher*, Hk: *nâ-âu sán*) manufactured by the Batavian *sinse* Si Ma In, which proved much more efficient against diphtheria than anything prescribed by Western doctors (Vorderman 1889, 568). As late as 1903 the people of Batavia insisted that a *sinse* should be put in charge of the city's efforts to combat malaria, cholera, and leprosy, following Surabaya's example (Hesselink 2011, 267).

61. Other Hokkien disease names encountered in Malay advertisements include *bongsiat* (nocturnal emissions; Ml. *ngompol*), *gahong* (rheumatic pains in the leg), *honghwee* (internal heat), *jangbwee* (buboes), *kamthjeng* (genital ulcers), *kek lim* (retention of urine), *keng kie poet twie* (irregular menstruation), *kioekin* (cramps), *lamsin* (weakness), *pektai* (leucorrhea), *pianswi* (total paralysis), *sekhong* (venereal diseases), *seteng* (small hard boils), *she li lat* (scrofula), *sheswaja* (syphilis), *shetjheng* (venereal ulcers), *thianpauw* (pus-filled ulcers), *tiooksiang* (injuries), *titjheng* (hemorrhoids), *tjia-besiauw* (indigestion), *tok* (toxins), *toyang* (impotence), and *twitjing* (spermatorrhea). A number of medical practices, too, were known and used beyond Chinese circles, including the treatment of rheumatic pains (*kihong*), injuries (*kisiang*), and dampness (*kisip*).

62. As considerable differences existed from one *sinse* to another, and between Hokkien and Hakka traditions, the seeds for pharmaceutical competition were sown long before commercialized printing entered the scene. See Vorderman 1889, 574–85 for a contemporaneous account.

63. This book was briefly mentioned by the Royal Batavian Society of Arts and Sciences, yet nobody felt the need to facilitate its publication (Salmon and Sidharta 2007, 177).

64. *Ilmoe Obat-Obattan Bergoena* 1890; *Kitab Obat Penjakit Pest* n.d.

65. See, for example, A. I. H. n.d. and Ong S. P. n.d.

66. See Poeze 1989 for a detailed study on (Chinese-)Indonesian students in the Netherlands.

67. Rudolph 1998, 319, 380–401.

68. See R. Lie 2017, 458 for an example. A similar controversy divided opinions in China around the same time (Salmon and Sidharta 2007, 178–80).

69. "Saja soedah berobat sama sinseh dan Doctor poenja lama tidak bisa baik, dari itoe saja datang di Padang berobat, saja panggil sinseh Tjiang Soei Heng lantas kasi obat, dan bloem stenga boelan saja poenja mata soedah baik" (*Radio* 1932).

70. *Thong Thian Piet Hiauw* 1912, 4. The first part means "Heavenly Cavern," the second is unclear.

71. *Thong Thian Piet Hiauw* 1912 39–40, 98–102.

72. "Gele Profeet" 1919. Another newspaper, too, recounted his hatred for shrewd businessmen ("Solosche Causerie" 1919).

73. "Kliwatan poenja Bodo" 1925.

74. "Notes from Java" 1924. Another Singaporean newspaper reports how, on his way to China, Tan Tik Sioe spent several days curing Singapore's Chinese inhabitants, who had arrived in great numbers to see him. Some of his talismans (*hoo*) were illegally being sold for twenty cents a piece ("The Chinese Hermit" 1924).

75. See Hartanto 1978, 42 for an account of his life as recalled by his friends. According to this source, Tan Tik Sioe was invited to Penang by a certain "Majoor Go Djoe Tok," a wealthy businessman he had once cured after no European doctor could do so. I suspect that his benefactor was the same person as the ship-owner, merchant, and tin-miner Khaw Joo Tok (1871–1951), given that the sound /k^h/ in the latter's name would have been pronounced as /g/ by speakers from East Java.

76. Tan T. S. S. 1932, 79, 98, 136.

77. "Kuat kan kita punya badan, dan boleh hilang kan macham-macham punya p'nyakit" (*Kabar Uchapan Baru*, October 22, 1928).

78. "kesturi (musk), mutiara (pearl), amber (ambar), dupa atau kemunian (frankincense; stanggi), Szechuan punya rusa kesturi [musk-deer], kala jinkeng [scorpion] dengan badan halipan [centipede bodies]" (*Kabar Uchapan Baru*, October 15, 1928).

79. "Speciaal boeat dipake oleh orang lelaki sadja, samatjem minjak wangi boeat plesiran jang tida ada lagi tandingannja dari kamandjoerannja" (*Sin Po Wekelijksche Editie* 1926).

80. "Teramatlah guna bagai perumpuan² sebab ia mengkhuat kan [*sic*!] dan membrikan sehat napsu dan badan nya" (*Kabar Kawat Malayu* 1924).

81. See Lin and Tsai 2014, 128–35 on medical advertising in early Republican China and Pernau 2019 on Sanatogen advertisements in India. Hoogervorst (2016, 294–95) provides some background on potency drugs in the Netherlands Indies.

82. Pik 1936.

83. See Chow 2014, 79–100 for a similar argument on postcoloniality and food practices in Hong Kong.

84. "koki jang pande masak djoega ada satoe artist, dan orang jang soeka makanan enak poen ada satoe orang jang soeka kunst. Maka boekan lajiknja mendapet gelaran 'loe 'ni kaja babi sadja'"; "Ini baek diperhatikan oleh orang Tionghoa jang berlepotan mentega atawa berdaki kedjoe" (B. H. 1929).

85. "Orang Tionghoa makan sembari berobat dan berobat sembari makan" (Liem 1940b, 15). On *ketjap*, see Liem 1940a, 13.

86. "Leloetjon dari Koran-Koran" 1927.

87. "Betoel banjak orang Timoer berladjar makan kedjoe, tapi Blanda tida koerang jang dojan bami, poejonghai dan tjaptjay" (Antjoah 1926, 762).

88. B. H. 1929.

89. "Eten 'bij den Chinees'" 1941.

90. For example, the first recipe requires *tjioe tjhing* (light soy sauce) and *hay mo kee* (blubberlip snapper), the second *pao hie* (abalones) and the third *pihi* (dried flounder), *djoehi* (squid), *bokdji* (edible fungus), *kintjam* (tuberose flowers), and *so-oen* (cellophane noodles) (De Vereniging van Huisvrouwen 1937).

91. The best known noodle types in the Sino-Malay literature were *bahmi* (wheat noodles), *bihoen* (rice vermicelli), *kweetiau* (flat rice noodles), *misoa* (salted wheat vermicelli), and *so-oen* (cellophane noodles). The Chinese also popularized new ways to prepare local food products, including *haysom* (sea cucumber), *hebie* (dried shrimps), *siham* (cockles), and *swikee* (edible frogs). See also Lombard 2005, 261 on Chinese culinary introductions in Maritime Southeast Asia.

92. Van Naerssen 1941, 85, 102; Lombard 2005, 321.

93. For example *bakkoet* (pigs' bones), *daging samtjam* (pork belly), *liongkoet* (pigs' spine), *tihi* (pigs' ear), *titee* (pigs' trotters), *tithauw* (pigs' head), *titouw* (pigs' tripe), and *tjaplek* (soft loin) (Tan K. G. 1941, 9). For Chinese-derived cooking techniques, see Kam 1974, 5 and Lombard 2005, 321.

94. *Kabar Slalu*, January 25, 1924.

95. Wilkinson 1932, 522. This sauce is also the basis of England's ketchup, which was originally made with mushrooms.

96. Liem 1940a. The word is already glossed as *soja* (soy) in Batten (1868, 197). A 1940 Malay-Mandarin self-study book likewise translates *ketjap* as *tjiang-yoe* (soy sauce) (The C. S. T. 1940, 265). This semantic shift also took place across the Straits of Malacca. A 1930 inventory published in the *Bintang Pranakan* of products for sale in Singapore reads "Kichap (soy sauce from China)" (Kichap [Towyu deri Tiong Kok]). In the Kapampangan-speaking parts of the Philippines, by contrast, the related word *kesiap* still refers to fish sauce. On the Hokkien precursor of both words, see Douglas 1899, 242.

97. "Sarang soendel Djepang dan boengah raja laen bangsa" (Liem 1940a, 11).

98. See, for example, the advertisements in *Kabar Kawat Malayu* (1924) and *Kabar Uchapan Baru* (1926).

99. See Ishwara 2012 and Bromokusumo 2013 for an introduction to Indonesia's Peranakan cuisine and F. Chia 1983, 107–17 on Malaya's Nyonya cuisine. To give but one example of a hybrid dish, East Java's *opor kaki babi* consists of Chinese-style pig's trotters in a Javanese-style spiced coconut sauce, flavored with five-spice powder (*ngohiang*) and shiitake (*hioko*) (Ishwara 2012, 227).

100. "makanan Njonja Betawi dan Pranakan; segala roepa Masakan tjara: Olanda, Djawa, dan Melajoe" (Lie T. L. 1915).

101. This reflects the historical situation that male ancestors were typically Chinese, whereas female ancestors were Southeast Asian (Sidharta 2011, 116–17).

102. Ie 1933; Tan K. S. 1935.

103. Freedman and Koo Siu Ling 2015. Also see Sidharta 2011, 115–16.

104. *Fu Nu Tsa Chih* 12 (1933): 16. Even in more recent Peranakan cookbooks, Chinese-inspired dishes feature in similar quantities as Indonesian and European ones (Eleonora 1959; Ishwara 2012).

105. Sidharta 2011, 117. Another example is the restaurant Tay Sam Yoen in Pantjoran, Batavia, which boasted having cooks from Hong Kong and Nanjing ("Restaurant Tay Sam Yoen" 1934).

106. In seventeenth-century Batavia, soldiers, sailors, and artisans relied on Chinese-run cookshops for their cheap meals (de Haan 1922, 508). Even in Cape Town, where a tiny community of Indies Chinese resided in the 1740s, their products, restaurants, and cooking skills drew European praise (Yap and Leong Man 1996, 8).

107. Hulsman 1926, 4.

108. As early as 1885, an inventory of food products for sale in Batavia lists 75 Chinese and 167 indigenous products, some of which were shipped in from Palembang, Singapore, Siam, Annam, and China (Vorderman 1885).

109. *Sin Po Wekelijksche Editie* 70 (1924): iii.

5. THE HUMORISTIC AND THE INVECTIVE

1. Leow 2016, 219; Fahmy 2011, 170.

2. See J. Jackson 2013 for a similar argument in the context of Madagascar.

3. Already in 1812, when Indonesia temporarily found itself under British rule, a number of satirical Malay poems appeared from the hands of Eurasian writers in Semarang's *Java Government Gazette*, castigating the English for their ignorance about life in the Indies and mocking their habits and speech (P. Lee 2014, 309–11). Also see Farid and Razif 2008 on subversive indigenous writings in the early twentieth century.

4. See Grijns 1976 on *lenong* and van der Putten 2015 on *boria*.

5. Tan S. B. 2006 and Johan 2019 provide examples from Malaysian popular culture and Goebel 2015 and Keppy 2019 from that of Indonesia.

6. Kwee T. T. 1947; Anderson 2016, 171–76.

7. Kim To 1911, 445. Incidentally, the pseudonym of the author's victim is itself a pun on Multatuli—the pen name of the anticolonial critic Eduard Douwes Dekker (1820–87)—and the Malay words *buta* (blind) and *tuli* (deaf).

8. See Wallace 1983 on Malay pronouns in general and Oetomo 1987 on pronouns in East Java's Peranakan variety.

9. "Sarang Tawon" 1949.

10. Liu P. S. 1926.

11. A. A.Aoe 1923.

12. "Tjonto dari Djaoe" 1926.

13. The patois of society's lower rungs—and in particular Java's underprivileged Eurasians—was sometimes referred to as *petjok* or *sinjo-taal*. It was equally derided in indigenous, Dutch, and Chinese publications.

14. J. S. 1923.

15. Tong Ketik 1929.

16. Kwee T. H. 1928, 1686.

17. A 1905 newspaper article in *Ik Po* gives examples of phrases used by the Chinese in Solo, along with their meanings in mainstream vernacular Malay ("Bahasa Tjina di Tanah Djawa" 1905). A 1939 *Sin Po* article contains similar examples taken from the colloquial language of Chinese in Lasem (Oei 1939a).

18. "Telur: Yaitu orang yang bertutur yang bukan bahasanya mengikut bahasa orang tiadalah betul pada hurufnya seperti [...] orang cina hendak berbahasa Melayu menyebut 'orang' katanya 'onang' atau menyebut 'udang' katanya 'ulang'" (Raja Ali Haji 1986–87, 246).

19. See Dharmowijono 2009, 141 n. 202, 250, n. 139, 385, Chambert-Loir and Kramadibrata 2013, 13, and Hoogervorst 2017, 306–9 on the linguistic othering of Singkeh speech in Dutch and Malay literature. Even Singkehs married into Peranakan families could be told apart by their inability to pronounce the /r/ and a number of other shibboleths. See F. Chia 1983, 51–52 and Gwee 2013, 31–32 for examples from the Straits.

20. *Soerabaijasch handelsblad*, October 11, 1883, 2. Note that this sentence does not rhyme—and is therefore far less memorable—without a Chinese accent (Ml: *Orang Djawa patjoel, Orang Tjina koempoel, Orang Wolanda angkoet*).

21. Vincy 1933, 117.

22. Tjie 1933, 70. Earlier that year, Japan withdrew from the League of Nations after having been criticized for its military incursions into Manchuria.

23. Kwee T. H. 1930b, 111.

24. Tan B. S. 1937, 40.

25. In the classical Malay literature, too, most Dutch officials spoke bad Malay. See van Ronkel 1918a, 859–60 and Hooker 1991, 541 for examples.

26. Even a Low Malay phrasebook intended for prospective German planters prescribed the use of this pronoun (Hüttenbach 1921).

27. *Oetoesan Borneo* 9 (1928): 1.

28. Lie K. H. 1891, 16.

29. Also see Kato 2003 on Malay equivalents for "I" in late colonial novels. The use of *orang* to form plural pronouns reflects a similar usage in Hokkien (*lâng*) and has become widespread in Malay contact varieties (Hoogervorst 2015, 261).

30. Tjiong 1924, 42.

31. Kinship terms included *engkoh* (older brother), *engkong* (grandfather), *enso* (sister-in-law), *entjek* (uncle), *entjim* (auntie), and *twatji* (older sister). Widespread honorifics were *hoedjin* (madam), *kaptwa* (captain), *kongsi* (lieutenant), *loohoedjin* (elderly lady), *loosianseng* (elderly gentleman), *sianseng* (sir), *siotjia* (young lady), *thauké* (business owner), *tongkoen* (boss), and *tongpao* (compatriot). *Liatwi* (all of you) was a common way to politely address a group of people, e.g., *liatwi pembatja* (all you readers).

32. Unlike its Hokkien precursor, the Malay form *goea* is pronounced disyllabically. It was retranscribed into Hokkien as *gû-ōa* in the *Ferry and Bridge of the General Language* (Lim T. T. 1878, 1).

33. The form *lú* is restricted to only a few Hokkien subdialects (Jones 2009b, 56–58), whereas "li" (*lí*) is given as the correct from even by scholars based in the Netherlands Indies (Lim T. T. 1878, 3; Tjoa T. K. 1904, 1).

34. Lim H. S. 1887, 133. Note, however, that in an 1894 Sino-Malay storybook from the Indies, we see a young boy using *loe* to his school master (*Boekoe Tjerita Siauw Soat* 1894, 28).

35. *Traveller's Malay Pronouncing Hand-Book* 1897, 34; *Kelly & Walsh's Handbook* 1919, iii.
36. Some examples can be seen in "Correspondentie-Artikelen over het Onderwijs" (1900, 539). See Traill 1982, 131–32 on Raffles's usage of the pronoun.
37. *Ien Po* 2 (1917): 2.
38. Lauw Botak 1931, 16.
39. As Oetomo (1987, 170) points out, this idiosyncratic usage reflects the historical confinement of Hokkien to the male domain, at least in the Netherlands Indies. The pronoun is still used in present-day Indonesia to mark stereotyped Chinese speech (Goebel 2015, 164–68). See Douglas 1899, 350 on the Hokkien precursor *óe* and F. Chia 1983, 54 on its usage in Baba Malay (*oi*).
40. S. O. S. 1930, 669.
41. Jones 2009b, 56.
42. Pekdjit 1941, 2.
43. The *Ferry and Bridge of the General Language* equates it with Malay *kita* (Lim T. T. 1878, 4), but the pronoun *kita* is itself complicated. It is unmistakably plural in standard Malay, but could be singular ("I") as well as plural ("we") in vernacular Malay. In Malay translations of European or Chinese novels, *kita* often substitutes "I" in the source text. In a Mandarin phrasebook titled *Hoa Woe Ho Pie* (Combining Chinese and Malay), *kita* is likewise used in its singular meaning (Chun 1920, 107).
44. Nio (1955a, 42) interprets them as politer versions of *goea* and *loe*. In mainstream Hokkien, *goán* and *lín* are the pluralized counterparts of *góa* and *lí*.
45. Boekit Doeri 1929, xvi.
46. See Oetomo 1987, 196 on Dutch pronouns in the 1980s Malay of East Javanese Peranakan.
47. "Soeka plesir dan tida maoe perhatiken roemah-tangga" (Pouw K. A. 1937, 11); "jang taoe banjak hal kemerdika'an bangsa Barat" (13); "Maen mata dan saling oendjoek sympathie dengen perkata'an-perkata'an moeloek jang dioetjapken dalem bahasa Blanda" (13).
48. Pouw K. A. 1937, 60.
49. Yang-Lioe 1937, 95.
50. Seen in Hoh Hoh Sianseng 1936.
51. Lee S. L. 1930, 40.
52. *Pembrita-India* 1 (1922): 23.
53. Around this period, *Kung Yen* received several warnings from the colonial government for "unacceptable anti-Japanese writing" (ontoelaatbaar anti-Japansch geschrijf) (Poeze 1994, 248, 305).
54. *Kung Yen* 143 (1939): 3.
55. *Bin Seng* 2 (1922): 1.
56. See Tan K. S. 1920 for a contemporaneous account on the beginnings of the Chinese boycott movement of Japanese products and stores.
57. *Perniagaän* 151 (1923): 1.
58. These included *andjing* or *asoe* (dog), *babi* (pig), *kadal* (lizard), *kalde* (donkey), *kampret* (small bat), *kerbo* (water buffalo), *monjet* (monkey), and *tjeleng* (wild boar). The word for animal itself (*binatang*) was also used in swearing.
59. These words were used as nouns as well as adjectives and included *badoet* (clown), *bodo* (dumb), *dogol* (dimwit), *edan* (insane), *gelo* (foolish), *gendeng* (idiotic), *gila* (crazy), *goblok* (stupid), *kepala-oebi* (yam-head), *koerang beres* (dysfunctional), *menta-mateng* (half-baked), *otak miring* (halfwit), *otak oedang* (shrimp-for-brains), *otak toempoel* (dim-brained), *sontolojo* (mad), *tjerobo* (insolent), and *tolol* (silly).
60. For example, I have never encountered in print the common Hokkien-derived word *tiko* (male pig), which could be used derogatorily for indigenous men.

61. See Abdul Mutalib Abdul Ghani (1991, 22, 25), who gives no explanation of this word. In addition, various Hokkien swear words can be found in an article published in the *Indisch Weekblad van het Recht* (Indies Law Weekly) on a defamation lawsuit (Hoogervorst 2017, 306).
62. Dixi 1927, 511.
63. Chandra 2006, 266–67.
64. *Sin Po Wekelijksche Editie* 356 (1930).
65. Vincy 1933, 107.
66. *Pewarta Soerabaia* 12 (1914), 1.
67. Kho 1947, 13.
68. A. S. B. 1926, 1412.

EPILOGUE

1. "Meskipun kebudajaan Tionghoa tidak membawa pengaruh setjara demikian rupa sehingga melahirkan bangunan² monumental seperti tjandi² Borobudur, Prambanan, dsb. tapi penulis² dan tamu² dari Tiongkok telah membangunkan sebuah monumen bersedjarah penting bagi Indonesia, merupakan tulisan² tentang Indonesia. Dilihat dari perspektip sedjarah dan budaja, maka tulisan² orang² Tionghoa tentang Indonesia didjaman kuno itu tidak kalah pentingnja daripada tjandi² Borobudur, Prambanan, atau Sewu" ("Kebudajaan" 1960).

2. "Pada hemat saja, kita harus memandangnja sebagai milik bangsa Indonesia, karena itu karja apa jang sekarang sudah mendjadi orang Indonesia dan karena itu tertulis dalam bahasa Indonesia, biarpun bukan bahasa Indonesia jang bagus dan pula bukan bahasa Indonesia jang resmi. Dan bagaimana dengan hasil-sastera pengarang Tionghoa-Peranakan jang telah menolak kewarganegaraan Indonesia dan kini mendjadi warganegara Tiongkok? Saja berpendapat, karja mereka ini, jang djumlahnja pasti ketjil dibandingkan dengan jang mendjadi bangsa Indonesia, djuga harus dipandang sebagai kepunjaan bangsa Indonesia. Karena karja itu memakai bahasa Indonesia, sekalipun bukan jang resmi, dan tertjipta dibumi Indonesia. Biar bagaimanapun hasil-sastera pengarang Tionghoa Peranakan, jang sekarang mendjadi bangsa Tionghoa, tidak dapat dianggap termasuk pada sastera Tiongkok, berdasarkan bahasa suasana tjeritera dan tempat-terbitnja" (Nio 1962, 158–59).

3. "Sebagian pengarang peranakan lebih memilih menonjolkan identitas ke-Indo-nesian-nya. Misalnya pengarang Abdul Hadi WM yang sudah membaur tuntas. Namun, ada pula pengarang peranakan yang masih mempertahankan identitas peranakannya, seperti Kho Ping Hoo, Marga T, dan Basuki Sudjatmiko. Identitas peranakan tercermin dalam karya mereka; kadang-kadang jelas, adakalanya samar-samar. Tetapi ini tidak berarti karya mereka "kurang Indonesia." Sebetulnya mereka orang Indonesia yang dilahirkan dan dibesarkan di bumi Garuda dan karyanya mencerminkan keadaan masyarakat Indonesia yang majemuk. Dari sudut sastra, mempertahankan identitas pribadi dalam karya mereka justru akan lebih memperkaya sastra Indonesia modern" (Suryadinata 2016b, 257).

4. "De oude cultuur is zoo machtig interessant, is zoo'n aardig studieobject" (Pané 1941, 21).

5. "Regional Language" 1949. "Nah, stijl Sin Po djadi diam-diam bantoe bentoek Blok Asia" (*Sin Po*, March 9, 1949, 2).

6. Alisjahbana 1934.

7. This exclusion of Dutch and Chinese words certainly improved its status in the eyes of ethnic Malays. According to the Malayan language engineer Zainal Abidin bin Achmad (1895–1973), "Indonesian" was widely regarded as a "chaotic and bad language" (bahasa

jang katjau dan buruk) in the 1930s, yet these attitudes disappeared in the 1940s and the two varieties even started to adopt each other's words (Alisjahbana 1948a, 72).

8. See J. B. Kwee 1977, 221, Kratz 1992, Chandra 2006, 260; 2011a, 93, and Suryadinata 2016b on the latter years of Sino-Malay print culture. Initially, standard Indonesian chiefly prevailed in nationalistically inspired music. Pané 1941 provides a contemporaneous account and van Dijk 2003 a historical study. For a study on the impact of Indonesian standardization on Jawi-literate Muslim intellectuals, see Fogg 2015. Heryanto 1995, Bertrand 2003, and Samuel 2005 discuss Indonesian standardization in postcolonial times.

9. See Mahdi 2006, 102 on the language of early films and Bodden 2010 on theater.

10. "jang memenuhi sjarat² tata-bahasa jang lazim sebagai pertanggungan-djawab moril terhadap bahasa nasional kita" (Gan n.d., 197).

11. Fahmy 2011; Leow 2016.

12. Alisjahbana 1934.

13. See Skinner 1967 for a contemporaneous account.

14. Pramoedya Ananta Toer, for example, faced imprisonment in 1961 for his benevolent attitudes toward the Chinese, as expressed in one of his monographs, "which aroused official military and civilian antagonism on account of its defence of the Chinese community at a time when discriminatory policies were being pursued by the government" (*Indonesia: Amnesty International Report* 1977, 59).

15. See Purdey 2006 for an overview of this period and Suryadinata 1972, Heryanto 1998, Coppel 2002, Chandra 2006, and Somers-Heidhues 2017 for background studies on Chinese-Indonesians during the Suharto presidency.

16. Clammer 1980, 61; Rudolph 1998, 49.

17. See Suryadinata 2007, Chong 2014, and Setijadi 2015 on Indonesia's resinicization and Pandiangan 2003 and Hoon 2006 on the contemporary Chinese-Indonesian press.

18. Budianta 2012. For more background on Chinese-Indonesian revitalization, see Herlijanto 2016 and Anggraeni 2017.

19. Some government-supported projects approach Chinatowns (*Pecinan*) as sites of heritage (Tjiook 2017). The same is true for Chinese mosques. See Suryadinata and Kwartanada 2016 for more background.

20. See Chong 2014, Stenberg 2015a, and Setijadi 2015 on the contemporary role of Mandarin and Winkelmann 2008 and Stenberg 2017 on Indonesia's Chinese-language literature, which was revitalized in 1996.

21. Examples are given in Hoon 2006 and Kuntjara 2007. These translingual practices can also be observed among young Indonesians of non-Chinese backgrounds who attend schools where Mandarin is taught or often socialize with Mandarin-speaking friends.

22. This observation was also made by Chandra (2006, 235–56, 298).

23. See Chandra 2006, 237, Sen 2006, and Olszewska 2014 for more background.

24. Salmon 2013d, 293–94.

25. Chua 2008, 232.

26. Chakrabarty 2000.

27. Hofmeyr 2013, 153.

28. We might think, for example, of a periodical like *Barhout* (1929–31), which was published in vernacular Hadhrami Arabic. Such sources contain important fragments of Indonesian history, in the same way that writings in Indonesian languages contain important (and oft-neglected) fragments of Dutch history.

29. Rutten and van der Wal 2014.

References

A. A. Aoe. 1923. "Angin Toefan dari Barat Mengamoek di Timoer." *Sin Po Wekelijksche Editie* 37: 589–91.
A. I. H. n.d. *Ilmoe Melahirken: Dari Boenting sampe Branak*. Batavia: Kho Tjeng Bie.
A. S. B. 1926. "Laloetjoehan jang Tida Disengaja." *Sin Po Wekelijksche Editie* 187: 1412.
Abdul Mutalib Abdul Ghani, ed. 1991. *Syair Siti Zubaidah Perang China*. Kuala Lumpur: Dewan Bahasa dan Pustaka.
Adam, Ahmat B. 1995. *The Vernacular Press and the Emergence of Modern Indonesian Consciousness (1855–1913)*. Ithaca, NY: Cornell University Press.
Adhikari, Mohamed, ed. 1996. *Straatpraatjes: Language, Politics and Popular Culture in Cape Town, 1909–1922*. Pretoria: J. L. van Schaik.
Albrecht, J. E. 1879. "Het Schoolonderwijs onder de Chineezen op Java." *Tijdschrift voor Indische Taal-, Land- en Volkenkunde* 25: 225–41.
Alisjahbana, Sutan Takdir. 1933–34. "Bahasa Indonesia." *Poedjangga Baroe* 1: 129–79.
Alisjahbana, Sutan Takdir. 1934. "Kedoedoekan Bahasa Melajoe-Tionghoa." *Poedjangga Baroe* 2, no. 1: 97–105.
Alisjahbana, Sutan Takdir. 1948a. "Bahasa Indonesia dan Malaja." *Pembina Bahasa Indonesia* 3: 72–73.
Alisjahbana, Sutan Takdir. 1948b. "Edjaan Bahasa Indonesia." *Pembina Bahasa Indonesia* 1: 7–10, 17.
Alisjahbana, Sutan Takdir. 1948c. "Soal Kesatuan Bahasa dan Bahasa Melaju-Tionghoa." *Pembina Bahasa Indonesia* 4: 97–100.
Amrith, Sunil S. 2013. *Crossing the Bay of Bengal: The Furies of Nature and the Fortunes of Migrants*. Cambridge, MA: Harvard University Press.
Anderson, Benedict. 1991. *Imagined Communities: Reflections on the Origin and Spread of Nationalism*. London: Verso.
Anderson, Benedict. 2008. "Exit Suharto: Obituary for a Mediocre Tyrant." *New Left Review* 50: 27–59.
Anderson, Benedict. 2016. *A Life beyond Boundaries*. London: Verso.
Ang, Ien. 2001. *On Not Speaking Chinese: Living between Asia and the West*. London: Routledge.
Anggraeni, Dewi. 2017. "Chinese Indonesians after May 1998: How They Fit in the Big Picture." *Wacana* 18, no. 1: 106–30.
Antjoah. 1926. "Timoer dan Barat." *Sin Po Wekelijcksche Editie* 152: 761–62.
Appadurai, Arjun. 1986. *The Social Life of Things: Commodities in Cultural Perspective*. Cambridge: Cambridge University Press.
B. 1932. "Indische Causerieën: Gedeukt Hollandsch." *Nieuwsblad van het Noorden*, November 9, 5.
B. H. 1929. "Makasan Tionghoa." *Sin Po Wekelijksche Editie* 306.
"Baba." 1906. "Fasal tauchang." *The Friend of Babas* 1, no. 1: 5–6.
Badings, A. H. L. 1883. *Hollandsch-Maleische en Maleisch-Hollandsche Samenspraken*. The Hague: A. Berends.
"Bahasa Melajoe." 1924. *Sin Po Wekelijksche Editie* 81: 473.
"Bahasa Tionghoa . . .!" 1929. *Hoakiao* 122: 2.

"Bahasa Tjina di Tanah Djawa." 1905. *Ik Po* 43: 3.
Bailey, Paul J. 2003. "'Unharnessed Fillies': Discourse on the 'Modern' Female Students in Early Twentieth-Century China." In *Women and Culture in Modern China (1600–1950)*, 327–57. Taipei: Academia Sinica.
Bakhtin, Mikhail. 1984. *Rabelais and His World*. Bloomington: Indiana University Press.
"Balzaalschittering . . ." 1936. *Sin Po Wekelijksche Editie* 668, Hollandsch Supplement, 26.
Batten, C. J. 1868. *De Djoeroe Basa Betawi*. Batavia: H. M. van Dorp.
Beete Jukes, J. 1847. *Narrative of the Surveying Voyage of H.M.S. Fly*. Vol. 2. London: T&W Boone.
Behrend, T. 1993. "Manuscript Production in Nineteenth-Century Java: Codicology and the Writing of Javanese Literary History." *Bijdragen tot de Taal-, Land- en Volkenkunde* 149, no. 3: 407–37.
Bernards, Brian. 2015. *Writing the South Seas: Imagining the Nanyang in Chinese and Southeast Asian Postcolonial Literature*. Seattle: University of Washington Press.
Bertrand, Jacques. 2003. "Language Policy and the Promotion of National Identity in Indonesia." In *Fighting Words: Language Policy and Ethnic Relations in Asia*, edited by Michael Edward Brown and Sumit Ganguly, 263–90. Cambridge, MA: MIT Press.
Bhabha, Homi K. 1994. *The Location of Culture*. London: Routledge.
Birch, E. W. 1969. "The Vernacular Press in the Straits." *Journal of the Malaysian Branch of the Royal Asiatic Society* 42, no. 1: 192–95.
Blagden, C. O. 1917–20. "Malay." *Bulletin of the School of Oriental Studies* 1: 97–100.
Bleeker, P. 1844. *Bijdrage tot de Kennis der Genees- en Artsenijmengkunde onder de Chinezen in het Algemeen en onder die te Batavia in het Bijzonder*. Batavia: Bataviaasch Genootschap.
Blommaert, Jan. 2008. *Grassroots Literacy: Writing, Identity and Voice in Central Africa*. London: Routledge.
Blussé, Leonard. 1990. "Doctor at Sea: Chou Mei-yeh's Voyage to the West." In *As the Twig Is Bent: Essays in Honour of Frits Vos*, edited by Erika Poorter, 7–30. Amsterdam: J. C. Gieben.
Blussé, Leonard. 2000. *Retour Amoy: Anny Tan—Een vrouwenleven in Indonesië, Nederland en China*. Amsterdam: Uitgeverij Balans.
Blussé, Leonard. 2014. "Of Hewers of Wood and Drawers of Water: Leiden University's Early Sinologists (1854–1911)." In *Chinese Studies in the Netherlands: Past, Present and Future*, edited by Wilt L. Idema, 27–68. Leiden: Brill.
Blussé, Leonard, and Nie Dening. 2018. *The Chinese Annals of Batavia, the "Kai Ba Lidai Shiji" and Other Stories (1610–1795)*. Leiden: Brill.
Bodden, Michael. 2010. "Modern Drama, Politics, and the Postcolonial Aesthetics of Left-Nationalism in North Sumatra: The Forgotten Theater of Indonesia's Lekra, 1955–65." In *Cultures at War: The Cold War and Cultural Expression in Southeast Asia*, edited by Tony Day and Maya H. T. Liem, 45–80. Ithaca, NY: Southeast Asia Program Publications.
Boekit Doeri. 1929. "Penghidoepannja Njonja Millionnair." *Hoakiao* 127: xi–xvi.
Boekoe Tjerita Siauw Soat: Kim Ko Kie Koan. 1894. Batavia: IJap Goan Ho.
Borthwick, Sally. 1983. *Education and Social Change in China: The Beginnings of the Modern Era*. Stanford, CA: Hoover Institution Press.
Brinkgreve, Francine, and Johanna Leijfeldt. 2017. "The Chinese-Indonesian Collections in the National Museum of World Cultures, the Netherlands." *Wacana* 18, no. 2: 275–314.

Bromokusumo, Aji Chen. 2013. *Peranakan Tionghoa dalam Kuliner Nusantara*. Jakarta: Gramedia.
Budianta, Melani. 2012. "Malang Mignon: Cultural Expressions of the Chinese, 1940–1960." In *Heirs to World Culture: Being Indonesian, 1950–1965*, edited by Jennifer Lindsay and Maya H. T. Liem, 255–81. Leiden: Brill.
Butatuli and Hemeling. 1913. *Boekoe Wet dan Rasia tentang Perhoeboengan antara Prampoean dan Lelaki*. Batavia: Tjiong Kone Bie.
Byrd, Cecil K. 1970. *Early Printing in the Straits Settlements, 1806–1858*. Singapore: Singapore National Library.
Candranegara. 1877. *Cariyos Purwalelana*. Second edition. Semarang: G. C. T. van Dorp.
Carey, Peter. 1992. *The British in Java, 1811–1816: A Javanese Account*. Oxford: Oxford University Press.
Chakrabarti, Pratik. 2014. *Medicine and Empire: 1600–1960*. Houndmills: Palgrave Macmillan.
Chakrabarty, Dipesh. 2000. *Provincializing Europe: Postcolonial Thought and Historical Difference*. Princeton, NJ: Princeton University Press.
Chambert-Loir, Henri. 1999. "Sair Java-Bank di Rampok: Sastra Melayu atau Melayu-Tionghoa?" In *Panggung Sejarah: Persembahan kepada Prof. Dr. Denys Lombard*, edited by Henri Chambert-Loir and Hasan Muarif Ambary, 335–64. Jakarta: École Française d'Extrême Orient.
Chambert-Loir, Henri, and Dewaki Kramadibrata, eds. 2013. *Katalog Naskah Pecenongan: Koleksi Perpustakaan Nasional Sastra Betawi Akhir Abad ke-19*. Jakarta: Perpustakaan Nasional Republik Indonesia.
Chan, Liang Wai. 2003. "The Go Collection of the Sinological Institute at Leiden University." MA thesis, University of Leiden.
Chan, Shelly. 2018. *Diaspora's Homeland: Modern China in the Age of Global Migration*. Durham, NC: Duke University Press.
Chandra, Elizabeth. 2006. "National Fictions: Chinese-Malay Literature and the Politics of Forgetting." PhD diss., University of California.
Chandra, Elizabeth. 2011a. "Fantasizing Chinese/Indonesian Hero: Njoo Cheong Seng and the Gagaklodra Series." *Archipel* 82: 83–113.
Chandra, Elizabeth. 2011b. "Women and Modernity: Reading the Femme Fatale in Early Twentieth-Century Indies Novels." *Indonesia* 92: 157–82.
Chandra, Elizabeth. 2013. "From Sensation to Oblivion: Boven Digoel in Sino-Malay Novels." *Bijdragen tot de Taal-, Land- en Volkenkunde* 169, nos. 2–3: 244–78.
Chandra, Elizabeth. 2015a. "Blossoming Dahlia: Chinese Women Novelists in Colonial Indonesia." *Southeast Asian Studies* 4, no. 3: 533–64.
Chandra, Elizabeth. 2015b. "Review of *Rethinking Chineseness: Translational Sinophone Identities in the Nanyang Literary World*, by E. K. Tan. Cambria Press, Amherst, NY, 2013." *South East Asia Research* 23, no. 2: 263–65.
Chandra, Elizabeth. 2016. "The Chinese Holmes: Translating Detective Fiction in Colonial Indonesia." *Keio Communication Review* 38: 39–63.
Chang Pin-tsun. 1998. "The Formation of a Maritime Convention in Minnan (Southern Fujian), c. 900–1200." In *From the Mediterranean to the China Sea: Miscellaneous Notes*, edited by Claude Guillot, Denys Lombard, and Roderich Ptak, 143–55. Wiesbaden: Harrassowitz.
Chatterjee, Partha. 1993. *The Nation and its Fragments: Colonial and Postcolonial Histories*. Princeton, NJ: Princeton University Press.
Chaudhary, Shreesh. 2009. *Foreigners and Foreign Languages in India: A Sociolinguistic History*. Delhi: Foundation Books.

Chen Mong Hock. 1967. *The Early Chinese Newspapers of Singapore, 1881–1912*. Singapore: University of Malaya Press.
Cheng Weikun. 1998. "Politics of the Queue: Agitation and Resistance in the Beginning and End of Qing China." In *Hair: Its Power and Meaning in Asian Cultures*, edited by Alf Hiltebeitel and Barbara D. Miller, 123–42. Albany: State University of New York Press.
Chia Cheng Sit. 1899. "The Language of the Babas." *Straits Chinese Magazine* 3, no. 9: 11–15.
Chia, Felix. 1983. *Ala Sayang!* Singapore: Eastern Universities Press.
Chiang, Howard. 2018. *After Eunuchs: Science, Medicine, and the Transformation of Sex in Modern China*. New York: Columbia University Press.
Chien Hung-yi. 2012. "Tuku Kao: Ben Tudi Ming de Yuanliu yu Dongya Shijie de Lianjie" [Toko: An Etymology of a Local Placename and Its Connections to the Maritime Asia]. *Taiwan xue zhi* 6: 77–100.
Chin, Grace V. S., and Tom Hoogervorst. 2017. "From Soetji to Soendel: Negotiating Race, Class and Gender in a Netherlands Indies Newspaper." *Intersections: Gender and Sexuality in Asia and the Pacific* 41: 13 pp.
"The Chinese Hermit." 1924. *The Straits Times*, August 18, 10.
Chong Wu Ling. 2014. "Democratisation and Ethnic Minorities: Chinese Indonesians in Post-Suharto Indonesia." PhD diss., National University of Singapore.
Chow, Rey. 1993. *Writing Diaspora: Tactics of Intervention in Contemporary Cultural Studies*. Bloomington: Indiana University Press.
Chow, Rey. 2013. "On Chineseness as a Theoretical Problem." In *Sinophone Studies: A Critical Reader*, edited by Shu-Mei Shih, Chien-Hsin Tsai, and Brian Bernards, 43–56. New York: Columbia University Press.
Chow, Rey. 2014. *Not Like a Native Speaker: On Languaging as a Postcolonial Experience*. New York: Columbia University Press.
Chua Beng Huat. 2008. "Southeast Asia in Postcolonial Studies: An Introduction." *Postcolonial Studies* 11, no. 3: 231–40.
Chun Foo Chun. 1920. *Hoa Woe Ho Pie*. Batavia: Chun Foo Chun, Lie Bok Sioe.
Clammer, John R. 1980. *Straits Chinese Society: Studies in the Sociology of the Baba Communities of Malaysia and Singapore*. Singapore: Singapore University Press.
Claver, Alexander. 2014. *Dutch Commerce and Chinese Merchants in Java: Colonial Relationships in Trade and Finance, 1800–1942*. Leiden: Brill.
Cohen, Matthew Isaac. 2006. *The Komedie Stamboel: Popular Theater in Colonial Indonesia, 1891–1903*. Athens: Ohio University Press.
Cohen, Robin. 2007. "Creolization and Cultural Globalization: The Soft Sounds of Fugitive Power." *Globalizations* 4, no. 3: 369–84.
Cohn, Bernard S. 1996. *Colonialism and Its Forms of Knowledge: The British in India*. Princeton, NJ: Princeton University Press.
Coppel, Charles. 1981. "The Origins of Confucianism as an Organized Religion in Java, 1900–1923." *Journal of Southeast Asian Studies* 12, no. 1: 179–96.
Coppel, Charles. 1997. "Emancipation of the Indonesian Chinese Woman." In *Women Creating Indonesia: The First Fifty Years*, edited by Jean Gelman Taylor, 22–51. Clayton, VI: Monash Asia Institute.
Coppel, Charles. 2002. *Studying Ethnic Chinese in Indonesia*. Singapore: Singapore Society of Asian Studies.
Coppel, Charles, and Leo Suryadinata. 1978. "The Use of the Terms 'Tjina' and 'Tionghoa' in Indonesia: A Historical Survey." In *The Chinese Minority in Indonesia: Seven Papers*, edited by Leo Suryadinata, 113–28. Singapore: Chopmen Enterprises.

"Correspondentie-Artikelen over het Onderwijs in de Maleische Taal voor Officieren." 1900. *De Indische Gids* 22, no. 1: 532–48.
Cushman, J. W., and A. C. Milner. 1979. "Eighteenth- and Nineteenth-Century Chinese Accounts of the Malay Peninsula." *Journal of the Malaysian Branch of the Royal Asiatic Society* 52, no. 1: 1–56.
D. H. 1867. "Stemmen van Inlanders: Bloemlezing uit de Samarangsche Couranten." *Tijdschrift voor Nederlandsch-Indië* 1, no. 2: 126–39.
de Haan, F. 1922. *Oud Batavia: Gedenkboek uitgeven ter gelegenheid van het 300-jarig bestaan der stad in 1919*. First Volume. Batavia: G. Kolff.
de Jonghe, A. 1967. *De Taalpolitiek van Koning Willem I in de Zuidelijke Nederlanden (1814–1830): De Genesis der Taalbesluiten en hun Toepassing*. Sint-Andries-bij-Brugge: J. Darthet.
Departement van Economische Zaken. 1935. *Volkstelling 1930. Deel VII: Chineezen en Andere Vreemde Oosterlingen in Nederlansch-Indië*. Batavia: Landsdrukkerij.
Derks, Hans. 2012. *History of the Opium Problem: The Assault on the East, ca. 1600–1950*. Leiden: Brill.
Dermout, J. 1894. *Piong Pan Ho: Oorspronkelijke Indische Roman*. Amersfoort: G. J. Slothouwer.
Dharmowijono, Widjajanti. 2009. "Van Koelies, Klontongs en Kapiteins: Het Beeld van de Chinezen in Indisch-Nederlands Literair Proza 1880–1950." PhD diss., University of Amsterdam.
Ding Choo Ming. 1978. "An Introduction to the Indonesian Peranakan Literature in the Library of the Universiti Kebangsaan Malaysia." *Journal of the Malaysian Branch of the Royal Asiatic Society* 51, no. 1: 54–61.
Ding, Picus Sizhi. 2016. *Southern Min (Hokkien) as a Migrating Language: A Comparative Study of Language Shift and Maintenance Across National Borders*. Singapore: Springer.
Dixi. 1927. "Soesie-Ngokeng dari Darah dan Daging." *Sin Po Wekelijksche Editie* 241: 511–12.
Dorleijn, Margreet, and Jacomine Nortier. 2017. "Metalinguistic Discourse on Multilingual Urban and Youth Speech Styles and Multilingual Awareness and Linguistic Practices." *Applied Linguistics Review* 10, no. 3: 1–11.
Douglas, Carstairs. 1899. *Chinese–English Dictionary of the Vernacular or Spoken Language of Amoy*. London: Presbyterian Church of England.
Drewes, G. W. J. 1981. "Balai Pustaka and Its Antecedents." In *Papers on Indonesian Languages and Literatures*, edited by Nigel Phillips and Khaidir Anwar, 97–104. London: School of Oriental and African Studies.
Duggan, Geneviève. 2001. "The Chinese Batiks of Java." In *Batik: Drawn in Wax*, edited by Itie van Hout, 90–105. Amsterdam: Royal Tropical Institute.
Edwards, E. D., and C. O. Blagden. 1931. "A Chinese Vocabulary of Malacca: Malay Words and Phrases Collected between A.D. 1403 and 1511 (?)." *Bulletin of the School of Oriental Studies* 6, no. 3: 715–49.
Eleonora. 1959. *Masakan Sehari-Hari*. Semarang: Liong.
Elson, R. E. 2008. *The Idea of Indonesia: A History*. Cambridge: Cambridge University Press.
Erkelens, Monique. 2013. "The Decline of the Chinese Council of Batavia: The Loss of Prestige and Authority of the Traditional Elite amongst the Chinese Community from the end of the Nineteenth Century until 1942." PhD diss., University of Leiden.
Errington, Joseph. 2008. *Linguistics in a Colonial World: A Story of Language, Meaning, and Power*. Malden, MA: Blackwell.

Esser, S. J. 1938. "Maleisch en Nederlandsch." *Koloniale Studiën* 22, no. 1: 154–68.
"Eten 'bij den Chinees' en Betalen volgens de Grieksche Calendas: Diefstal door het Keelgat!" 1941. *Sin Po Wekelijksche Editie* 962: 25.
F. 1928. "Kenapa Banjak Prampoean Tida Kawin?" *Sin Po Wekelijksche Editie* 291: 471–74.
Fabian, Johannes, ed. 1990. *History from Below: The "Vocabulary of Elisabethville" by Andre Yav. Text, Translations, and Interpretive Essay*. Amsterdam: John Benjamins.
Fahmy, Ziad. 2011. *Ordinary Egyptians: Creating the Modern Nation through Popular Culture*. Stanford, CA: Stanford University Press.
Farid, Hilmar, and Razif. 2008. "Batjaan Liar in the Dutch East Indies: A Colonial Antipode." *Postcolonial Studies* 11 no. 3: 277–92.
"Fasal tauchang." 1906. *The Friend of Babas* 1, no. 3: 3–4.
Finnane, Antonia. 2007. *Changing Clothes in China: Fashion, History, Nation*. London: Hurst.
Fogg, Kevin W. 2015. "The Standardisation of the Indonesian Language and Its Consequences for Islamic Communities." *Journal of Southeast Asian Studies* 46, no. 1: 86–110.
Fokker, A. A. 1891. "De Waarde van het Maleisch als Beschavingsmedium." *Tijdschrift voor het Binnenlandsch Bestuur* 5, nos. 1–6: 82–88.
Fokker, A. A. 1906. *Kitab Tjonto Soerat-Soerat Melajoe*. Leiden: E.J. Brill.
Foulcher, Keith. 2000. "Sumpah Pemuda: The Making and Meaning of a Symbol of Indonesian Nationhood." *Asian Studies Review* 24, no. 3: 377–410.
"Fox-Trot-Lek." 1924. *Sin Po Wekelijksche Editie* 96: 699.
Franken, J. L. M. 1953. *Taalhistoriese Bydraes*. Amsterdam: A. A. Balkema.
Freedman, Paul, and Koo Siu Ling, eds. 2015. *Culture Cuisine Cooking: An East Java Peranakan Memoir*. Eindhoven: Lecturis.
Frost, Mark Ravinder. 2005. "Emporium in Imperio: Nanyang Networks and the Straits Chinese in Singapore, 1819–1914." *Journal of Southeast Asian Studies* 36, no. 1: 29–66.
G. 1935. "Bahasa Melajoe." *Keng Po Speciaal Nummer*, 41–44.
Gallop, Annabel Teh. 1990. "Early Malay Printing: An Introduction to the British Library Collections." *Journal of the Malaysian Branch of the Royal Asiatic Society* 63, no. 1: 85–124.
Gallop, Annabel Teh. 2009. "Was the Mousedeer Peranakan? In Search of Chinese Islamic Influences on Malay Manuscript Art." In *Lost Times and Untold Tales from the Malay World*, edited by Jan van der Putten and Mary Kildine Cody, 319–38. Singapore: NUS Press.
Gan Kok Liang. n.d. *Thian San Tjhit Kiam*. Semarang: Pustaka Silat.
García, Ofelia, and Li Wei. 2014. *Translanguaging: Language, Bilingualism and Education*. Houndmills: Palgrave Macmillan.
Gartenberg, Gary Nathan. 2000. "Silat Tiles: Narrative Representations of Martial Culture in the Malay/Indonesian Archipelago." PhD diss., University of California.
Gee, James Paul. 2000–1. "Identity as an Analytic Lens for Research in Education." *Review of Research in Education* 25: 99–125.
"Gele Profeet." 1919. *De Sumatra Post*, May 2, 2.
"De gelijkstelling der Chineezen." 1940. *Sin Po Wekelijksche Editie* 920: 27.
George, Abosede A. 2014. *Making Modern Girls: A History of Girlhood, Labor, and Social Development in Colonial Lagos*. Athens: Ohio University Press.
Giddens, Anthony. 1990. *The Consequences of Modernity*. Cambridge: Polity Press.
"Gila Hormat." 1928. *Djawa-Tengah Review* 3, no. 6: 32.

Godley, Michael R. 1981. *The Mandarin-Capitalists from Nanyang: Overseas Chinese Enterprise in the Modernization of China, 1893–1911*. Cambridge: Cambridge University Press.
Goebel, Zane. 2015. *Language and Superdiversity: Indonesians Knowledging at Home and Abroad*. Oxford: Oxford University Press.
Goerz. 1938. "Bahasa Melajoe jang Orang Disoeroe Peladjarin." *Sin Po Wekelijksche Editie* 801: 22–23.
Govaars-Tjia, Ming Tien Nio. 1999. "Hollands Onderwijs in een Koloniale Samenleving: De Chinese Ervaring in Indonesië, 1900–1942." PhD diss., University of Leiden.
Grijns, C. D. 1976. "Lenong in the Environs of Jakarta: A Report." *Archipel* 12: 175–202.
Grijns, C. D. 1991. "Bahasa Indonesia Avant la Lettre in the 1920s." In *Papers in Austronesian linguistics, No.1*, edited by H. Steinhauer, 49–81. Canberra: Pacific Linguistics.
Groeneboer, Kees. 1993. *Weg tot het Westen*. Leiden: KITLV.
Gwee Thian Hock, William. 2013. *A Baba Boyhood: Growing up during World War 2*. Singapore: Marshall Cavendish.
Gyssels, Kathleen. 2007. "Creoles." In *Imagology: The Cultural Construction and Literary Representation of National Characters. A Critical Survey*, edited by Manfred Beller and Joep Leerssen, 131–35. Amsterdam: Rodopi.
Habermas, Jürgen. 1989. *The Structural Transformation of the Public Sphere: An Inquiry into a Category of Bourgeois Society*. Cambridge, MA: MIT Press.
Hageman, J. 1860. "Bijdragen tot de kennis van de Residentie Soerabaja." *Tijdschrift voor Nederlandsch-Indië* 22, no. 1: 17–34.
Han Bing Hwie. 1923. *Sair Tjerita Penjakitnja Rahajat Tiongkok*. Batavia: Lie Tek Long.
Hanboen dalem Holl. Chin. School. 1926. Malang: Comité Penggerak Hanboen dalam Holl. Chin. School.
Hartanto, John Surjadi. 1978. *Biografi Rama Moortie: Tan Tik Sioe Sian. Pertapa di Lereng Gunung Wilis*. Surabaya: Indah.
Hau, Caroline S. 2014. *The Chinese Question: Ethnicity, Nation, and Region in and Beyond the Philippines*. Singapore: NUS Press.
Hee Wai-Siam. 2019. *Remapping the Sinophone: The Cultural Production of Chinese-Language Cinema in Singapore and Malaya before and during the Cold War*. Hong Kong: Hong Kong University Press.
Heng, Derek. 2008. "Shipping, Customs Procedures, and the Foreign Community: The 'Pingzhou ketan' on Aspects of Guangzhou's Maritime Economy in the Late Eleventh Century." *Journal of Song-Yuan Studies* 38: 1–38.
Herlijanto, Johanes. 2016. "What Does Indonesia's Pribumi Elite Think of Ethnic Chinese Today?" *ISEAS Perspective* 32: 1–9.
Hermawan, Eddy. 1994. *Yindunixiya Xi Zhaowa Kejia Hua*. Beijing: Zhongguo Shehui Kexue Chubanshe.
Herudjati, P., ed. 2008. *Pengaruh Dialek Melayu-Tionghoa pada Perkembangan Bahasa Indonesia (Tentang Bahasa dan Sastra Melayu-Rendah)*. Semarang: Masyarakat Tjerita Silat & Fakultas Sastra UNDIP.
Heryanto, Ariel. 1995. *Language of Development and Development of Language: The Case of Indonesia*. Canberra: Australian National University.
Heryanto, Ariel. 1998. "Ethnic Identities and Erasure: Chinese Indonesians in Public Culture." In *Southeast Asian Identities: Culture and the Politics of Representation in Indonesia, Malaysia, Singapore, and Thailand*, edited by Joel S. Kahn, 95–114. London: I.B. Tauris.

Hesselink, Liesbeth. 2011. *Healers on the Colonial Market: Native Doctors and Midwives in the Dutch East Indies*. Leiden: KITLV Press.
Hidayatullah, Moch. Syarif. 2012. "*Bustān al-Kātibīn*: Pengaruh Tata Bahasa Arab dalam Tata Bahasa Melayu." *Manuskripta* 2, no. 1: 53–77.
"Hikajat Bahasa Blanda di Indonesie." 1926. *Sin Po Wekelijksche Editie* 156: 821–22.
Hill, A. H. 1955. "The Hikayat Abdullah." *Journal of the Malayan Branch of the Royal Asiatic Society* 28, no. 3: 3–354.
Hirth, F. 1888. "The Chinese Oriental College." *Journal of the China Branch of the Royal Asiatic Society* 22: 203–19.
Ho Engseng. 2006. *The Graves of Tarim: Genealogy and Mobility across the Indian Ocean*. Berkeley: University of California Press.
Hoffman, John E. 1979. "A Foreign Investment: Indies Malay to 1901." *Indonesia* 27: 65–92.
Hoffman, John E. 1995. "Sumpah Pemuda: International Malay on Oath." In *Makalah pada Kongres Bahasa Melayu Sedunia*, 535–52. Kuala Lumpur: Dewan Bahasa dan Pustaka.
Hofmeyr, Isabel. 2013. *Gandhi's Printing Press: Experiments in Slow Reading*. Cambridge, MA: Harvard University Press.
Hoh Hoh Sianseng. 1936. *Feuilleton: Kang Ouw Tay Hiap*. Bandung: Tjerita Silat.
Hoogervorst, Tom G. 2015. "Tracing the Linguistic Crossroads between Malay and Tamil." *Wacana* 16, no. 2: 249–83.
Hoogervorst, Tom G. 2016. "Manliness in Sino-Malay Publications in the Netherlands Indies." *South East Asia Research* 24, no. 2: 283–307.
Hoogervorst, Tom G. 2017. "What Kind of Language Was 'Chinese Malay' in Late Colonial Java?" *Indonesia and the Malay World* 45, no. 133: 294–314.
Hoogervorst, Tom G. 2021. "Gained in Translation: The Politics of Localising Western Stories in Late-Colonial Indonesia." In *Translational Politics in Southeast Asian Literatures: Contesting Race, Gender and Sexuality*, edited by Grace V. S. Chin, 100–131. New York: Routledge.
Hoogervorst, Tom G. Forthcoming. "'Do You Love China or Not?': Late-Colonial Textbooks to Learn Mandarin through Malay." In *Sinophone Southeast Asia: Sinitic Voices across the South Seas*, edited by Caroline Chia and Tom Hoogervorst. Leiden: Brill.
Hoogervorst, Tom G., and Henk Schulte Nordholt. 2017. "Urban Middle Classes in Colonial Java (1900–1942): Images and Language." *Bijdragen tot de Taal-, Land- en Volkenkunde* 173, no. 4: 442–74.
Hooker, Virginia Matheson. 1991. *Tuhfat al-Nafis: Sejarah Melayu Islam*. Kuala Lumpur: Dewan Bahasa dan Pustaka.
Hoon Chang-Yau. 2006. "'A Hundred Flowers Bloom': The Re-emergence of the Chinese Press in Post-Suharto Indonesia." In *Media and the Chinese Diaspora: Community, Communication and Commerce*, edited by W. Sun, 91–118. London: Routledge.
Horton, William Bradley. 2020. "Shifting Communication: Language Learning during the Japanese Occupation of Indonesia." *Akita Daigaku Kyōiku Bunka Gakubu Kenkyū Kiyō* 75: 67–75.
Huang Huimin. 2004. "Xinma Baba Wenxue de Yanjiu." MA thesis, National Chengchi University.
Huffman, James L. 1997. *Creating a Public: People and Press in Meiji Japan*. Honolulu: University of Hawai'i Press.
Hulsbosch, Marianne. 2014. *Pointy Shoes and Pith Helmets: Dress and Identity Construction in Ambon from 1850 to 1942*. Leiden: Brill.

Hulsman, Leo. 1926. "Batavia . . . De Stad der Schaduwen." *D'Oriënt* 50: 2–5.
Hung, Tzu-hui. 2011. "Living with, among, and as Others: Creolizing Transpacific Chinese Diaspora." PhD diss., Stony Brook University.
Hunter, Emma. 2015. *Political Thought and the Public Sphere in Tanzania: Freedom, Democracy and Citizenship in the Era of Decolonization.* Cambridge: Cambridge University Press.
Hüttenbach, Heinrich. 1921. *Anleitung zu Enlernung der Malayischen Sprache.* Medan-Deli: Varekamp.
Hwang, E. T. H. 1935. *Kitab Logat Baroe: Tionghoa-Melajoe.* Shanghai: Modern Languages Association.
Hwat San. 1929. "Pendoedoek Suriname." *Hoakiao* 131: 15–16.
Ie Tjoen Leng. 1933. *Vegetarianisme atawa Tjia Tjai.* Buitenzorg: Doenia Ilmoe.
Ikeya, Chie. 2008. "The Modern Burmese Woman and the Politics of Fashion in Colonial Burma." *Journal of Asian Studies* 67, no. 4: 1277–1308.
Ikeya, Chie. 2011. *Refiguring Women, Colonialism, and Modernity in Burma.* Honolulu: University of Hawai'i Press.
Ikeya, Chie. 2018. "Talking Sex, Making Love: P. Moe Nin and Intimate Modernity in Colonial Burma." In *Modern Times in Southeast Asia, 1920s–1970s*, edited by Susie Protschky and Tom van den Berge, 136–65. Leiden: Brill.
Ilmoe Obat-Obattan Bergoena pada Sekalian Orang Lelaki dan Prampoean jang Dapet Roepa-Roepa Penjakit. 1890. Batavia: Yap Goan Ho.
Indonesia: Amnesty International Report. 1977. London: Amnesty International Publications.
Injo Bian Hien. 1931. *Nasib.* Batavia: Samideo.
Ishak, Md. Sidin Ahmad. 1998. *Penerbitan & Percetakan Buku Melayu.* Kuala Lumpur: Dewan Bahasa dan Pustaka.
Ishwara, Helen. 2012. "Aneka Rupa Masakan Peranakan." In *Indonesian Chinese Peranakan: A Cultural Journey*, edited by Lily Wibisono, Mary Northmore, Rusdi Tjahyadi, and Musa Jonatan, 222–47. Jakarta: Kompas Gramedia.
Iskandar, Teuku. 1981. "Some Manuscripts Formerly Belonging to Jakarta Lending Libraries." In *Papers on Indonesian Languages and Literatures*, edited by Nigel Phillips and Khaidir Anwar, 145–52. London: School of Oriental and African Studies.
J. S. 1923. "Lelakonnja 'Nir Petroes." *Sin Po Wekelijksche Editie* 33: 523–25.
Jackson, Jennifer. 2013. *Political Oratory and Cartooning: An Ethnography of Democratic Processes in Madagascar.* Malden, MA: Wiley-Blackwell.
Jackson, R. N. 1965. *Pickering: Protector of Chinese.* Kuala Lumpur: Oxford University Press.
Jap Tjion Lian. 1926. "Pandji Woeloeng." *Hoakiao* 6: 38–40.
Jedamski, Doris. 1992. "Balai Pustaka: A Colonial Wolf in Sheep's Clothing." *Archipel* 44: 23–46.
Jedamski, Doris. 1997. "De Taalpolitiek van de Balai Poestaka." In *Koloniale Taalpolitiek in Oost en West: Nederlands-Indië, Suriname, Nederlandse Antillen en Aruba*, edited by Kees Groeneboer, 159–85. Amsterdam: Amsterdam University Press.
Jedamski, Doris. 2014. "Translation in the Malay World: Different Communities, Different Agendas." In *Asian Translation Traditions*, edited by Eva Hung and Judy Wakabayashi, 211–45. Manchester: St. Jerome Publishing.
Johan, Adil. 2019. "Cosmopolitan Sounds and Intimate Narratives in P. Ramlee's Film Music." *Journal of Intercultural Studies* 40, no. 4: 474–90.
Jones, Russell. 2009a. "The Chiangchew Hokkiens: The True Pioneers in the Nanyang." *Journal of the Malaysian Branch of the Royal Asiatic Society* 82, no. 2: 39–66.

Jones, Russell. 2009b. *Chinese Loan-Words in Malay and Indonesian*. Kuala Lumpur: University of Malaya Press.
Judge, Joan. 2008. *The Precious Raft of History: The Past, the West, and the Woman Question in China*. Stanford, CA: Standford University Press.
K. H. N. 1926. "Onderwijs Hoakiao di Indonesia." *Hoakiao* 14: 9–11.
K. W. S. 1931. "Hoakiauw dan Onderwijs." *Sin Po Wekelijksche Editie* 411.
"Kaboeroekan." 1926. *Sin Po Wekelijksche Editie* 157: 833–34.
Kam Seng Kioe. 1974. *Masakan Tionghoa Asli*. Semarang: Loka Dhi Sastra.
Kang Pei-te. 2017. "Shiba, Shijiu Shiji Badaweiya Tangren dui Zhimindi Xingzheng Tixi de Wenhua Renzhi Fuyu Yu Chong Su Yi 'Gong'an Bu' Zhong de Guanzhi, Jigou." *Hanxue Yanjiu* 35, no. 1: 261–90.
Kaptein, Nico. 1993. "An Arab Printer in Surabaya in 1853." *Bijdragen tot de Taal-, Land- en Volkenkunde* 149, no. 2: 356–62.
Kato, Tsuyoshi. 2003. "Images of Colonial Cities in Indonesian Novels." In *Southeast Asia over Three Generations: Essays Presented to Benedict R. O'G.*, edited by James T. Siegel and Audrey R. Kahin, 101–5. Ithaca, NY: Cornell University Press.
"Kebudajaan: Sebuah Mata-Rantai Hubungan antara Tiongkok dan Indonesia Purba." 1960. *Republik*, February 3, 3.
Keessen, Jan. 2009. *Cardinal Men and Scarlet Women: A Colorful Etymology of Words that Discriminate*. Milwaukee: Marquette University Press.
Kelly & Walsh's Handbook of the Malay Language for the Use of Tourists and Residents. 1919. Singapore: Kelly & Walsh.
Keppy, Peter. 2019. *Tales of Southeast Asia's Jazz Age: Filipinos, Indonesians and Popular Culture, 1920–1936*. Singapore: NUS Press.
"Keputusan Kongres Bahasa Indonesia I: Surakarta, 25–28 Juli 1938." 1983. *Pembinaan Bahasa Indonesia* 4, no. 4: 208–30.
Kern, H. 1881. "Over Eene Oudjavaansche Oorkonde van Çaka 782." *Verslagen en mededelingen der Koninklijke Akademie van Wetenschappen* 2, no. 10: 79–115.
Khadiv-Jam, Hoseyn, ed. 1994. *Masīr-i Ṭālibī: Yā Safarnāma-i Mīrzā Abū Ṭālib Khān*. Tehran: Islamic Revolution Publishing and Education Organization.
Kho An Kim. 1947. *Pendjara Fasis atau Dari Neraka ke Neraka*. Medan: Toko Boekoe Djaman.
Khoo Joo Ee. 1998. *Straits Chinese: A Cultural History*. Amsterdam: Pepin Press.
Kim, Diana S. 2020. *Empires of Vice: The Rise of Opium Prohibition across Southeast Asia*. Princeton, NJ: Princeton University Press.
Kim To. 1911. "I, II-I." *Sin Po* 28: 444–47.
King, Michelle T. 2009. "Replicating the Colonial Expert: The Problem of Translation in the Late Nineteenth-Century Straits Settlements." *Social History* 34, no. 4: 428–46.
Kitab Obat Penjakit Pest jang Soedah Banjak Menoeloeng. n.d. Batavia: Kho Tjeng Bie.
"Kliwatan poenja Bodo." 1925. *Hoakiao* 4: 21.
Klöter, Henning. 2005. *Written Taiwanese*. Wiesbaden: Harrassowitz.
Klöter, Henning. 2011. *The Language of the Sangleys: A Chinese Vernacular in Missionary Sources of the Seventeenth Century*. Leiden: Brill.
Knight-Achjadi, Judi, and Asmoro Damais. 2005. *Butterflies and Phoenixes: Chinese Inspirations in Indonesian Textile Arts*. Jakarta: Mitra Museum Indonesia.
Knörr, Jacqueline. 2014. *Creole Identity in Postcolonial Indonesia*. New York: Berghahn.
Koks, J.Th. 1931. *De Indo*. Amsterdam: H.J. Paris.
Kong Yuanzhi. 2005. *Silang Budaya Tiongkok-Indonesia*. Jakarta: Bhuana Ilmu Populer.
Korbannja Setan Bantal. n.d. Batavia: Kwee Seng Wie.

Kratz, Ernst Ulrich. 1992. "Peranakan Writing and Indonesian Literature after Independence." In *Le Moment "Sino-Malais" de la Littérature Indonésienne*, edited by Claudine Salmon, 133–47. Paris: Association Archipel.
Kuiper, Koos. 2005. "The Earliest Monument of Dutch Sinological Studies: Justus Heurnius's Manuscript Dutch-Chinese dictionary and Chinese-Latin *Compendium Doctrinae Christianae* (Batavia 1628)." *Quaerendo* 35, nos. 1–2: 109–39.
Kuiper, Koos. 2010. *The Go Collection: Introduction and Catalogue*. Leiden: Leiden University.
Kuiper, Koos. 2017. *The Early Dutch Sinologists (1854–1900): Training in Holland and China, Functions in the Netherlands Indies*. Leiden: Brill.
Kuitert, Lisa. 2020. *Met een drukpers de oceaan over: Koloniale boekcultuur in Nederlands-Indië 1816–1920*. Amsterdam: Prometheus.
Kuntjara, Esther. 2007. "The Hybrid Language of the Chinese in Indonesia: A Perspective on Language Pluralism and the Implications in Social Relationships." In *Chinese Diaspora since Admiral Zheng He with Special Reference to Maritime Asia*, edited by Leo Suryadinata, 353–70. Singapore: Chinese Heritage Centre.
Kwa Kian Hauw, David. 2009. "Ragam Pakaian Kaum Peranakan." In *Peranakan Tionghoa Indonesia: Sebuah Perjalanan Budaya*, edited by Heru Kustara, 130–63. Jakarta: Intisari.
Kwa Kian Hauw, David. 2016. "Tionghoa dalam Budaya Betawi." In *Tionghoa dalam Keindonesiaan: Peran dan Kontribusi bagi Pembangunan Bangsa*, edited by Leo Suryadinata and Didi Kwartanada, 2:19–26. Jakarta: Yayasan Nabil.
Kwartanada, Didi. 2013. "The Tiong Hoa Hwee Koan School: A Transborder Project of Modernity in Batavia, c. 1900s." In *Chinese Indonesians Reassessed: History, Religion and Belonging*, edited by Sai Siew-Min and Hoon Chang-Yau, 27–44. New York: Routledge.
Kwartanada, Didi. 2014. "Translations in Romanized Malay and the Revival of Chineseness among the Peranakan in Java (1880s–1911)." In *Translation in Asia: Theories, Practices, Histories*, edited by Jan van der Putten, and Ronit Ricci, 119–35. Manchester: St Jerome Press.
Kwartanada, Didi. 2017. "*Bangsawan Prampoewan*: Enlightened Peranakan Chinese Women from Early Twentieth Century Java." *Wacana* 18, no. 2: 422–54.
Kwartanada, Didi. 2018. "Mandarin Comes to the South Seas: The Making of Chinese Education in Early Twentieth Century Java." *Asian Culture* 42: 37–54.
Kwee, John B. 1977. "Chinese Malay Literature of the Peranakan Chinese in Indonesia, 1880–1942." PhD diss., University of Auckland.
Kwee Kek Beng. 1935. "De Chineesche pers in Nederlandsch-Indië." *Koloniale Studiën* 19, no. 1: 194–224.
Kwee Kek Beng. 1936. "Westersche Invloeden op het Maleisch." *Koloniale Studiën* 20, no. 1: 89–109.
Kwee Seng Tjoan. 1917. *Tjerita Anak Prampoean di Bikin Sebagi Parit Mas*. Batavia: Kwee Seng Tjoan.
Kwee [Seng Tjoan]. 1929. *English & Malay Dictionary*. Batavia: Kwee Seng Tjoan.
Kwee Tek Hoay. 1928. "Almarhoem Toean Gouw Peng Liang." *Panorama* 99: 1683–87.
Kwee Tek Hoay. 1930a. *Boenga Roos dari Tjikembang*. Batavia: Panorama.
Kwee Tek Hoay. 1930b. *Zonder Lentera*. Batavia: Panorama.
Kwee Tek Hoay. 1934a. "Edjaän jang Tida Lengkep." *Moestika Romans* 5, no. 54: 981–83.
Kwee Tek Hoay. 1934b. "Merosotnja Pembatjaän Melajoe Tionghoa." *Moestika Romans* 5, no. 50: 597–99.

Kwee Tek Hoay. 1934c. "Toneelgezelschap Dardanella poenja Bahasa Melajoe." *Moestika Romans* 5, no. 54: 773–75.
Kwee Tek Hoay. 1934d. "Edjaän jang Rapih." *Moestika Romans* 5, no. 55: 822–24.
Kwee Tek Hoay. 1935a. "Apatah jang Masih Koerang dalem Bahasa Melajoe?" *Moestika Romans* 6, no. 68: 276–79.
Kwee Tek Hoay. 1935b. "Kapentingannja Tanda pada Hoeroef 'E.'" *Moestika Romans* 6, no. 62: 867–69.
Kwee Tek Hoay. 1935c. "Tjatjat-Tjatjat Ketjil dalem Edjaän." *Moestika Romans* 6, no. 65: 64–66.
Kwee Tek Hoay, trans. 1936. *Rubaiyat dari Omar Khayyam*. Batavia: Moestika.
Kwee Tek Hoay. 1938–41. *Drama di Boven Digoel*. 4 vols. Cicurug: Moestika.
Kwee Thiam Tjing. 1947. *Indonesia dalem Api dan Bara*. Malang: Tjan Tjoe Som.
Kwik Khing Djoen. 1923. *Kitab Vortaro*. Batavia: Sin Po.
"Lagi Satoe Djoeroe Terbang Prampoean Tionghoa." 1932. *Sin Po Wekelijksche Editie* 508: 611.
Lalla, Barbara, and Jean D'Costa. 1990. *Language in Exile: Three Hundred Years of Jamaican Creole*. Tuscaloosa: University of Alabama Press.
Lao Jen. 1928. "Prampoean jang Kapingin Djadi Lelaki." *Sin Po Wekelijksche Editie* 287: 403.
Laobing. 2003. "Shitan Yihua Wenxue de Lishi Fazhan Yu Qianjing" [A preliminary discussion of the historical development and prospects of Sino-Indonesian literature]. *Shijie Huawen Wenxue Luntan* 1: 8–10.
Later, J. F. H. 1915. "De Maleische Pers." *De Indische Gids* 37, no. 2: 1264–72.
Latif Yudi. 2008. *Indonesian Muslim Intelligentsia and Power*. Singapore: ISEAS.
Lauw Botak. 1931. *Ratoe Doenia atawa Bebrapa Hal jang Penting dalem Congres Journalisten Indonesia*. Semarang: Kamadjoean.
Lean, Eugenia. 2007. *Public Passions: The Trial of Shi Jianqiao and the Rise of Popular Sympathy in Republican China*. Berkeley: University of California Press.
Lee, Peter. 2013. "Cross-Dressing Chameleons." *The Peranakan* 1: 4–9.
Lee, Peter. 2014. *Sarong Kebaya: Peranakan Fashion in an Interconnected World, 1500–1950*. Singapore: Asian Civilisations Museum.
Lee Soen Liang. 1930. "Njonja mantoe modern." *Hoakiao* 155: 40–46.
Lee, Thienny. 2016. "Dress and Visual Identities of the *Nyonyas* in the British Straits Settlements: Mid-Nineteenth to Early-Twentieth Century." PhD diss., University of Sydney.
"Leloetjon dari Koran-Koran." 1927. *Sin Po Wekelijksche Editie* 243: 542.
Leo, Philip. 1975. *Chinese Loanwords Spoken by the Inhabitants of the City of Jakarta*. Jakarta: L.I.P.I.
Leow, Rachel. 2016. *Taming Babel: Language in the Making of Malaysia*. Cambridge: Cambridge University Press.
"Letters of a Javanese Princess." 1922. *The Spectator* 128, no. 4895: 500–1.
Lewis, Su Lin. 2009. "Cosmopolitanism and the Modern Girl: A Cross-Cultural Discourse in 1930s Penang." *Modern Asian Studies* 43, no. 6: 1385–1419.
Lewis, Su Lin. 2016. *Cities in Motion: Urban Life and Cosmopolitanism in Southeast Asia, 1920–1940*. Cambridge: Cambridge University Press.
Lg. 1930. "Siapa jang Ngawoer?" *Hoakiao* 147: 15–16.
Li Minghuan. 2003. "From 'Sons of the Yellow Emperor' to 'Children of Indonesian Soil': Studying Peranakan Chinese Based on the Batavia Kong Koan Archives." *Journal of Southeast Asian Studies* 34, no. 2: 215–30.
Liaw Yock Fang. 2016. "Buku Tata Bahasa Modern Pertama." In *Tionghoa dalam Keindonesiaan: Peran dan Kontribusi bagi Pembangunan Bangsa*, edited by Leo Suryadinata and Didi Kwartanada, 1:184–205. Jakarta: Yayasan Nabil.

Lie In Eng. 1918. *Tjerita Nona Hong Giok atawa Bidadari dari Doenia!* Batavia: Lie Tek Long.
Lie Kim Hok. 1891. *Melajoe Betawi.* Batavia: Albert & Rusche.
Lie Kim Hok, trans. 1912. *Pembalesan Baccarat.* Batavia: Hoa Siang In Kiok.
Lie Kim Hok, trans. 1914. *Tjerita Dji Touw Bwe.* Batavia: Kho Tjeng Bie.
Lie Kim Hok, trans. 1919. *Boekoe Tjerita Nio Thian Laj.* Batavia: Kho Tjeng Bie.
Lie, Ravando. 2017. "Dr Oen Boen Ing: Patriot Doctor, Social Activist, and Doctor of the Poor." *Wacana* 18, no. 2: 455–84.
Lie Swie Goan. 1915. *Tjerita Satoe Prampoean jang Gaga.* Batavia: Lie Tek Long.
Lie Tek Long. 1915. *Boekoe Masakan Betawi.* Batavia: Lie Tek Long.
Lie Thiam Tjin. 1929. "Sedikit tentang Bahasa." *Hoakiao* 125: 11–12.
Liem Thian Joe. 1933. *Riwajat Semarang, 1416–1931.* Semarang: Ho Kim Yoe.
Liem Thian Joe. 1939a. "Journalistiek Tionghoa-Melajoe." *Sin Po Wekelijksche Editie* 840–45: 21–23, 24–25, 15–19, 24, 21–24, 14–16.
Liem Thian Joe. 1939b. "Soerat Kabar Hoeroef Tionghoa di Java." *Sin Po Wekelijksche Editie* 847–49: 21–24, 8–10, 15–16.
Liem Thian Joe. 1939c. "Tjerita-Tjerita Tionghoa dalem Bahasa . . . Djawa." *Sin Po Wekelijksche Editie* 832: 5–7.
Liem Thian Joe. 1940a. "Ketjap . . . !" *Sin Po Wekelijksche Editie* 915: 11–13.
Liem Thian Joe. 1940b. "Dapoer Tionghoa." *Sin Po Wekelijksche Editie* 892: 10–15.
Lim Hiong Seng. 1887. *A Manual of the Malay Colloquial.* Singapore: Koh Yew Hean Press.
Lim Kong Chuan. 1877. *Tong Yi Xin Yu.* Singapore: Koh Yew Hean Press.
Lim Kong Chuan. 1883. *Hua Yi Tong Yu.* Singapore: Koh Yew Hean Press.
Lim Tjay Tat. 1878. *Kitap Tong Gi Tjin Liong.* Batavia.
Lin Pei-yin and Weipin Tsai. 2014. *Ideas, Information and Knowledge in Chinese Societies, 1895–1949.* Leiden: Brill.
Lin, Philip T. 2015. *Taiwanese Grammar: A Concise Reference.* Greenhorn Media.
Liu, Lydia H. 1995. *Translingual Practice: Literature, National Culture, and Translated Modernity—China, 1900–1937.* Stanford, CA: Stanford University Press.
Liu P. S. 1926. "Iseng-Iseng Ini Hari." *Hoakiao* 13: 2.
Liu, Petrus. 2011. *Stateless Subjects: Chinese Martial Arts Literature and Postcolonial History.* Ithaca, NY: Cornell University Press.
Locher-Scholten, Elsbeth. 2000. *Women and the Colonial State: Essays on Gender and Modernity in the Netherlands Indies, 1900–1942.* Amsterdam: Amsterdam University Press.
Lohanda, Mona. 2005. "The Passen- en Wijkenstelsel: Dutch Practice of Restriction Policy on the Chinese." *Jurnal Sejarah* 12: 58–76.
Lombard, Denys. 1972. "La Grammaire Malaise de Lie Kim Hok (1884)." In *Langues et Techniques, Nature et Société*, edited by Jacques Barrau, Lucien Bernot, Georges Condominas, Mariel Jean Brunhes Delamarre, Francis Leroy, Alexis Rygaloff, and Jacqueline M. C. Thomas, 197–203. Paris: Klincksieck.
Lombard, Denys. 1977. "Les Maîtres de Silat d'Origine Chinoise, Contribution à l'Histoire des Arts Martiaux dans l'Archipel." *Archipel* 14: 33–41.
Lombard, Denys. 2005. *Nusa Jawa: Silang Budaya.* 2 vols. Jakarta: Gramedia Pustaka Utama.
Lombard, Denys, and Claudine Salmon. 1993. "Islam and Chineseness." *Indonesia* 57: 115–31.
Look Lai, Walton. 1993. *Indentured Labor, Caribbean Sugar: Chinese and Indian Migrants to the British West Indies, 1838–1918.* Baltimore: John Hopkins University Press.
Lu Pao Ru. 1935. *Correspondentie Dagang.* Batavia: Samideo.

Lubis, Koko Hendri. 2018. *Roman Medan: Sebuah Kota Membangun Harapan*. Jakarta: Gramedia Pustaka Utama.

Mahadevan, Sudhir. 2015. *A Very Old Machine: The Many Origins of the Cinema in India*. Albany: State University of New York Press.

Mahdi, Waruno. 2006. "The Beginnings and Reorganization of the *Commissie voor de Volkslectuur* (1908–1920)." In *Insular Southeast Asia: Linguistic and Cultural Studies in Honour of Bernd Nothofer*, edited by Fritz Schulze and Holger Warnk, 85–110. Wiesbaden: Harrassowitz Verlag.

Mahdi, Waruno. 2012. "Bifurcation of Commercial Tradition in West Indonesia, 1850–1930, as Reflected in Contemporaneous Malay Print Publishing." *Asian Journal of Social Science* 40: 100–32.

Mahdi, Waruno. 2016. "Linguistic Variety in Later Nineteenth-Century Dutch-Edited Malay Publications." *NUSA* 60: 107–85.

Mahmood, Datin Seri Endon. 2004. *The Nyonya kebaya: A Century of Straits Chinese Costume*. Singapore: Periplus.

Maier, Henk. 1991. "Forms of Censorship in the Dutch Indies: The Marginalization of Chinese-Malay Literature." In "The Role of the Indonesian Chinese in Shaping Modern Indonesian Life," special issue, *Indonesia*, 67–81.

Maier, Henk. 1993a. "Beware and Reflect, Remember and Recollect: Tjerita Njai Soemirah and the Emergence of Chinese-Malay Literature in the Indies." *Bijdragen tot de Taal-, Land- en Volkenkunde* 149, no. 2: 274–97.

Maier, Henk. 1993b. "From Heteroglossia to Polyglossia: The Creation of Malay and Dutch in the Indies." *Indonesia* 56: 37–65.

Maier, Henk. 2004. *We Are Playing Relatives: A Survey of Malay Writing*. Leiden: KITLV.

"Masok terbilang." 1931. *Bintang Pranakan*, February 7, 3.

Maters, Mirjam. 1998. *Van zachte wenk tot harde hand: Persvrijheid en persbreidel in Nederlands-Indië 1906–1942*. Hilversum: Verloren.

Mazzaferro, Gerardo, ed. 2018. *Translanguaging as Everyday Practice*. Cham: Springer.

McHale, Shawn Frederick. 2004. *Print and Power: Confucianism, Communism, and Buddhism in the Making of Modern Vietnam*. Honolulu: University of Hawai'i Press.

McKeown, Adam M. 2008. *Melancholy Order: Asian Migration and the Globalization of Borders*. New York: Columbia University Press.

Mian Yan, Margaret. 2006. *Introduction to Chinese Dialectology*. Munich: Lincom Europa.

Mignolo, Walter D. 2009. "Epistemic Disobedience, Independent Thought and De-Colonial Freedom." *Theory, Culture & Society* 26, nos. 7–8: 1–23.

Mill, J. V. G. 1970. *Ma Huan: Ying-Yai Sheng-Lan: "The Overall Survey of the Ocean's Shores."* Cambridge: Cambridge University Press.

Mills, J. V. G. 1938. "The Expression Tho-Kho." *Journal of the Malayan Branch of the Royal Asiatic Society* 16, no. 1: 137–38.

Mohamad, Maznah. 2008. "Malay/Malaysian/Islamic: Four Genres of Political Writings and the Postcoloniality of Autochthonous Texts." *Postcolonial Studies* 11, no. 3: 293–313.

Moriyama, Mikihiro. 2005. *Sundanese Print Culture and Modernity in 19th-Century West Java*. Singapore: Singapore University Press.

Naregal, Veena. 2001. *Language Politics, Elites, and the Public Sphere: Western India under Colonialism*. London: Anthem Press.

Nio Joe Lan. 1932. "De Omgangstaal der Chineezen in Indonesië." *De Indische Gids* 54, no. 2: 1089–94.

Nio Joe Lan. 1937. "De Indo-Chineesche Literatuur." *De Indische Gids* 59: 32–47, 231–46, 311–29.

Nio Joe Lan. 1939a. "De Eigen Onderwijsvoorziening der Chineezen." *Koloniale Studiën* 23, no. 1: 67–94.
Nio Joe Lan. 1939b. "Het Chineesch-, Hollandsch- en Engelsch-Maleisch." *De Indische Gids* 61, no. 1: 408–19.
Nio Joe Lan. 1940. *Riwajat 40 Taon dari Tiong Hoa Hwe Koan—Batavia (1900–1939)*. Batavia: Tiong Hoa Hwe Koan.
Nio Joe Lan. 1943. "Maleische Bewerking van Chineesche Literatuur." *Cultureel Indië* 5: 170–77.
Nio Joe Lan. 1955a. "Kata-kata 'gu' dan 'lu' di Indonesia." *Bahasa dan Budaja* 3, no. 3: 41–44.
Nio Joe Lan. 1955b. "Perkembangan & Berachirnja Bahasa Melaju Tionghoa." *Buku Kita* 1, no. 1: 301–4, 347–49.
Nio Joe Lan. 1961. "Bahasa Melaju Tionghoa." *Bahasa dan Budaja* 4, nos. 5–6: 201–15.
Nio Joe Lan. 1962. *Sastera Indonesia -Tionghoa*. Jakarta: Gunung Agung.
"Notes from Java." 1924. *Malaya Tribune*, December 26, 2.
Nothofer, Bernd. 2004. "A Comparison of Klinkert's Low and High Malay Translations of the Gospel according to St. Matthew as Part of his Translation of the New Testament." In *Menabur Benih, Menuai Kasih: Persembahan Karya Bahasa, Sosial dan Budaya untuk Anton M. Moeliono pada Ulang Tahunnya yang ke-75*, edited by Katharina Endriati Sukamto, 453–63. Jakarta: Universitas Katolik Indonesia Atma Jaya.
Nova Hino. 1911. "Hoakiauw di Hindia Olanda." *Sin Po* 28: 438–43.
O. & Y. 1921. *Sat Tjoe Po atawa Iboe Kedjem jang Memboenoeh Anaknja lantaran Pertjinta-an Haram*. Batavia: Tan Thioen Soe.
Oei Liong Thay. 1939a. "Badean dari Lasem." *Sin Po Wekelijksche Editie* 835: 20–21.
Oei Liong Thay. 1939b. "Kabetoelan & Hokkhie." *Sin Po Wekelijksche Editie* 827: 5–9.
Oetomo, Dédé. 1987. *The Chinese of Pasuruan: Their Language and Identity*. Canberra: Australian National University.
Oetomo, Dédé. 1988. "Multilingualism and Chinese Identities in Indonesia." In *Changing Identities of the Southeast Asian Chinese since World War II*, edited by Jennifer Cushman and Wang Gungwu, 97–106. Hong Kong: Hong Kong University Press.
Oetomo, Dédé. 1991. "The Chinese of Indonesia and the Development of the Indonesian Language." In "The Role of the Indonesian Chinese in Shaping Modern Indonesian Life," special issue, *Indonesia*, 53–66.
Oey, Eric M. 2013. "*Lie Sie Bin Yoe Tee Hoe*: Six Malay/Indonesian Translations of a Chinese Tale." In *Literary Migrations: Traditional Chinese Fiction in Asia (17th–20th Centuries)*, edited by Claudine Salmon, 315–35. Singapore: ISEAS—Yusof Ishak Institute.
Oi Yan Liu. 2014. "Encountering Competing Empires: Journeying Chinese Communities in Southeast Asia under Chinese, Dutch, and British Imperial Rule." PhD diss., Cornell University.
Oldham, W.F. 1891. "Singapore, Straits Settlements." *The Gospel in All Lands*, January, 209–12.
Oliver, Pasfield, ed. 1708. *The Voyage of François Leguat*. London: Hakluyt Society.
Olszewska, Dobrochna. 2014. "Indonesian 'Chineseness': The Image of the Chinese Diaspora in Indonesian Film. Character Portrayal and Interethnic Relations." In *Media in China, China in the Media: Processes, Strategies, Images, Identities*, edited by Adina Zemanek, 179–94. Cracow: Jagiellonian University Press.
"Onderwijs Tionghoa di Indonesia." 1935. *Sin Po Jubileum Nummer*.
Ong, Aihwa. 1992. *Flexible Citizenship: The Cultural Logics of Transnationality*. Durham, NC: Duke University Press.

Ong Swi Pan. n.d. *Anomi*. Batavia: Ong Swi Pan.
Ong-Tae-Hae. 1849. *The Chinaman Abroad*. Shanghai: Mission Press.
Ong, Walter J. 2012. *Orality and Literacy: The Technologizing of the Word*. London: Routledge.
Palmer, John D. 2007. "Who Is the Authentic Korean American? Korean-Born Korean American High School Students' Negotiations of Ascribed and Achieved Identities." *Journal of Language, Identity, and Education* 6, no. 4: 277–98.
Pan, Lynn. 1990. *Sons of the Yellow Emperor: A History of the Chinese Diaspora*. Boston: Little, Brown.
Pandiangan, Andreas. 2003. "Chinese Press after the New Order: Caught Between the Continuity of Idealism and the Logic of the Market." *Asian Ethnicity* 4, no. 3: 401–19.
Pané, Armijn. 1938. "Tentang Boekoe² Melajoe Tionghoa." *Pandji Poestaka* 103/4: 77–80.
Pané, Armijn. 1941. "Gamelan tegenover Krontjong, Droom tegenover Werkelijkheid." *Poedjangga Baroe* 4, no. 1: 9–30.
Paradijs. 1920. *Boekoe Sair "Park."* Batavia: Liauw Tjin Kwie.
Pat Taij Tjoe. 1930. *Sair Perdjaka*. Batavia: Kwee Seng Tjoan.
Paulus, J. 1917. "Chineezen." In *Encyclopaedie van Nederlandsch-Indië*, vol. 1: A–G, edited by J. Paulus, 480–87. The Hague: Martinus Nijhoff.
Pekdjit. 1941. "Poetra Fortuna." *Sin Po Wekelijksche Editie* 928: 1–4.
Pena Baek. 1940. "Literatuur Tionghoa-Melajoe." *Sin Po Wekelijksche Editie* 870.
Perelaer, M. T. H. 1886. *Baboe Dalima: Opium Roman*. Rotterdam: Elsevier.
Pernau, Margrit. 2019. "Modern Masculinity, Bought at Your Local Pharmacist: The Tonic Sanatogen in 20th-Century Indian Advertisements." *Tasveer Ghar—A Digital Archive of South Asian Popular Visual Culture*, http://www.tasveergharindia.net/essay/sanatogen-masculine-advert.html.
"Perubahan Edjaan dengan Huruf Latin untuk Bahasa Indonesia." 1953. *Bahasa dan Budaja* 2, no. 1: 6–7.
Pijnappel, J. 1865. "Laag-Maleisch." *De Gids* 29: 148–59.
Pik. 1936. "Eenige Suggesties voor de Tegenwoordige Vakscholen." *Sin Po Wekelijksche Editie* 717: 27–28.
Plomp, Marije. 2012. "The Capital of Pulp Fiction and Other Capitals: Cultural Life in Medan, 1950–1958." In *Heirs to World Culture: Being Indonesian, 1950–1965*, edited by Jennifer Lindsay and Maya H. T. Liem, 371–95. Leiden: Brill.
Poeze, Harry. 1986. *In het Land van de Overheerser*, vol. 1: *Indonesiërs in Nederland 1600–1950*. Dordrecht: Foris Publications.
Poeze, Harry. 1988. *Politiek-Politioneele Overzichten van Nederlandsch-Indië: Bronnenpublikatie*, vol. 3: *1931–1934*. Dordrecht: Foris Publications.
Poeze, Harry. 1989. "Indonesians at Leiden University." In *Leiden's Oriental Connections, 1850–1940*, edited by Willem Otterspeer, 250–79. Leiden: E.J. Brill.
Poeze, Harry. 1994. *Politiek-Politioneele Overzichten van Nederlandsch-Indië: Bronnenpublikatie*, vol. 4: *1935–1941*. Leiden: KITLV.
Pollock, Sheldon. 2006. *The Language of the Gods in the World of Men: Sanskrit, Culture, and Power in Premodern India*. Berkeley: University of California Press.
Pols, Hans. 2018. *Nurturing Indonesia: Medicine and Decolonisation in the Dutch East Indies*. Cambridge: Cambridge University Press.
Post, Peter. 2019. *The Kwee Family of Ciledug: Family, Status, and Modernity in Colonial Java. Visualising the Private Life of the Peranakan Chinese Sugar Elite*. Volendam: LM Publishers.
Pouw Kioe An. 1937. *O, Prempoean!* Malang: Paragon Press.

Pouw Peng Hong. 1931. *The Standard English–Malay Dictionary*. Batavia: The Chinese & English Book Company.
Price, Richard. 2001. "The Miracle of Creolization: A Retrospective." *New West Indian Guide* 75, nos. 1/2: 35–64.
Prins, W. F. 1933. "De Bevolkingsgroepen in het Nederlandsch-Indische Recht." *Koloniale Studiën* 17, no. 2: 652–88.
Protschky, Susie, and Tom van den Berge, eds. 2018. *Modern Times in Southeast Asia, 1920s–1970s*. Leiden: Brill.
Proudfoot, Ian. 1994. *The Print Threshold in Malaysia*. Clayton: Monash University.
Proudfoot, Ian. 1998. "Lithography at the Crossroads of the East." *Journal of the Printing Historical Society* 27: 113–31.
Purdey, Jemma. 2006. *Anti-Chinese Violence in Indonesia: 1996–1999*. Honolulu: University of Hawai'i Press.
Quinn, George. 2013. "Liang Shanbo yu Zhu Yingtai: A Chinese Folk Romance in Java and Bali." In *Literary Migrations: Traditional Chinese Fiction in Asia (17th–20th Centuries)*, edited by Claudine Salmon, 336–58. Singapore: ISEAS—Yusof Ishak Institute.
"Raden Adjeng Kartini dan Bangsa Tionghoa: Kartini ada anak . . . Taopekong!" 1930. *Sin Po Wekelijksche Editie* 386: 323.
Rafael, Vicente L. 2016. *Motherless Tongues: The Insurgency of Language amid Wars of Translation*. Durham, NC: Duke University Press.
Rafferty, Ellen. 1984. "Languages of the Chinese of Java: An Historical Review." *Journal of Asian Studies* 43, no. 2: 247–72.
Raffles, Thomas Stamford. 1814. "A Discourse Delivered at a Meeting of the Society of Arts and Sciences in Batavia, on the Twenty-Fourth Day of April 1813, being the Anniversary of the Institution." *Verhandelingen van het Bataviaasch Genootschap* 7: 1–34.
Raja Ali Haji. 1986–87. *Kitab Pengetahuan Bahasa yaitu Kamus Logat Melayu Johor Pahang Riau Lingga*. Reprint, Pekanbaru: Departemen Pendidikan dan Kebudayaan.
Rea, Christopher, and Nicolai Volland, eds. 2015. *The Business of Culture: Cultural Entrepreneurs in China and Southeast Asia, 1900–65*. Vancouver: UBC Press.
Reed, Christopher A. 2004. *Gutenberg in Shanghai: Chinese Print Capitalism, 1876–1937*. Honolulu: University of Hawai'i Press.
"Regional Language." 1949. *Bangkok Post*, January 29, 2.
Respess, Amanda, and Lisa C. Niziolek. 2016. "Exchanges and Transformations in Gendered Medicine on the Maritime Silk Road: Evidence from the Thirteenth-Century Java Sea Wreck." In *Histories of Medicine and Healing in the Indian Ocean World: The Medieval and Early Modern Period*, edited by Anna Winterbottom and Facil Tesfaye, 1: 63–97. Houndmills: Palgrave Macmillan.
"Restaurant Tay Sam Yoen." 1934. *Het Nieuws van den Dag*, December 24, 2.
Ricci, Ronit. 2013. "The Malay World Expanded: The World's First Malay Newspaper, Colombo, 1869." *Indonesia and the Malay World* 41, no. 120: 168–82.
Rieger, Thomas. 1992. "La Guerre Sino-Japonaise dans la Littérature Indonésienne." In *Le Moment "Sino-Malais" de la Littérature Indonésienne*, edited by Claudine Salmon, 105–32. Paris: Association Archipel.
Rieger, Thomas. 1996. "From Huaqiao to Minzu: Constructing New Identities in Indonesia's Peranakan Chinese Literature." In *Identity in Asian Literature*, edited by Lisbeth Littrup, 151–72. London: RoutledgeCurzon.
Ritter, W. L. 1855. "De dubbele moord." *Biäng-Lala* 4, no. 1: 162–235.

Roces, Mina. 2005. "Gender, Nation and the Politics of Dress in Twentieth-Century Philippines." *Gender & History* 17, no. 2: 354–77.

Rockhill, W. W. 1915. "Notes on the Relations and Trade of China with the Eastern Archipelago and the Coast of the Indian Ocean during the Fourteenth Century. Part II." *T'oung Pao*, 2nd series, 16, no. 2: 236–71.

Rudolph, Jürgen. 1998. *Reconstructing Identities: A Social History of the Babas in Singapore*. Aldershot: Ashgate.

Rush, James R. 1960. *Opium to Java: Revenue Farming and Chinese Enterprise in Colonial Indonesia, 1860–1910*. Ithaca, NY: Cornell University Press.

Rutnin, Mattani Mojdara. 1993. *Dance, Drama, and Theatre in Thailand: The Process of Development and Modernization*. Chiang Mai: Silkworm Books.

Rutten, Gijsbert, and Marijke J. van der Wal, eds. 2014. *Letters as Loot: A Sociolinguistic Approach to Seventeenth and Eighteenth-Century Dutch*. Amsterdam: John Benjamins.

S. O. S. 1930. "Cultuur 'Baba.'" *Sin Po Wekelijksche Editie* 355: 669–700.

Sai Siew-Min. 2006. *Representing the Past of Chinese Language Education: Language, History and Chinese Identities in Indonesia*. Ann Arbor: University of Michigan Press.

Sai Siew-Min. 2013. "The Nanyang Diasporic Imaginary: Chinese School Teachers in a Transborder Setting in the Dutch East Indies." In *Chinese Indonesians Reassessed: History, Religion and Belonging*, edited by Sai Siew-Min and Hoon Chang-Yau, 45–64. New York: Routledge.

Sai Siew-Min. 2016. "Mandarin Lessons: Modernity, Colonialism and Chinese Cultural Nationalism in the Dutch East Indies, c.1900s." *Inter-Asia Cultural Studies* 17, no. 3: 375–94.

Sai Siew-Min. 2019. "Dressing Up Subjecthood: Straits Chinese, the Queue, and Contested Citizenship in Colonial Singapore." *Journal of Imperial and Commonwealth History* 47, no. 3: 446–73.

Sai Siew-Min and Hoon Chang-Yau, eds. 2013. *Chinese Indonesians Reassessed: History, Religion and Belonging*. New York: Routledge.

Salmon, Claudine. 1971. "Le *Sjair* de l'"Association Chinoise" de Batavia (1905)." *Archipel* 2: 55–100.

Salmon, Claudine. 1974. "Aux Origines de la Littérature Sino-Malaise: Un Sjair Publicitaire de 1886." *Archipel* 8: 155–86.

Salmon, Claudine. 1976. "À Propos de la Première Traduction Malaise du Haigong Xiao-hong-pao Quan-zhuan." In *Études d'Histoire et de Littérature Chinoises: Offertes au professeur Jaroslav Průšek*, 209–25. Paris: Bibliothèque de l'Institut des Hautes Études Chinoises.

Salmon, Claudine. 1980. "La Notion de "Sino-Malais" est-elle Pertinente d'un Point de Vue Linguistique?" *Archipel* 20: 177–86.

Salmon, Claudine. 1981. *Literature in Malay by the Chinese of Indonesia: A Provisional Annotated Bibliography*. Paris: Editions de la Maison des Sciences de l'Homme.

Salmon, Claudine. 1984. "Chinese Women Writers in Indonesia and Their Views of Female Emancipation." *Archipel* 28: 149–71.

Salmon, Claudine. 1986. "L'Édition Chinoise dans le Monde Insulindien (Fin du XIXe s. – Début du XXe s.)." *Archipel* 32: 113–39.

Salmon, Claudine. 1991. "A Critical View of the Opium Farmers as Reflected in a *Syair* by Boen Sing Hoo (Semarang, 1889)." In "The Role of the Indonesian Chinese in Shaping Modern Indonesian Life," special issue, *Indonesia*, 25–51.

Salmon, Claudine. 1996. "Ancestral Halls, Funeral Associations, and Attempts at Resinicization in Nineteenth-Century Netherlands India." In *Sojourners*

and Settlers: Histories of Southeast Asia and the Chinese in Honour of Jennifer Cushman, edited by Anthony Reid, 183–214. St. Leonards: Allen & Unwin.
Salmon, Claudine. 2000. "The First Chinese Language Newspaper of Java (1852–1857?)." Asian Culture 24: 79–89.
Salmon, Claudine. 2006. "Women's Social Status as Reflected in Chinese Epigraphs from Insulinde (16th–20th Centuries)." Archipel 72: 157–94.
Salmon, Claudine. 2009a. "Malay (and Javanese) Loan-words in Chinese as a Mirror of Cultural Exchanges." Archipel 78: 181–208.
Salmon, Claudine. 2009b. "The Chinese Community of Surabaya, from Its Origins to the 1930s Crisis." Chinese Southern Diaspora Studies 3: 22–60.
Salmon, Claudine. 2013a. "A Note on Javanese Works derived from Chinese Fiction." In Literary Migrations: Traditional Chinese Fiction in Asia (17th–20th Centuries), edited by Claudine Salmon, 235–47. Singapore: ISEAS—Yusof Ishak Institute.
Salmon, Claudine. 2013b. "Introduction." In Literary Migrations: Traditional Chinese Fiction in Asia (17th–20th Centuries), edited by Claudine Salmon, 1–36. Singapore: ISEAS—Yusof Ishak Institute.
Salmon, Claudine. 2013c. "Malay Translations of Chinese Fiction in Indonesia." In Literary Migrations: Traditional Chinese Fiction in Asia (17th–20th Centuries), edited by Claudine Salmon, 248–76. Singapore: ISEAS—Yusof Ishak Institute.
Salmon, Claudine. 2013d. "Writings in Romanized Malay by the Chinese of Malaya: A Preliminary Inquiry." In Literary Migrations: Traditional Chinese Fiction in Asia (17th–20th Centuries), edited by Claudine Salmon, 277–314. Singapore: ISEAS—Yusof Ishak Institute.
Salmon, Claudine. 2019. "Contact Languages on the South China Sea and Beyond (15th–18th Centuries)." Asian Culture 43: 20–43.
Salmon, Claudine, and Denys Lombard. 1974. "Les Traductions de Romans Chinois en Malais (1880–1930)." In Littératures Contemporaines de l'Asie du Sud-Est, edited by P.-B. Lafont, and Denys Lombard, 183–201. Paris: L'Asiathèque.
Salmon, Claudine, and Denys Lombard. 1997. "Confucianisme et Esprit de Réforme dans les Communautés Chinoises d'Insulinde (Fin XIXe–Début XXI Siècle)." In En Suivant la Voie Royale: Mélanges Offerts en Hommage à Léon Vandermeersch, edited by Jacques Gernet and Marc Kalimowski, 377–407. Paris: École Française d'Extrême Orient.
Salmon, Claudine, and Myra Sidharta. 2007. "Traditional Chinese Medicine and Pharmacy in Indonesia—Some Sidelights." Archipel 74: 165–204.
Salmon, Claudine, and Myra Sidharta. 2018. "Sino-Insulindian Private History Museums, Cultural Heritage Places, and the (Re)construction of the Past." Asian Culture 42: 1–28.
Samuel, Jérôme. 2005. Modernisation Lexicale et Politique Terminologique: Le Cas de l'Indonésian. Paris: Peeters.
Sandrow, Nahma. 1996. Vagabond Stars: A World History of Yiddish Theater. Reprint, Syracuse: Syracuse University Press.
Santa-Maria, Luigi. 1980. "Une Contribution Marginale à la Lexicographie Malaise: Deux Dictionnaires du Malais Parlé (Seconde Moitié du XIXe s.) presque Oubliés." Archipel 19: 143–54.
"Saorang Tionghoa." 1949. Sin Po, June 16, 3.
"Sarang Tawon." 1949. Sin Po, August 4, 2.
"Satoe tindakan baroe." 1926. Hoakiao 20: 6–7.
Schlegel, Gustaaf. 1891. "Chinese-Malay and Javanese Literature in Java." T'oung Pao 2, no. 2: 148–51.

Schlegel, Gustaaf. 1900. "The Secret of the Chinese Method of Transcribing Foreign Sounds." *T'oung Pao*, 2nd series, 1, no. 1: 1–32.

Schottenhammer, Angela. 2015. "China's Emergence as a Maritime Power." In *The Cambridge History of China*, vol. 5, pt. 2: *Sung China, 960–1279*, edited by John W. Chaffee and Denis Twitchett, 437–525. Cambridge: Cambridge University Press.

Selapar bin Kenyang. 1931. "Fikiran dalam Mengukur." *Saudara*, May (accessed through the Malay Concordance Project, http://mcp.anu.edu.au).

Sen, Krishna. 2006. "'Chinese' Indonesians in National Cinema." *Inter-Asia Cultural Studies* 7, no. 1: 171–84.

"Seorang Parisienne-tjina." 1903. *Bintang Hindia*, March 1, 50.

Seow Phi Tor and Seow Chin San, trans. 1936. *Flying Swords: The Twenty-Four Heroes*. Singapore: Oon Sye Chin.

Setijadi, Charlotte. 2015. "Being Chinese Again: Learning Mandarin in Post-Suharto Indonesia." In *Multilingualism in the Chinese Diaspora Worldwide: Transnational Connections and Local Social Realities*, edited by Li Wei, 141–57. London: Routledge.

Setijadi, Charlotte, and Thomas Barker. 2010. "Imagining 'Indonesia': Ethnic Chinese Film Producers in Pre-Independence Cinema." *Asian Cinema* 21, no. 2: 25–47.

Shellabear, W. G. 1913. "Baba Malay: An Introduction to the Language of the Straits-Born Chinese." *Journal of the Straits Branch of the Royal Asiatic Society* 65: 49–63.

Shih Shu-Mei. 2007. *Visuality and Identity: Sinophone Articulations across the Pacific*. Berkeley: University of California Press.

Shiraishi, Takashi. 1990. *An Age in Motion: Popular Radicalism in Java (1912–1926)*. Ithaca, NY: Cornell University Press.

Sidharta, Myra. 1992. "Contemporary *Peranakan* Women Writers." In *Le Moment "Sino-Malais" de la Littérature Indonésienne*, edited by Claudine Salmon, 165–84. Paris: Association Archipel.

Sidharta, Myra. 2004. *Dari Penjaja Tekstil sampai Superwoman: Biografi Delapan Penulis Peranakan*. Jakarta: KPG.

Sidharta, Myra. 2007. "The *Putri China* and Their Daughters." In *Chinese Diaspora since Admiral Zheng He with Special Reference to Maritime Asia*, edited by Leo Suryadinata, 267–77. Singapore: Chinese Heritage Centre.

Sidharta, Myra. 2011. "The Dragon's Trail in Chinese Indonesian Foodways." In *Chinese Food and Foodways in Southeast Asia and Beyond*, edited by Tan Chee-Beng, 107–23. Singapore: NUS Press.

Sie Boen Lian. 1938. "Gambang Kromong Muziek." *Mededeelingen van het China Instituut* 2: 78–88.

Siegel, James T. 1997. *Fetish, Recognition, Revolution*. Princeton, NJ: Princeton University Press.

Siow Choon Leng. 1924. "Negri Canton, bukan-nya negri Macao." *Kabar Slalu*, January 18, 8.

Situmorang, T. D., and A. Teeuw, eds. 1952. *Sedjarah Melaju menurut Terbitan Abdullah*. Jakarta: Djambatan.

Skinner, William G. 1967. "The Chinese Minority." In *Indonesia*, edited by Ruth T. McVey, 97–117. New Haven, CT: Human Relations Area Files.

Skinner, William G. 1996. "Creolized Chinese Societies in Southeast Asia." In *Sojourners and Settlers: Histories of Southeast Asia and the Chinese in Honour of Jennifer Cushman*, edited by Anthony Reid, 51–93. St. Leonards: Allen & Unwin.

Soenoto, S. Faizah. 1988. "Seri Roman Melayu Cina." In *Texts from the Islands: Oral and Written Traditions of Indonesia and the Malay World*. Proceedings of the 7th

European Colloquium on Indonesian and Malay Studies, edited by Wolfgang Marschall, 365–80. Berne: University of Berne.
"Solosche Causerie." 1919. *Bataviaasch Nieuwsblad*, November 18, 2.
Somers-Heidhues, Mary. 1996. "Chinese Settlements in Rural Southeast Asia: Unwritten Histories." In *Sojourners and Settlers: Histories of Southeast Asia and the Chinese in Honour of Jennifer Cushman*, edited by Anthony Reid, 164–82. St. Leonards: Allen & Unwin.
Somers-Heidhues, Mary. 2017. "Violent, Political, and Administrative Repression of the Chinese Minority in Indonesia, 1945–1998." *Wacana* 18, no. 1: 94–105.
Song Chong Sin. 1921. *English–Malay Dictionary*. Batavia: Kho Tjeng Bie.
Song Ge. 2017. "Note sur le Musée-Bibliothèque des Chinois peranakan de Tangerang, Jakarta." *Archipel* 93: 219–28.
Stenberg, Josh. 2015a. "Multilingualism and the West Kalimantan Hakka." In *Multilingualism in the Chinese Diaspora Worldwide: Transnational Connections and Local Social Realities*, edited by Li Wei, 123–40. London: Routledge.
Stenberg, Josh. 2015b. "*Wayang Potehi*: Glove Puppets in the Expression of Sino-Indonesian Identity." *Journal of Southeast Asian Studies* 46, no. 3: 391–416.
Stenberg, Josh. 2017. "The Lost Keychain? Contemporary Chinese-Language Writing in Indonesia." *Sojourn: Journal of Social Issues in Southeast Asia* 32, no. 3: 634–68.
Stenberg, Josh. 2019. *Minority Stages: Sino-Indonesian Performance and Public Display*. Honolulu: University of Hawai'i Press.
Stewart, Charles, ed. 2007. *Creolization: History, Ethnography, Theory*. Walnut Creek, CA: Left Coast Press.
Su, Ching. 1996. "The Printing Presses of the London Missionary Society among the Chinese." PhD diss., University of London.
Sunarti, Sastri. 2013. *Kajian Lintas Media: Kelisanan dan Keberaksaraan dalam Surat Kabar Terbitan Awal di Minangkabau (1859–1940-an)*. Jakarta: KPG.
Suryadi. 2019. "Roman Medan: The Nature and Sociopolitical Context of a Corpus in Sumatran Popular Literature, 1930s–1960s." *Malay Literature* 32, no. 2: 207–38.
Suryadinata, Leo. 1971. *The Pre-World War II Peranakan Chinese Press of Java: A Preliminary Survey*. Athens, Ohio: Ohio University.
Suryadinata, Leo. 1972. "Indonesian Chinese Education: Past and Present." *Indonesia* 14: 49–71.
Suryadinata, Leo. 2003. "The Contribution of Indonesian Chinese to the Development of the Indonesian Press, Language and Literature." In *Chinese Studies of the Malay World: A Comparative Approach*, edited by Ding Choo Ming and Ooi Kee Beng, 82–96. Singapore: Eastern Universities Press.
Suryadinata, Leo. 2005. *Pribumi Indonesians, the Chinese Minority and China: A Study of Perceptions and Policies*. Singapore: Marshall Cavendish.
Suryadinata, Leo. 2007. "Ethnic Chinese Political Participation and the Revival of Chinese Culture: Post-Suharto Developments." In *Chinese Diaspora since Admiral Zheng He with Special Reference to Maritime Asia*, edited by Leo Suryadinata, 331–38. Singapore: Chinese Heritage Centre.
Suryadinata, Leo. 2013. "Post-War Kung Fu Novels in Indonesia: A Preliminary Survey." In *Literary Migrations: Traditional Chinese Fiction in Asia (17th–20th Centuries)*, edited by Claudine Salmon, 393–413. Singapore: ISEAS—Yusof Ishak Institute.
Suryadinata, Leo. 2015. *Prominent Indonesian Chinese: Biographical Sketches*. Singapore: ISEAS Publishing.
Suryadinata, Leo. 2016a. "Berapakah jumlah orang Tionghoa di Indonesia?" In *Tionghoa dalam Keindonesiaan: Peran dan Kontribusi bagi Pembangunan*

Bangsa, edited by Leo Suryadinata and Didi Kwartanada, 1:lvii–lxiii. Jakarta: Yayasan Nabil.
Suryadinata, Leo. 2016b. "Dari Sastra Peranakan ke Sastra Indonesia" In *Tionghoa dalam Keindonesiaan: Peran dan Kontribusi bagi Pembangunan Bangsa*, edited by Leo Suryadinata and Didi Kwartanada, 1:245–57. Jakarta: Yayasan Nabil.
Suryadinata, Leo, and Didi Kwartanada, eds. 2016. *Tionghoa dalam Keindonesiaan: Peran dan Kontribusi bagi Pembangunan Bangsa*. 3 vols. Jakarta: Yayasan Nabil.
Susanto, Dwi. 2015. "Masyarakat Peranakan Tionghoa dalam Karya Sastra Peranakan Tionghoa Indonesia pada Paruh Pertama Abad XX: Kajian Sosiologi Sastra." PhD diss., Gadjah Mada University.
Sutrisno, Evi. 2017. "Moral Is Political: Notions of Ideal Citizenship in Lie Kim Hok's *Hikajat Khonghoetjoe*." *Wacana* 18, no. 1: 183–215.
Sweeney, Amin. 1980. *Reputations Live On: An Early Malay Autobiography*. Berkeley: University of California Press.
Sykorsky, W. 1980. "Some Additional Remarks on the Antecedents of Modern Indonesian Literature." *Bijdragen tot de Taal-, Land- en Volkenkunde* 136, no. 4: 498–516.
T. F. 1937. "Toekang Gambar dan Istrinja: Dari Bankier djadi Kunstenaar." *Sin Po Wekelijksche Editie* 747: 5–9.
T. K. S. 1930. "Sampe di Mana Moesti Merdika?" *Hoakiao* 148: 22–23.
T. P. B. n.d. *"Nerbomwek": Nasehat en Recepten boewat Orang Mendjadi Waras en Koewat*. Pekalongan: Fortuna.
"Tambahsia: Suwatu Cerita yang Betul Sudah Kejadian di Betawi antara Tahun 1851–1856." 2002. In *Kesastraan Melayu Tionghoa dan Kebangsaan Indonesia: Jilid 5*, edited by Marcus A. S. and Pax Benedanto, 1–148. Jakarta: KPG.
Tan Beng Hok, trans. 2009. *Memoar Ang Yan Goan, 1894–1984: Tokoh Pers yang Peduli Pembangunan Bangsa*. Jakarta: Yayasan Nabil.
Tan Boen Kim. 1915. *Njai Aisah atawa "Djadi Korban dari Rasia."* Batavia: Tjiong Koen Bie.
Tan Boen Kim. 1929. *Koempoelan Tjonto-Tjonto Rekest Hindia*. Telukbetung: The Trial.
Tan Boen Soan. 1937. *Kembang Latar*. Malang: Paragon Press.
Tan Chee-Beng. 1981. "Baba Chinese Publication in Romanized Malay." *Journal of Asian and African Studies* 22: 158–91.
Tan Chee-Beng. 1988. *The Baba of Melaka: Culture and Identity of a Chinese Peranakan Community in Malaysia*. Petaling Jaya: Pelanduk Publications.
Tan Chee-Beng. 2003. "Baba Malay Poetry Publications and Babas' Contribution to Malay World Studies." In *Chinese Studies of the Malay World: A Comparative Approach*, edited by Ding Choo Ming and Ooi Kee Beng, 97–139. Singapore: Eastern Universities Press.
Tan Djit Seng. 1913. *Impian dari Kota Nadem*. Batavia: Kho Tjeng Bie.
Tan Eng Kiong. 2013. *Rethinking Chineseness: Translational Sinophone Identities in the Nanyang Literary World*. Amherst: Cambria Press.
Tan Kee Gwan. 1939. "Bahasa Melajoe Rendah." *Sin Po Wekeljksche Editie* 835: 17–19.
Tan Kee Gwan. 1941. "Lagi Sekali tentang Pengaroenja Bahasa Tionghoa atas Bahasa Melajoe." *Sin Po Wekelijksche Editie* 951: 8–10.
Tan Khoen Swie. 1935. *Atoeran Masak Vegetarisch*. Kediri: Tan Khoen Swie.
Tan Kim Sen. 1920. *Hikajat Gerakan Boycott Japan*. Batavia: Loa Moek En.
Tan Pow Tek. 1916. *Shair Renchana Piatu*. Kuala Lumpur: The Khee Meng.
Tan Soe Djwan. 1940. *Kitab Too Tik King*. Kediri: Tan Khoen Swie.
Tan Sooi Beng. 2006. "Performing the Language of Inclusion: Multilingualism and Humour in Malay Comic Songs." In *Between Tongues: Translation and/of/in*

Performance in Asia, edited by Jennifer Lindsay, 224–41. Singapore: Singapore University Press.
Tan Tik Sioe Sian. 1932. *Montjo Prodjoh: Boengah Tjepaka Tjina II*. Batavia: Kho Tjeng Bie.
"Tanda djaman." 1930. *Haokiao* 133: 4–5.
Tarlo, Emma. 1996. *Clothing Matters: Dress and Identity in India*. London: Hurst.
Teekenpen. 1926. "Djadi Merah Tegen Wil en Dank." *Sin Po Wekelijksche Editie* 150: 735–36.
Teeuw, A. 1972. "The Impact of Balai Pustaka on Modern Indonesian Literature." *Bulletin of the School of Oriental and African Studies* 35: 111–27.
Teeuw, A. 1981. "Review of *Literature in Malay by the Chinese of Indonesia: A Provisional Annotated Bibliography* by Claudine Salmon. Paris: Editions de la Maison des Sciences de l'Homme, 1981." *Bijdragen tot de Taal-, Land- en Volkenkunde* 137, no. 4: 537–39.
Tejapira, Kasian. 1992. "Pigtail: A Pre-History of Chineseness in Siam." *Sojourn: Journal of Social Issues in Southeast Asia* 7, no. 1: 95–122.
Termorshuizen, Gerard. 2001. *Journalisten en Heethoofden: Een Geschiedenis van de Indisch-Nederlandse Dagbladpers, 1744–1905*. Amsterdam: Nijgh & Van Ditman.
Than, Tharapi. 2014. *Women in Modern Burma*. London: Routledge.
The Chih-hua, ed. 1936. *T.H.H.K. Tegal Djawa, 1906–1936*. Tegal: THHK.
The Chung Shen-Tjia. 1940. *Küoyu Zonder Goeroe. Part Two*. Surabaya: New China.
Thong Thian Piet Hiauw. 1912. Telukbetung: The Trial.
Tio Ie Soei. 1958. *Lie Kimhok (1853–1912)*. Bandung: L.D. Good Luck.
Tio Tek Hong. 2007. *Keadaan Jakarta Tempo Doeloe: Sebuah Kenangan 1882–1959*. Jakarta: Masup Jakarta.
Tjan Kwan Nio. 1992. "Kisah Hidupku." In *Le Moment "Sino-Malais" de la Littérature Indonésienne*, edited by Claudine Salmon, 154–64. Paris: Association Archipel.
Tjie Tek Goan. 1933. *Naga Poeti*. Surabaya: Hahn.
Tjiong Soen Liang. 1924. *Pantoen Tjapgome*. Batavia: Goan Hong.
Tjiook, Wiwi. 2017. "Pecinan as an Inspiration: The Contribution of Chinese Indonesian Architecture to an Urban Environment." *Wacana* 18, no. 2: 556–80.
Tjiook-Liem, Patricia. 2009. "De rechtspositie der Chinezen in Nederlands-Indië 1848–1942." PhD diss., University of Leiden.
Tjoa Boan Soeij. 1922. *Sair Swatoe Tjerita jang Betoel Soeda Kedjadian di Tanah Betawie dari Halnja Oeij Tambah Sia*. Batavia: Kho Tjeng Bie.
Tjoa Tjoe Kwan. 1897. *Penjoeratan pada Menjataken Hoeroef Tjina jang Beroepa Gambar*. Batavia: Albrecht.
Tjoa Tjoe Kwan. 1904. *Tjiap Kian Siang Tam*. Surakarta: Tjoa Tjoe Kwan.
Tjon Sie Fat. 2009. *Chinese New Migrants in Suriname: The Inevitability of Ethnic Performing*. Amsterdam: Amsterdam University Press.
"Tjonto dari Djaoe." 1926. *Sin Po Wekelijksche Editie* 170: 1.
Traill, H. F. O'B. 1982. "The 'Lost' Manuscript of the Hikayat Abdullah 'Munshi.'" *Journal of the Malaysian Branch of the Royal Asiatic Society* 55, no. 2: 126–34.
The Traveller's Malay Pronouncing Hand-Book. 1897. Singapore: Singapore and Straits Printing Office.
Tong Ketik. 1929. "Moesti Rajahken Lebih Rameh." *Sin Po Wekelijksche Editie*.
Tshoa Tsoe Koan. 1889. *De Feestdagen der Chineezen*. Batavia: Albrecht & Rushe.
Tsuchiya, Kenji. 1991. "Popular Literature and Colonial Society in Late Nineteenth-Century Java: *Cerita Nyai Dasima*, the Macabre Story of an Englishman's Concubine." *Southeast Asian Studies* 28, no. 4: 467–80.
Uchida, Keiichi. 2017. *A Study of Cultural Interaction and Linguistic Contact: Approaching Chinese Linguistics from the Periphery*. Göttingen: V&R Unipress.

Usman, Zuber. 1955. "Dari Bahasa Melaju ke Bahasa Indonesia." *Buku Kita* 1, no. 1: 15–17, 59–60.
v. d. Kop, H. Tobi, and T. J. Bezemer. 1915. *Vademecum voor het Indische Leven*. Wageningen: A. Ophorst.
Valentyn, François. 1726. *Omstandig Verhaal van der Geschiedenissen en Zaaken het Kerkelyke ofte den Godsdienst betreffende*. Vol. 3. Dordrecht: Joannes van Braam.
van de Stadt, P. A. 1912. *Hakka-Woordenboek*. Batavia: Landsdrukkerij.
van der Burg, C. L. 1926. *Boekoe Segala Roepa Penjakit dan Obatnja*. Batavia: Kho Tjeng Bie.
van der Meer, Arnout H. C. Forthcoming. *Performing Power: Cultural Hegemony, Identity, and Resistance in Colonial Indonesia*. Ithaca, NY: Southeast Asia Program Publications, an imprint of Cornell University Press.
van der Meij, Dick. 2017. *Indonesian Manuscripts from the Islands of Java, Madura, Bali and Lombok*. Leiden: Brill.
van der Molen, Willem. Forthcoming. *Leven in Drie Culturen: Ko Ho Sing (1825–1890), Een Chinese Javaan in Nederlands-Indië*.
van der Putten, Jan. 1997. "Printing in Riau: Two Steps toward Modernity." *Bijdragen tot de Taal-, Land- en Volkenkunde* 153, no. 4: 717–36.
van der Putten, Jan. 2015. "Burlesquing Muharram Processions into Carnivalesque Boria." In *Shi'ism in South East Asia: 'Alid Piety and Sectarian Constructions*, edited by Chiara Formichi and Michael Feener, 203–21. London: Hurst.
van der Tuuk, Herman Neubronner. 1856. "Iets over de Hoog-Maleische Bijbelvertaling." *Bijdragen tot de Taal-, Land- en Volkenkunde van Nederlandsch-Indië* 5, no. 1: 171–83.
van der Tuuk, Herman Neubronner. 1864. "Review of *Handleiding bij de beoefening der Maleische Taal en Letterkunde voor de kadetten van alle wapenen, bestemd voor de dienst in Nederl. Indië* by J. J. de Hollander. Breda: Koninklijke Militaire Academie, 1864." *De Gids* 29: 525–32.
van der Tuuk, Herman Neubronner. 1886. "Klassiek Maleisch?" *De Indische Gids* 8, no. 2: 974–80.
van Dijk, Kees. 2003. "The Magnetism of Songs." *Bijdragen tot de Taal-, Land- en Volkenkunde* 159, no. 1: 31–64.
van Doren, J. B. J. 1853. *Bijdragen tot de Kennis der Zeden, Gewoonten en Geaardheid der Chineezen*. Utrecht: N. de Zwaan.
van Hoëvell, Wolter R. 1849. *Reis over Java, Madura en Bali in het Midden van 1847, 1e Deel*. Amsterdam: van Kampen.
van Naerssen, Frits Herman. 1941. "Oudjavaansche Oorkonden in Duitsche en Deensche Verzamelingen." PhD diss., University of Leiden.
van Ronkel, Ph.S. 1918a. "Daendels in de Maleische Litteratuur." *Koloniaal Tijdschrift* 7, no. 2: 858–75, 1152–67.
van Ronkel, Ph.S. 1918b. "Maleisch." In *Encyclopaedie van Nederlandsch-Indië*, vol. 2: H–M, edited by S. de Graaff en D. G. Stibbe, 654–58. The Hague: Martinus Nijhoff.
van Ronkel, Ph.S. 1921. *Supplement-Catalogus der Maleische en Minangkabausche Handschriften in de Leidsche Universiteits-Bibliotheek*. Leiden: E.J. Brill.
van Wijk, D. Gerth. 1881. "Eenige Opmerkingen naar Aanleiding van 's Heeren Klinkert's Beoordeeling der Mal. Spraakkunst van Dr. J. J. de Hollander." *Tijdschrift voor Indische Taal-, Land- en Volkenkunde* 26: 182–94.
Vaughan, Megan. 1991. *Curing their Ills: Colonial Power and African Illness*. Cambridge: Polity Press.
"Verboden toegang voor Chineezen." 1939. *De Tijd*, September 28, 2.

De Vereniging van Huisvrouwen. 1937. *Recepten van Chinese gerechten*. Semarang: De Bruin.
Verslag Congres Budyåtåmå. 1909. Yogyakarta: Ltd previously known as H. Buning.
Vikør, Lars S. 1988. *Perfecting Spelling: Spelling Discussions and Reforms in Indonesia and Malaysia, 1900–1972*. Dordrecht: Foris Publications.
Vincy, Leo. 1933. *Hambanja Satoe Soedagar Radja Oewang*. Surabaya: Tan's Drukkery.
Vleming, J. L. 1925. *Het Chineesche Zakenleven in Nederlandsch-Indië*. Weltevreden: Volkslectuur.
Voorhoeve, P. 1964. "A Malay Scriptorum." In *Malayan and Indonesian Studies: Essays Presented to Sir Richard Winstedt on His Eighty-Fifth Birthday*, edited by John Bastin and R. Roolvink, 256–66. Oxford: Clarendon Press.
Vorderman, A. G. 1885. "Beschrijvende Catalogus van Chineesche en Inlandsche Voedingsmiddelen van Batavia." *Bijdragen tot de Taal-, Land- en Volkenkunde* 32, no. 1: 123–59.
Vorderman, A. G. 1889. "De Chineesche Behandelingswijze van Keeldiphtheritis." *Geneeskundig Tijdschrift voor Nederlandsch Indië* 24: 559–649.
Wade, Geoff. 2007. "Chinese Economic Activities in Java in the Late Eighteenth Century as Reflected in the Batavian Kong Koan (公館) Records." *Chinese Southern Diaspora Studies* 1: 116–37.
Wahab Ali, Abdul. 2012. *Kemunculan Novel dalam Sastera Moden Indonesia dan Malaysia: Satu Kajian Perbandingan*. Kuala Lumpur: Institut Terjemahan & Buku Malaysia.
Wallace, Stephen. 1983. "Pronouns in Contact." In *Essays in Honor of Charles F. Hockett*, edited by Frederick B. Agard, Gerald Kelley, Adam Makkai, and Valerie Becker Makkai, 573–89. Leiden: E.J. Brill.
Wan Boon Seng, trans. 1931. *Chrita Dulu-Kala Bernama "Sam Ha Lam Tong" di Zeman Song Tiow*. Singapore: Wan Boon Seng.
Wan, Margaret B. 2009. *"Green Peony" and the Rise of the Chinese Martial Arts Novel*. Albany: State University of New York Press.
Wang Gungwu. 1958. *The Nanhai Trade: A Study of the Early History of Chinese Trade in the South China Sea*. Kuala Lumpur: Journal of the Malayan Branch of the Royal Asiatic Society.
Wang Gungwu. 1996. "Sojourning: The Chinese Experience in Southeast Asia." In *Sojourners and Settlers: Histories of Southeast Asia and the Chinese in Honour of Jennifer Cushman*, edited by Anthony Reid, 1–14. St. Leonards: Allen & Unwin.
Wang Tai Peng. 1994. *The Origins of Chinese Kongsi*. Petaling Jaya: Pelanduk Publications.
Wang Xiaomei. 2012. "Emergent Grammatical Structures of Bahasa Pasar: Based on Hakka-Malay and Cantonese-Malay Glossaries." *GEMA Online™ Journal of Language Studies* 12, no. 3: 856–83.
Watson, Cyril William. 1974. "Sair Nona Fientje de Feniks: An Example of Popular Indonesian Fiction in the First Quarter of the Century." *Asian Studies* 12, no. 1: 119–36.
Weinbaum, Eve, Lynn M. Thomas, Priti Ramamurthy, Uta G. Poiger, Madeleine Yue Dong, and Tane E. Barlow, eds. 2008. *The Modern Girl around the World: Consumption, Modernity, and Globalization*. Durham, NC: Duke University Press.
Wellington Koo, Madame. 1943. *Hui-lan Koo*. New York: Dial Press.
Wellington Koo, Madame. 1975. *No Feast Lasts Forever*. New York: Quadrangle.
Wen Zi Chuan. 1979. "Keren zai Bincheng." In *Binglangyu Keshu Gonghui Sishi Zhounian Jinian Kan*, 707–33. Penang: Penang Hakka Association.

Wertheim, Wim F. 1997. "Political Status of the Chinese in Pre-War Netherlands Indies: Secret Documents from 1924–1932." *Indonesian Law and Administration Review* 2: 6–27.
Wheatley, Paul. 1961. *The Golden Khersonese*. Kuala Lumpur: University of Malaya.
Wickramasinghe, Nira. 2014. *Metallic Modern: Everyday Machines in Colonial Sri Lanka*. New York: Berghahn.
Widmer, Alexander, and Veronika Lipphart, eds. 2016. *Health and Difference: Rendering Human Variation in Colonial Engagements*. New York: Berghahn.
Wieringa, Edwin P. 2007. *Catalogue of Malay and Minangkabau Manuscripts in the Library of Leiden University and Other Collections in the Netherlands*. Vol. 2. Leiden: Leiden University Library.
Wieringa, Edwin P. 2020. "Mother's Tongue and Father's Culture: A Late Nineteenth-Century Javanese Versification of Master Zhu's Household Rules (*Zhuzi Zhijia geyan*)." *Wacana* 21, no. 3: 384–407.
Wilkinson, R. J. 1985. *A Classic Jawi-Malay-English Dictionary*. Reprint, Melaka: Baharudinjoha.
Wilkinson, R. J. 1932. *A Malay-English Dictionary (Romanised)*. Vol. 1. Mytilene: Salavopoulos and Kinderlis.
Williams, Lea E. 1960. *Overseas Chinese Nationalism: The Genesis of the Pan-Chinese Movement in Indonesia, 1900–1916*. Glencoe, IL: The Free Press.
Winkelmann, Christine. 2008. *Kulturelle Identitätskonstruktionen in der Post-Suharto Zeit: Chinesischstämmige Indonesier zwischen Assimilation und Besinnung auf ihre Wurzeln*. Wiesbaden: Harrassowitz.
Wirawan, Yerry. 2011. "Pers Tionghoa Makassar Sebelum Perang Dunia Kedua." *Archipel* 82: 49–82.
Woodrich, Christopher A. 2016. "Inside Gazes, Outside Gazes: The Influence of Ethnicity on the Filmmakers of the Dutch East Indies (1926–1936)." *Plaridel* 13, no. 2: 1–21.
Woodrich, Christopher A. 2017. "Lie Kim Hok: Penulis Proto-Feminis Tionghoa Indonesia." In *Dari Doing ke Undoing Gender: Teori dan Praktik dalam Kajian Feminisme*, edited by Wening Udasmoro, 153–66. Yogyakarta: Gadjah Mada University Press.
Woolf, Virginia. 1986. *The Second Common Reader*. San Diego: Harcourt Brace Jovanovich.
Worsley, Peter. 2004. "Gouw Peng Liang's Novella, Lo Fen Koei: Patrons and Women. An Account of the Peranakan Chinese Community of Java in the Late 19th Century." *Archipel* 68: 241–72.
Yamamoto, Nobuto. 2019. *Censorship in Colonial Indonesia, 1901–1942*. Leiden: Brill.
Yang-Lioe. 1937. *Pelita Penghidoepan*. Malang: Paragon Press.
Yap Kim Hong. n.d. *Sair Nasehat Orang Moeda Lelaki dan Prampoean*. Batavia: Lie Tek Long.
Yap, Melanie, and Dianne Leong Man. 1996. *Colour, Confusion, and Concessions: The History of the Chinese in South Africa*. Hong Kong: Hong Kong University Press.
Yen Ching-hwang. 1976. "The Confucian Revival Movement in Singapore and Malaya, 1899–1911." *Journal of Southeast Asian Studies* 7, no. 1: 33–57.
Yen Ching-hwang. 2003. "Hokkien Immigrant Society and Modern Chinese Education in British Malaya, 1904–1941." In *Chinese Migrants Abroad: Cultural, Educational, and Social Dimensions of the Chinese Diaspora*, edited by Michael W. Charney, Brenda S. A. Yeoh, and Tong Ghee Kiong, 114–44. Singapore: Singapore University Press.

Yo Tien In, trans. 1939. *Kang Ouw Djie Sie Hiap*. Tasikmalaya: Boe Hiap.
Yong Heming and Jing Peng. 2008. *Chinese Lexicography: A History from 1046 BC to AD 1911*. Oxford: Oxford University Press.
Yoo, Genie. 2018. "Wars and Wonders: The Inter-Island Information Networks of Georg Everhard Rumphius." *British Journal for the History of Science* 51, no. 4: 559–84.
Zhu, Yun. 2017. *Imagining Sisterhood in Modern Chinese Texts, 1890–1937*. Lanham: Lexington Books.

Index

The letter *f* following a page number denotes a figure.

Abdullah bin Abdul al Kadir. *See* Munsyi Abdullah
Abu Taleb Khan, Mirza, 78
advertisements, 75, 87, 109–11, 118
Afrikaans, 18, 54, 66–67, 138–39
Al-Jaum, 110, 114
Anderson, Benedict, 5, 54–55
angmoh, 182n33
Annals of Batavia, 30–31, 114
Antologi Sastra pra-Indonesia (Pramoedya Ananta Toer), 55
Arabic script. *See Jawi*
Arabs, 31–32, 44, 110, 135–36
archival collections, 17
assimilation, 10–11, 26, 154–57
attire. *See* clothing

Baba, 9, 31–32. *See also Peranakan*
Baba Malay, 56–57, 59–61, 84–90, 137
Badings, Adriaan Herm Louis, 55
bad language, disclaimers of, 53–54, 72–74, 92–93, 155
Bahasa Indonesia. *See* Indonesian
Bakhtin, Michael, 4, 41
Balai Poestaka, 12, 24–25, 76, 79, 91–92
Baperki, 156
Batavian Malay (book). See *Melajoe Betawi*
Batavian Malay (dialect). *See* Low Malay
Bazaar Malay. *See* Low Malay
Betawi Malay. *See* Low Malay
Bible translators, 52, 57, 63
Bintang Hindia, 102
Bintang Pranakan, 84–85
Blagden, Charles Otto, 56
Boekoe Masakan Betawi (Lie Tek Long), 122
Boekoe Sair Kabaikannja Orang jang Hendak Melepas Thauw-tjang (Tjia Ki Siang), 107–8
borrowing. *See under specific languages*
Boven Digoel, 67, 94
boycotts, 119–20, 144
British Malaya, 8, 46, 56–57. *See also* Singapore; Straits Settlements

cacography, 18, 44–45, 128, 146–47
Candranegara, Raden Mas Adipati Arya, 32
Cantonese, 35, 40, 59, 122
Cape Town, 18, 181n18, 201n106
capitalism, 5
cartoons, 42–44, 104, 130–31, 145–47
censorship, 16, 24, 147–49
Chia Cheng Sit, 37–38, 88–89
China. *See* Ming dynasty; Qing dynasty; Republic of China; Song dynasty; Tang dynasty
Chinese accent. *See* /r/: pronounced as /l/; *Singkeh*: accent of
Chinese Council, 39, 44
Chinese cuisine, 119–24
Chinese-Indonesians
   history, 7–10
   modern language practices, 27, 205n21
   position in Indies, 20–22
   position in Indonesia, 150–57
   scholarship on, 17, 154, 157–59
   terminology, 7, 30–37
Chinese (language). *See under specific Sinitic varieties*
Chinese literature, 79, 81, 89–90, 95
"Chinese-Malay" (language), 41–42, 52, 65–66, 138–39
Chinese newspapers, 45–46, 83
Chinese Revolution, 3, 16, 33, 45, 107, 132
Chinese script, 37, 61, 71–72, 115–16. *See also* transcription, Chinese
Christianity, 61, 87–88, 107
Chulalongkorn, 95
Chung Hwa Hui (Indies), 48
Chung Hwa Hui (Netherlands), 115
class, 11, 107, 110–11, 130, 154–55. *See also* elites; middle classes
classical Malay. *See* High Malay
clothing, 21–22, 104–13
code-mixing. *See under specific languages*
colloquial Malay. *See* Low Malay
"coolies." *See* laborers
communism. *See* left-wing groups

235

INDEX

Confucianism, 45
cookbooks, 120–22
copyright, 79–80
cosmopolitanism, 2, 153
"creole," 36–37
cuisine, 119–24
cynicism. *See* humor

dandies, 43, 98–99, 110–12
Daoism, 117
dialectal differences (Malay)
    Borneo, 135–36
    British Malaya, 89–91, 102, 110, 183n52
    Java, 41, 120–21
    Sumatra, 41, 90, 193–94n54
dictionaries, 49, 57–63
digitization, 15–16, 159, 179n59, 179–80n78
disclaimers. *See* bad language, disclaimers of
Drama di Boven Digoel (Kwee Tek Hoay), 67
dress. *See* clothing
Dutch cuisine, 122
Dutch (language)
    borrowing from, 20, 41, 98, 102–4, 115, 145–48
    code-mixing with, 26f, 38, 48, 66, 113
    education in, 11, 42–50
    pidginized, 21–22, 104, 129–31, 141–42
    pronouns, 140–42
Dutch (people)
    language attitudes (*see* language attitudes)
    Malay spoken by (*see* Malay [language])
    mimicry of (*see* mimicry)

eating, with hands, 122, 129
education. *See* girls' education; *and under specific languages*
elites, 11, 54
Egypt, 18, 125–26, 155
English
    borrowing from, 39, 98, 103, 136
    code-mixing with, 50, 68, 84–85
    dictionaries, 62
    education in, 42, 47–48
entrepreneurship. *See* print entrepreneurship
Eurasians, 44–45, 130–31
    authors, 90
    collaboration with, 3, 87
    terminology, 21, 31
    Europeanized Malay. *See* mimicry

fashion, 107–13
femininity. *See* gendered practices
feminism, 102–3
Ferry and Bridge of the General Language (Lim Tjay Tat), 59, 202n32, 203n43

fiction and nonfiction, 79, 94–100
Fokker, Abraham Anthony, 52, 63
food, 119–24
food stalls, 122–23
"foreign orientals," 20–21, 142, 179n73
forms of address, 137–38
Fuhri, Eduard, 82
Fujian, 29, 39

Gandhi, Mohandas Karamchand, 158–59
Gan Kok Liang, 53, 155
gelijkstelling, 21
gendered practices
    culinary, 122, 124
    dress, women's, 106–13, 117
    liberalization, women's, 97–99, 102–4
    medicines, commercial, 118–19
    modern girls, 21–22, 25, 129
    self-defense for women, 96
    terminology, 31–32, 98–99
girls' education
    criticism, 119, 141–42
    emergence, 45–47, 115
    school uniforms, 109
Gouw Peng Liang, 69, 70, 90, 132
Guangzhou, 29
guidebooks, stylistic, 72–73

/h/, in word-final position, 74–75
Haan, Mattheus de, 114
hairstyle, 21–22, 104, 106–13
Hakka, 32, 40, 59, 139
Hambanja Satoe Soedagar Radja Oewang, 133–34, 147
Harahap, Parada, 36, 69, 143
health, 113–19
heritage, 150–57
heteroglossia, 41, 125–26
Heurnius, Justus, 53
Heutsz, Joannes Benedictus van, 119–20
High Malay, 12–13, 54, 64–70, 88–90
Hikajat Khonghoetjoe (Lie Kim Hok), 45
Hoakiao (periodical), 16–17
hoakiao (term), 34–35
hoana, 35–36, 109
Hoëvell, Wolter Robert van, 78
Hokkien, 39–40
    borrowing from, 32–35, 96–100, 105–6, 114, 130–39
    code-mixing with, 35, 38, 43, 84–85, 121
    education in, 42–50
    mixed expressions, 21, 104, 115–17, 130, 145
    romanization, xvii, 49, 71–72, 85
    study of, 52–53, 61
Hollandsch-Chineesche School, 48

Hoorn, Joan van, 114
humor, 19, 89, 93, 125–28, 146–49. *See also* translingualism: translingual puns
hybridity, 7, 101–2, 108, 121–22

identity. *See* orientation, cultural
Ik Po, 83
Im Yang Tjoe, 6, 69
Indians, 8, 142. *See also* minorities, as cultural entrepreneurs
Indonesia (term), 7, 36
Indonesia dalem Api dan Bara (Kwee Thiam Tjing), 126
Indonesian (language)
  emergence, 13, 26, 154–55
  standardization, 70, 75–76
Injo Bian Hien, 112
insults, 20–21, 33–36, 135, 145–46
Islam, 29, 30, 151–52
  Islamic texts, 83

Japan, 45, 94, 107, 124, 191n16
Japanese (language), 49, 184n84
Japanese occupation, 11, 50, 122, 148, 154
Japanese (people), 20, 143–44
  Malay spoken by, 126, 134
Java Malay. *See* Low Malay
Javanese (language), 23, 29, 37–38, 43, 81, 117–18
  accent, 128, 139, 145–46 (*see also* /r/: rolling)
  borrowing from, 133, 144
  newspapers, 61, 82–84
  pronouns, 135
  script, 37, 61, 71
Jawi, 63, 71, 81–84, 149
Jews, 44. *See also* minorities, as cultural entrepreneurs
jokes. *See* humor

Kang Ouw Djie Sie Hiap, 96–97
Kang Youwei, 45, 49
Kartini, Raden Adjeng, 102, 114
Kats, Jacob, 52, 69
Kembang Latar (Tan Boen Soan), 134–35
ketjap, 119, 121
Kho An Kim, 148
Kiao Seng, 87
Ki Hadjar Dewantara, 68
Kitab Vortaro, 62
KITLV, 12, 14, 16, 55
Klinkert, Hillebrandus Cornelius, 64
Koks, Joseph Theodore, 56
Kommer, Herman, 90, 193n40
Kong Koan. *See* Chinese Council

Ko Tsching Dschang, 53
Kung Yen, 143
Kwee Seng Tjoan, 105–6
Kwee Tek Hoay, 6, 16, 90, 94, 132
  on Malay, 41, 59, 64, 66–72, 74–75, 92
Kwee Tek Hoay, works of
  Drama di Boven Digoel, 67
  Zonder Lentera, 134
Kwee Thiam Tjing, 6, 90
  Indonesia dalem Api dan Bara, 126

/l/, pronunciation as /r/, 134. *See also* /r/
laborers, 23, 30, 118, 119
Lamb, Charles, 87–89
language attitudes
  Dutch, 36, 52–57, 63–64, 102, 128, 153
  Malayan, 57, 133, 204–5n7
  Sumatran, 57, 64, 91–92
language planners, 13, 63–64
Later, Johan Frederik Hendrik August, 91
Latin script. *See under specific languages*
Leguat, François, 31
Leiden University, 16, 40, 53, 115
Lee Choo Neo, 115, 197n35
Lee Soen Liang, 1–2, 141–42
left-wing groups, 16, 24, 36, 156
legal equation, 21
lexicon. *See* words, analysis of
Liang Qichao, 45
Lie Kim Hok, 6, 83, 94, 102
  Malay style, 66, 69, 70, 74
Lie Kim Hok, works of
  Hikajat Khonghoetjoe, 45
  Melajoe Betawi, 59, 72, 136
  Siti Akbari, 95
Liem Khing Hoo, 6, 94
Liem Thian Joe, 6, 89, 119, 121
  Riwajat Semarang, 54
Lie Tek Long, 122
Lim Boon Keng, 45, 49, 75, 115
Lim Hiong Seng, 59–61, 137
Lim Hock Chee, 90
Lim Kong Chuan, 58–60
Lim Tjay Tat
  Ferry and Bridge of the General Language, 59, 202n32, 203n43
  Mr. Tjoepeek Lie's Family Instructions, 85
literacy, 6, 18, 77, 177n20
Lu Pao Ru, 61, 73f
loanwords. *See under specific languages*
loe (pronoun), 137–38
Louw Djeng Tie, 97
Low Malay, 11–13, 19–20, 40–42, 54
  advantages of, 63–70, 87–90

INDEX

Ma Huan, 29
Malay–Cantonese Glossary, 59
Malay (language), 11–13, 40–42
 dialects (*see* dialectal differences [Malay])
 Europeanized (*see* mimicry)
 pidginized, 40, 53, 64
 romanization (British Malaya), xvii, 75, 90–91
 romanization (Indies), xvii, 59, 71–75, 85–91, 118–19
 Sinicized, 90, 94, 130–33
 spoken by Dutch, 12, 55–56, 134–35, 138
 spoken by Japanese, 126, 134
 spoken by *Singkeh*, 23, 42, 133
 study of, 52–61
 varieties (*see* High Malay; Low Malay; Service Malay)
 wordlist, oldest, 29, 57–58
Malay literature. *See* fiction and nonfiction; poetry
Malay press
 history, 77–87
 importance for the Chinese, 3
 language practices of, 91, 102
 newspapers, 80–87, 143–44
Malay, scholars of
 British (*see* Blagden, Charles Otto; Medhurst, Walter Henry)
 Chinese (*see* Kwee Tek Hoay; Lie Kim Hok)
 Dutch (*see* Klinkert, Hillebrandus Cornelius; Ophuijsen, Charles Adriaan van; Pijnappel, Jan; Ronkel, Philippus Samuel van; Tuuk, Herman Neubronner van der)
 Malayan (*see* Munsyi Abdullah; Raja Ali Haji; Zainal Abidin bin Ahmad)
 Sumatran (*see* Pané, Armijn; Takdir Alisjahbana, Sutan)
Malaysia, 125–26, 155
Mandarin, 24, 42–50, 61, 89, 156
Manual of the Malay Colloquial, A (Lim Hiong Seng), 59–61, 137
manuscripts, 71–72, 77–78, 81
martial arts, 95–97
Marxism. *See* left-wing groups
masculinity. *See* gendered practices
mass culture, 5, 18, 79–80, 101
mass media. *See* mass culture; printing
Medan, 109, 148
 literature from, 13
Medan Prijaji, 158
Medhurst, Walter Henry, 53
medicine, 113–19

Melajoe Betawi (Lie Kim Hok), 59, 72, 136
metalinguistic discourse, 51
methodology, 17–22
middle classes, 6, 25, 113, 153
Mijer, Pieter, 80
mimicry, 20–22, 94, 103–4, 112, 129–31
Ming dynasty, 29, 106
minorities, as cultural entrepreneurs, 3, 11, 152, 157
missionaries, 53, 61, 75, 81–83, 192n31, 192n33. *See also* Bible translators
misspelling. *See* cacography
mistranslation, 148
mocking. *See* humor; selfing and othering; Westernization
modernity, 3–4, 25, 101–4, 109–13, 124. *See also* progress
Moestika Romans, 69–70, 72
"Moesti Rajahken Lebih Rameh," 47, 104–5, 130–32
Mr. Tjoepeek Lie's Family Instructions (Lim Tjay Tat), 85
Munsyi Abdullah, 64, 78–79, 83, 138, 151
Muslims. *See* Islam

Naga Poeti (Tjie Tek Goan), 134
naming practices, 129–30, 141–42, 155–56
Nasib (Injo Bian Hien), 112
Na Tian Piet, 90
 Shaer Almarhoem Beginda Sultan Abubakar di Negri Johor, 85–87
nationalism
 Chinese, 9, 24, 42–50
 Indonesian, 5, 13, 16, 46, 70, 154–55
National Library of Indonesia, 15–16, 156
"native speakers," 11–12, 38–39
neologisms, 49, 102, 155
New Order. *See* Suharto
newspapers, 77–79. *See also* Chinese newspapers, Malay press: newspapers
Nio Joe Lan, 6, 27, 53, 91, 150–51
njonja, 31–32
"Njonja mantoe modern" (Lee Soen Liang), 1–2, 141–42
Njoo Cheong Seng, 6, 16, 69, 94
nyonya, 31–32

Oei Hui Lan, 110
Oeij Kim Tjoan, 109
Oeij Tambah Sia, 107
Oei Tiong Ham, 107, 110
Oetoesan Borneo, 135–36
Oldham, William Fitzjames, 56–57

INDEX

Ophuijsen, Charles Adriaan van, 12, 54, 64
   spelling system, 70, 75
opium, 30
O, Prempoean! (Pouw Kioe An), 140
orientation, cultural, 101, 106–8, 127, 148, 151
orthography, xvii, 53–55, 70–76, 128
othering. *See* selfing and othering
owe (pronoun), 138–39

Pané, Armijn, 13, 91–92, 154, 189n77, 196n3
Pané, Sanoesi, 186n14
Pantoen Tjapgome, 1–2, 67, 137
pantun, 92–93, 95
Pat Taij Tjoe, 112
Pendjara Fasis (Kho An Kim), 148
Peranakan, 9, 31–33, 35, 48
   cuisine, 122
   dress, 108
   language competencies, 37–38, 44–45, 138–39
   See also *Baba*
Perniagaän, 143
Petjok. *See* Dutch: pidginized
Phrasebook for Chinese and Foreigners (Lim Kong Chuan), 58–60
phrasebooks, 38, 40, 47, 58–61, 137
pidginization. *See* Dutch (language); Malay (language)
Pijnappel, Jan, 56
Pingzhou Table Talks, 29
plurilingualism, 11–12, 38–39, 49–50
"Poetra Fortuna," 38, 139
poetry, 92–93, 95
popular culture. *See* mass culture
potency drugs, 118–19
Pouw Kioe An, 6
   O, Prempoean!, 140
Pramoedya Ananta Toer, 196n92, 205n14
   Antologi Sastra pra-Indonesia, 55
print capitalism, 5
print entrepreneurship, 5–7, 77–80, 152
   medicine, influence on, 114–15, 118
   stylistic choices, 11–13, 101–2
   See also minorities, as cultural entrepreneurs
printing, 77–87
print languages, 5, 77, 128, 158
progress, 4, 78, 80. *See also* modernity
pronouns, personal, 135–42
public sphere, 5, 24, 97–98, 102, 153
puns. *See* translingualism: translingual puns
purity, of language, 51–52, 63, 139

Qing dynasty, 3, 30, 39, 45, 106–8, 132–33
Quanzhou, 29
   dialect of Hokkien, 39, 58–59
queue. *See* hairstyle

/r/
   pronunciation as /l/, 33, 56–57, 133, 149, 202n19
   rolling, 128, 129–30, 143, 146–47
Raffles, Thomas Stamford, 40, 138
Raja Ali Haji, 64, 133, 151, 188n42
Rama-Moortie. *See* Tan Tik Sioe San
reading practices, 24, 77–81, 91
   individualized, 37, 71–72, 77
registers (linguistic), 12, 127
religion. *See specific religions*
Republic of China, 4, 46, 106–10, 132, 155
restaurants, 120–23
Riau, 63
Riau Malay. See High Malay
Riwajat Semarang (Liem Thian Joe), 54
resinicization, 35–36, 43–44, 48, 156–57
retailers. *See* shop owners
romanization. *See under specific languages*
Ronkel, Philippus Samuel van, 56–57
Rumphius, Georg Eberhard, 114

Sair Perdjaka (Pat Taij Tjoe), 112
Sair Tan Keng Siang, 99
Salmon, Claudine, 14–15, 157–58
Samarangsch Advertentie-blad, 82–84
sarcasm. *See* humor
Sarekat Islam, 46, 78, 97
Sartika, Dewi, 45
Sastradarma, Raden Arya, 32
satire. *See* humor
Schlegel, Gustaaf, 53, 188n38
schwa /ə/, 74
Selam, 32
Selompret Melajoe, 83, 189n82
selfing and othering, 125–35
   ethnic designations, 30–37
   Singkeh, othering of, 23, 42, 133
   Westernized Chinese (*see* Westernization)
   See also /l/; /r/
self-styling. *See* mimicry; selfing and othering
Semarang, 91, 121
sensitive issues, 94–100
Service Malay, 12, 40
sex, 97–99
sexology, 99
School Malay. See High Malay

Shaer Almarhoem Beginda Sultan Abubakar di Negri Johor (Na Tian Piet), 85–87
Shanghai, 110
shop owners, 38–39, 109–10, 124
Siam, 95, 191n16, 197n24
silat, 95–97
Singapore, 44–47, 56–57, 75, 83–87, 118–19
Singkeh, 32–34, 108, 122
   accent of, 23, 42, 133 (*see also* /r/: pronounced as /l/)
Sinology, 40, 53
Sino-Malay newspapers. *See* Malay press: newspapers
Sino-Malay texts, 10–17, 154–59
Sinophone Studies, 9–10
Sin Po, 16–17, 45–46, 144
   on language, 62–63, 75–76
Sip Ngo Im, 57
Siti Akbari (Lie Kim Hok), 95
skin complexion, 22
slurs. *See* insults
Soerat Chabar Batawie, 82–83
Soerat Kabar Bahasa Melaijoe, 82
Soewandi Spelling System, 70, 75–76
Soewardi Soerjaningrat, 68
Song dynasty, 29
South Africa, 47, 69, 138–39, 158–59. *See also* Afrikaans; Cape Town
Southern Min. *See* Hokkien
soy sauce, 119, 121
spelling. *See* orthography
Sri Lanka, 83, 191n16
Sriwijaya, 29
Stadt, Peter Adriaan van de, 57
Standard Hakka Glossary of the Malay Language, 59
standard Indonesian. *See* Indonesian (language)
Straits Chinese Magazine, 87–89
Straits Settlements, 8, 84–87, 108–9, 115. *See also* Singapore
students, 42–43, 115
style (linguistic). *See* Malay; mimicry
Suharto, 13–14, 54, 155–56
Sukarno, 155
Sumatran Malay. *See* High Malay
Sundanese (language), 145–46
   borrowing from, 99, 115, 133
Sun Yat-sen, 3, 107, 109
Surabaya, 44, 83, 108–9, 184n70, 184n79
Suriname, 36–37, 182n22, 182n30
Swahili, 18, 158, 188n52
swearing. *See* insults

syair. *See* poetry
Syair Siti Zubaidah, 145–46

Taiping Rebellion, 30, 82
Takdir Alisjahbana, Sutan, 67–68, 76
Tamil, 83, 118
Tan Boen Soan, 6
   Kembang Latar, 134–35
Tang dynasty, 29, 34, 192n31
Tan Hong Boen, 6, 69
Tan Tik Sioe San, 97, 117–18
Tat Seng Pian, 114–16
Teochew, 39–40, 136
Thailand. *See* Siam
theater, 6, 67, 133, 137, 155
THHK (Tiong Hoa Hwee Koan), 42–50, 61–62, 105–6, 109
Tong Thian Piet Hiauw, 117
tionghoa, 7, 33
Tiong Hoa Wi Sien Po, 102
Tirto Adhi Soerjo, 78, 158
Tjan Kwan Nio, 53–54
Tjerita Anak Prampoean di Bikin Sebagi Parit Mas (Kwee Seng Tjoan), 105–6
Tjia Ki Siang, 107–8
Tjie Tek Goan, 134
tjina, 33–34
Tjoa Tjoan Lok, 83
Tjoa Tjoe Kwan, 37, 61, 83, 114
Tjoe Bi Tia, 114
tones, Chinese, 58–59, 72
Totok, 32–33, 45–49
transcription, Chinese
   of Dutch words, 58
   of Malay words, 57–59
translanguaging, 17–18
translated works, 87–93, 95
translingualism
   translingual practice, 17–18
   translingual puns, 55, 89, 104, 134, 142, 146–49
transliteration. *See under specific languages*
Tuuk, Herman Neubronner van der, 54
typesetters, 93

Ureca, 156

Valentijn, François, 54
vernacular (language), 4–5
   in popular literature, 88–94, 98–100
   as research tool, 18–20, 153, 157–59
violence. *See* martial arts
visuality, 12, 97–98, 111

VOC, 30, 32, 57, 106, 114
vocabulary. *See* words

Wahid, Abdurrahman, 156
Wang Dahai, 32
waroeng, 122–23
Westernization, 25
   mockery of, 21–22, 129–30, 104, 140–42
   versus resinicization, 43–44, 48
women's magazines, 102, 122

words, analysis of, 17–22, 101–2, 133, 155.
   See also insults; translingualism: translingual puns

Yi Jing, 29

Za'aba, 204–5n7
Zainal Abidin bin Ahmad, 204–5n7
Zhangzhou, 29
   dialect of Hokkien, 39, 53, 58–59
Zonder Lentera (Kwee Tek Hoay), 134

www.ingramcontent.com/pod-product-compliance
Lightning Source LLC
Chambersburg PA
CBHW030536230426
43665CB00010B/920